Remembering Reinhold Niebuhr

Remembering Reinhold Niebuhr

Letters of Reinhold and Ursula M. Niebuhr

Edited by Ursula M. Niebuhr

HISTORY & WORLD AFFAIRS

HarperSanFrancisco

A Division of HarperCollins*Publishers*

FIRST EDITION

Library of Congress Cataloging-in-Publication Data
Niebuhr, Reinhold, 1892–1971.
    Remembering Reinhold Niebuhr : letters of Reinhold and Ursula M. Niebuhr / edited by Ursula M. Niebuhr.—1st ed.
        p.   cm.
    1. Niebuhr, Reinhold, 1892–1971—Correspondence.   2. Niebuhr, Ursula—Correspondence.   3. Theologians—United States—Correspondence.   I. Niebuhr, Ursula.   II. Title.
BX4827.N5A4   1989
230'.092'2—dc20   89–45259
ISBN 0–06–066234–4   CIP

---

91   92   93   94   95   RRD(H)   10   9   8   7   6   5   4   3   2   1

This edition is printed on acid-free paper that meets the American National Standards Institute Z39.48 Standard.

For our children
and grandchildren
and other members of the family.
Also, for all of Reinhold's friends and
former students.

Contents

Preface

Letters, especially family letters, are the primary source for any biography. Yet using them raises various questions. Should the intimate exchanges between husband and wife, for example, be exposed to the outside world?

Reservations such as these prevented me from making earlier use of these letters. But in the last few years there have appeared accounts of Reinhold's views, theological and political, and descriptions of his life and character so inaccurate as to be distasteful to our family and also to his friends and former students.

Accordingly, it seemed both right and proper for me to show what manner of man Reinhold Niebuhr really was, as teacher and preacher, as husband and father. Our letters to each other, with letters from our friends, should, so I thought, disclose the quality of his humanity.

The task for me, already approaching eighty and not in good health, was daunting. I had so many letters of his and mine as well as so many others. The first task for me was to read and to select. I did not type, and many of the letters were handwritten and very difficult to decipher.

But I had wonderful friends who encouraged and helped me. Margaret Clarke transcribed and typed the first draft of the manuscript. Others came to her rescue, copying or continuing the transcription: Barbara Swan, Susan De Gersdorff (who spent her last Harvard vacation transcribing letters handwritten on thin air-mail stationery) Diane Roosa, Mary Misch, and lately, Geraldine McEvoy.

Good friends and neighbors helped me greatly. Sally Begley and Anne Klein literally sustained me. Also, I would like to thank Dr. John Burton and Dr. Joel Colker, whose diagnostic skill and treatment helped me and the manuscript to survive.

My thanks also go to the friends who have allowed me to use letters: Mrs. Lewis Mumford, Professor Arthur Schlesinger, Jr., and Dr. Hans Christoph von Hase; Professor Edward Mendelson for permission for the Auden letters; Mrs. Elizabeth al Qadhi and Mr. Charles Strachey for permission to use their father's letter.

My thanks also go to David Wigdor, Assistant Chief of the Manuscript Division of the Library of Congress, for his encouragement and help in many ways.

I would like to mention my old friend Marion Pauck for many things but especially for her translation of Dr. Hans Christoph von Hase's letter of July 1935. Our own daughter, Elisabeth Sifton, always apprehensive about my health, was available for expert advice. Our son, Christopher, was infallible in points of historical exactness and dates. He was responsible for the chronological outline of his father's life and much proofreading and correcting.

Spelling and punctuation in the original letters have usually been corrected or standardized for this edition, but in some cases, such as the W. H. Auden letters, the original text has not been changed. I and the publisher's editors have supplied identifications and other explanatory information in notes and within brackets in the text of letters. We have tried to give helpful information without being overwhelming. A person mentioned in a letter who is not known today or outside our circle of friends is identified the first time the name appears. Quotations from the Bible are usually from the King James Version and the English Revised Version, but sometimes the letter writer was quoting from memory and used a mixed text.

Biographical Chronology: Reinhold Niebuhr

1892	June 21 – Born in Wright City, MO
1910	Graduates from Elmhurst Pre-Seminary, Elmhurst, IL
1913	June 11 – Graduates from Eden Seminary, Webster Groves, MO
	June 29 – Ordained, German Evangelical Synod, Lincoln, IL
1914	B.D., Yale Divinity School
1915	M.A., Yale Graduate School
	Called as pastor, Bethel Evangelical Church, Detroit, MI
1916	Publishes "Failure of German-Americanism" and "The Nation's Crime Against the Individual" in the *Atlantic Monthly*
1917	Named Executive Secretary, War Welfare Commission, German Evangelical Synod
1923–24	Visits Britain and Europe, in seminars led by Sherwood Eddy
1927	*Does Civilization Need Religion?*
1928	Named Associate Professor, Union Theological Seminary, New York, NY
1929	*Leaves from the Notebook of a Tamed Cynic*
1930	Named Professor, Union Theological Seminary, New York, NY
	D.D. (Hon.), Eden Seminary, Webster Groves, MO
1931	December 22 – Marries Ursula Keppel-Compton in Winchester Cathedral, England
1932	*Moral Man and Immoral Society*
	D.D. (Hon.), Grinnell College, Grinnell, IA
1934	September 11 – Christopher born
	Reflections on the End of an Era

1935	*An Interpretation of Christian Ethics*
1937	*Beyond Tragedy*
	Delegate to Oxford Conference
1939	January 13 – Elisabeth born
	Gifford Lectures, University of Edinburgh
1940	*Christianity and Power Politics*
1941	*The Nature and Destiny of Man,* Vol. 1
	Christianity and Crisis founded
1942	D.D. (Hon.), Yale University
1943	*The Nature and Destiny of Man,* Vol. 2
	D.D. (Hon.), Oxford University
1944	*The Children of Light and the Children of Darkness*
	D.D. (Hon.), Harvard University
1946	*Discerning the Signs of the Times*
	D.D. (Hon.), Princeton University
1947	Warwick Lectures, University of Aberdeen and University of Glasgow
	Olaf Petri Lectures, University of Uppsala
	Co-Chairman, Founding Conference of Americans for Democratic Action
	D.D. (Hon.), University of Glasgow
1948	Chairman, The Church and the Disorder of Society Commission, World Council of Churches Conference, Amsterdam
1949	*Faith and History*
	Delegate to UNESCO Conference, Paris
1952	*The Irony of American History*
	Suffers strokes
1953	*Christian Realism and Political Problems*
1955	*The Self and the Drama of History*
1957	Read paper on "Relations of Christians and Jews" before joint faculties of Jewish Theological Seminary and Union Theological Seminary

1958	*Pious and Secular America*
	Visiting Scholar, Institute of Advanced Study, Princeton
	Elected to American Academy of Arts & Letters
1959	*The Structure of Nations and Empires*
1960	Retires from Union Theological Seminary
1961–62	Teaches at Harvard University (lectures with Paul Sigmund published in 1969 as *Democratic Experiences*)
1963	*A Nation So Conceived* with Alan Heimert
	Debate with James Baldwin
1964	Awarded Presidential Medal of Freedom
1965	*Man's Nature and His Communities*
	Foreword for *Mississippi Black Paper*
1967	D.Phil. (Hon.), Hebrew University, Jerusalem
1971	June 1 – Dies, Stockbridge, MA
1974	*Justice and Mercy*, Ursula Niebuhr, ed.
1986	*The Essential Reinhold Niebuhr*, Robert McAfee Brown, ed.

A bibliography prepared by D. B. Robertson, *Reinhold Niebuhr's Works,*
lists all his writings as well as articles about him. Union Seminary
in Richmond, VA, has the Reinhold Niebuhr Audio Tape Collection.
Some of his letters and other papers have been deposited in the
Library of Congress.

Biographical Chronology: Ursula M. Niebuhr

1907   Born at Southampton, England

1922–24   Attends St. Catherine's School, Bramley

1924–25   Enrolls at University College, Southampton
            Passes London Intermediate Arts B.A.

1925–26   Prepares for Oxford
            Wins history scholarship, St. Hugh's College

1926–30   Studies history
            In 1927, changes to the Honour School of Theology

1930   Receives First Class Honours in theology

1930–31   Holds Mills Fellowship at Union Theological Seminary, New
            York, NY
            Awarded S.T.M.

1931   December 22 – Marries Reinhold Niebuhr in Winchester
            Cathedral, England

1941   Appointed Lecturer in Religion, Barnard College, Columbia
            University, New York, NY

1946–65   Appointed Associate Professor, Executive Officer, Department
            of Religion, Barnard College

1952   D.D. (Hon.), Trinity College, Toronto

1961–62   On leave from Barnard College
            Honorary Fellow, Institute for Independent Study, Radcliffe
            College

1965–71   Works with Reinhold Niebuhr until his death

1966–68   Teaches part-time at Simon's Rock College, Great Barrington,
            MA
            Trustee, Simon's Rock College

1973   Scholar in Residence at Ecumenical Institute for Advanced
        Theological studies at Tantur outside Jerusalem
1978   D.D. (Hon.), General Theological Seminary, New York, NY

Introduction

What Was Your Husband Like?

It was Palm Sunday, 1980. The Ecumenical Institute for Advanced Theological Studies in Jerusalem had arranged for a bus to take those who wanted to join the procession on the Mount of Olives to commemorate the events of the first Palm Sunday. Our group started at Bethany with a brief visit to the Church and the Tomb of Lazarus. The appropriate passage from Scripture had been read to us, and we had joined in a few prayers. Then we walked up and over the hill to Bethphage, following the path taken by Jesus.

Religious communities from all over Jerusalem, from the orders, convents, monasteries, schools, and other places for religious instruction and work in the city also joined the gathered crowd. We were marshaled and directed to wait until the procession could be formed. For the first time since the unification of Jerusalem in 1967 the Eastern Calendar coincided with the Western Calendar, so the group was larger than usual. Approximately ten thousand pilgrims would be in the procession. There were memories of other Palm Sundays when the weather had been chilly or wet, but this day was beautiful and bright.

While we waited some of us sat down on the grass beside the pebbly path. A quiet and sensitive-looking woman sitting by my side asked, "Would you tell us about your husband? What was he like? Of course we have read a lot of his writings, but would you not be able to tell us about *him?*"

The speaker was a Korean nun, Sister Kim, a graduate student at Harvard University. She had told me a little about her work at Harvard, and I gathered that she had spent some time at the Ecumenical Institute, where I had been briefly before other meetings in Jerusalem.

The question about my husband came suddenly and unexpectedly in the context of the occasion. I did not answer at once. How could I describe in a couple of sentences the energetic, dynamic human being with whom I had lived? Where should I start?

Nearby were acquaintances from the U.S.A. One was a seminary teacher of New Testament, a member of my own Episcopalian church. It was forty years ago, he told me, that he had been a student at Union Theological Seminary and had known my husband. (He looked to me much too young to have been a student forty years ago.) Should I ask him to help me describe Reinhold? There hardly seemed time to start. But noticing that another onlooker was looking at a watch to note the time, I remembered how constant was Reinhold's preoccupation with time. So often he was looking at his watch, for he was speedy, quick, and efficient, and got more things done in a short space of time than anyone else I had ever known. I found myself saying rather weakly, "Well, he really would not be happy here, doing nothing, waiting for a procession to start." I turned to this American scholar who had known him, and asked him, "Reinhold would not be happy here?" He gave a hearty laugh, "That's for sure. He would be streaking through here in a flash."

But this seemed rather irrelevant. How could I explain to this lady with her inherited culture from the Far East that my husband was a dynamic Westerner, with all the energy not only of an American but of Western Man incarnate. So I started to tell her how Reinhold was someone possessed with an itch to work and to action, which in his case was translated into words, either the written or typed words, or into speech.

Descartes had said "Cogito, ergo sum," but Reinhold would have said, "Scribo, ergo sum." He thought and wrote, I think, simultaneously. He also could think on his feet, but that did not mean that he did not do an enormous amount of homework, reading, gathering material from a wide range of sources. He never regarded himself as a scholar in the usual, more restricted sense of someone who would be intrigued or fascinated by variant readings in a text, or the clues that catch the attention of the academic detective. He described himself as a parson with a journalistic urge, who somehow had strayed into the academic world and hovered on the fringes of the political world. He read quickly, noting at the back of the book passages he wanted to refer to later, and he had an extraordinarily good memory for these passages. Sometimes he and I would be reading the same book. He was the hare and I was the tortoise. But usually this hare got as much out of it as the careful tortoise. Occasionally I would catch him out. He might mark a passage that he liked as a possible illustration for something he wished to say or write. But he had read a little too quickly and had not realized that the passage was a quotation and did not express the thought of the author of the book. But these faux pas were few and infrequent, and no one was more amused or apologetic than he to have been caught out.

He wrote many book reviews, and those who have studied his
have found those reviews a vivid illustration of how his interests ra
Many of his friends thought that some of his better writing was done in his
shorter pieces, for instance in the editorials he wrote for the paper he
started in the early forties, *Christianity and Crisis,* or in book reviews written
for the *New York Times* or the *Herald Tribune,* or for *The Nation* and other
journals.

As he often emphasized, he was not a systematic thinker in the conventional sense, but he had a systematic approach to problems of understanding and expression. One of my own colleagues once exclaimed when we
were listening together to a talk Reinhold was giving to Columbia University
students, "Gosh, what a mind he has. He instinctively has the systematic
approach to the understanding of problems." But he repeatedly tried to
show that his thought was not systematic in the same sense as that of his
colleague Paul Tillich but that it was pragmatically shaped by the changing
historical situation and the way in which it impinged on his understanding
of the Christian faith. He took his categories from what he had learned
from the Bible, particularly the Prophets and the words of Jesus, and from
those thinkers who have so shaped the expression of thought in our Western tradition. St. Augustine probably was his favorite. He turned instinctively to those who meditated upon the contradictions in human nature and
stood also under the sense of the transcendence of God. So Augustine,
Pascal, and later, Kierkegaard, as well as Luther, were important and form-
ative in his thinking and writing.

Sister Kim's question, however, remained. What was he like? How was
I going to answer this question? After all, we were so close that it would be
almost as is I were trying to describe myself. And yet we were so different.
The hesitation, and to a certain degree the inhibition, in trying to tell others
what he was like, stays with me.

His letters show him as a devoted father, and our married life as warm
and happy. The words of a prayer that Reinhold used when performing
marriage ceremonies was a description of our own experience: ". . . by
whose Providence these Thy children have found each other and learned to
love and cherish each other." It is now many years since he died on June 1,
1971. I have been cowardly in trying to write about his life, because what
I knew best was our life together. Neither of us felt happy with autobiography.

Wystan Auden, our good friend for many years, agreed with us. He
thought that autobiographies were written, if not with an eye for posterity,
with an eye on good returns for the money. Yet it was Wystan who
encouraged Reinhold after his stroke—or rather his strokes—in 1952 to

write about himself. It was a good instinct, I think, although Wystan was not always tactful in trying to persuade Reinhold. Facetiously, he used to say, "It is worth making money out of misery," or something nasty and commercial like that. But I know he thought that Reinhold's analysis of himself after his illness and experience with repeated vascular occlusions might also be helpful to others, with the curious sense of not being the full and whole self after an illness that was not only weakening but also left behind it a sense of a disturbance and a disruption of the integrated person. This was interesting to Wystan and to me. I re-read Freud; I read the English physiologists and neurologists, such as Russell Brain on the brain (a delightful coincidence in name which amused all of us in the same way as John Wisdom's being the professor of philosophy at Cambridge). Trying to understand what had happened to Reinhold after these injuries to his neurological system and wondering which of his brain cells had been knocked out, turned me back to re-read the Gifford Lectures given by Lord Sherrington the year before Reinhold gave his at the University of Edinburgh in 1939.*

Lord Sherrington's lectures have a wonderful passage describing the brain as like a switchboard when the contacts are made and the lights go on. Quite obviously some of Reinhold's lines of communication to the brain had been damaged. Luckily, his speech and his general intellectual processes seemed not to have suffered. I did suspect that there had been some disturbance in the part of the brain where higher abstract relationships might be comprehended. I noticed that after his strokes he was much more interested in reading historical and objective discussions of events. He always had been interested in history and biography and the stuff of political ethics, but now for the more abstract arguments of philosophy and systematic thought he seemed not to have much appetite or interest.

But the question that had been asked me, "What was your husband like?" covered how he was in the earlier years as well as in these later, more difficult years. I have often told how we met and how vivid, dynamic, and interesting he was to me. I used to say that I had never been bored either by him or by anything he said. (Sometimes he used to accuse me of having a rather low boredom level.)

Not only was this so in conversation but also in his more formal utterances, whether a lecture, a political speech, or a sermon. When he worked on his sermons, he would take some theme from Scripture, and he would mull over it, and then perhaps use it for a short address at Union Theolog-

*Charles Sherrington. "Man on His Nature," The Gifford Lectures (Edinburgh, 1937–38). Cambridge: The University Press, 1951.

ical Seminary in the weekday morning chapel service at half past eight, when the address lasted only a few minutes. If the theme and his discussion of it seemed meaty enough, he would mull over it further and develop it into a longer sermon of about twenty-five minutes or so for a Sunday morning service held in the seminary chapel. Later, he would take the same text and in a sense the same theme, and preach on it at Harvard, Yale, or Princeton. I used to say that the theatrical companies would try out a play in the provinces, Boston or Philadelphia, before bringing it to Broadway, but Reinhold would try it out first on Broadway (Union Theological Seminary at Broadway and 122nd Street) and then take it to the provinces, to Yale, Princeton, or Harvard.

In every preacher, there is something of the actor. Wystan Auden, who often gave readings of his poetry, used to exchange somewhat ribald remarks with Reinhold about the fact that both he and Reinhold were ham actors when they "performed." Reinhold was very aware of this, and rather troubled by it. If he would mention in his sermon the subtle temptation of talking about his lacks and sins and need of grace, he would be thinking as he talked about his condition (how consciously he would not know), "Aren't I doing a good job with this?" So he was very aware of the double edge of the so-called successful preacher. So was I, and often I was rather embarrassed by the enthusiastic listeners who would come up and tell me what a wonderful sermon it was. Somehow to receive the bouquets and congratulations after the service and then go off to a good Sunday lunch seemed wrong. I would mutter that the prophet was supposed to sit under a juniper tree, as Elijah did. And even if those that Reinhold had been slaughtering for the sake of the Lord were not physically the priests of Baal, yet some of the aspects of human nature, either individual or social, which he had been analyzing in his sermon surely should have left him as well as us seeking the shade of the juniper tree, and repeating, with Elijah, "O Lord, take away my life, for I am no better than my fathers" (1 Kings 19:4).

Reinhold was really very generous with my critical attitude about his preaching. Coming from a different tradition liturgically, I regarded sermons as only part of the offering of worship. In the Eucharist, the homily, or so I thought in those days before the revision of liturgies, should be short and used to "point" some aspect in the Gospel for the day. This seemed to be for me the satisfactory solution for, or resolution of, different psychological movements in the act of worship. I could see a place for a preaching service, for the Protestant sermon, or the university sermon, for that matter, but it seemed to me then, and it still does, that this was *not* liturgy or worship. The rather formless service that had grown up in the American college and university chapels was usually a mixture of a very short morning prayer,

om the Anglican Book of Common Prayer, with the usual psalm
ive reading from the Psalter, a couple of hymns and a couple of
prayers, depending again on the churchmanship or the tradition of the
college chaplain. Such might be a suitable background, all things considered, for a sermon that was searching, well presented, and not too long, but to me this was not worship. For me worship involved the emptying of the self and the offering of the self objectively expressed in the sequences of liturgy.

In this way, the sermon should lead on to some liturgical expression of the movement of the soul under the scrutiny of conscience and of the judgment as well as the mercy of God. To have a cheerful hymn and a still more cheerful slapping of back and shaking of hand outside was inappropriate. Reinhold endured this critical attitude of mine in a very tolerant way. He would cheerfully tell other people that preaching was his art form and the Lord had given him a wife who didn't like sermons. I would counter with, "Unless they are *your* sermons, darling." This happened to be quite true. I did like his sermons. I also believed they were his art form and also that they were done extraordinarily well, not only from the point of view of the shaping but also in substance, so that they did reach out and touch the heart and conscience as well as the mind.

Reinhold did not preach from a written text. He mulled over the theme, memorizing some of his illustrations and quotations, with perhaps half a page of rough notes as a sort of outline. They were for his own sake, not to be referred to in the course of the sermon but as markers on the way when he was thinking about it beforehand. His prayers he did write out, and when preaching, for instance in the chapel at Union Theological Seminary, two or three of these would be used in the service as well as for a concluding collect or prayer. He had been quite influenced by Anglican prayers, and we assembled a fair assortment of others, ancient and modern, which also helped shape his own expression. He had a sense of style and, like Winston Churchill in his speeches, preferred to use simple words rather than ponderous, many-syllabled alternatives.

He preached, therefore, freely from the outline he had in mind, and he was able to relate illustrations and occasional ad lib comments with extraordinary effect. He would stand very still, using only his voice and sometimes an outstretched finger for emphasis. I used to tease him about this outstretched finger, particularly noticeable after his stroke had lamed his left hand. For me, it reminded me of the words in the Gospel of Luke: "If I by the finger of God cast out demons, then is the Kingdom of God upon you."

He felt that preaching was his vocation. He wrote, "For nearly forty years I preached almost every Sunday in various parts of the country. . . .

'Making sense' out of the symbols and professions of faith has always been the responsibility of the preacher and teacher. The preacher is the mediator of God, God's judgment and also of his mercy."

Growing Up in England

When in 1931 I told my friends and family in England that I was going to marry a thirty-nine-year-old bald-headed professor of Christian ethics, many of them thought I had fallen in love with the embodiment of ideas and concerns in which I had been interested. It was not quite so simple as that, but there was perhaps an element of truth in what they said.

During my years at Oxford I had become more and more interested in religion. I changed my school, therefore, from modern history to theology. My College of St. Hugh's generously allowed me to retain my scholarship which had been awarded to me in history. This was financially helpful, and I was also grateful for the honor.

The history I had been studying at Oxford, and before that at the University College of Southampton, often showed the interaction of religion with political and social forces. The Wars of Religion, the Reformation, the Crusades—all these seemed to suggest that religion made everything worse. It sanctified political power and intensified the horrors of warfare.

These questions had bothered me even as a child. Growing up in South- ampton, where my father was a doctor, there was much history all around us. Southampton, an important port, had been invaded by Danes, Romans, and Normans. We would walk along the western sea front and see the West Gate through which Edward III had marched with his troops. His invasion of France culminated in the Battle of Crecy. Later, Henry V passed the same way, again to invade France, and to win the Battle of Agincourt. So when I read Shakespeare's play and reverberated to "Tomorrow is St. Crispin's Day. . ." I knew part of the scenario.

On our walks with nurse or governess, there was much to observe and wonder about. Not only were there associations of kings and conquerors but also religious foundations. There were many ancient churches, including St. Michael's, where Philip V of Spain worshiped the day before he wed Mary, queen of England, in Winchester Cathedral. Also, abbeys and priories abounded, so that often I wondered about the connection of the warlike kings with those who built the abbeys, now "bare ruined choirs," such as Netley and Beaulieu.

I was brought up in the conventional way of the period, customary for the professional, slightly upper-middle class. The nursery was our kingdom, ruled over by a nurse. Later, the nursery became the schoolroom and a governess was in charge. Languages were an essential part of our education, so we learned French and German from our governesses who came, alternately, from France and Germany.

The World War of 1914–18 interrupted this sequence and, of course, my education. Our brothers were at school, first a day school nearby and then at a boarding public school. My older sister attended a day school not far away, but I, regarded as delicate, stayed at home. Governesses became scarce. Women had gone off to more interesting and patriotic jobs. A succession of Belgian refugee nursery-governesses came, who were supposed to look after me. This was a charitable exercise on the part of my parents but not exactly educational for me.

The outbreak of war affected more than my education. Southampton was the port through which thousands of soldiers and supplies passed. The common, a large tract of land (365 acres), had supplied camp space for soldiers in the Hundred Years War of the fourteenth and fifteenth centuries, and again in the seventeenth and eighteenth centuries in the War against Spain, and later still, in the Napoleonic War. We children walking up the avenue could see the common where we had walked and played covered with army huts and tents. Now, of course, it was out of bounds for us. Down the avenue, which was only a couple of hundred yards from our house, would march hundreds of soldiers. I might stand, with governess and dog, and watch. In the first year or so, I wondered, Was I growing taller, or were the soldiers growing smaller? Later I learned that Kitchener's Army of 1915–16 indeed was composed of small men from city offices, mines, and factories. My medical father, too old for active service, working overtime as so many doctors had been called up, was also on call for examining recruits, particularly for heart and related ailments. I remember his remarking on the various different physical conditions, comparing the desk-bound office workers to the shipyard navvies (unskilled laborers) or postmen who walked on their delivery rounds.

But after Kitchener's Army came the colonials: Anzacs* from Australia and New Zealand, tall and bronzed; and then later still the Americans, again tall. I still remember their shiny leather boots and belts.

But if the war filled our historical canvas, yet we were praying for peace. Somehow, this never seemed quite valid. Even in church, it was more exciting to sing "Onward, Christian Soldiers" with the Royal Engineers in their uniforms as part of the congregation than it was to intone "Peace, Perfect Peace." Yet, of course, we all longed for peace and for the war to be over.

When the war was over and peace was declared, life for many was very difficult. Many families had lost young sons; my brother in the Officers'

---

*Anzacs is an acronym for Australian and New Zealand Army Corps.

Training Corps was not eighteen when the armistice was signed, so escaped the fate of so many of his contemporaries. In other ways also, life was difficult. Even people in ordinary households found that it was hard to maintain, in their pleasant but inconvenient houses, the kind of life they were accustomed to. I recall also the activities of trade unions and the numbers of the unemployed.

But life was interesting to a rather innocent girl of eleven. My mother found an excellent teacher to take on a couple of other adolescent girls and me in a tutorial class. Miss Aldridge had been head mistress of a good private school for girls but had retired and given up her school. Being somewhat bored after a year or so, she agreed to this plan, with the help of a recent graduate of Oxford to take us for mathematics and Latin.

I realize what extraordinary luck I had then and at other times and places to have had interested and interesting teachers. We studied a lot, especially history and literature, learned a lot, and inquired a lot. When we read the *Lyrical Ballads,* we also learned about the French Revolution, and reverberated to Wordsworth's loss of ideological vision. When we read Milton, learning many of his poems by heart, we also studied his times. We roamed, if not wildly, certainly widely, and to this day, I recall many of the associations and passages of literature we learned.

Boarding school followed a couple of years later and at the ages of thirteen to fifteen, I was at St. Catherine's, Bramley. Again, I was lucky. Although conventional in its setup and even conventual, with school uniforms, silence in the corridors, high church Anglican liturgical observance with chapel twice a day, there was much which I regarded then and now as important. There were splendid teachers. Miss Gertrude Hardy, sister of the famous mathematician G. E. Hardy was our Latin mistress. She was a Fabian, had a flat in Chelsea, and knew the Sidney Webbs and Bernard Shaw, and lent us all sorts of literature that were not strictly classical! Her colleagues also were good and the classes small and interesting. The services in the school chapel also were important for me. The school chaplain was a superannuated clergyman, but the chapel mistress was a good musician. We learned much church music and sang plainsong and liturgical settings such as those by Tallis. The chapel mistress went to London for classes with Gustav Holst, who himself taught at St. Paul's School for Girls, so we were kept up-to-date.

I left St. Catherine's before I was sixteen; I had passed the School Certificate Examination well enough to have gained exemption for necessary matriculations for Oxford, Cambridge, and London. But Oxford did not welcome adolescents. Also, I needed to win a scholarship. In order to get in at one of the women's colleges, it was necessary to attain Scholarship Standard. Also, scholarship aid was necessary.

Again I was lucky. In those postwar years the local University College, where my sister had been studying modern languages, had acquired some excellent scholars. Why not enroll there, and study for the first part of the London B.A.?

Here I stayed for a whole year, which I much enjoyed. I chose history, English, logic, and Latin as my subjects. Also, important for me, I met an entirely different sort and condition of young men and women, and realized how restricted socially my upbringing had been.

After passing the London Intermediate B.A., I was anxious to concentrate on getting a scholarship at Oxford. I worked with a young historian, V. T. Harlow, who later became the Beit Professor of Colonial History at Oxford. He supervised my reading and I wrote essays for him on a variety of historical subjects. Again, I was lucky. He was a good historian and interesting teacher. He and his wife became my lifelong friends.

My family had always been Cambridge, for generations and centuries. My brother had studied classics and law there, and it was even rumored that family money earlier had helped with the founding of Girton College (for women). But after the war, when women were admitted to both universities, Cambridge gave them only titular membership, while Oxford gave them full membership. Also, the women's colleges at Cambridge were more remote. The female titular undergraduates bicycled in for lectures wearing hats, not caps and gowns. I went to Cambridge for interviews and found I was much more drawn to my first love, Oxford. Therefore, winning a scholarship to St. Hugh's fulfilled my hopes and dreams.

Grateful as I was for this chance to go to Oxford, I was also grateful to my parents who made it possible. We were not well off, and university education, even in those days, was relatively expensive, even with some scholarship help.

My sister Barbara, a few years older than I, was a great source of support in many ways. She often was an advocate with my parents on my behalf, which I did not know at the time.

My father was a hard-working doctor; his own family had been conventionally upper class, although impoverished. The men in the family always went into the army, the navy, or the church. My father had rebelled against this convention and wanted to study medicine, which was regarded as *not* upper class. Most of the distinguished doctors at that time seemed to be Scottish. Luckily for him, an aunt, no doubt a quiet rebel herself, sold some property and bought a house near London so my father might commute to Guys Hospital to pursue his medical education. Although conservative in his politics, nonetheless he was critical of conventional behavior, and I think from his own experience he had learned to be sympathetic about concerns and questions of others.

The patients he enjoyed looking after were the workers in the shipyards and in other working-class jobs. He had been in favor of the Insurance Act of 1911, which came in when Lloyd George was chancellor of the exchequer. Many of his patients were "on the Panel," covered by this national insurance. I recall him telling my mother that he tried to persuade teachers and even curates to go on the Panel rather than feel obligated to pay fees as private patients.

He was born in the close of Hereford Cathedral, and he and my mother met in the palace of the bishop of Norwich. I used to think that this was appropriate, and that my mother particularly seemed to fit into the milieu of a cathedral close. But such was not to be. Southampton, a provincial and commercial town, expanding as a busy port for transatlantic shipping, was not where she felt most at home. The cathedral, with its liturgy, its music, and its tradition remained as a standard for her and also, to a certain extent, for my father.

Both of them were more than conventionally religious. My father, whenever possible, sang in the choir of a nearby church on Sunday evening— 6:30 evensong was then a popular service. Both of them disliked High Church practices of the Anglo-Catholic variety, and they found equally uncongenial the services of the very Low Church. The standard for them was that of the cathedral service.

We always had family prayers. Before breakfast we assembled in the dining room, the maids in their morning uniforms sitting in a row in front of the sideboard. The family was at the other end of the room, with my father at the end of the long dining room table with the Bible and Book of Common Prayer in front of him. A passage from Scripture was read and then we all stood up, turned around, and knelt against the Chippendale chairs upon which we had been sitting. Always included was the collect for the season and the Lord's Prayer. Once a parrot given us by one of my father's patients, who was a steward on one of the liners, burst into ribald and obscene speech in the middle of prayers. I looked to see what others were doing and I shall never forget the look on the face of my elder brother, who was home from his public school for the holidays. Prayers were dissolved; cook disappeared muttering words about "the doctor's bacon," and after this, the parrot and his cage were banished from family prayers.

My mother was very devout; the liturgy and the teachings of the church meant much to her. In my childhood, I had to learn a collect from the Book of Common Prayer every week until I knew all the collects of the liturgical seasons; then I proceeded to the Gospels for each week. Last, I learned the Epistles. On Sunday afternoon in the drawing room, I would recite what I had learned, while my mother explained difficulties of interpretation and tradition.

We were lucky living not far from Winchester and not so very much further from Salisbury Cathedral. A great treat was when my father, on a Sunday afternoon, would drive us over for the afternoon service at Salisbury, the early English architecture of which he preferred to Winchester. This was very special: a drive through country we knew and loved, and again a service we loved.

But for me Winchester was even more special, especially as I grew older. It was almost within walking distance. Often I could bicycle there, or take a bus part of the way and then walk over the downs and drop down to the River Itchen by the Hospice of St. Cross, and then continue to the cathedral.

It had a library of interest to scholars, and some of its reference volumes then were housed up in the south transept. I was allowed to use these, so I would climb up the stone stairway in the walls, until I reached a landing, from which I could look over the chancel and also glimpse a sweep of the nave. Winchester is the largest of English cathedrals, over 560 feet long. Architecturally, it is Norman with perpendicular details and additions. Sometimes, as I read, a choir practiced below, and the voices of boy choristers would ascend and transport me to yet another world.

Oxford also gave me history and beauty. Not only wonderful places in which to study, such as the Bodleian Library, but also to walk through college quadrangles or narrow streets on the way to tutorials or lectures somehow caught me up to all those in the past who had studied there, who had asked questions, and had wondered about life and its meaning.

My first year at Oxford, 1926, was the 700th anniversary of the death of St. Francis. Oxford had been founded by the Franciscans, who came from Paris in 1224. They cared for the poor, the sick, and lepers but also were excellent teachers. The eminence of Oxford in the thirteenth century was due to the Franciscan friars.

The commemorative celebration for St. Francis provided yet another strand to my thinking about life. The Franciscan values of the simple life, holy poverty, and yet learning, was this what one strove for? One of the essays I wrote for a tutor my first term was a comparative study of the discipline of St. Francis and St. Dominic.

The questions asked by these men centuries ago somehow were related to the questions I was asking. As my first year continued I wondered more and more whether I could study the history of the Christian faith I had inherited, and which had formed English life and history. This faith had built the very churches, the abbeys, and cathedrals I knew and loved, as well as Oxford itself.

Luckily, my moral tutor (the Oxford equivalent of a faculty advisor), a medieval historian herself, was sympathetic with my questions and was interested when I inquired whether I might change my school from that of history to theology. She discussed this with the principal, Miss Gwyer, and it was agreed before the end of my first year that I might follow my desire.

The principal of the College undertook to be my moral tutor and put me in the care of Canon B. H. Streeter, the synoptic scholar, for my academic tutor. He was an interesting character, famous for his work in the synoptic problem, and although he was not a good undergraduate tutor, he taught me much by the way—in the study of textual criticism, for example.

For the following years, I wandered widely. At Oxford, lectures in themselves are not important unless they are interesting in themselves. Those listed as introductory or basic, I soon discovered were intended for theological students, as theological colleges abounded, representing different denominations and churchmanship. Attendance at lectures was not required, although in those days one was supposed to let one's tutor know which lectures one was attending.

Canon Streeter suggested I go to the lectures of C. H. Dodd—"Quite a good scholar, quite remarkable, you should try him out"—at a non-Anglican college, Mansfield. So I penetrated this Nonconformist institution. Very different from the setting and feel of other Oxford colleges, where lectures were held in dining halls or in drafty and often beautiful old chambers, Mansfield felt more like University College, Southampton, with earnest seekers after truth, taking down notes and obviously meaning business. And C. H. Dodd *was* remarkable. I went to his lectures on "Synoptic Data for the Life of Christ," "Recent Tendencies in the Criticism of the Fourth Gospel," and later, lectures on some of our Greek texts of the New Testament.

At the end of my second year, Canon Streeter left for the U.S.A. where he was to give a series of lectures. I acquired another tutor, L. B. Cross, fellow of Jesus College, who was a Hebrew and Old Testament scholar. He not only tutored me in his subject but helped me plan for the other requirements in the curriculum. These included the New Testament in Greek and specific patristic texts—among others, St. Athanasius, Tertullian, and St. Augustine—in the original languages, Latin and Greek.

I continued going to lectures, had occasional tutorials with specialists in some specific field, and occasionally attended "informal instruction," the Oxford equivalent of a seminar. One such was described as the "Rabbinic Background to the New Testament." I turned up to find myself the only one who wanted to study this subject. It was offered by Herbert Loewe, a scholar well known and respected in the field of biblical and Judaic literature. I learned a lot from him, for he put the New Testament Gospels into their proper setting with the natural references to, and often the presuppositions of, Jewish literature.

Already I had acquired Claude Montefiore's two-volume commentary on the Synoptic Gospels. Sometimes Dr. Loewe would illustrate a reference and then ask me, "Did you find that in Montefiore?" and laugh triumphantly if I had not. The two were friends and some years later together they brought out *A Rabbinic Anthology*. These sessions brought home to me what is so easily forgotten, that Jesus was a Jew. This discovery made me very critical of many New Testament commentaries and critical works, for they all assumed and presumed that Jesus was Christian.

Another special occasion was the Bampton Lectures of 1928. K. E. Kirk, afterwards bishop of Oxford, gave the series on "The Vision of God" in the university church. It was a brilliant and learned discussion of the Christian doctrine, the Summum Bonum. The lectures were published in 1931; I gave Reinhold a copy, which he much used and marked.

As many and varied as the academic offerings in theology were, Oxford also offered the questing soul a variety of liturgical usage. Christ Church Cathedral and the chapels of Magdalen and New College all had splendid choirs and beautiful singing. Of the many parish churches, there were some High or Anglo-Catholic in their liturgy, others broad or evangelical Low Church. The Society of St. John the Evangelist, the well-known monastic order of Anglicanism, was situated outside Oxford at Cowley, so that society was known generally as the Cowley Fathers. [In this century Cowley became the center of the Morris Cowley automobile, named for William Morris (later Lord Nuffield). In my day, elderly scholars remembered Morris as having a bicycle shop on Long Walk Street, where he mended their tire punctures.] There were churches, and also colleges and houses belonging to the Roman Catholics and the nonconformists.

I remember the Quaker scholar Douglas Steere, later a professor at Haverford College, asking me at a tea party whether I felt more sense of the numinous in a meeting of Quakers or in a high-sung Eucharist. This question remained with me for several reasons. First, it was considered very American to ask such a question at a tea party. Inhibited English folk did not discuss personal faith or sex at a tea party. I knew and liked my questioner. He was studying the thought of Baron von Hügel, whose work had influenced me. Douglas Steere's dissertation was supervised by my own tutor Canon Streeter.

Steere's question also reflected the period, for Rudolph Otto's book *The Idea of the Holy* had come out the year I went up to Oxford. Thus the concept and the word "numinous" were current.

Other books that had come out about the same time and had influenced me included R. H. Tawney's *Religion and the Rise of Capitalism* and R. G. Collingwood's *Speculam Mentis,* which had come out a couple of years earlier. Sir Edwyn Hoskyns of Cambridge a couple of years later translated Karl Barth's *Epistle to the Romans.* We were also reading the German Formgeschichte scholars and, of course, Bultmann and Dibelius.

Scientists also stirred winds of philosophical speculation. The work of A. N. Whitehead, whose *Religion in the Making* had been widely read, acquainted us with the concept of process and reality, while Lloyd Morgan challenged us to think about emergent evolution. Joseph Needham of Cambridge caught the attention of many with his book *The Sceptical Biologist.*

Many other books of all kinds were coming out in the middle twenties. The novels of E. M. Forster, Aldous Huxley, Virginia Woolf, D. H. Lawrence, Sinclair Lewis, and Thornton Wilder were read and discussed. Likewise, Lytton Strachey's *Eminent Victorians* was enjoyed and argued about with energy. Was he to be our English Voltaire? Many poems of T. S. Eliot had come out—often muttered quotations used to be heard—and Robert Graves was giving us verses. Those of Yeats and Ezra Pound also made us argue. I had met them both at Rapallo, on the Italian Riviera, where my father was thinking of retiring. My father sometimes played chess with W. B. Yeats, and I believe also with Ezra Pound.

My own generation at Oxford already was producing poets: C. Day Lewis, W. H. Auden, Stephen Spender (who was immortalized as an "Isis Idol"), and Louis MacNeice. These last two looked very much as a poet should look, elegant and romantic, while Auden did not.

There were also some who became prominent in the political world. Quentin Hogg, now Lord Hailsham, was president of the Union (debating society) my last year. Dick (R. H.) Crossman and Hugh Gaitskell both were contemporaries of mine.

Such belong to my store of memories of Oxford in those years. For me it had been a season and a place where there had been opportunity to learn and to read, also to talk and listen. But now that I had my First Class Honours, what was I going to do immediately or what was I going to plan for?

Such questions beset any recent graduate, but I was lucky in having friends, senior academics, who were wise and who helped me. I was not to decide my life work the first two months of my postgraduate existence. Better, one told me, to read and think and get a research fellowship, and go on asking questions. "Read something quite different from what you have been doing," suggested E. L. Woodward. "Read Dante, read Luther, read the Bible in German, read anything except those second century second-rate church fathers you have been working on," another friend advised. "Go abroad, learn another language, get out of Oxford," and so on, and so on. My name had been put in for a research fellowship. But in the field of theology, all graduate fellowships were limited to what were called "Clerks in Holy Orders." Incidentally, the same was true for the higher degrees in theology, but a couple of years later some of my academic teachers and friends changed that by action of the Hebdomanal Council. This was establishment Oxford!

Jobs of various sorts and kinds were suggested. C. H. Dodd, who had been one of my examiners in my finals, had been appointed to a chair at Manchester University. He suggested I might be his assistant, and I would have the advantage of the excellent Rylands Library. Canon Raven, whom I knew slightly as he was a friend of Canon Streeter, had organized a school of religion at the cathedral at Liverpool—what about a part-time job there? So it went on and on. Sir Flinders Petrie, the great pottery archaeologist, was collecting volunteers for his dig. . . . I was very tempted, for archaeological research was always alluring. (This was the period when Sir Leonard Wooley had thrilled us all with his discovery of the layers in Ur of the Chaldees that showed there had been the physical flood in that area, stories of which appear in Sumerian, Assyrian, and Hebrew literature.)

Other friends, however, remarked that if I were interested in "bread for the hungry"—in other words, education and concern for those who needed it—I should not go hunting for "dead bones." There was truth in this. I had thought of working in the East End of London at St. Margaret's, a settlement house, and perhaps studying at the same time.

One rather interesting challenge came from my own Anglican church. I was recommended for a job teaching at a college for the training of deaconesses. I visited the college to investigate. The Order of Deaconesses had been reinstituted in the days of the evangelical revival of Anglicanism in the nineteenth century. The women were ordained, and performed all sorts of useful work, usually in local parishes. They *were* ordained, but the ordination in no way was equivalent to the Order of Deacons for men. Nor were they permitted to perform any part of liturgical services in the church. Also, if a deaconess married, her ordination was annulled.

This last was most intriguing and altogether illogical, not only to me but to many others, who, as I had, studied the whole history and theology of orders in the church for Bishops, Priests, and Deacons. At the root of all this was the fear of the woman, or of sex, which had so infiltrated our theology and ecclesiastical life. Some of my friends were anxious that I, theologically educated, should test this by offering myself as a candidate for ordination as a deaconess, and then see what might happen!

Meanwhile, V. T. Harlow, a friend who had helped to prepare me for Oxford, noticed an advertisement in the university *Gazette* for a traveling fellowship to come to Union Theological Seminary in New York City for a year. The English committee consisted of two Anglican professors—one from Oxford, one from Cambridge—and two nonconformist ones. My name was submitted, and all of them—three of the four I knew—warmly supported me and put me at the top of the list. When my name and sex reached Union Seminary, the president, Henry Sloane Coffin, cabled back, "No, no woman accepted," or words to that effect.

When the English committee received this news, they were irritated. They thought it was ridiculous and cabled back to Dr. Coffin, apparently telling him not to be silly, and that my academic record was far superior to that of any of the men on the list.

Meanwhile I, quite happily, was considering all sorts of possibilities when a cable arrived saying Union Seminary would let me come! I was rather inclined to let it all go, but my eminent friends at Oxford and Cambridge thought it in the interests of everyone that I should go.

Therefore, after various rearrangements, I set sail for this land of opportunity. I did not know then what fate might befall me.

How I Met Reinhold Niebuhr

"I think I would like to listen to some of the natives," I said. "After all, the Scottish professors I have read and know about, so there is not much point in going to *their* lectures."

It was 1930, and I was speaking to a Scot, a delightful, erudite Highlander, John Baillie, so I knew I was safe in making such a remark. He had taught in the U.S.A. at Auburn Presbyterian Seminary in upper New York state, and then had gone to Queen's University in Kingston, Ontario. After becoming well known in the theological world, he had been invited to become professor of systematic theology at Union Theological Seminary. He and his tall, English wife, Jewel, had just settled in their academic quarters when I arrived from England. He had been assigned to me as one of my two supervisors for research, and he was helping me to arrange the best use of my time.

The curriculum at Union Theological Seminary, although it was regarded as a graduate institution, seemed to me to be pregraduate rather than postgraduate in its academic program. After taking "schools" in theology at Oxford, and getting a "First," I had looked forward to the freedom of independent study and concentration on a particular subject of research. As my fellowship only extended to the eight-month academic year, it was obvious that all I would be able to do would be to start on this: to do some preparatory reading, organize the field in which I wanted to concentrate, and listen and imbibe what American theologians were thinking, doing, and writing. I had read a good deal in the learned journals of New Testament scholars particularly, such as C. C. Torrey, Ropes, and Henry Cadbury on the text of the New Testament and the historical setting and interpretation of the New Testament documents. But what about the others? This was what Professor Baillie and I had been discussing as well as the philosophy of John Dewey, whose influence prevailed at Columbia University and Teachers' College "across the street" from Union Theological Seminary. Should I read American philosophy? I had read a little of William James, whose *Varieties of Religious Experience* had interested me enough to make me want to read more, and then there was Josiah Royce and, of course, A. N. Whitehead from England, now at Harvard. Some of my more senior friends at Oxford had obtained Commonwealth Fellowships in order to study with him, but I was not interested in philosophy as much as in understanding the historical situation which colored and shaped the philosophy. So what was I to do in these few short months?

Professor Baillie was most understanding. He shared this same view of the possibilities of postgraduate research, so together we worked out a "schedule" for me that would satisfy the academic authorities at the seminary and yet would give me time and freedom to start something of interest and usefulness for further study.

"But they will want you to take a degree," he said, looking at me somewhat quizzically.

"Heavens!" said I. "What, after less than eight months of study? What sort of degree would that be?" I was scandalized.

"Yes, an M.A." he said. "And what is more, the dissertation for that degree will have to be in on April 1st." He looked at me most apologetically.

"April the 1st! April Fools' Day! How absolutely idiotic! Why on earth?" I got up from my chair. I felt ready to go back to England, to throw the fellowship in their faces. What an insult to this serious, embryonic scholar. My mind went back to the notice for this fellowship in the Oxford University *Gazette*. It was a humbug. I felt cheated.

Professor Baillie was most conciliatory. He understood completely, and he explained that apparently some holders of a similar fellowship from Scotland had not justified their opportunities and had spent their time going to night clubs and speakeasies, so the degree requirement was put in as a restraint. As he told me this, I got angrier and angrier, but I did not want to show it to this kind, courteous, delightful, newfound friend. How could I tell him that Scottish theological students, doomed no doubt to some grim parish in a granitelike village or in gloomy Glasgow were taking the last fling at the fleshpots of New York before such a fate. But such were not models for scholarly research. He came to my rescue.

"Look here," he said, "we will work out something that will be all right. You read what you would like, tackle some book you want to read or some period in which you want to read, and I will talk to Professor Scott, your other supervisor. You think out a topic that sounds all right, and then you can write an essay for him and me just as you might report on your reading and then we will use that as your thesis."

I sputtered somewhat at this; it was kind of him but somehow did not do justice to my yearnings to be a proper research person embarking on my subject. But Professor Baillie was being so nice, so I conceded, "Well, I suppose, perhaps I could do it as a sort of prolegomenon." Somehow that long word was impressive enough in its sound to restore a little of my *amour propre*.

Professor Baillie assented eagerly, "Yes," he said, "that would be splendid. Draft an approach to your subject, and then indeed entitle it as a prolegomenon!" We discussed this further and worked out a sort of program. I was to go to his own lectures, and, returning to my initial comment, he suggested I should listen to the lectures of one of the American scholars. There did not seem to be too many of them in the more academic subjects; the native teachers seemed to be teaching practical subjects such as pastoral theology and parish work, religious education, and so forth. The famous Dr. Harry Emerson Fosdick, who was minister of the neighboring Riverside Church, which had only recently been erected and then opened, lectured three times a week on what was called the English Bible, a very effective interpretation of biblical material for clergy, teachers, and church workers.

"There is a new man here," Dr. Baillie said. "He has only been here a year or two, and he gave his inaugural lecture a week or two before you arrived. He is a remarkable chap, had a parish in Detroit, is very intelligent and most interesting." He looked across his desk at me and with that charming intense speech of a Highland Scot, he added, "You'll *love* him." I did not want to sound snobbish or supercilious, but I was rather amused at his comment and thought how nice it was that Professor Baillie was so enthusiastic about his colleague.

Professor Baillie then relayed an invitation from his wife for me to come to dinner with them and with the German Fellow, who had come from Berlin. His name was Dietrich Bonhoeffer. I had already met him and thought him rather too Teutonic and too Prussian for my taste. We had talked about the German scholars whom I had read, but he was not very forthcoming although he and I shared a few similar reactions to some American customs and conditions, particularly the fact that academic buildings were maintained at the temperature of 85 to 90 degrees Fahrenheit.

It was not long before I met the "new man" from Detroit. It came about by chance as I was leaving the office of a distinguished professor who had welcomed me as bringing news from scholars in his field at Oxford. When we had finished our conversation, he said, "I hope you will see something of this country outside these academic halls."

"Oh yes," I said, getting up to go and thinking in a flash of the amusing and interesting places I had already been "outside these academic halls." Then I added, "Today I've been asked to lunch with the editors of the *New Republic*. I've been reading through the back numbers for the last year or so to prepare me for the occasion, and I wonder if you could help me. I am not quite sure of their political stance, for example, in the election of 1928 and the Al Smith campaign." But then I thought that perhaps this was not in the realm of my kind host.

He also got up, looking a little baffled. "I don't read the *New Republic*. I know there are some very good literary critics who write for it, but I would not want to, or venture to . . ." He opened the door of his office, and warmly and kindly said that he would be glad to welcome me to his seminar and asked me to come back and tell him more about some of my former tutors at Oxford who worked in his field.

"Here comes a colleague of mine," he said. "You certainly ought to meet him. Now, *he* would be able to help you about the *New Republic* and its political views.

"Professor Niebuhr," he raised his voice, "I wonder if you have met our new English Fellow?"

A tall figure had been walking rapidly down the corridor more or less in the direction of the professor's office and was turning right to go down the stairs but turned back on hearing the words addressed to him. A tall, rather bald gentleman with a ruddy countenance and piercing blue eyes stretched out his hand. "Pleased to meet you." My host hastily introduced us and continued, "Miss Keppel-Compton was inquiring about the politics of the *New Republic*."

"The *New Republic*, well—." There followed a rapid description and analysis of the varying political stances that the writers of the *New Republic* had shown over the past few years. I listened, interested, but was entirely unable to assimilate all of these details despite my reading of the back numbers. Yet I was fascinated by the flow of words and vigor of description.

The professor stopped himself, took out his watch, looked at it, and thrust forward his hand, "Happy to talk to you some time about American politics. I would like to ask you about things in England, too." He turned and went down the stone staircase two or three steps at a time.

"A rather refreshing academic," said I to myself as I bade a final farewell to the older professor. I hoped I would remember something of what I had recently learned, as I took my way via elevated railway and subway to the offices of the *New Republic* on Varick Street.

It was all rather exciting to be asked to such an occasion. I had had friends whose fathers or other relations wrote for the *Spectator* or the fairly new *Weekend Review* or the *Manchester Guardian,* but never had I been asked to luncheon with the editors of these illustrious journals. Naturally, therefore, I felt somewhat tremulous and hoped I would not betray my Oxford and English background by displaying dreadful ignorance about American affairs.

But I need not have worried. The editor, Bruce Bliven, looking benign behind his spectacles, welcomed me, and as soon as I saw his wife Rosie, I forgot my apprehensions. I sat at lunch between Bruce Bliven and Malcolm Cowley. The conversation ranged from Creole cooking, about which Stark Young discoursed at length, to Joe Cook. This last name worried me. Joe Cook—who was he? Had I missed some important political candidate? I found American names, which seemed sometimes quite ordinary, often were the same as the names of colleges and universities. Al Smith, of course, had nothing to do with Smith College. Brown University had not produced a Brown candidate, although I knew the Browns of Rhode Island as a very distinguished family. But Cook—Cook County? I seemed to remember that had something to do with politics in Chicago. Was that named after Joe Cook? Oh heavens! My host, Bruce Bliven, must have sensed my perplexity, and he explained the nature of Joe Cook's eminence. "He was a music hall star." Mr. Bliven, who wrote a weekly column for the *Manchester Guardian,* was very adept at explaining American life to English readers, and he proceeded to translate and explain other aspects of American life, none of it—on that occasion, however—in the political realm.

I don't think I shall ever forget that occasion. It was a delightfully warm autumn day in late October or early November, and I remember writing home to say it was wonderful to walk about New York in a silk dress. How dated that sounds today! I knew that in England, either in my native Hampshire or at Oxford, the sturdy tweed suit with a warm sweater, and probably a raincoat as well, would have been my garb. So the sun and the light and the vivid bright shadows in New York thrilled and stirred me. What a wonderful place—how nice everybody was, and how clean it was compared to London. This was the autumn of 1930, and how pleasant I found it all.

Part I

Letters and Memoirs
1931-1939
Reinhold and Ursula Niebuhr

One

1931
Engaged But Apart:
Transatlantic Letters

"You will love him." So Professor John Baillie charmingly had said when discussing with me which lecture courses I should attend. Not only did I discover that I *did* love Reinhold but he had been discovering he was in love with me.

That academic year of 1930–31 passed all too quickly. I had to write a dissertation before April 1st. Also, I had wanted to get the flavor of American thought in various theological areas. I attended a seminar where recent cosmologies of A. N. Whitehead and Lloyd Morgan were analyzed and discussed. I attended Reinhold's lectures, as did Dietrich Bonhoeffer and the other fellows from abroad.

Friends of mine from Oxford heard rumors of my involvement with Reinhold, and a charming couple came over to see what the situation was and, if possible, to dissuade me from any foolish course of action with somebody they had never heard of. Very kindly they bore me off to Washington for the Easter weekend, and we had a splendid time. Afterward I was able to introduce them to Reinhold, but they were still a little apprehensive.

By the beginning of May we were engaged. Professor John Baillie and his charming wife Jewel asked us both to dinner and we told them the happy secret. Their affectionate friendship was to mean much to both of us in the years to come.

But plans for our own immediate future were complicated. Reinhold had a busy summer schedule, speaking at many student and other conferences, and also teaching at the summer school at Union Seminary and at its annual Ministers' Conference. In between, he was also working on *Moral Man and Immoral Society*. There were family problems for him as well. His mother, Lydia, had lived with him ever since her husband's death and since Reinhold's ordination. Only twenty-two years older than Reinhold, she enjoyed living in the parsonage and helping him with the parish in Detroit. She told me that she had not missed her husband after he had died, as "Reinhold has taken his place." She, as also Reinhold, had assumed that she would live with us.

Such a prospect alarmed me. I returned to England to see my own family and friends, and to ponder the situation with the man I had promised to marry.

Despite everything, we were too much in love to do anything else but marry, which we did on December 22, 1931, in Winchester Cathedral.

Black Mountain, NC
July 14, 1931

Dearest Ursula:

Now you can read my letters. A new portable typewriter which I ordered some time ago came yesterday. I celebrated by getting off my speech to be delivered in Cleveland at the World YMCA Conference, and which must be translated into sixteen languages and must therefore be in their hands this week. The stuff I wrote is not worth putting into one language, but I will put up a bluff if they want me too. Played with one of the executives at Blue Ridge at golf yesterday afternoon and beat him because he was a little worse than I. It was my first game in three years and therefore pretty bad.

Your report on the family was, of course, very interesting to me. It is rather sad that your mother should not have a place for the evening of her life more suited to her needs than Woodhall. Is there any possibility of changing things still? We men are a self-sufficient lot who might well take advice more frequently than we do. Your plans about going to Oxford for a good part of my stay suits me very well. How about spending a little time in London? You haven't forgotten that I am supposed to hang around the Round Table Conference[1] a little if it starts on September 6th. My present information is that the committee on structure begins [then] and that Gandhi will be present for it. I don't suppose that very much will happen in the first weeks, however.

Now that I have a typewriter I am going to try to work seriously on my book. I can't think without a machine. It has become a part of my mental equipment since I have used one consistently since I was 16. It is such a job to know just where to dig in. I feel like an architect who is laying the foundations for a big building on a hillside and wonders just where the surveying job is to begin. I am almost tempted to defer work on the book a little longer and try to do an article for the *Atlantic*. I haven't missed an annual article for them for eight years now and if I don't do it now, it won't be done.

Meanwhile the time slips by, and it is little more than a month before I will see you. What a reunion that will be. I have so many things I want to talk about. And then also I don't want to talk at all but just know your presence. Good-bye my dearest. I must run off to the mail.

Semper idem,

Reinie

1. *Round Table Conference called by Lord Irwin (later Lord Halifax) and Gandhi at Kingsley Hall.*

Black Mountain, NC
July 14, 1931

Dearest Ursula:

Though I have written you once today, I am going to write again, the pretext being the enclosed letter from Dot Hackett.[1]

After spending a week resting up I am beginning to feel like myself and am ready for some real work. I have done a good deal of reading in spite of the feeling of lassitude, and now I am going to work on my courses. Also I am getting ambitious for an article in the *Atlantic*. Think I will write on "The Peril of American Power." Getting a typewriter in my hands again gives me all kinds of ambition.

Sorry you missed the [Sherwood] Eddys in London. Perhaps you saw them after all? They won't be back to the U.S.A. until we're old married folks. Mrs. Page and daughter Mary arrived today. They have a cottage not very far from ours. We are close enough so that we can get together and work out our *World Tomorrow*[2] stuff, yet we can be as alone as we want. Kirby[3] and I play tennis together every other morning. I beat him this morning for the first time. He is a little too good for me. My tennis is too soft for a real player. Heard a rumor yesterday that Pit[4] is being considered rather seriously for the presidency of Princeton. I don't know whether I desire that for him or not. He will end as a college president some day, but Princeton is too much of a nice country club. Asked him about it two weeks ago and he said he wasn't interested.

Here I go gossiping about all sorts of things. Didn't get a letter from you today. You have no idea how much time I put in going to the post office three miles away. Thus you keep me from the American ideal of efficiency.

Your devoted,

Old Man

1. *Former student at Union Seminary, recently married.* 2. World Tomorrow: *a liberal journal.* 3. *Kirby Page; fellow editor of* World Tomorrow *and a well-known pacifist writer and speaker.* 4. *Henry Pitney Van Dusen; later president of Union Seminary.*

Black Mountain, NC
July 16, 1931

Dearest Ursula:

This morning's mail brought me two letters from you and all the interesting enclosures. The bishop [of Southampton, Cecil Boutflower] is certainly good. I knew our marriage would be "mixed" nationally speaking and perhaps in a few other ways, but it never occurred to me to think of it as mixed religiously speaking and I don't suppose it did to you. That letter from such a nice man shows how little nonconformist means in England even to this day, at least from the perspective of "the church." When I think of religion's many little parochialisms I am inclined to agree with Briffault about it. Mrs. Moffatt's[1] reactions are good too. Of course I don't rate with Pit and a mere English girl can't compete with a Scotch one from the Moffatt perspective, so we will have to be satisfied with an afterthought from that quarter. We should worry, in good American parlance. I shudder to think of all the little slights which you will have to suffer for marrying into the department of Christian ethics. For most of your compatriots on the faculty that is worse than marrying a non-Anglican from the bishop's viewpoint. That was a nice letter from Doris.[2] The German girl who added the postscript is a buxom German lass of the kind you find in the storybooks only that she has more brains.

I love your letters except that they give me an inferiority complex. I can really get a picture of your life from your letters while all I can do in my letters is to say, "The weather is nice today and it is not quite as hot as it was yesterday." Last night I finished my Union lectures, at least one set of them. The other set of five will be done a little later. I am not doing as much work as I expected. I read a lot but not to much purpose, and my work on my courses has not been started.

I like your suggestion about getting a car, if we can. I'm going to leave arrangements pretty much in your hands. The only proviso as far as I am concerned is that we must spend about four days or so in London or very close to it. That will be necessary only if the committee on structure actually convenes on September 6th and Gandhi is in London. I am not going to bother him with an attempt at an interview for the *World Tomorrow,* but I will have to try to get something from his entourage and something on the general intent of the meeting. For the rest I will leave it all to you. The idea of spending some time in Oxford appeals to me very much. But don't forget that I'm a bashful soul. I want to meet your best friends of course but not all of those brilliant people who are on the periphery of your Oxford career. That's a very nice letter from Professor Harlow.[3] I am certainly anxious to meet him and Mrs. Harlow and I shall write him shortly.—Looking over the sentence previous to the last, I find that there is something the matter with it. But I will let you laugh at it without correcting it.

You are worried about my sentence from Virginia about making "each other miserable in love." What I mean is that sometimes I have a fear that I won't make you happy because I am a rather unimaginative cuss, and there are many things about the feminine mind and about the human soul that I do not understand. You know that I believe that real love can overcome all difficulties, only I worry sometimes about putting your love to too severe a test. And yet I don't worry either. I know what we have already experienced together is proof against all of life's vicissitudes. Douglas Steere,[4] whom I met, as I think I told you, at Williamstown and who was more enthusiastic about our adventure than anyone else, gave me some interesting testimony which I appreciated for its very honesty. He said, "When I tell you that marriage is wonderful I don't belittle the difficulties. My wife and I are much happier now than we were two years ago. The period of feeling out the places where we hurt each other is over and it has been rather glorious to find how love grows rather than diminishes as you overcome the initial difficulties."

Am reading Parker's *Human Values* today. Remember I gave that book to you in the hall one day when you were working on a paper for me. I didn't give it to you at that, for I have the selfsame book here. It is really quite good and gives me a point or two for my work. I enclose a very brief outline of my book [*Moral Man and Immoral Society*] which does not satisfy me at all. I can't really get started on it. But it shows the kind of material I want to deal with though probably in an entirely different sequence. It has been so long since I have done consistent and consecutive thinking that I can't get down to it. If I were an artist, I would write numerous short stories and never get to a real novel. My resolution peters out before I finish the larger task.

Sent you a fountain pen for your birthday today. I will write you a birthday letter later but just mention the fact in case the package arrives before the day. I thought I remembered that you lost your pen and hence the gift which had to be chosen from a very limited supply of things down here in the woods.

Once I get started I want to say so many things that I can't really say on paper. I'll store most of them up for August 22nd. Meanwhile I am with you day by day and hour by hour.

Yours forever,

Reinie

1. Mrs. James Moffatt, wife of biblical scholar who translated the Bible. 2. A former student. 3. Professor V. T. Harlow; Oxford expert on colonial British history. 4. A Quaker scholar who taught at Haverford College. U. N. had known him when he was studying at Oxford with her tutor Canon B. H. Streeter.

Black Mountain, NC
August 3, 1931

Dearest Ursula:

Since I haven't heard from you for several days, all I can do is to write a few unimaginative words, for if you don't prime my pump no water flows. Here it is but two days from breaking up camp. I have bought my ticket so I feel like the end is drawing nigh. It has been a very delightful vacation, not quite as much work was done as I anticipated, but I was pretty tired when I arrived. I enclose a letter from the *Atlantic* which I received in the same mail yesterday in which I sent my letter off to you. This means that my annual article for the *Atlantic* has again been accepted. I think I wrote you that it is on "The Peril of American Power." It's the kind of article which might feed the prejudices of the friend in Woodhall who thinks that Americans are so terrible. But of course there is no animus in my indictment. I am beginning to think that all human beings react very similarly under identical conditions. Am going to make an index on all my reading this month for the book and then write "finis" to that work. On the boat I am going to work only on my courses.

Will be with you so shortly now that I can already see you standing on the dock.

Yours in bondage,

Reinie

Enroute
August 6, 1931

Dearest Ursula:

The acquisition of a portable typewriter for use during my vacation makes it possible to write a letter on a train. It is against the Pullman code to do so, but since there is no one in the smoker with me, the porter hasn't stopped me thus far. I left Black Mountain last night and will arrive in Cleveland at 3:45 this afternoon. I thought I would write you now for, except I get a letter on the train soon, it will not precede me to England. I can hardly believe that I am off in nine days and will be with you in a little more than two weeks.

As the day arrives I am filled with more and more longing and with more and more trepidation, the one being relevant to you and the other to the host of people who will have to "look me over." I shouldn't be such a fool, but I might as well confess the worst. I hope in arranging our program you can allow about four days for London. Gandhi will arrive on September 6th according to present plans and C. F. Andrews, who is going to have charge of his household, is a good friend of mine. I think he will arrange so that we can participate in some of the smaller meetings of Gandhi's delegation held at Kingsley House. I would like to get a little glimpse of the inner circle and pick up as much as I can of the why and wherefore of Indian politics. After reading a good deal about the situation I think what you report about Lord Irwin's [later Lord Halifax, viceroy of India] pessimism is quite in line with all the facts. The conference will probably not succeed except some kind of miracle occurs.

The enclosed pictures were taken two days before my leaving Black Mountain and I brought them along to send to you. One of them will show you how much tan I acquired in my daily morning tennis match with Kirby [Page] and in my occasional efforts at berry picking. The mountains are full of blackberries and Hulda [R.N.'s sister] and I picked enough to give Mother a jelly supply for the winter (for both families mother declares). Thus we frugally combined foresight with pleasure and sunbathing.

Besides meeting your father and mother, I have become especially anxious to know your sister. She seems to have a delightful sense of humor. Of course I am not surprised at that. But tell her to go easy on those limericks.

A fellow has disturbed my isolation and looks askance at my machine, so good-bye until "Der Tag."

Yours,

Reinie

Union Theological Seminary
New York, NY
August 9, 1931

Dearest Ursula:

It is Sunday night, and I am in my office after two meetings today to get ready for my two classes tomorrow. I don't feel very much like working in this heat but it has to be done. I wonder what you will make of our American summers. Luckily we won't have to spend many of them in the city but every once in a while I will have to serve at the summer school. Pit tells me that his wife is quite washed out by the heat. They are away with his folks at Cape Cod over this weekend. Saw Pit in Cleveland before coming here.

All kinds of folks want to be remembered to you, the Frames,[1] the [Harry Emerson] Fosdicks (who are sailing Wednesday for Germany), the Moores,[2] my brother, etc., etc. Am having dinner with my two brothers and Beulah,[3] tomorrow night. Am writing this while Dr. Fosdick is holding forth in my place at the vesper service. As I am becoming a little more sensible, I refused to talk three times today.

When I think that a week from today I will be on the ocean England bound, I get all excited. In some ways a whole aeon seems to have passed since we last saw each other. When I realize that the next wait will be longer than this one, I see what a problem is involved. But I had better not say too much about that since my last efforts along this line seem to have gotten me into trouble. It will be wonderful though to have those days in which to make definite plans and prepare for the finals. If I could express myself properly I could tell you how much my whole life has been changed by the fact and the thought of your love and the idea of a partnership between us through the years. It will be glorious even though I am afraid my thoughtlessness will give you more than one moment of misery. But I'll try to cultivate the graces of a decent, domesticated male.

Yours in eternal love,

Reinie

1. *James Frame was professor of New Testament at Union Seminary.* 2. *John Moore; graduate student at Union Seminary.* 3. *R.N.'s two brothers were Helmut Richard and Walter; Walter was married to Beulah.*

Woodhall Spa
Lincolnshire, England

Sunday Morning
August 9, 1931

Darling:

. . . This morning I am looking forward to another Sunday morning a fortnight ahead and I wonder about it all. Two more weeks, and it is just over eight weeks since we said good-bye at Boston. They have been such odd weeks, I don't know any time in my life I have found more trying.

. . . Going back to the "I and Thou" business, there *does* have to be a lot of faith, doesn't there? I always find myself imagining that you feel about me, in the same sort of way I feel about you, just because we both love and are in love. But I don't suppose that is altogether valid, is it? Anyhow, so my reason and even imagination tell me. But if I listen to my reason and even to my imagination, I would never dare to let myself go and talk to you as I do. So I shut my ears to these voices of reason and imagination and walk or rather write—in faith. Of course, faith may be too good a name for what in this case probably is a gigantic self-delusion and egoistic projection of my own feelings. It is really all very difficult.

. . . Monday was most exciting; I had four letters from you, and the *World Tomorrow* followed the next day. The letters were most cheering, darling, the ones written the last days in July and on August 1st, one letter especially made me feel very happy. You too apparently had been feeling the same things that I had, which made the fact that our belonging to each other more certain.

And the *World Tomorrow* was good too. The editorial seemed first rate, also your book reviews. And I enjoyed amazingly that article on Vladeck;[1] I am longing to hear you tell me more about him. Who wrote that article? I am also wanting to know what the atmospherics of the Socialist Party are at the moment, and the results of your cogitations with Norman Thomas.[2]

What masses we'll have to talk about, and yet we won't want to talk all the time. I always look back to the times when we just sat together, and knew each other without speaking, rather than the times when we were talking, don't you? And that's what I am waiting for each day now. I think of you lecturing, speaking, preaching, among all the people and in the heat of New York. Then I think of the days ahead and am lost in glad anticipation.

[U.M. K-C.]

1. *Charney Vladeck; editor of the* Jewish Daily Forward.   2. *Leader of Socialist Party; perennial party candidate for president.*

Union Theological Seminary
New York, NY
August 11, 1931

My Dearest:

As the day draws near and as I wait for three days without mail from you, I see more than ever all that you mean to me and how foolish I am in my inability to express myself and tell you all that. I sit down and write you my humdrum letters when what I ought to be saying is something quite different, about how completely my life has been changed by our love and how much I look into the future with all its problems with a great deal of joy, knowing that we will be facing it together. I also ought to say how sorry I am to be such a poor correspondent. But I'll try to say all the things I can't say in a letter when I see you. I have been making pictures of you constantly at the dock in Southampton, with me craning my neck to see whether I could get a glimpse of you. It will be fun. —Just had a note from Coffin[1] asking me to come and see him before I sail. I don't know how he thinks I am going to do that. Arnold[2] is still languishing in jail on a serious charge. Can't get out on bail which means that they are going to try to deal with him as harshly as possible.

Have to speak twice tonight, once to student movement people and later to the Columbia socialist crowd. The summer school group here this summer is rather inferior. Most of them are parsons who have little conception what it is all about.

John Bennett[3] sends me excerpts from a letter from John Naish.[4] He says, "He is a fortunate man. I had heard that she was engaged but did not know until I met her that he was the man. Of course I know the *Tamed Cynic* so it was delightful to know that she was to have a husband worthy of her." I'll subscribe at least heartily to the first sentence and hope that the second is not too far from the truth.

Yours in impatience,

Reinie

1. *Henry Sloane Coffin; president of Union Seminary.*   2. *Arnold Johnson; a Union Seminary student concerned with workers and their rights, who later became a state (Ohio) and national communist leader.*   3. *Professor and later president of Union Seminary.* 4. *Oxford tutor of U.N.*

Woodhall Spa
Lincolnshire, England

Friday Night
August 14, 1931

Darling:

. . . Four letters came from you today, the last days you had in Black Mountain, and one written on the train, with photos of you and your family. They were quite good, one specially good of you. And, I loved your letter, but then I always do. I am afraid I am not going to get my letters from you next week, as you sounded as if you weren't going to write much longer. But—I suppose I *can* wait nine days before I see you.

I am going off on Monday to stay with Mrs. Preston, Bob's [R. H. Keppel-Compton, U.N.'s brother] mother-in-law, at Bedford before going down to Bishop Cecil [Boutflower] at Winchester on Friday. She, Mrs. Preston, is a very beloved friend, and one of the most gallant ladies that I know. She is very alone now, and rather crippled in gait and health at that, with a broken hip bone that never joined up properly. She lives at Bedford with very devoted maids and enjoys her friends, and lives a very restricted life in the gayest spirit. She used to be very active and alive in every way, and now her bad health and loneliness cut her off from so much. But she is still a good sport and a wise one.

I laughed over the letter from the *Atlantic* editor. . . . "Had a great conversation about the confessional, clergy and human nature." Can't you see it? or rather hear it? To talk about the confessional with the soup, clergy—as the pièce de résistance, and human nature bringing in the dessert! But, he showed an expected wisdom about your article. I want to see it.

I had such a nice letter from Douglas Steere this morning. I'll show it to you the week after next now. Also, I had one from your friend Bishop Scarlett[1] last Monday in which he spoke most charmingly about you, and about you and me. It was terribly nice of him to write. I am longing to meet him as well as all your other friends.

Incidentally, you didn't get the point of my "reactions" to the meeting of some of your acquaintances and even of Walter and Beulah. I was perhaps amused that I was treated with such care as if I was either a corpse or a sin or a problem or anything that wasn't terribly ordinary and natural. I don't think I have got the appropriate sense of the numinous for some of the conventional occasions of this life. I only want to giggle when other people seem to be too serious.

I am listening to Mozart's G Minor on the gramaphone and it's bringing back other occasions listening to the Lerner Quartet. Chamber music I love, and this is great. I think Mozart here is portraying the soul of Harlequin. . . . Man playing with the illusion of freedom within the determined sphere of his own little world, and making or trying to make his own harmony within the scale allowed him.

Anyhow, I am glad over the harmony that happened to have happened with us. I don't think I could ever have achieved the harmony by myself. But perhaps no one can achieve that by him or herself. Now, I look forward to one long harmony with you, darling.

Ursula

1. *William Scarlett; Episcopal Bishop of Missouri.*

Union Theological Seminary
New York, NY
September 23, 1931

My Dearest:

I didn't get a chance to write that letter last night, Arnold and Allen[1] sat in my office until midnight and I couldn't get rid of them. They are very much confused and don't quite know what to do. Harrowing experiences such as they have had leave a mark on the human spirit, or rather they leave marks some of them ennobling and some of them more dubious. I think Arnold will do some work here and spend his weekends speaking for the miners. I am trying to prevent him from joining up with the communists. He has resigned from the Socialist Party as being too conservative.

Pit is nicely ensconced in an apartment big enough for social events, but the darn place costs $140 a month. We might be able to swing that for a few months.

. . . The students are standing outside before a closed door while I write this letter and they are becoming urgent so I'll have to open up to them. Our opening convention begins in an hour. I have 18 applicants for my seminar but only 10 places, so I'll have to weed out eight and that's a job.

Am anxiously awaiting your first letter. Your book by E. L. Woodward[2] was here on my arrival, but I haven't had a chance to get at it yet.

Yours devotedly,

R.

1. *Allen Keedy; student of R.N.'s.* 2. Three Studies in European Conservatism *(1929).*

New York, NY
September 24, 1931

The grind has begun. Yesterday, Jimmy Frame started off with a very brilliant address on the cultivated minister. Classes begin today. Many ask about you and send love, and also many of the students including Bill Pickford. Pickford went to a summer colony, all equipped with flannels and swell clothes, to find out that he was a minister to poor farmers and miners.

. . . I find it difficult to concentrate upon my work and I suppose I will do horrible stuff in the next months. I shall depend greatly on moral support from your letters which will soon be arriving regularly I am sure. Jim Dombrowski[1] and I are having lunch together this noon and he is now waiting for me. Arnold has decided to continue his studies. So we are getting a little more settled. The communist organizer came around yesterday, nice young woman who has considerable influence with Arnold, but he has held out against her. The English Fellow for this year has just called to say he is coming up to see me.

Yours ever and always,

Reinie

1. *Graduate student and assistant in Department of Christian Ethics.*

Union Theological Seminary
New York, NY
September 26, 1931

My Dearest:

Two letters from you came this morning and I am glad. I received one from the hotel and the other where you were staying with the Wells.[1]

We had our retreat[2] yesterday. For some strange reason most everyone turned out. Pit and I did the talking. We took absolutely the opposite sides of the question; his speech being full of counsel about sanity, caution, circumspection, etc., etc. I took a rather different line without joining issues with him, though it was rather apparent to the listeners that we were further apart than we have ever been. Had a long talk with Dr. Coffin the other night. He is terribly worried about some of the students and will more and more be inclined to bring pressure against radicalism. It's not going to be easy to steer an honest and at the same time a sane course.

Have a delicious feeling of being unhurried this morning. I can go over the weekly journals without just skimming the articles and get a lecture or two ready for next week. Started out with a class of 50 in Philosophy of Religion but my Ethics course is smaller. Have reduced my seminar from 18 to 12. This noon we have our staff meeting at the *World Tomorrow*. The rest of the day will be given over to pure study.

. . . Just at this point some students came in to disturb my quiet and ask about their work for this year. Some sent regards to you. *Time* magazine just called up to ask whether I was responsible for the memorial to the President.[3] So it goes. Writing you this gossip I can't help thinking how nice it will be to do all things together when that time comes.

Yours impatiently,

[R.N.]

1. *Close friends of Keppel-Comptons; he was a clergyman with very similar concerns to R.N.*   2. *Seminary picnic/retreat (usually to Riverdale) for students and faculty.*   3. *Sent from Socialist Party; R.N. was not responsible.*

Union Theological Seminary
New York, NY
October 1, 1931

. . . I just had a terrible longing for you last night and wished that I might just talk and talk with you about the, well about everything. Things have become rather tense around here. Although this country does not face nearly the same difficulties which England faces, we are used to so little that everyone is panicky. Dr. Coffin is less himself than I have ever seen him. He worries about the radical students being here at the seminary and has been closer to trying to tell me what I ought to do than he has ever before dared. Pit's nice wife meanwhile finds it very strange that religious people should mix in political questions at all, and I have a slight suspicion that he will become more conservative. Meanwhile it is foolish to think of nothing but caution when dealing with our American people on social and political issues because there is so very little active political intelligence.

John Bennett visited with us yesterday after a committee meeting downtown. He is to be married on the 30th of this month. He has been busy detaching the Student Movement[1] from the general YMCA. or at least helping to lead the forces which is accomplishing this laudable enterprise.

[R.N.]

1. *An organization of young Christian men and women who did not want to be associated with the YMCA.*

Union Theological Seminary
New York, NY
October 3, 1931

. . . Had two letters from you this morning so I feel quite good, also had a letter from the Commissioner General of Immigration about the trouble of getting you into the country.

I will send you that *Atlantic* article[1] if I can lay hold of it. The new one isn't out. The other article I've sent to the *Forum*. I had a nice letter from Mrs. Baldwin[2] of New Canaan, Connecticut, saying that she liked my article on religion and radicalism. I mention this because it was a very nice letter and you had told me that you had met her and liked her very much. I have not known her myself.

We had the "Round Robin" last night with groups of students coming in every 15 minutes. John Parks,[3] whom you may not remember, had one group and he said to me, "Do you remember who was in my group last year?" I confessed ignorance. Whereupon he said "That young blond lady in the black dress who came from England was in my group" and that he had felt quite important because so many people asked him, "Who is the striking young lady?" But here I am feeding your vanity. But I somehow like the young man telling me the story.

Thank the Lord I have another weekend for catching up on my work. I have to write three editorials for the *World Tomorrow* today, and tomorrow [they] will have to be used for a *Christian Century* article. Meanwhile I have about two dozen books for you. I wish I could push some of those on to you.

[R.N.]

1. *"The Religion of Communism,"* by R.N.   2. *Founder of the National Urban League, aunt of Roger Baldwin (founder of the American Civil Liberties Union) and herself a Bowles.*   3. *Seminary student.*

Woodhall Spa
Lincolnshire, England
October 2, 1931

Darling:

I got such a nice letter from you this afternoon, the second so far—very welcome. It's odd—I long for your letters just as ever I did when you came over, but there's also a different feeling as well. That different feeling is a happier one and that is why I am telling you.

I can just imagine Pit Van Dusen all nicely ensconced. I am sure he is acquiring the married look, too. It's to be noticed in the set of the coat collar, particularly obvious with an overcoat. Do look hard and see if he's got it yet. Men vary in the degree in speed in which they accomplish it. Pit is just the kind which shows it quite soon, only don't tell him so. I don't think you will ever get it, somehow. I suppose it is because you are so much always on the move.

However, to return to Pit, and their apartment which we might take over. It does sound a terrible lot to pay in rent. Of course, already my romantic soul is going to be frightfully depressed because I and the man I love are not going to start married life in a garret on two pennies a week! I remember explaining, with all the earnestness of twenty-two years and proportionate innocence to a gentleman of thirty-four, that I *couldn't* marry a man who was already "settled," [the luckless individual in question was a rather bright young headmaster, and incidentally a Cambridge Blue (varsity athlete)] with a respectable income and household and all the rest of it. I must, so I then declared, marry someone with whom I could start along with on the road Life. I drew a most attractive picture of two bare-legged young things, setting out with high ideals and a sense of humor, who would then show the world what love and laughter could do together, and I remember ending up by explaining it would all be *such* fun and I was quite good at making artistic seats out of grocer's packing cases!

So much for my departed youth and romantic hopes, but after all it was only a year and a half ago that I sat on a down in the Cotswolds and gave expression to all these views. And—they die hard. So I shall welcome the day, when the call comes to move, and we shall shoulder our pack and jog off together somewhere else. . . .

. . . I hope all goes well with you, darling. Please, you must be explicit with me about yourself if you can bear to. Otherwise I shall worry . . . I mean, explicit about your state of mind and feelings about things. And, if you dare worry about me, well I may feel that you are being adventuresome as it is about *me*. You are having to bet, to gamble, or anything else you like on me, after all you know. And you mustn't expect to have known ahead of time what my future reactions to conditions, situations and circumstances will be, otherwise it won't be at all interesting. I am doing the same to you. I refuse to think now "Will Reinhold want me to do this, or that, or the other?—Will Reinhold be worried if I want, or don't want this, that, or the other?" I know you, and the sort of person you are, and I know that the untoward is even liturgically provided for in the taking of each other for worse as well as for better. But I don't see the point of imagining occurrences when the worse may be the actual, do you? I, as also the Devil, can quote Scripture to my own purpose. So I will say, "For by Hope we are saved, but Hope that is seen is not Hope; for who hopeth for that which he seeth? But if we hope for that which we see not, then do we with patience wait for it" (Romans 8:24)—and if you are still worried by doubts that rise, I shall say, very firmly, "There is no fear in love . . . and he that gambles on me and on love is not so ultra-rational. It is in accordance with the rationality of the

Christian ethic of love!" I hope you like my sermon, after all it is very sincere, and *highly* moral!

Ever your own,

U.M.

Union Theological Seminary
New York, NY
October 4, 1931

Dearest:

Here is the record of my second Sabbath day spent at home. I have one more before the grind of sprouting incessantly begins. I didn't go to church and I read instead [Robert] Bridges' *Testament of Beauty*. Also sampled Bertrand Russell's new book, *The Scientific Outlook*. Another interesting pot boiler.

Tried to find Jim D. to come for a walk but couldn't find him so took a walk all by myself along Riverside Drive and became very sentimental thinking of the many walks we have taken there. I saw many a loving couple on the park benches and became even more sentimental, thinking it kind of foolish to be separated so long but wondering if this isn't a good thing to get myself in shape before I inflict myself upon you. I came home to write my sermon for next Friday. Religion and love must be closely related for I thought out a sermon while I was really thinking of you. I won't tell you what it was about or what it is about! But I think it is rather more poetic than most of my efforts.

This is my complete diary for the day. Tomorrow I am going to try and revamp my Ethics course and then work out a socialist speech for Tuesday night when I must speak at some socialist rally.

R.N.

Woodhall Spa
Lincolnshire, England
October 5, 1931

Darling:

I am not going to tell you about my efforts to be domestic, while the household was short of help. It mightn't be good for you to know how many times I burnt my fingers and saucepans and said "Damn," so I'll tell you instead that although it was Sunday I did *not* go to church. Instead, I "cleansed the sinner" (that's a corporal work of mercy, you know) by washing my hair, and then had a nice little worship service sitting Buddha-wise in front of the fire drying my hair and listening to a Mozart quartet. I even moralized to myself upon the parabolic character of themes and patterns and harmonies. Then for intellectual stimulation, I digested the *Observer,* i.e., Garvin [editor of *Observer*], and then the *Spectator,* etc., Bertrand Russell has a new book out, *The Scientific Society*—even more pessimistic. I read a review of *Dynamite* by Harold Laski, who grouped it into the nemesis of American business! (And—also the menace of America!) I want to get hold of the new little effort of J. A. Hobson, that sounds rather Tawneyish and also rather like you, so I gather from the review. I'll let you know about it if it is any good.

This evening I went for a long walk all around Tattershall, do you remember that is where we saw the castle and Collegiate Church? I walked back as it was getting quite dark, with wonderful sunset streaks of glory across a rather leaden Lincolnshire sky. Church bells were ringing, and the country *smelled* good. I'm always rather aware of smells, and I love the smell of autumn. I smelled some honeysuckle and nearly fell into a deep ditch trying to locate it, which was a rude interruption of my romantic reverie.

This evening I have been reading T. F. Powys'[s] *Mr. Weston's Good Wine*. Mr. Weston is God, a traveling wine merchant. Most entertaining, or least so in bits.

Now I'm getting all excited over the thought of tomorrow being Monday with a possible post from you. Dear, O dear, I wish we could be saying in "two months' time."

You won't forget to tell me scraps about what you are doing, will you? I want to know what you are talking about, either in your chapel addresses or any special presentations in your lectures. I want to hear about everything you are doing.

Love—as ever & always,

U.M.

Woodhall Spa
Lincolnshire, England
Monday, October 6, 1931

Dearest:

It was good to get two letters from you this morning, those of the 24th and 25th. Also, I had two long letters from Dr. [James] Frame and Dr. Foakes Jackson;[1] both with reports on you, your appearance, your behavior, and speech. I'll send the former's to you anon. It is so good, will you thank him for it? I'll write to him soon.

. . . *Later, same day:* After having those two letters this morning, the afternoon post brought three others: written on the 26th and 28th. So imagine my joy and satisfaction. It is/was good to hear about things too, the retreat and the opening chapel service. Only you must not be so merely factual in your accounts—I love to hear that you spoke, but I would more love to hear a line or two on what you spoke about. Dr. Frame was very enthusiastic about your chapel prayers, incidentally, and also blew me up for sending you so unnecessarily soon back when you had arranged not to be there for the first Friday morning service with your address. You awful old hypocrite; your sins, or rather your overscrupulous conscience, has been found out. You certainly render the things that are due unto Caesar with exactitude. But also my own amour propre forbids me letting it be known how anxious you were to get back to your own soil and work!

I'm interested to hear about Pit's attitude; can it be that marriage has produced an intensification of the "Safety First" virtues? Just quote to him my favorite few lines:

"Unless I take my part of danger in the raging sea; a devil rises in my heart far worse than any death to me."

But I did love his letter to you. Thank you so much, darling, for sending it. I love what he said, "From one who has done it, to one who is about to." Honestly though, Pit *is* a tremendously satisfying and satisfactory friend.

I am sorry you haven't been feeling so fit, and very tired. Do take care of yourself and don't work so hard. Dr. Jackson said you looked younger and happier than he had seen you, also bronzed and quite unintellectual, no, I must find what he said exactly, so I'll quote, "Well bronzed and quite rustic and unintellectual. . . . I was pleased to have a good report to give you about him." The dear old boy also wrote, "I'm delighted he made such a good impression on your family. Your mother is about right; he is a very great man and has a brilliant future before him, but he has overdone it and is a bit of an ass with his conscientious scruples. I have been thinking of other people all my life, and have not even the satisfaction of an approving conscience." Further he gave me his opinion that what you needed was "good humored chaff and an affectionate wife who would make you into a rational human being." So—! I don't think I shall make you into anything, I don't think I *want* to, to begin with. You are much too nice as you are even though you do have "over-conscientious scruples."

Give my best love to your family. And also to my friends: Bill Pickford, Marty Keeler and Allen Keedy, and of course, Arnold—(I do sympathize for and with the last two) and the Black brothers and Doc Reardon and, of course, Joe Haroutunian. Give my love also to anyone else who looks as if they would like it, especially dear Gaylord White,[2] and tell him I shall be thinking of that pleasant Princeton trip he took me on just a year ago, and all our talks at Union Settlement[3] and elsewhere. Of course, give Pit my best and so on and so on ad infinitum.

How are the *World Tomorrow* people? How is Devere Allen? Has he decided against going to the *Nation* and will stay with you?

Do give him my regards.

U.M. K-C.

1. *Elderly distinguished English scholar who taught at Union Seminary.* 2. *Professor of Applied Christianity at Union Seminary. White was very devoted to R.N. and had been most hospitable and kind to Ursula when she came to Union on her fellowship. He had also been the first headworker at Union Settlement (1901–23).* 3. *Settlement house founded by Union Seminary, located in East Harlem.*

Woodhall Spa
Lincolnshire, England
October 7, 1931

Darling:

The days pass, but although they go without me ever doing anything tremendously interesting, yet they go all too slowly. Three weeks ago we said good-bye just about this time. But I am counting the weeks, eleven weeks now, until you'll be here again.

I've just escaped from one of the duty "tea fights" below in the drawing room. Terrible—yet more retired parsons and parsonic relics abound in this place. However I've been bestowed buns and brightness all 'round and answered the conventional questions "I expect you're getting very busy now?" And inquiries after trousseau and my domestic education and of course, about *you!* Actually, today is the first time I have been able to be the conventional young thing, even to the extent of thinking about trousseau!

"Uncle Felix" [Canon Blakiston] came in to chat this afternoon, and sent many messages to you. He was so cheering, and preached a little to me about the sin of being intense, and said "religious and moral people always ran an extra risk in that direction." I've never been considered religious or moral before, however, he went on to say that he felt sure that the Almighty put the fishes in the sea to show over-worried men that one part of the created soul was to swim about in the enjoyment of what they had.

The domestic crisis is easier. A new temporary cook has eased the strain. The parents are thinking a little bit about going to Exmouth, so Mother is going down there tomorrow to see what she thinks about it. I think she would prefer it to this part of the world. She has been very sporting about a possible move; it might be better for her.

Such a dull letter, forgive it.

Love, [U.M. K-C.]

P.S. Dorothy and Eddie Wells sent us a heavenly dark old oak carved bread and cheese board, with bread knife. They thought we would like something Winchesterish, so it has the Winchester College figure and motto, "Manners mayketh Man." They remembered that you said you liked the English habit of having a loaf of bread on a board in the dining room.

Union Theological Seminary
New York, NY
October 8, 1931

Dearest:

Nothing has happened since I wrote you on Sunday night. This is Tuesday morning. I went to sleep in chapel this morning, Dr. Moffatt[1] speaking. Had a dreary hour in my Ethics class. Been interviewing students ever since. This is the uninteresting life of an academic. I am enclosing my weekend schedule for the second semester so you may see that things are not as terrible with regard to everything. At least on some of the dates, Chicago, Williams, and Wellesley, I hope you will come with me, which means there will only be nine weekends when we have to be separated.

By the way, the box of books we got together came through all right, and I didn't have to pay any duty on them, as they came under my $100 limit.

I have just had a talk with Dr. Coffin and he is going, after all, to write the State Department, so that we can get you into the country in spite of you being an alien. Dr. Coffin will give me a letter to Secretary

Stimson[2] through which I will get a letter to the American consul which I am sure will fix everything up all right. I have to have two Americans who know me to sign my paper in London. Luckily, the Elliotts[3] are on sabbatical and perhaps they can meet us at the embassy after the wedding.

[R.N.]

1. Professor of New Testament at Union Seminary.   2. Secretary of State; New York lawyer.   3. Harrison and Grace Elliott; he was a colleague of R.N.'s at Union Seminary; signed affidavit for U.N. to enter U.S.

Union Theological Seminary
New York, NY
October 13, 1931

My Dearest:

I have just mailed two letters to you and then the ones on S.S. *Paris* came from you. While I'm waiting for Mr. Savage[1] of Scribner's to come up, I'll send you another word and will send this on the *Europa*. You asked about my health. It is improving. I still miss a night or two of sleep but I'm getting along fairly well. The pressure is simply terrible. It seems that everyone wants to see you just when you want to study or must get out a lecture. As long as there is such constant pressure on me, I think I'll have to give up doing a decent scholarly job.

Pat Malin gave a very brilliant paper before our socialist group yesterday. Do you remember him—the young economist who married a rich Quaker girl [Biddle] and they live in spartan simplicity? Caroline came along with him and stayed at our house. They are going to have a baby and in the modern fashion seem to want the whole world to know it. The refectory table conversation was about what the baby was to be named.

Tonight I am going to write my lecture over again on Egyptian religion and also the one in my Philosophy of Religion course. I am really not studying philosophy of religion enough to be lecturing on it. I will have to go purely into the field of ethics sooner or later.

Your letters are a great inspiration to me. I get just as much fun out of being loved as you do. I don't know which is more fun, loving or being loved. But anyway I like both kinds of joy.

R.N.

1. William Savage; religion editor at Scribner's; consulted R.N. about possible publication of books.

Union Theological Seminary
New York, NY
October 14, 1931

My Dearest:

I have sent one letter on S.S. *Aquitania* but I think I can still catch it this afternoon and your generous letters received this morning prompt me to write another letter even though I ought to be studying the *New York Times* to understand the Manchurian situation more perfectly, for my afternoon current events course. You can't imagine how much your letters help me. I know I ought to write more in detail just because I enjoy it when you do. So I'll try—

Arose this morning at 7:15. Wondered if Ursula would find that too early. Breakfasted at 7:45. Went to chapel because I thought Dr. Burkitt[1] from Cambridge would be speaking, but found I was mistaken. Dr. Ralph Sockman[2] spoke and I don't like his speaking because he is too smooth. Wonder whether every preacher must not strike the critical observer like that, talking about excellences and sacrifices which he himself does not embody.

Nine o'clock, read all of Ursula's letters so failed to reread my notes for the lecture course. Both lectures were particularly atrocious this morning. Wonder if I have completely lost my grip. I just talk and get nowhere.

Twelve noon, went home to lunch. Saw Dr. Burkitt and Dr. Foakes Jackson going together to the refectory for luncheon. These English do find each other and why shouldn't they? Delivered Ursula's messages to Joe Haroutunian and Doc Reardon. Both these are still without a job. The world is always hardest on the personalities of finest grain. I like these two fellows tremendously and they're both in rather a desperate situation.

One o'clock, ascended the stairs to my office to write a letter to Ursula. Amen.

This little diary brings us to the present moment. What more could you ask for? I received the literature about the North German Lloyd Trips this morning. Should we come back second class or third class? Tourist accommodation is so good that I don't know whether we could justify better ones, and yet we will have that kind of trip only once. What do you say? Winter rates, second class on the *Bremen* will cost us only $150; so I think we will take that.

You say $140 rent per month is a lot of money for an apartment. It is too much for what we get. . . . As for starting life with me in the garret, you may not be able to do that but you will have a chance to end with me there. I do appreciate your lack of insistence on security most particularly. I am really getting afraid of this job. To teach ethics in such a place of secure vantage as this in a distressed world is really beginning to worry me. So perhaps in a couple of years, we will venture out. I am really beginning to think this place won't be able to stand the kind of teaching that this era needs, and why should one demand the right to criticize everything in a system which gives one such ease? I'd rather win my own freedom than have the feeling that Dr. Coffin is preserving a free pulpit for me and paying the price while I do nothing but spout. . . .

My health, it is much better than it has been. Have started playing tennis twice this week and I feel better for the exercise. Part of the difficulty has been just that.

I send you all my love and devotion. It will be great fun to plan the future together. I feel particularly joyful that it may have some adventure in it for us both. I may be afraid of adventure in some respects but I am now getting more afraid of security. It will be such fun to think of yourself as taking care of someone in one moment and in the next think of being taken care of.

Yours altogether,

R.N.

1. *Professor at Cambridge University known for his work on Christian origins. Author of Church and Gnosis.* 2. *Well-known New York preacher; pastor of Methodist Church on Park Avenue.*

Woodhall Spa
Lincolnshire, England
Thursday, October 14, 1931

My Dearest One:

I had your October 7th letter with one of the day before—today. The first letters I had since October 1st from you, so I was glad to get them. It was the letters you wrote after getting mine (the one I wrote in answer to your boat letters). But, I think I was more hurt by the one I got than by those boat letters. . . .

However—having wasted a few hours in tears and trouble of soul, I can now laugh at myself for being so neurotic, and perhaps can control myself enough to write a letter to you, a letter which will not hurt, worry, or upset you.

I *do* trust you, darling, Don't you believe that? Do you think I could say that I could marry you and come over and live in a place I don't frightfully like, and which is all so different from what I am accustomed to, and am at ease amongst, *unless* I had the greatest trust in you and in your love? Do you think I could contemplate even coming into such an entirely alien atmosphere, or into such an insecure situation as that which is the outcome of your domestic mores, unless I had entire confidence in you? If I had ever once thought of my security, or of my peace of mind, or ease of conduct, I wouldn't have dared to think that I could carry things through, and be your wife under the present circumstances. But, I don't. I just know that my love for you is such that all fear and doubt is *wrong,* and I put enough value on that love to feel I can gamble on all else in the world besides.

But you say, "I cannot trust you, for you veto my suggestions." Yet I cannot *pretend* to agree when I do not, can I? Do you think that "trust" is synonymous with perfect "agreement" or "compliance" with everything you say and feel?

However, that is all over and done with now. I have made my protest about things and you know how I feel. That is enough for me now and I leave all the rest to you.

If it would make things happier for you, and easier for your mother, I'll write, "Go and live with your mother, and satisfy her happiness and your conscience. All is over with this tiresome woman in England." Would that make things any better? After all, I am young enough to start again! If you would prefer that but do not want to do the breaking off of our engagement, from motives of chivalry, at least be *honest.* Tell me. I would willingly provide for you and your mother's happiness, "authentic happiness," by my breaking off the engagement. I would do so without asking you, now straight away, but somehow that would seem hardly fair. So, promise me if you cannot bear the strain of two loyalties, tell me, then I [will] withdraw from the competition in foreign markets!

I am not being facetious, or bitter, or sarcastic but dead serious. I do care about your happiness, and I don't worry about mine frightfully. As I have said before, I don't think happiness comes by minding about it. If I appreciate your position and knowing you as well as I do, I know also a little bit of what you are feeling and suffering. So I wish I could tell you I do understand, but promise to tell me what you feel.

Ever yours,

U.M. K-C.

Woodhall Spa
Lincolnshire, England
Friday, October 15, 1931

Darling:

I had hoped for another letter from you this morning, but perhaps my luck will be this afternoon. Meanwhile, even if I don't hear from you, I am feeling the whole time with you, and knowing instinctively that you are worried about this and about that. Fretted by the would-be controlling atmosphere about you in the shape of Dr. Coffin and the conservatism about you; full of concern lest your mother should be having too hard a time to part from a son that she has had for nearly 40 years to herself. Worried lest I will not "fit in" with your existing loyalties. Hurt, because you feel I do not understand the nature of these loyalties. And, all these pulls, in the midst of hard work and exhausting pressure of teaching, writing, and thinking. Isn't that a bit of how it is, darling? . . .

But, you must not be bitter with me because I feel differently about certain things. I do understand your feelings, but because of my feelings, I can't entirely "sym-pathize" in the true sense of "feel with" you on all points. I would be a hypocritical humbug were I to pretend that I did. But I do understand; but, as I said before, intellectual and psychological "understanding," even the Scriptural "understanding of the heart," does not always carry with it emotional "sympathy."

So much for how I feel. Now for you, I *am* unhappy about you. I cannot bear to think that you look forward to the future as being full of "every kind of hell." And, it may be that "you know right now in the present that you love me, and wish every day I were with you," but if that implies doubt of the existence of a similar feeling in the future well, we must just face it, also "right now," before we go any further.

I wrote last night in answer to the letter I got from you which you wrote on October 7th, apropos of my letter to you upon reception of your boat letters. But this letter coming via S.S. *Bremen* quick boat may reach you first, so I'll say again what I said there.

If you really cannot bear the strain of two loyalties pulling at you, either now or in the future, you must be *honest* with me and tell me so, now. I don't want you [to] feel you are "bound" to me in any way or to have any chivalrous notion about not wanting to break our engagement. If you really feel you cannot do as our English Prayerbook requires of "those coming together in Holy Matrimony"—namely that "forsaking all others, keep thee only unto her as long as ye both shall live"—well, if you cannot feel you can do that, in honesty and singleness of heart, *and* in gladness of soul, then the only thing to do, is not to go on with this venture of love and of getting married.

I have not got enough confidence in myself to enter into competition in any market, least of all in the market of love and loyalty. And, if, as appropriately, the American tariff is too high, well, the English import can be discouraged, and can stay at home.

I know you well enough by now to realize the strength of your instincts; that if your instincts work in the way you describe in every letter, well, there is no gainsaying it, and we must realize the fact. I have said with reiteration and emphasis, that I am willing to gamble on everything, for I put enough value on what your love is and means to me. But, you, knowing yourself, may not be able to feel this, and if again you do not, we must realize it.

So, would it be more for your "ultimate happiness" if you were to break all this off? You *must* promise to be absolutely honest. I would rather have the absolute truth than chivalrous evasions of it. I think I am strong enough in my feelings about you to prefer to know that you were happy and unified living with your mother, than to know you were torn in spirit and vexed in soul because I loved you and wanted you to live with me.

As I said yesterday in my letter, I would write now and break off our engagement but I think it is only fair to put it to you first.

I want you to take this seriously, and very seriously to consider it. I am not being hysterical, or wishing to force an issue, or to force your hand in any way. I have told you how I feel, how I feel toward you and I feel toward the other thing. Now I just want to know how you feel. And, in view of your feelings it might be for your and Mrs. Niebuhr's "ultimate happiness" for you and Miss U. Keppel-Compton to part company now, once and for all.

So it is up to you. And all I say is, be *honest* with yourself, *and* with me. There can be no happiness via half-measures or partial expressions of your true feelings. As I said before, on a certain fateful Wednesday the 6th of May, I love you well enough to care for your happiness most. Therefore, I know I love you well enough to let you go and bid good-bye. It would be my "love-be-wi-ye" as well as "God-be-wi-ye."

Yours ever, in truth *and in love,*

Ursula

Union Theological Seminary
New York, NY
October 16, 1931

My Dearest:

. . . Had chapel this morning and gave the "poetic" talk I worked out ten days ago about which I wrote you. Had a rather decent class in Philosophy of Religion this morning. My Ethics class isn't going so well for some reason or other. Tonight I have to speak at the annual conference of the F.O.R. [Fellowship of Reconciliation]. Tomorrow my brother Helmut is coming in from New Haven with his family. Am anxious to show Helmut your photo. He doesn't know what you look like at all.

I am a little distressed about Jim Dombrowski. He's not been at all cordial since I came back this autumn. He tries to, but fails. I don't know just what is the matter. He has, like some of the other students, become very sympathetic to communism under the stress of American conditions at the moment and it may be that he thinks that I don't go far enough in my radicalism. I don't know whether that is it.

Please send me that immigration application some time with your part filled out. I want to leave one copy in Washington before I go so that we'll only have to refer by cable to it.

The young professor from Princeton who used to be here has just come in and interrupted this letter. He went into ecstasies when he saw your photograph, which I have here at the office. Incidentally, I turn to your photographs more sentimentally than I like to admit to reassure myself that you really "belong to me." I wonder how it is possible for all this to have happened and my heart is filled with gratitude for the wonder of our love.

Heber Harper, who teaches at Columbia, and is an old friend, wants me to come to tea at his house because his wife, whom I know but not very well, is so anxious to talk to me about our marriage. She's all excited about it because she was your age when [she and] Heber, [then] my age, were married eight years ago. She says it's just right that way. I don't feel quite so old when I hear such things from friends. Mrs. Nevin Sayre, wife of the secretary of the F.O.R., an English woman, stopped me at the meeting of the F.O.R. to say that she would claim the right to invite us to dinner before any others had the chance. She's terribly anxious to meet you and she is a lovely woman whom you will like to know, and I feel sure about that.

You haven't told me yet about the bon mots of Barbara's.[1] I bet she pulls more than one fast one at our expense. But that is American slang which you won't understand.

Saturday morning: I didn't mail the letter yesterday because no boat was leaving and the boat that leaves today is not quick. Mail seems to come more or less in weekly installments and go about the same way.

Had a great crowd out last night for the F.O.R. meeting. Devere Allen and I spoke. Devere is still dickering with the offer from the *Nation,* but I don't think he will take them up. They are obviously too worried about his ability to carry on. Just had a note from Dr. Coffin this morning saying he had heard from Stimson's secretary saying they were looking up how they could best facilitate our affairs. Dr. Coffin closes his letter with these words: "I emphasized to Secretary Stimson the deserving service that you always render to the Republican Party!" Helmut and his family have arrived and the house is full of Niebuhrs as Walter's wife and child also came. They are all very anxious to meet you. At this point Helmut came up to the office and we have spent an hour talking over our academic jobs as well as the general state of the universe. He is a great comfort, that fellow and brother of mine, about as sensible as anyone I know.

I hope I'll have some mail from you on Monday. I need it badly. Had a talk with Mrs. Baldwin this morning, the nice old lady you visited on your way to Maine last year. It was the first time I had met her. She told me how nice you are. Funny how you like to hear that even if you know it.

Yours devotedly,

R.N.

1. *Older sister of Ursula U.N.*

Union Theological Seminary
New York, NY
October 18, 1931

My Dearest:

Here it is Sunday night, another day wasted as far as catching up with any significant work which is piled up and which I wanted to do over the weekend. Preached in Englewood [NJ] this morning at Dwight Morrow's church, and a very horrible sermon it was due to lack of preparation. I sat up and talked with my brother until the small hours last night. To my consternation, Dr. Foakes Jackson showed up at church and disconcerted me by his presence. Fortunately it looked as if he slept through the sermon but appearances may be deceiving. The old boy may have been wide awake and would know what a terrible discourse it was. Perhaps he will write to me about it.

I rushed home for a family dinner with the whole family. This afternoon I went to see whether Jim Dombrowski would take a walk with me and found a tea going on in his room with King Gordon's[1] cousin from Canada doing the honors and a bunch of students in. Zilla Hawes came and we had an interesting discussion. All about politics, of course. They had been discussing Harry Ward[2] and myself before I came, trying to determine the difference between our positions. I told them that was very simple. I didn't have as much "guts" as Harry Ward when it came to the realities of the social struggle.

Tonight I am trying to get some of my course material in shape because I must run from one thing to another tomorrow. Federal Council of Churches meeting, socialist, dentist, dinner with Francis Henson,[3] etc., etc. One of those hectic days which make one feel futile and foolish when it is all over. I have had an invitation from the Coffins to have lunch with Dr. Burkitt on Wednesday. He asked to have me invited, wanting no doubt to look over the man who dares to take an English girl from her native hearth. I hope I won't disappoint him too much. I have been too busy to hear a single one of his lectures. Will have to try to go next week. I know next to nothing about gnosticism, which is his topic, and I don't know whether that is a good reason for going or for staying away.

I hope I hear from you in the morning. I think a boat or two must have come in on Saturday, though I haven't had a chance to look it up in the paper today. I'm anxious to know just how you're feeling and hoping against hope that my continued note of worry in my letters won't make you disgusted with me. It's four weeks now since I returned and only two more months until we will be a married couple. There is enough thrill in that to overcome all worries if only you will trust me in spite of my difficulties.

Next morning, Monday, the 19th: I am going to write you a few more lines this morning because I realize there won't be another chance today. Just received your cable and I appreciate it. Particularly since no letters came I was greatly bucked up by the thoughtfulness of your cable. I know that if we trust each other we can make a go of it. I do so appreciate the trust you have in me though we do have such differences about important matters. . . . Just the assurance of your trust although I have had it before, always gives me new courage.

Now I must go off to a foolish meeting in town. And spend the rest of the day in conferences while my academic work—I must soon lecture on ethics of world religions about which I know precisely nothing—languishes. Among other things we are organizing at present demonstrations against official violence in some of the worst industrial areas. Don't know how far we will get with it. America is still in the frontier period in all these matters. But I don't know whether any nation has much on us at that. When it comes to handling industrial problems, all modern nations are brutal with varying degrees.

Yours ever,

[R.N.]

1. Assistant in Department of Christian Ethics; Canadian Rhodes scholar. 2. Colleague and professor of Christian ethics. 3. Active in Student Christian Movement.

Union Theological Seminary
New York, NY
October 20, 1931

Dearest:

I just mailed you two letters and here's another because I forgot some good and bad news. I have been elected president of the Fellowship of Reconciliation, a job I'd really like to accept, but I told them I would do so only if I could relinquish my chairmanship of the League for Industrial Democracy. I have put it up to Norman Thomas. I think the F.O.R. would be the most ideal organization for me to keep in contact with the outside world and its problems, something as [Harry] Ward does through the American Civil Liberties.

The other matter is I have received notice that the Indian Committee has unanimously requested the committee which controls the Barrows Lectures to appoint me for the year 1933–34. This Indian lectureship is controlled by the University of Chicago and requires a year's absence in the Orient for the purpose of lecturing at all the Indian universities. Since we hope we might have a family by that time, I doubt whether I will accept even if the election does fall on me as now seems likely. But at any rate it is interesting.

The bad news is that the dentist wants $600 to put my teeth, bridgework, etc., etc., into condition.

And finally, please accept my humblest apologies for all the silly things I have said in my letters. When I remember how I love you, I don't think I mean half of them. I still hope you may be pleasantly disappointed when we really live together after all the fears I have given you.

Yours ever,

R.

Union Theological Seminary
New York, NY
October 23, 1931

My Darling:

Here it is Friday night, the first "at home"[1] begins in an hour and a half. I feel rested for the first time in over a week because I took the afternoon off and had a sleep, then played tennis with Jim, Pat Malin, and Styron. Just held a little session down in the social room in which the students tried to decide between propaganda and education as the way of arriving at truth, or rather whether education was ever anything but propaganda. Jim and I seem to be getting a little closer together again. I missed his friendship so much that I feel better for being on a more intimate footing with him again. It is curious how this Russian business is captivating the imagination of many of our best fellows, Francis Henson, Jim, etc., etc.

Had dinner last night at the Coffins with the Burkitts. It was a very delightful evening. Dr. Coffin had warned me ahead of time that the Burkitts were thoroughly "unreconstructed" politically and socially and that we had better stay off political issues. He felt that since they regarded his political ideas as dangerous, they would certainly not take to mine. The E. F. Scotts[2] had told the Burkitts that Dr. Coffin was altogether too sympathetic to radical opinion in the seminary so you may imagine what they told them about me. The Burkitts will probably feel genuinely sorry for you. We did stay off political topics. Burkitt is a very charming fellow and entertained us royally with all sorts of reminiscences. By the way, we talked about the wedding and they asked who was going to be my best man. I told them about the necessity of having an unmarried man and they said that idea was erroneous. If it is, I wonder if it would not be best to ask Sonny Elliott[3] to serve. He is not a particularly close friend of mine, but we will be living with them for some years probably. But I rather like the idea of asking your cousin. Please let me know what you think would be best.

I have been genuinely sorry all day for all the terrible things I have written while in the depths of worry and I hope you haven't taken them too seriously. All day I have had in the back of my mind, even while I was lecturing, "If only I could speak to Ursula and tell her I am not quite as much a damn fool as my letters make me appear." I think I will send a cable tomorrow and try to express myself though that is not easy in a cable. Your friend Grace Wilson received a letter from you today and I did not. I began to speculate whether you had received a particularly ugly letter from me and had so stopped writing. This strain of separation is getting on my nerves as much as anything.

Tomorrow I am going to Philadelphia, then will rush back for a speech in Brooklyn on Sunday afternoon and then I go to Toronto. I probably won't get back until Wednesday morning, but will write you from Toronto. I'll probably also write tomorrow before I go, but perhaps you may not hear from me on Sunday.

I'll have to stop now and go home for the "at home." I'll be thinking about what our first "at home" together will be like. I do hope you will forgive me for my depressed comments and not be completely disgusted with me. I am pretty bad but I do so love you and long for you and still hope to be able to make you happy. Give my love to your father and mother and Barbara. Hope you haven't had to tell them how terrible I am when I get depressed.

Devotedly,

R.

1. *Reception for students at faculty homes—an "open house."*   2. *E.F. Scott was Professor of New Testament at Union Seminary.*   3. *Harrison Elliott.*

Woodhall Spa
Lincolnshire, England
Sunday, October 25, 1931

Dearest:

I am just wondering what you are feeling like, in mind and soul, now. It is so difficult having to wait ten days before one knows how the other one is. So I am thinking of you, and wondering if you still are happy about the future, and I am praying that you are, for I would so love to be joyful with you about it.

Dorothy Morrison, the great friend of mine I spoke of, arrived yesterday. It is so good to have her here again, to talk with and to laugh with. She used to live in Southampton, she and her mother, while her father, Captain Morrison, was abroad, as he was Commodore of the Royal Mail

Line. . . . It was especially after I left my boarding school, and during the time I was working at Southampton University College, that I got to know her properly. Dorothy was up at Oxford, before my day, and read history, but did not finish—her mother's health and other concerns interfered. She was also very interested in theology, and so we used to read and think about some of our problems of understanding theology together.

Now her mother is dead—she died of cancer two years ago. Dorothy, a young lady of means and ability, good looks and all the rest, has elected to work as a diocesan educator and organizer for the Missionary Council at Liverpool. It sounds rather like a job that Canon Raven and the Manchester Diocese people suggested for me, if I had not come over on the fellowship to New York.

She arrived yesterday just the same as ever: handsome, humorous and lively. It has been such fun; it has been very tonic both for Mother and even Daddy [who] has been laughing and enjoying all her bon mots and recital of life as now lived in Liverpool.

This afternoon we all went over to Houghton Hall, the place of the Hon. Mrs. Lenox Linsly. You'll remember that fantastic evening we had when she so kindly asked us to dinner? After all it wasn't so long ago, only two months. You and I sailed off, and, as Daddy needed the car, we bicycled, you, looking rather too tall for our gardener's bicycle, and I using the house parlor maid's, in, of course, our evening clothes. But we arrived triumphantly, and you really carried everything off awfully well.

I was telling Dorothy Morrison about that evening. How Mrs. Linsly had invited her neighboring lord of the manor, who also was a clergyman, and held the family living! I remember explaining to you afterwards how that this "squirson" is, of course, becoming less and less, as this sort of "family living" is regarded, even in the conservative Church of England, as not being the proper thing. But that was not the point of the dinner. Do you remember how this gentleman turned to you and said, "I understand you are a specialist in Christian ethics. What would your advice be about the farmers who kill the foxes?" I am sure you realized that he, as well as being the squire and also the rector, was also master of the hounds! Anyhow, you won my entire admiration for asking him instead some wonderful question which in a way shoved that difficult question aside, and soon we were discussing pigs, which both Mrs. Linsly and he had on their farms, which were, of course, also attached to these manor houses.

Dorothy enjoyed this story immensely as I do in retrospect. And on this Sunday afternoon, we were all asked over there to tea. It was suddenly frightfully cold, but there was a wonderful autumn sunset, and on arrival, we all went to look over the new poultry and new pigs in the farm attached to the Hall. It is a very English habit to wander, even in the depths of winter which this was not, over the garden and grounds, and to inspect the pigs! Then we came back to tea, and tea around a blazing log fire in the old dining hall, again all this was very English. There were no little lace tea napkins or any super-refinements, but lots of old comfy arm chairs, homemade scones, old-fashioned lamps, lots of books and needlework and people indiscriminately placed on the floor, in chairs if dogs allowed, and on sofas. Mrs. Linsly's cousins were staying with her, charming people, the younger generations of which I had known at Oxford. Odd other people dropped in, casually, "Hullo, isn't it slightly chilly? What?" To be greeted as casually in return, "And what are you doing here?" And the answer might come like this, "Oh, just canvassing the farmers on the Sabbath, don't you think that's a good idea? But to visit you was a pleasant thought, also tea at this juncture."

So it went on, and I wished you had been there. I do rather revel in the casual friendliness such as does flourish in this absurd country. It probably would seem too casual to others, though, and almost rude. I was buttonholed by the Tomlins—Lord Tomlin, went on a legal mission to U.S.A. last year, and had the most interesting time there. So he was full of interest about all things American, in the political, academic, and economic spheres. He himself is a K.C. [King's Councillor], and was therefore rather critical of certain legal procedures and practices [in the U.S.A.]. Also he could not quite get over the material criteria which he found existing in the mind of so-called intellectuals. He told me how when some university, Harvard or Yale, both were mentioned in this connection, was giving him an L.L.D., or the American equivalent in honorary degrees, the president of the university emphasized with pride the earning capacity of their best graduates. He guided Lord Tomlin to a board on which were recorded, not their intellectual achievements, or their academic honors, but their subsequent incomes, estimated according to the lofty standard of dollar worth! He also remarked that in England, he is regarded as almost a Tory, but in America he would be a radical of radicals! Such were the reactions of a typical English political legal observer, who has served many colonial appointments and home offices too. All rather interesting, I thought.

I must stop, it really is quite cold. We are having lovely weather, fine and beautiful, but so cold. Hard frosts, which are odd for this month. So we shiver and run about, pile on more woolen clothing, and get pink noses and cheeks. It's marvelous weather for walking, though, one can walk for miles and miles, Dorothy and I went for a ten-mile tramp this morning and came home ravenous and happy, having ambled over plowed fields, heath and fen, in a glorious frosty sunshine. We missed our dogs, and I wanted you! I always do but the time is now only just over eight weeks. Do you realize that? That is, unless you decide to chuck up the whole business.

Love, ever yours,

U.M. K-C.

Union Theological Seminary
New York, NY
November 2, 1931

My Dearest:

It is four o'clock in the afternoon and I have been doing little else but reading your letters and writing to you since I came into the office at seven in the morning. Now I must write an introduction to Lynn Harold Hough's[1] book. He was hurt by the way I did not let him know about our engagement. He's very much attached to me in spite of our differences, and the fact I'm marrying an English girl just thrills him all over because he has a very romantic attachment to England. He preaches in the City Temple in London every summer and thinks that everything the English do is right. We will have to go out and see him sometime, even though his artificial speech will appall you. His speeches were rather terrible to bear. But when I was a youngster and he a famous preacher in Detroit, he was kind and took me in and introduced me around and has been a most affectionate friend ever since. Now I have to write an introduction to his new book and I don't know quite what to say because his gospel and mine are at the opposite ends of the poles.

Just now the package with the book by Hobson arrived and the other with your photograph. The photograph is just the right size for a desk picture and I am going to have it framed immediately. Thank you for it and for the Hobson book, which I hope to read tonight. Now I'll have to go to work. This business of mooning about you all day is hard on the regular job. Won't it be nice when we can take out our affection in a more satisfying way? I am sending you this month's *World Tomorrow.* I wrote the editorial on France and on the English elections and the article on Russia but nothing else, but it's a fairly good number.

Yours in love eternal,

Reinhold

My Dearest:

Later: After mailing my two letters to you, I want to add another one. I just think and think about you all day. I am so grateful for your love, which is willing to trust me so much. Then I get creepy all over thinking of how your family and friends will pity you for marrying an American who has no proper sense of married life and is still tied to his mother's apron strings. I haven't honestly ever had that reputation in this country. Mother, though she lives with me, has interfered with my life very considerably less than Pitney Van Dusen's mother, for instance. But what is the good of talking? I am merely exhibiting wounded pride and mixed up with that is a very real concern for your future. Yet somehow I feel so much more certain than ever before. I'll really try to be a decent husband and anyhow I think we are going to have so much fun working all things out together that a great deal of this will seem like an evil dream when we think back on it.

Now I am going to have some dinner and go back to work on my courses. I finished the introduction to Hough's book and tonight will devote myself to a few editorials, Chinese ethics, and Schweitzer's *Mysticism of the Apostle Paul.* In this way I mix things up and never get to the bottom of anything.

Yours forever,

Reinhold

1. *Prominent Methodist clergyman; became dean at Drew Theological Seminary in New Jersey.*

Union Theological Seminary
New York, NY
November 3, 1931

My Dearest:

This is the end of a day such as I would like to have frequently in order to catch up with my work. Spent the whole morning in my office. Played tennis in the afternoon, then went out with the Lymans[1] to New Jersey across the new George Washington Bridge—that bridge is really wonderful. And now I have the evening for solid study. I have worked one lecture out on the ethics of early English law, worked on another on the ethics of Hindu religion, prepared the stuff for Current Events class on the Round Table Conference and now am trying to determine the difference between Catholic and Protestant mysticism. No wonder I never get any expert knowledge on anything. This darn ethics job covers too wide an area from religion to economics.

The rest of the week is going to be a nightmare. Sometime or other I will have to prepare a sermon for both Yale and Smith for I preach at those two institutions next Sunday. I wonder when I can manage to do that.

Meanwhile, I have been rereading your letters and contemplating on how selfish I have been to worry about my problems while you, after all, had a solid one of your own trying to preserve confidence in me while most of the folk around you are probably pitying you for marrying such a one as I. That you should have such confidence in me in spite of those fears fills me with gratitude and a sense of responsibility and a curious sense of serenity. I feel certain that when we are together we will see each other's problems and not only our own. We do have a considerable gulf to bridge between varying preconceptions as well as national and personal prejudices. But I feel if you can love me after all my tiresome worries, everything will be all right. I just have a more solid confidence in the ability of our mutual love to bridge difficulties.

I never thanked you for your letter about being willing to share anything with me which duty might seem to dictate. I think we will always have a decent roof over our head, but I am getting terribly afraid of teaching ethics in the welter of this kind of a civilization from the security of a professor's chair. I rather think we can make life more adventuresome and vigorous than that. There is so much unconscious hypocrisy in all this academic life. We just had our pay for unemployment benefits. Most of the students are so aroused by the sorry state of the unemployed that they gave more than last year, some going on a more meager diet. Meanwhile, the professors gave less than last year though their salaries are worth 20% more than two years ago. All this makes some of the students rather cynical. The students with meager incomes of $1,000 give $25 and professors with incomes of $8,000 give $35 or $50 at the most. When I think of all that sort of thing, I feel like giving up all pretension of being a scholar. I never will be anyway and I don't like the lack of sensitivity of scholars to the world around them.

I want so much to talk to you by the hour about all this and it thrills me to think that I won't have to go it alone wherever it may be that we will decide on together.

I asked Jim whether he had a new tie as you asked about it, he said he hadn't. We talked about the wedding and Jim suggested I ought to ask Marcus Knight[2] to be best man. What do you think of that? He was a good friend of mine, or is. Perhaps it would be a good idea.

I would like to go on and on and write about our future. But these letters are such a poor substitute for something better. Now I have to go back to work and find out more about Catholicism and Protestantism.

Yours forever,

Reinhold

1. *Eugene W. and Mary E. Lyman; he was professor of philosophy of religion; she lectured on the English Bible.* 2. *English clergyman; had been an English Fellow 1929–30.*

Westminster, England
November 5, 1931

Dearest One:

I got your letter of October 28th via the *Aquitania* this morning. I have now reached such a state of befuddlement over what you call our "problems" and "difficulties" that I feel that it is all *wrong* to be so dismal and fearful.

. . . After all, marriage between those who love each other as we do ought to be full of wonder and of joy, not something to be entered on fearfully or as potentially full of terrible and alarming occasions for the two married folk as for those outside. If your mother *really* loves you, she will want you to be happy (that is why I *cannot* understand Pit's remark, which I thought hardly tactful, or conscious of what unselfish mother love is.) If I were a mother, I would consider it an insult to my love for others to consider anything as a beloved child's happy marriage as "tragic." To call a step which involves a son's fulfillment as a man and as a citizen "tragic" for the mother who bore him is surely to equate mother love with mere animal maternal possessive instinct. Darling, I am not being unsympathetic with your mother's problem here. I do feel what I say very strongly, and I am a woman, and I hope to be a mother. I know I shall never feel anything tragic which comes to me apropos of you or of any children I might bear unless it involves their unhappiness or their moral failure. If I were a bad woman who seduced you, or ruined your career, then I feel your marriage to me might be as "tragic as death," for it might mean the ruin of a good man. But I just do *not* see (I honestly am befuddled, darling, and don't please be bitter with me about this) how anything that is going to make you happy can really be as "tragic as death" for Mrs. Niebuhr. I think that love for a person, if it not be compatible with wanting the happiness of that person, *that* is being as "tragic as death."

My idea and ideal of what true mother love is is "absolutist." And to think that it is *you* who have tried to convince me that we had to be absolutists in order to avoid the enervating compromises that attend a pragmatic adherence of the Aristotelian mean!

Darling, don't be offended by what I have just said. For it is not only that mother love, but that any love ought to feel that way. For instance, suppose you had wanted to break off our engagement because you felt your happiness consisted in staying the son and not being the husband. And suppose I agreed because I saw your happiness was that way. Well, that ought not to be "tragic as death," ought it? I would say to myself, "I love him; therefore I want his happiness; therefore what he is doing is right for him." I would be rather annoyed if such noble renunciation was regarded as tragic.

Do you see what I mean at all? Or is this another of my presuppositions which you do not understand?

As I have said before, all I know is that I love you terribly. So to be honest, I am glad you do not want to break off what we are going to do together. But I do want you to feel that it's a joyful thing we are doing. How can we let the joy of it shine out unless we yield to the full wonder of it and be spiritually spontaneous and natural about it? Loving you makes me want to love everyone a little bit more. If I am going to be hedged about with fearful precautions lest someone's feelings will be hurt or the tensions be caused, well, my joy and love will go back, shrivel, and subside. Do let me love you, properly, joyfully. After all, joy is the best solvent of the tragic sense of life, though it is not appropriate on occasions which are regarded as "tragic as death." So tell me it isn't all that tragic; tell me that it is right and lovely and wholesome and joyous our love and that we hope to be married. Surely joy and love cannot hurt anyone's feelings, can they?

I am very tired and quite sleepy. I am here in Barbara's little flat, occupying the daybed in the sitting room. Her American friend was occupying it earlier in the week and I have been gathering bits from American papers; *Nations, New Republics,* etc. which she left behind. Made me quite homesick for U.S.A. Barbara now is out, at a party, with fireworks and Guy Fawkes, as it is November 5th! But I have subsided by the fireside and a drink to nurse a bad headache in bed. Darling, please try and remember that your happiness will be my happiness, therefore it is our happiness. I am glad you still want me to marry you; I almost feared at times you did not, and any time you change your mind, let me know. I do want you to feel that our life will be wonderful and most deeply joyful, that is, if *you really* want us to be together.

Yours forever, utterly and entirely,

U.M. K-C.

Westminster, England
Friday, November 6, 1931

Darling One:

I have just spent the day being busy and doing nothing. I achieved a birth certificate and passport photos and saw about my wedding dress, etc., etc. I had lunch with Barbara in the City and viewed her financial milieu and in the evening we both went off to see a ballet. And we also saw one of Purcell's operas, *Dido and Aeneas*. Monica Ratcliffe, Peggy's younger sister, was in the chorus incidentally. We sat with Peggy Ratcliffe[1] and another friend and I learned with amusement that her father, S. K. Ratcliffe, is going on S.S. *Bremen* on December 30th!! Peggy feels we ought to warn him off, as he, knowing me so well, might be rather *de trop* with you and me. But I think you might enjoy him, so I think it is all right and we will let him stay with his booking. You and he can talk about Russia and international affairs when you get tired of holding my hand!

I met Mrs. Stringfellow Barr, Barbara's nice American friend, today. She is interesting and a charming-looking person. She knows Union Seminary quite well and used to stay at the president's house as she knew the Francis Browns[2] very well, a MacLure. Her own husband was at the University of Virginia, and is very much a Virginian who is related to all the other Virginians! She was very funny on the subject, also upon the amusing provincialdom of the faculty circle at Emory University [where her husband was a visiting professor]! She was very amusing about U.S.A. generally; she is herself American with a Spanish grandmother and a father who was an Orientalist and taught and lived at Oxford.

It was she who heard you preach this past summer. Now she seems to be over here for some time. Barbara tells me that her husband suggested she better keep away if she didn't really feel happy with their university circle! So here she is. Of course, she knows crowds of interesting people in England and loves it here, but it seems rather tragic and wrong, I feel. Everyone says her husband is charming, but apparently they are both a little too brilliant and highly strung as well as over-stimulating each other to be together nonstop. Another American lady whose academic husband is on sabbatical told Barbara and me that she thought English families had no home life. "English mothers don't even keep their sons at home!" This was apropos of the fact that she couldn't find a decent school for her small son of 7 or 8 to go to other than a boarding school, and therefore had to send him away. She was loud in lament, "Why in America, we keep our sons at home. They learn to consider us: You send them away to school and they become too self-sufficient at once!"

So I do think you were absolutely right in saying that all our presuppositions are different, partly owing to national differences. But, then, I can't help being English!

Why am I telling you this? I didn't mean to, but perhaps it does illustrate the fact that our national instincts were different, and now that I am leaving England, I am realizing it.

U.M. K-C.

1. *A contemporary of U.N.'s at Oxford. Her father was a well-known journalist and a popular lecturer in the U.S., where he came every year.*   2. *Brown was the former president of Union Seminary.*

Union Theological Seminary
New York, NY
November 6, 1931

My Dearest:

No mail from you since Tuesday and you've probably fared no better for the boats are not running very regularly any more. Another week of work is done. I had really a pretty good lecture this morning, about the first this year that gave me any satisfaction. So I feel a little more satisfied with the world. I'm taking things a little easier this afternoon, going to a League of Industrial Democracy meeting this afternoon. Then my second "at home" tonight. Tomorrow I'll have to work hard on my weekend engagements, as I am preaching at Yale and at Smith College on Sunday. The invitations for next year are beginning to pour in, and I am in a continual quandary to know what to do. Would like to ask you about each one of them, and I think I'll postpone answering most of them until we can decide together.

I bought the passages for the boat this morning, by telephone, and so the day seems to be very near. I got an outside cabin, second class, a cabin which in the summer season is used for first class. The weeks go by so quickly now. There won't really be much until we will actually be on that boat together, a respectable old married couple. Just think of it. There are always so many things that I want to tell you about and ask you about. I imagine I'll have to send half a dozen cables when the time draws near because I've forgotten something. You won't forget to buy your own wedding ring and I'll buy mine here! It would be nicer if I could buy one for you, but how do I know how big your finger is?

. . . I feel serene and confident with regard to the future. Many questions and problems raise themselves in my mind but I am so sure they can be solved if we really try to understand each other's position and trust each other that I worry no more. Perhaps you have begun to worry? I hope not. I wouldn't blame you considering the misgivings which many of your friends must have.

I forgot to tell you about John Bennett's address. It is Auburn Seminary, Auburn, NY. I don't know whether I told you that Kay, his sister, was through here a week ago on her way to the wedding. John was married just a week ago. She said, "I am going to tease John after the wedding until I force some classical remark out of him which I can quote for years to come—and then I will let him alone."

I think I'll preach a sermon at Yale on the text "Not many mighty, not many noble, not many wise after the flesh are called." I will either work that up or use the sermon which you helped me prepare on the text from Isaiah. I haven't used that a second time and with the pressure under which I work, the sermon has to do duty more than that. Have you ever had a chill run down your back as you thought of the horrible necessity of listening to me say the same thing over and over again in the years ahead? It will be a good discipline for me and prompt me to try to say something new. Now I have to rush off to the meeting. My thoughts are constantly with you.

In haste,

R.N.

Graduate Club
New Haven, CT
Saturday, November 7, 1931

My Dearest:

I didn't get a chance to write to you today before coming here. Just had dinner with my brother Helmut and Florence and their two kiddies. Played a game of dominoes with them and then came back here to finish the work on my sermon. I won't get a chance to write tomorrow as I will be hopping off from here to Smith College. . . .

Yours,

Reinhold

Union Theological Seminary
New York, NY
November 9, 1931

My Dearest One:

This is Monday morning and I haven't heard from you since last Tuesday. That is a long time. I wish these boats were not on winter schedule. There are so many things I wonder about and I long for your letters, if only to have you tell me that you love me in spite of all the bother about my family and what has gone on between us. I know you do, but a week without letters is a trial.

I didn't write to you yesterday. The whole day was one grand rush. Preached at Yale in the morning, and President Angell asked me to reconsider my decision to come to Yale. I told him there was small chance. I had a hurried lunch with my brother and then went on to Smith where I spoke in the afternoon. I spent the evening with President and Mrs. Nielson. He is a Scotsman and she is German and both of them are as brilliant and as witty as any two people I know. I don't know when I have spent a more delightful evening. Mrs. Nielson had a great time twitting her husband about his "nineteenth-century liberalism." She reads a great deal of German philosophy and has imbibed some of the German pessimism. She also got off to both of us for the arts and trickery of the orator. It was really great fun. I couldn't help thinking of us again and again during the evening as I took in this family scene with its revelation of perfect understanding across a national boundary. I told them about you, and they were very much interested in our romance. I think you'll have to come along when I go there next year.

As I didn't get much sleep last night, I'm not in very good shape to do my work today. I had to get up at 6 this morning and the darn berth was too warm to sleep for the few hours that I was on the train. Will have to spend the day getting lectures ready on the ethics of Egyptian religion. It is a shame to lecture on such a subject when you know next to nothing about it. I have just read two books on the subject. From now to Christmas, my class in Ethics will be a nightmare because I am traversing territory with which I have very little familiarity. The weather is wonderful now. And it is a shame to be living in the city and have so much work to do. I wish I could get away for about a week. I have just finished arranging my schedule for Chicago and we ought to have an interesting time there, for we will be there for four days. I haven't taken too many engagements so we will have a little time for other things.

I am still hoping I'll hear from you today, but it is probably a vain hope. But these days of agony are drawing to a close.

Yours devotedly,

R.N.

Union Theological Seminary
New York, NY
November 10, 1931

My Dearest:

I have been walking around in a daze all day. The ships which came in today and yesterday had no mail for me. It is over a week since I last heard from you. I cannot imagine what has happened since several boats have come in without mail. The last time I heard from you was when you wrote on Sunday the 25th. I suppose that your mail is catching slow boats now as I am with my mail, but I should have heard at that. . . .

I ought not to worry when I don't hear from you, but after what you have written about how people in England worry about your decision to marry me I get all jumpy when I don't hear from you for such a long time. And it's only six weeks until we will be married too. It will be great to have all those worries over and know that we have each other and will begin living our lives together. You may think me a pretty self-sufficient duck, but I really cannot imagine my life alone any more. I think of all things in terms of what you may think or want to do about them. In spite of my fears I still hope for good news.

I had a decent class in Ethics this morning after spending about three solid days in preparation for it. The rest will probably be punk again. For I do not have that much time to prepare lectures on subjects about which I know so little. I returned an hour ago from a Federal Council[1] committee meeting. A waste of two hours which might have been spent more profitably. I wonder whether committees ever arrive anywhere. I am almost inclined to agree with your friend Leonard Hodgson[2] that one ought to stick to one's knitting and forego these conferences.

Now I am going back to study the ethics of Egyptian, Chinese, and Indian religion! I wish I knew something about those subjects. I just don't. I'll scratch the surface and bluff my way through.

I am living on hope for good news tomorrow.

Yours always,

R.N.

1. *Federal Council of Churches*, the organization headquartered in New York City that coordinated Protestant denominations; later became the National Council of Churches.
2. Theological scholar, then canon of Winchester Cathedral; later canon and professor at Christ Church, Oxford.

Union Theological Seminary
New York, NY
November 22, 1931

My Dearest:

I write you this word of love and devotion on the day which is just one month from our nuptials, to use a phrase which newspaper headlines have stereotyped. One month from today and we will belong to each other forever. It is both a joyous and a solemn thought. We will share a great deal of joy together and inevitably some sorrow and we will try to multiply the former and divide the latter by sharing it.

Have just come up to send you a brief note. I spent part of the afternoon advising with Arnold [Johnson] who is trying to decide whether to go back to Kentucky to stand trial or whether to remain here as the Kentucky courts would undoubtedly prefer. He is in a great quandary what to do and I am not clear either. Another part of the afternoon was used in visiting with the Lymans. Prof. Lyman has been sick for a week. They send their love to you. Now we must run off to the Lehmans[1] for supper. The weather is unbelievably warm. We have not had such an autumn here since 1847. The temperature today is about as warm as [it] usually [is] about the end of August. I worked up some real perspiration just walking leisurely in the park with Arnold. So I won't be used to your chilly island when I arrive there. I wish you might be here today and we could have a real walk in Riverside Park. Mrs. Bruce Bliven[2] wrote the other day and reminded me that it was just a year ago that she met me while going to the F.P.A.[3] luncheon with you. That made me think. Remembering how distinctly conscious I was of your presence at that luncheon, I came to the conclusion that I had really fallen before the holiday season where I have officially placed the point of the beginning of my disintegration as a self-sufficient bachelor. Very important matter of chronology, don't you think?

I will have to run along now. This is the briefest letter I have written in a long while. But there is nothing new to write. My letters are like my sermons—the same old story in only a slightly new form. Give Barbara my love and do let me know all this bright stuff she has touched off at my expense.

With all devotion,

Reinhold

1. *Paul and Marian Lehman; he was a graduate student who won a scholarship to study with Karl Barth.* 2. *Close friend of U. K-C.; wife of the editor of the* New Republic. 3. *Foreign Policy Association.*

Union Theological Seminary
New York, NY
November 24, 1931

My Dearest:

It is Tuesday 12:30 which means that in one hour more four weeks from today we will be walking down the aisle all ready to be married. And the world will never know what a historic occasion that is in the lives of two humble people. I received a nice batch of letters from you this morning and fed my soul on them and I can even expect another letter tomorrow as one of the big boats comes in today. The steamship companies have been kinder to me lately. You are always kind with the regularity of your letters but sometimes the companies are most unkind.

. . . Tonight I have to attend the executive meeting of our League of Independent Political Action[1] and see whether we are going to try to put a ticket in the field next year against the two old parties. We probably haven't strength to do it. I am sending you the last issue of the *World Tomorrow*. It will probably give your cousin Julian Piggott a case of nausea if he reads it so don't show it to him. It isn't a particularly good number, by the way. I haven't had the chance to write anything for a long while, and I won't have any further opportunity until I get on the boat. I wonder whether we will have to have about three hours a day set aside for work on the way back, you to answer or write all the thank you letters and I to work on my courses.

You know it is rather nice to anticipate letters from one's beloved without fearing they may contain something which reflects a misunderstanding. I am so glad we found peace and understanding before we actually come to live together. I do not mean we won't have to face some pretty difficult problems and probably we won't always understand each other. I look forward to the years before us with only joy and gratitude.

Yours devotedly,

Reinhold

1. *Embryonic organization founded in New York City in December 1928 by Norman Thomas, John Dewey, and Paul Douglas for third-party programs and action.*

My Dearest:

Have just come back from my political meeting where we conferred with John Dewey, Oswald Villard of the *Nation,* Devere Allen, etc., on the possibilities of a new party next year. We didn't realize how much we were academics and really unable to bring a new party to birth, but it was interesting. Villard who sat next to me asked me all about you and then said that he had recently been at a party where they talked about you and me and that someone said you had the whole academic world at your feet and then were foolish enough to go and marry an old bald-headed professor. I accepted the compliment with great pride. I think maybe the Blivens have been talking to him and Devere Allen added a little sauce.

Had a letter from [Harry] Ward today. He is a complete communist by now and says that nothing he reads from us, that is, in our magazines, interests him. It all seems to belong to an old world while he is in the world which represents the future. I just wonder what he will be like when he comes back.

I don't know whether I will have a chance to write to you tomorrow, three classes, faculty executive committee meeting, dinner with Bishop Scarlett, and after that the theatre will take up the whole day. Now I have to get to work on Buddhistic ethics. You can't imagine how I am slaving for my courses this year. This is my fourth year and it is as hard as ever. I wonder whether I will ever know enough to make this work a little easier. One ought not to come into this academic work as late as I did. This stuff ought to be gathered in the years when I was running around doing practical work.

But now I must get to work. Glad you bought yourself something out of that money. Please spend the rest of it not on household stuff but for yourself. Don't forget the ring. I haven't bought mine yet. We decided on plain gold, did we not? If this is wrong, cable me.

> *Yours in true devotion, love and gratitude,*
>
> *Reinhold*

Union Theological Seminary
New York, NY
November 25, 1931

My Dearest One:

I didn't expect to write you today as it was too crowded, but a very tragic incident has changed things. Dr. Gaylord White died an hour ago and all classes have been suspended. He had not been sick at all, but died just before chapel this morning of heart failure. He was such a wonderful soul that I just can't think of his being dead. What a strange thing life is. In one moment you have life and personality in all the richness and variety and uniqueness of a single soul and the next moment a blank. My waning faith in immortality always receives new strength when I face such ultimates as the death of a dear friend. He really was one of our choicest spirits and makes some of these ranting theologians with their prejudices and egotism seem very small indeed.

I received some awfully nice letters from you this morning and I thank you for them. I think I must have been reading your letters just about the time of Dr. White's death. Incidentally, I have substituted your letters for chapel this fall, which means that I have cut many a chapel. When a letter from you is in the box, I go to my office and enjoy it and leave chapel go hang. "I have married a wife therefore I cannot come." I haven't married her yet but the tie is definite and the love as great. Your letters are so full of love and devotion that you scare me a little at times, and I think to myself you have created in your imagination a different me than the real one and that I will disappoint you when you have to put up with all my foibles. But I do think that love makes it possible to put up with one another's foibles. If people really didn't love one another, they couldn't stand intimacy for human nature is just peculiar enough to make that impossible without real love.

Sitting here and writing to you at my leisure where I expected a full day of work makes me think of the strain it may be for you to have to live with one so enmeshed in so many things. Not that I expect to go on at this crazy pace all my life, but I am afraid I will never be a man of leisure except in the summer months. There are too many things to be done for leisure. Dr. Coffin is terribly worried about me having such close connections for the wedding. "If you disappoint your in-laws and a bride, don't say I didn't warn you," he says. But to get there a day earlier I have to leave almost a week earlier as the other boats are so much slower, and I can't imagine a boat being over 24 hours late. Perhaps I can't imagine it partly because we have such incredible summer weather still. Every day is supposed to be the end of it, but it still is as warm as August today. It is [a] great boon for the suffering unemployed.

Now I must go and see if I can be of any use to the Whites.

With all love and devotion,

Reinhold

Union Theological Seminary
New York, NY
December 2, 1931

My Dearest One:

The faculty meeting lasted too long for me to go to Brooklyn and anyway there were two more letters from you, very nice letters, too, and so I came back to my office to do some work and write some lectures. You are wonderful. Your love and your willingness to bear with my quirks as well as joys fills me with radiant hope. As the time approaches, it will be pretty difficult to bear the waiting and the longing. Life was certainly meant for two people like us to be together. The arrangements about going to Oxford are certainly splendid. The Crosses[1] are wonderful in their helpfulness. I wrote out, with Hulda's help, the wedding announcement addresses last night so that part of the preliminaries is ready. I'll be gone this weekend so will perform any other preliminaries the last weekend.

I hope these letters reach you before some of my more depressed ones come. Please don't be afraid of me. I trust you and love you even when I go into a tailspin, which I really never had before in my life.

Yours in complete love,

Reinhold

P.S. I do have the items you mentioned, a travelling kit and a cigarette case, but not a silk dressing gown. But what is the idea of presents for me? No sense in that. The groom is only a necessary evil at a wedding.

1. *Leslie and Gertrude Cross; he was an Old Testament scholar and Fellow of Jesus College, Oxford.*

Union Theological Seminary
New York, NY
December 3, 1931

My Dearest Ursula:

I ran out between classes this afternoon and bought the wedding ring at a neighborhood jeweler. It is a plain gold band which is not too different from yours. As I have two meetings tonight and leave tomorrow noon for a weekend trip to the University of Illinois from which I will not return until Wednesday, my days here seem to be actually about over. I feel as if I were getting on the boat tomorrow although it is really twelve days away. I do feel sorry I wrote you those terribly depressed letters, I really don't feel any anxiety, although I know there is some unresolved conflict about my mother. But I look forward to everything now in joy and confidence.

The students went out yesterday to help organize the Brooklyn Edison people and this morning's paper had a good story on they're being slugged by hired gangsters of the company. Dr. Coffin was so excited about the possible effect upon the Board because Jim Dombrowski's name was mentioned in the story. So that again I am beginning to feel that my days here will not be many. Pit has been made dean of students in place of Gaylord White and I'm depending upon that to be a check on Dr. Coffin because Pit is, for all of his innate conservatism, rather wiser than Coffin in dealing with such issues. But we shall see what we shall see.

I am enclosing a letter from my brother which reveals him rather clearly and I thought you would appreciate reading it. The occasion for the letter was a pamphlet on sex, the one I told you about when Mr. [Sherwood] Eddy gave it to me. My brother found it in my office this summer and asked to take it home with him as he had never studied anything like that. This letter represents his reaction.

I am enclosing one of the announcements of the wedding, which are all addressed and ready. Did the work after midnight last night. I may send the whole box to you tomorrow in order to save me carrying it in my luggage. Sorry to write in such a hurry. I have to leave now to go to a dinner of the Student Movement which Pit has arranged.

Yours devotedly,

R.N.

Union Theological Seminary
New York, NY
December 8, 1931

My Dearest:

Here it is Tuesday and I haven't written you since Saturday. I just picked up the *Times* and see that [S.S.] *Hamburg* leaves tomorrow, and I think if I get a letter on that boat it will arrive before I will. I am writing this in the smoker of a Pullman on my way to New York. I am on the train all day and am working out my three courses for tomorrow. I spoke to 1,200 Congregationalists last night in Chicago and got a midnight train out. On Sunday I spoke to three audiences of university students at the

University of Illinois. It has been a pretty strenuous weekend which has become a little more than a weekend, almost like an English weekend. Yesterday noon I had to speak to the alumni of Union Seminary in Chicago as well.

Two weeks from tonight we will be all married and starting our life together. It hardly seems true and yet it is. One wonders how one can contain one's emotion when the time arrives. It will be wonderful, I know, our life together. I do hope you won't find me too difficult in my moods and vagaries. I am confident that love does have an alchemy which knows how to dissolve difficulties and we'll resolve ours I am sure. I could wish that I had a little easier second semester so that we would have more time together. But we will make the most of what we have.

I hope you are not having too strenuous a time in your last days at your home. I am, by the way, doing no shopping for Christmas gifts for your family or for the Crosses hoping we can do that together after we reach Oxford. There is little time for it now and hardly any sense in lugging things over when everything nice can be had over there.

Spent part of yesterday with Dr. Morrison and Paul Hutchinson of the *Century*.[1] Paul is one of my most intimate friends. They expect us to stay with them in June. Dr. Morrison said, "I had some fear that you never would be married because of your home conditions and because of your gracious mother who made things so easy for you. I hope you will live alone, at least for the time being." I assured him we would. Whereupon he said, "I thought you would have the sense to do that. Mrs. Morrison and I have been talking about it and hoping you would, yet we realized that little mother would have to go through some ordeal the first few months." So you see that some people who regard what we are doing as perfectly natural and necessary nevertheless see some of the pain.

I have been filled with remorse all day as I sat thinking about some of the first letters I wrote over a week ago which you are receiving now. I hope you can forgive me for them. When I look forward to two weeks from tonight I don't want to think of anything else.

Yours devotedly,

Reinhold

1. *Dr. Charles C. Morrison had been Publisher of the* Christian Century *since 1908, and Paul Hutchinson was its editor. The* Century *was an interdenominational Christian weekly established in 1884 and renamed* Christian Century *in 1900.*

Two

1933
Memoir:
Comic Interlude

It was late summer, in 1933. Reinhold Niebuhr was traveling through the Berkshires to the hill village of Heath, in western Massachusetts. He was looking forward to a last few days after a busy summer. He had been in England with his wife Ursula visiting her relations and their friends. He had left her there, so that he might return to teach in the summer school at Union Theological Seminary in New York City. His wife had suffered a rather serious miscarriage on board an ocean liner on her birthday, August 3. After surgery and a hospital stay, they had been lent a delightful old house at Heath, Massachusetts, where she might spend a convalescent couple of weeks, and where Reinhold might also have a breathing space before the Seminary term started in mid-September.

He had been attending a weekend conference of congenial liberal-minded clergy and academics. They called themselves the Fellowship of Socialist Christians, and had supported Norman Thomas in his campaign for the presidency in 1932. But now it was the Age of Roosevelt. Many new frontiers were being explored in the social and economic realm. As the historians have noticed, Roosevelt was moving along the path of trial and error. In the big corner cabin suite next to Ursula on the ocean liner, was U.S. Secretary of State Cordell Hull and his wife returning from the bungled London Monetary and Economic Conference.

Such was the background, and Reinhold Niebuhr, as he drove, meditated on these and many other subjects. Arriving at Lenox, he failed to pause at a stop sign by Trinity Church. A policeman at that corner strode over deliberately to scold the man driving the shabby little car with a New York license. "Buddy, can't you read?" he said, glaring at the weary academic within. "Let me have a look at your license," and he reached out his hand.

Reinhold brought out his driving license, but it had expired a couple of days earlier. The policeman's wrath was expressed vividly. "What do you think you are doing? Don't you keep the law in New York? Come along, buddy, we will have to take you to the police station."

A somewhat chastened Reinhold, in the shabby little car, followed the policeman to the Lee Police Station and was there deprived of any article that might be used to damage himself, or, presumably, the station or the police.

Meanwhile, in the beautiful grounds of the Manse at Heath, Ursula was lazily convalescing. She was alone save for a delightful large lady who had been procured as cook and housekeeper for those few weeks. The Manse was a lovely pre-Revolution house which their friend Mrs. Ethel Moors had purchased many years earlier, and which she generously lent to friends of varying shades of political and denominational coloring for short and longer periods.

In the calm of a Sunday afternoon, the telephone rang. It was Reinhold.

"Hello, darling," said Ursula. "Where are you?"

"In jail in Lee, Massachusetts," replied her husband.

"How simply marvelous! How did you achieve that? Was this after your meeting?"

"No, I didn't stop for a traffic sign in Lenox."

"And they put you into jail for that?" His English wife seemed somewhat outraged at such extreme police tactics.

"The trouble is they want money!"

"What! They want to be bribed?"

"No, I have to have money to put up bail, and I've only got a couple of dollars, you see."

"Heavens, wouldn't they accept the typewriter as a sort of equivalent?"

"No. Can you get hold of some of our friends and see if anybody could drive down with some money?"

"Yes, I'll try—don't worry. Meditate, darling. Try all the different disciplines of meditation and contemplation. Try the Ignatian method."

"Don't be silly. Try and get some money quick." Reinhold rang off.

Ursula pondered. She was several miles from the village of Heath, where indeed they had friends. Those who had cash were more likely to be those who came for the summer vacation. Unfortunately, they were mostly clergy. There was Bishop Gilbert the suffragan of New York, whom she knew was away preaching or at some theological conference. Dr. and Mrs. Angus Dun—he later was to be bishop of Washington, DC—were also away. There were a couple of farms within a mile or so, but Ursula was not supposed to walk that distance and she had no mode of locomotion. What was she to do?

Light from heaven struck her. The Gardner Days in Williamstown! The Rev. Gardner Day was the rector of St. John's at Williamstown. He was a good friend, and he and his wife Katherine had been married a few months after Reinhold and Ursula had been married. Katherine was the sister of a very close friend of Reinhold's, John Bennett, who later was to be his colleague at Union Theological Seminary and later become president there. Reinhold and Ursula had seen a good deal of Katherine and Gardner Day the previous summer, which the Niebuhrs had spent at Heath, often coming to Williamstown to use the Williams College Library and to see other friends in that delightful place.

As rector of St. John's, Gardner would have access to money. Perhaps he might even use, on loan, some of the morning's offering? Delightful possibilities of all sorts flocked to Ursula's mind. Praying to heaven for help, she telephoned the Gardner Days. Blest be her prayers, for they were at home. The situation appealed to their neighborly altruism and also to the strain of fantasy that Katherine Day particularly possessed and that was a great bond between her and the Niebuhrs.

"[Verily] the Lord hath been on our side" (Ps. 118:6). Ursula returned to the chaise lounge in the garden, humming her favorite Anglican chants. After all, it would be the hour of evensong in the cathedrals she knew so well, and she would be able to rejoice, feeling indeed that the Lord would not leave his own to languish in prison.

Meanwhile, Gardner and Katherine Day proceeded down Route 7 to Lee, accompanied by two large, gray afghan hounds. Gardner had been able to procure enough money, almost enough for a king's ransom. The Niebuhrs were too tactful to inquire the source of such affluence, but the Lee police accepted it duly as appropriate bail.

Gardner Day, wearing his clergyman's collar, entered the police station with his wife and the two dogs. His wife was tall and striking, with a wonderful combination of dramatic appeal and humor. Gardner, one of the most handsome and distinguished of men, was a splendid foil to his wife's presence. They entered the cell. Katherine Day dramatically threw herself on her knees in front of Reinhold, clasped her hands together and then liturgically exclaimed, "Let us pray." Rising from her knees, she bestowed upon the policemen a copy of a book that Reinhold Niebuhr had published the year before: *Moral Man and Immoral Society*.

The police seemed somewhat startled. There were the large, gray afghan hounds; there was this distinguished looking gentleman in his clergyman's collar; there was this fantastic lady—and all on a late Sunday afternoon.

The prisoner was released, and the Days, accompanied by the chastened Reinhold, betook themselves to Route 7 and proceeded up to the further reaches of western Massachusetts.

The memory of all this remained. Reinhold had had experience of prison in the days before student uprisings and the clamor of the later sixties. It affected his sensibilities, the lack of anything to do, the fact that the police took away his typewriter and the Sunday newspaper.

His wife chided him, "Darling, why on earth didn't you have a clergyman's collar with you, and a Bible obviously opened to some important passage?"

"Of course I had a Bible; it was in my suitcase, but you know I never wear a clergyman's collar."

"But didn't you have something else, your traveling communion set or something to show that you were a kosher clergyman?" Reinhold disdained such obvious "perks" of the clerical profession. "I always thought a little jesuitical casuistry was lacking in your education," Ursula remarked. "It is awfully useful, you know, particularly in crises."

In later years, living at Stockbridge, the Niebuhrs sometimes wondered if the Lee Police Station still possessed that copy of *Moral Man and Immoral Society*.

Three

1936
Transatlantic Exchange

Early in 1936 I had disturbing news about my mother's health. Reinhold and I thought it important that I go to England to see her, and to take our son Christopher, eighteen months old, with me. My parents were then living at East Moseley, near Hampton Court Palace, an easy distance by suburban train from London. So, apart from the pleasure of being at home with them, and especially with my mother, it was quite easy to see my friends in London and catch up on what so many of my friends were doing. My sister Barbara, also concerned about my mother, had come home to help with the general situation.

I was delighted to discover, both through casual reading of periodicals and from my friends, that Reinhold's writings were becoming well known in England. Alan Richardson, who was to become dean of York Minster but who was currently editor at the Student Christian Movement in London, had written several articles, as had the literary critic John Middleton Murry, to mention just two.

Later, Reinhold was to join me for the summer and we were able to find a charming thatched cottage not too far from Oxford, or London, where he might both work and get a little rest after his term. He was entranced with the ability in England to get the books he needed from the London Library, or from the Times Book Club, or from Oxford so that he could work not only on his serious academic lectures, but also for his articles and reviews on current affairs.

Union Theological Seminary
New York, NY
April 3, 1936

Dearest One:

I have had you terribly on my mind today, worrying about you and wondering how you are faring, how the old boy is behaving, whether the nurse your mother was getting is as helpful as she seemed, whether you were seasick, etc., etc. It seemed a shame to let you go like that last night. I won't let you travel alone with this infant again. It must be too difficult. I only hope it won't be too ghastly.

I am writing this before going to the Lymans' for dinner. I am all dressed up in my "soup and fish." I have been thinking a good deal about that college [Sarah Lawrence] proposition. I believe that it is so important to get a foothold in the academic ladder that we ought even to postpone an infant for a year in order to get you started. In the same way, I believe that it would be good if you wrote Miss Warren[1] immediately expressing your regret that you could not meet the [search] Committee before you departed, and asking whether it would help to come back early. I don't think a chance like this ought to be missed. In fact, I get quite excited about it when I think of the possibilities. But, of course, I don't want to impose the decision upon you. Only it does seem to me important.

I sat up last night until 2 A.M. preparing my classes, consequently I slept all the afternoon recuperating. Then I had a handball game, dressed, and now it is dinner time. Consequently, I have to hurry to get this letter off to catch the *Ile de France*. The house is terribly empty. I have fortunately not been in it except to sleep. It is 7 P.M. and I must hurry. Give my love to your mother and to Barbara and to your dad and give the old boy a kiss for me.

Much love,

R.N.

1. *President of Sarah Lawrence College, Bronxville, NY.*

Union Theological Seminary
New York, NY
April 9, 1936

Dearest One:

I rather hoped a little that you would send me a cable today. I knew you would consider it an extravagance and yet wished I had asked you to do so. But after all you could do no more than say "arrived safely" and that would not tell me how much trouble you had on board or whether you were seasick. I hope things were not too bad. I am waiting anxiously for the first mail. I preached my first Lenten service yesterday at 5. The night before I preached at Trinity Lutheran Church. We will have to go there sometime as they really have a nice liturgy though the pastor is a little too smooth to suit me. Today I am going to rest after Bill Savage comes in an hour. I am very tired after hectic days this week. I have to read six theses over the weekend, but that is not so bad.

Wilhemina is leaving next Wednesday. I think I had better let Bridget come in a few hours every other day. I think that will do it. Wilhemina has put up the new curtains and changed the covers on the furniture, so everything is as ordered. Jim Dombrowski is still here and probably will be for another month.

Kagawa[1] spoke here in the Social Room. He was terribly offended by my criticism of him and mentioned it in his speech. His address was romantic but interesting. He is a resourceful little fellow. He filled a blackboard up with cryptic figures as he spoke which no one could understand. After the meeting, students asked whether they could come up to the apartment for a chat, and about 25 showed up to discuss the speech and everything else. And so to bed.

Everyone here is asking about you. Dr. Coffin told me to come in for any meal when I felt lonely. Mrs. Coffin was standing by without seconding the invitation, so I will hardly accept it. I dropped in on Tuesday night after the service at the Van Dusens' where they had a party for John Baillie.[2] It wasn't too much fun. They were all paired off and there was no general discussion, so I had to talk for an hour with nice Miss Adelaide Case.[3] I know you don't like general discussion, but this tête-à-tête gets my goat unless you draw someone very interesting in the lottery.

I am full of contrition in my loneliness of all the failures I have made this winter in properly considering you. So you will find me all attention while the contrition lasts. I put it like that because one does not easily overcome native defects. In fact, I am fatalistic about that and doubt whether anyone ever changes native defects. I am terribly anxious to hear how everyone is and how you find life over in England, and how the old boy is behaving. I would like to be with him and give him his orange juice again in the morning.

Much love,

R.N.

1. *Toyohiko Kagawa; religious leader in Japan who preached pacifism rather akin to Gandhi's in India, and author of* The Religion of Jesus *(1931). R.N. had published an article, "The Political Confusions of Dr. Kagawa," in* Radical Religion *(Winter 1936).*   2. *Professor of systematic theology at Union Seminary.*   3. *Professor of education at Teachers College of Columbia University and later professor of religious education at Episcopal Theological Seminary in Cambridge, MA.*

Union Theological Seminary
New York, NY

Easter Morning
April 12, 1936

Dearest One:

It is Easter morning and I miss you terribly. It is several days before a decent boat sails, but I'll write you my Easter letter. Poor Tillich[1] sailed yesterday and gave me his proofs for a glance at them before turning them over to Bill Savage. The translation is simply terrible. It gave me a pain in every bone. Consequently I spent all last night and all this morning working on them. I have only finished about one-third. I will turn over the rest to the Stanleys.[2] I can't devote any more time to them much as I would like to whip the stuff into shape. At that, I am caught up with my work. During the free weekend I wrote a sermon for next Sunday and one for Friday morning, three lectures, and read seven theses. This afternoon I will go to the Cathedral [of St. John the Divine] for Easter hymns, etc., so that the spirit of the day will not escape me entirely.

I am letting Wilhemina go on Tuesday. I'll give her some extra days off. I have not made any arrangements for the apartment yet. I think I'll have Bridget in twice a week and do the rest myself.

I have gotten enough rest and relaxation to be able to sleep a little better, so I am feeling quite fit again but awfully lonely. All things are relative. You may think me a cold fish and self-sufficient, but I am really so much married that I feel as if I had lost my personal identity.

This week's program is: Monday in Springfield, Tuesday, dinner at General Seminary, Thursday, dinner with Prof. MacMurray[3] at the Van Dusens', Friday, Theological Society, Saturday, Clergy Meeting at Harrisburg, PA, Sunday sermon here. That is why I prepared a lot of stuff in advance.

I wonder what you and Christopher are doing this morning, and how your mother is and how you find things in general. If only I had asked you to cable. Betty Van Dusen [Pitney Van Dusen's wife] asked me whether I had had a cable. I told her no. She wanted to know whether I had asked for one and I answered that I forgot to. She said, "Exactly what Pit and I did last time. He expected a cable and I didn't send one because I thought it extravagant." Still, maybe I'll hear from you over the weekend.

Next morning, Monday: [I] went to the Cathedral yesterday afternoon and stayed until Milo Gates [the dean] started to preach, then I took a little walk. Worked some more on Tillich's translation. By the way, I gave him your address. You can reach him in care of Edinburgh House, Eden Gate. He hopes to see you but doubts whether he can be allowed out. J. H. Oldham has him dated practically every day.

I am getting ready to go to Springfield this noon. I do wish I knew how you are and whether you are happy. Tell the old boy not to forget me. Tell him I'm the guy that gives him his orange juice in the morning, or did.

Love to your mother, to Barbara, etc.

Yours,

R.N.

1. *German theologian at Union Seminary.* 2. *Clifford Stanley; a graduate student at Union Seminary, and his wife.* 3. *Professor John MacMurray; professor of philosophy; later at Edinburgh.*

Union Theological Seminary
New York, NY
Thursday, April 16, 1936

Dearest:

I have just come up from the Van Dusens' apartment where a company of us spent an interesting evening with Prof. MacMurray. He was really very good. Douglas Steere, Dean Wicks, and Prof. Green from Princeton also were there.

Just before going, I received my first letter from you, unexpectedly. It was a short note written just after you arrived at your home and made me certain that you had written before and I had not received your letter. You refer to Christopher being sick on board but give no particulars.

I had to write tonight because beginning with chapel in the morning, every hour of the day is literally occupied. I may even have to cancel some of my engagements in order to go to Buffalo for the organization meeting of the State Committee of the Socialist Party. That would come up just when I could not afford the time. I will be in Harrisburg on Saturday and come back in time to preach here on Sunday. The advantage in hopping about is I don't have to be in this empty house. It really is very empty without you.

I feel hounded today. I am writing this note after class. I am leaving in an hour and a half by plane for Buffalo. The Organization Committee requires every vote and they have tearfully implored me to cancel all engagements to go to Buffalo.

Much love, will write more leisurely tomorrow.

Yours,

R.N.

East Moseley
Surrey, England
April 18, 1936

Darling:

. . . I had hoped that you would give Tillich a letter to hand to me; and now, although I am sure you will have written by the boat he came on, I won't get it until Monday, alas!

It was fun meeting Tillich. We, I and (The Rev.) Hugh Lister, met him at Paddington Station. We fed him on a British lunch (a mixed grill and a double Bass [ale]) and took him around London on the top of a bus, and then put him on his train for Blickling Hall, the noble seat (really lovely) of Lord Lothian, near Norwich, for a weekend theological conference. Tillich was really very funny—rather like Christopher [18 months], solemn and emphatic, but very nice, and also amazed at the freedom of our railway stations, and at how polite everybody was! So Hugh Lister and I explained that democracy and feudalism had a few saving heritages left!

Hugh Lister is your disciple. He goes everywhere clasping your book [*Moral Man and Immoral Society*]! Who is publishing the *Interpretation of Christian Ethics* over here? He said he got them easily, but I forgot to look at his copy, to see where and how and who is putting it out. So please answer this question.

He also said he had sold, so to speak, lots of copies the last week or two. He really was awfully nice; young, dark hair, nice looking, easy and well spoken. He had on a casual but well-cut black and grey pin-striped suit, grey waistcoat, dog collar, and old grey felt hat. Tillich was *frightfully* impressed by his appearance, and asked me in an awestruck whisper, "And he is very noble?" Actually, he is the son of a doctor (he is one of *the* Listers, the medical family, Lord Lister, chloroform and all the rest). He was a railway engineer, then took Holy Orders and a bit later, became a socialist. He is a curate at an Anglo-Catholic church at Hackney, and runs the Eton College Mission there. He also does trade union organizing and tries to make the populace class conscious! He is not an intellectual, but no one's fool, and being very nice and terribly nicely English, is a *most* suitable choice to impress Tillich! He also helps Joe Oldham, with the World Council of Churches, etc., hence our going together to meet Tillich.

He is *not* a Reckett-Demant, etc., crowd; he regards them all too "liberal"—they talk about love, and he does not like their politics. He regards them also as a bit too sacramental in their emphases, doctrinally. He himself is an Anglo-Catholic, but liturgically, and feels that the test of a man is what he thinks about sin, social and otherwise. That is why he follows you rather than Reckett & Co. Father Noel[1] he regards as hot air. I shall now try and see what *I* think about all these characters. [Reckett and his friends ran an Anglo-Catholic socialist journal called *Christendom* to which U.N. had subscribed.]

So it was all rather fun, talking and discussing these odd points with him and with Tillich. Hugh Lister is dying for you to preach over here and told me how Edward Shilleto[2] came back from U.S.A., and at some gathering or other was asked what had struck him most in U.S.A. He then said "Reinhold Niebuhr," not quite as broadly as that, but something like that. And continued, "Quite seriously, I will tell you, it was a man I heard preach and speak and his name was Reinhold Niebuhr."

So "one up," old Shilleto! You would laugh at how I lap up all this about you in my own country! . . .

Ursula

1. *Anglo-Catholic priest.*   2. *English writer.*

Union Theological Seminary
New York, NY

Sunday Morning
April 19, 1936

Dearest:

I have prepared my sermon and while I let it simmer, I will give you an account of myself. I have had only that one batch of letters and am hoping for better news of you and Christopher when I get back.

On Friday, I started to fly to Buffalo. I have no luck with aviation. The pilot was ordered down at Elmira because of fog in Buffalo. "A man was killed on this route two weeks ago," said the pilot, "and they are taking no chances." I spent the night in Elmira. The Norman Thomas faction, incidentally, had twenty votes to spare, so they really didn't need my vote though they solemnly swore they did. I got up at 6 at Elmira, rode 6 weary hours on a bus, addressed a Methodist ministers meeting in Harrisburg and caught a train at 4 for NYC. I came home in time to prepare a sermon and to get a good night's rest, so I do feel chipper this morning, except the house is terribly empty.

Had a note from Mrs. Fosdick last night saying that Bishop Scarlett would be dining with them, that Dr. Fosdick is absent and would I complete the table for dinner. So I am going over there after the service.

The past week has been terribly hectic. Dr. Coffin has been very nasty. The students asked to participate in the nation-wide Peace Demonstration on Wednesday. They talked it over with the Student-Faculty Committee, which reported favorably. Coffin, for some unknown reason, was terribly upset and emotional. He wanted his vote recorded in the negative and also leave to record his objections. On Friday morning when I had a chapel service, he started out: "You fellows make me tired. I'm sick of this place and wish I had accepted a church. I'm going to carry this matter to the Board." So I went to the mat and was just as nasty as he. I said, "You make me tired, too. I feel just as much like quitting and taking a church as you do. I particularly object to having disciplinary matters settled by the faculty, carried to the Board as if we were a lot of children to be overruled by our elders." So we locked horns more definitely than in years. He was so childish that even Dr. Lyman who is so mild thought it very queer. The end of the season seems to leave him with frayed nerves. But my nerves are frayed too. What children we are.

On Wednesday night, George Lansbury[1] and Dr. Fosdick opened a big peace campaign in Carnegie Hall. Kirby Page is positively feverish about it. There will be a broadcast with Lansbury, Mrs. Roosevelt, and Kirby Page. Nationwide hook-up.

Two more weeks of hard work, then the worst will be over.

Later, afternoon: I preached my morning sermon on the two texts "Except ye become as little children" (Matt. 18:3) and "When I became a man, I put aside childish things" (1 Cor. 13:11). Will Scarlett and Dorothy Fosdick[2] honored me with their presence. I went over after the service and had dinner with them. They all want to be remembered to you. I took Scarlett down to Broadway, and then went to the hospital where Jim Dombrowski is getting along nicely. He will get back here on Wednesday.

Incidentally, MacMurray was superb the other evening. Everyone was very much impressed by him. He spoke among other things about God and mutuality. Someone asked him how God had anything to do with social life. Said he, for instance: "A married couple have had a falling out. They love each other, which means they are attached to each below and above the level of reason. At the level of reason, there is a rift, which means they interpret certain experiences from different perspectives. Perhaps they do not understand each other at all. Such a situation requires forgiveness, but there can be no forgiveness on the conscious level because there they are two individuals who have hurt each other and therefore are too busy defending themselves, which means that attack continues, for there is attack in every defense. How is such a situation resolved? Only if by some accident, or by discipline, the matter is viewed from some perspective which each of them is quite unable to take as a conscious or rational position. This," said he, "is the experience of grace and forgiveness. They find each other through God indirectly and not through a direct approach."

I give the exposition as exactly as I know how. Douglas Steere leaned over and said, "Isn't that a fresh and natural approach to a profound problem?" I agreed nonchalantly that it was, without revealing that I was really deeply moved and felt a little of the grace he was talking about. I knew how truly we loved each other and felt that some of the difficulties we have had were not altogether strange or hopeless, and silently praying for that grace. Don't you think that is good, dear? And after all, while we still face problems, some of them really have been solved on the level at which he speaks. About being united both below and above the level of reason, I could testify anew with considerable emotion. For without you, life is just halved. Everything seems stale when it is not shared with you. I did not like preaching this morning without you there, even though I did not have to be so careful about the hymns!

Next morning, Monday: Have just had my breakfast and see from the *Times* that I can mail this on S.S. *Georgic.* Have you had early morning tea in bed? Ain't that wonderful!

Much love,

R.N.

1. *Leader of the British Labour Party until 1935.*   2. *One of Harry Emerson Fosdick's daughters.*

East Moseley
Surrey, England
April 20, 1936

. . . Had a most amusing day with Tillich: first met him and then Barbara joined us, Joe Oldham carting off his suitcase, etc. We took him to the National Gallery as he wanted to see the Italian pictures. Pictures mean everything to him, more than I had realized, so we spent two hours there. Then we took him to a Dickens inn, The St. George and the Vulture, for lunch. He is fearfully thrilled and impressed by it all, and thought that the driver of the taxicab which we took because a sudden ghastly shower descended, "looked so noble, he looked like a general in the army, and was so polite." He's *most* impressed by the English manner. So he was really quite delightful to take around.

Then Barbara's friend turned up and played his part. He was the exact type I had already gathered from Barbara. Tillich played up to him and also enjoyed meeting him, as a type he wouldn't have met at his official theological and academic gatherings. (He was a banker and in the City, and incidentally *quite* conservative). His father, Mr. Gooderaham, used to be Governor of the Tower of London, and so on his instructions we went bounding forth to inspect the Tower. Quite fun, but it was still raining. Then we took Tillich to a home-made tea place I knew of, and delivered him at 32 Russell Square for his conference. The place turned out to be the Student Conference Hostel where Peggy Ratcliffe is sub-warden, so we all met together and had another cup of tea. Edwyn Bevan,[1] who had been at the same conference with Tillich, came up and talked to me about you and about your brother Richard, and asked all sorts of questions and wants to meet you. [This famous scholar had been at school with my uncle, Arthur Spencer Compton, and I had known him because of this connection and because of his sister who lived in Oxford; also I had gone to the special lectures he gave at Oxford—he was a kind of floating, stratospheric scholar who gave special lectures at most of the universities.] He also talked to me about my Uncle Arthur, who was his great friend and about my grandparents, etc. After all this, the theologians descended to hear Tillich read his paper, so Barbara and Peggy Ratcliffe and I drifted out and home.

Tillich was much impressed by his weekend at Blickling Hall. "It was like a house of a prince, not like a feudal lord's; it was royal rather than noble." And he loved the family pictures, the Holbeins and Van Dycks and also the wonderful park, also the butlers and the early morning tea brought to his bedroom! He told me modestly that Lord Lothian had liked him, so he quite liked Lothian, who took him [on] a long walk in the afternoon! Canon Raven and Edwyn Bevan, as I told you, were there and others whom you and I know.

He is spending a night at Hackney with your admirer Hugh Lister. I think he is getting quite a good picture of England. Lord Listowel [a socialist peer and a friend of ours] was going to take him around the Houses of Parliament tomorrow, but the Budget Speech is on, and so we may have to forget that. We shall take him to the Tate [Gallery], and then look in on the Wedgewood Benns[2] close by, before putting him on the train at Victoria Station for the Oldhams. . . .

U.M.N.

1. *Well-known scholar, especially on the Greco-Roman world of the New Testament.*
2. *Wedgewood Benn, Lord Stansgate, later secretary of state for air, and his wife, Margaret.*

East Moseley
Surrey, England
April 23, 1936

Darling One:

. . . We had another amusing day with Tillich on Tuesday. I met him at the Russell Square Hostel where he had been giving one of his papers, on God and history, etc. Margaret Delmar, Barbara's friend (whose father was professor of English at Berlin University) was coming to meet us, as Tillich was to look up some academic exiles at the Warburg Institute, of which she has been the secretary. We met, went to the Tate Gallery, where we had lunch, and then looked at pictures. Tillich and Margaret Delmar (whom Barbara always thinks is rather like Mrs. Tillich) got on famously.

After this, we went in to see the Wedgewood Benns, who, as you will remember, live almost next door to the Tate, and had tea with them. Wedgewood was splendid; he asked Tillich just the right questions and was most intelligent, really more perspicuous than I have ever known him on the subject of England and Germany. The Benns *do* make people do and be their best, don't they? And Tillich was fearfully impressed with their interest and niceness. Then we went on a few more yards, to Thames House and the Warburg Institute, and from thence to Victoria Station where I delivered Tillich up to Joe Oldham.

[Later]: I have just left John Baillie at Charing Cross Station, he was proceeding to Euston Station for Scotland and I to Waterloo Station to go home. It was great fun seeing him, and he was greatly "stimulated" (his own word) by his American trip. He and [John] Middleton Murry[1] talked the whole way over on the boat, apparently, and John Baillie quite fell for him, and really got hold of him and his odd lovable personality in a most understanding way. I hope John M. Murry liked him as well. I had taken John Baillie to see the Benns, the *other* Benns, Sir Ernest[2] and Lady Benn, who have a flat in the same building where John's club, the Author's Club, is. Ernest Benn looks like a paterfamilias conservative version of Wedgewood. Very nice to us. I am lunching with Lady Benn, and going to a matinee on Wednesday. I enjoyed a good dinner and talk with John Baillie.

He is such a dear. But he made me feel homesick for you. John the Scot is so appreciative of the U.S.A. and of its citizens, especially of people like you. In a way I feel it is good to be here, good for me to be on my own a bit in England, and see all my English friends and perhaps forget some of my U.S.A. ones. But then seeing someone like John, the quintessential Scot who loves U.S.A., makes me become homesick for U.S.A. again!

Tomorrow I shall be taking Tillich to lunch with Lord and Lady Listowel. They have asked the economist Graham Hutton, the left-liberal sub-editor of the *Economist,* so it ought to be quite fun. Tillich is frightfully funny about all these people, he wants to know if they are "feudal" or "bourgeois," and doesn't understand how one can be upper middle class, or just a gentleman or a lady in the socio-moral sense that you so dislike!

[*Later*]: Just to tell you about lunch with Tillich at the Listowels. Tillich met me there, looking fearfully brushed up in his Sunday get-up, black coat and grey trousers, etc. He thoroughly enjoyed himself, discovered mutual acquaintances with Lady Listowel (she is Hungarian, and a journalist), and agreed with them politically and was very happy with this. He said to me afterwards—"Ach, your English friends, they agree with what I think and what I thought about Germany—and the British attitude and the French, etc. They did when I was in New York and they think the same now!"

Graham Hutton, who runs the *Economist* now, was also very congenial, nice, and intelligent. He is going to U.S.A. in October, to study the banking possibilities.

We discussed mostly the political situation in this country. The conservative Old Guard; Churchill; the Chamberlains; and Baldwin[3] and the almost suppressed younger ones like Anthony Eden;[4] and the effect all this had on any foreign policy. Of course, we discussed in and out of season the political international situation. The Listowels [he is a Labour peer]—especially she—and Hutton were almost more pessimistic than Tillich. She and Tillich had crossed over on the same boat, but they never spotted each other. She is very amusing about her table companions, acrobatic dancers. Tillich was quite disappointed that he had not seen her on board. . . . Later he remarked to me. "I like your friends. The Countess, she rang me up in the bath." Tillich is really quite a snob.

Love—so much,

U.M.

1. *John M. Murry; English literary critic.*   2. *Older brother of Wedgewood Benn.*
3. *Stanley Baldwin; prime minister of Great Britain 1924–29 and 1935–37.*
4. *Conservative British politician; at Foreign Office in late pre-war days, critical of Neville Chamberlain's appeasement of Hitler; later British prime minister.*

Union Theological Seminary
New York, NY
Thursday, April 23, 1936

Dearest:

The S.S. *Bremen* sails today so that I have another chance to send you a line. Last night I was so desperately tired I would have given anything for an evening at home. But I had to manage the meeting for Jim [Dombrowski] as he is still at the hospital. It was held at the home of a wealthy old widow who covers her ignorance and futility by being a patron of the arts and of left-wing causes. Her apartment is a sight. I know little about art, but discovered she knows nothing. We had only about thirty people come, but Bertha Daniels spoke with real charm, although too long, about the work of the Highlander Folk School.[1]

George Lansbury was really superb yesterday. What he says is simple and not profound. He is a vivid example of the power of pure character and really is a remarkable old man. England at its best. I would like to rub him under the noses of all those who speak of the "lower classes." I also wish that our Americans could catch something of the unity of your English culture unconsciously revealed by men such as Lansbury. . . . On the international situation he is pretty much a washout. Just to say that we must not apply sanctions because it may lead to war seems a hopeless and irrelevant counsel just now. . . . Kirby Page sends his love to you. He is shepherding Lansbury about with great affection and diligence and is completely wearing himself out in this peace campaign. I feel like an old man on the sidelines as I note his enthusiasm. Or is it the sloth of fatalism creeping over me?

Two more weeks of grinding work and then a little relief. If only I didn't have as many meetings all scheduled. I will be running from one thing to another after the close of the seminary. Most of the things are sudden however, and I feel they are important and a real obligation.

I do hope the old boy is improving and you managed to find some help. William Savage is coming in a moment. I have spent the morning trying to get *Radical Religion* into shape. I tried to correct an article by Winnifred [Wygal]. It was so confused, so full of jargon and so generally inadequate that I finally gave it up and returned it to her. These are the trials of editing.

Much love,

R.

1. *School in Tennessee started by Myles Horton, a student of R.N.'s.*

East Moseley
Sussex, England
April 28, 1936

Darling One:

We are just off to Hampshire, for Catherine Wells'[s] [daughter of Eddie and Dorothy Wells] wedding. Mother is coming, a great triumph, and she is thrilled. It is quite a lovely day, springlike and warm, relatively, with a golden light. So we start at 12:30; the wedding is about 3:00 at Overton. We shall go by train, as Daddy can't get away, and the train is quite comfy but slow.

S. K. and Peggy [Ratcliffe] came down and spent the day here yesterday. He was quite full of beans and talked non-stop as usual but Daddy and Mother rather liked it, and he was really rather sweet with them.

(Continued, en route to Overton): We are now at Basingstoke, of Gilbert and Sullivan fame. The train to Overton is a little local puff-puff, and is full of weddingish sort of people, and they all look *very* English!

Later [same day]: Now we are back and have had dinner. It was a very nice wedding and all *frightfully* English, almost *New York*ishly English. Distinctly of a type, ancient top hats on top of weather-beaten country and clerical faces, and all the females unfashionably distinguished with everyone speaking clerical Oxford English, not the fashionable London-Oxford Cockney, such as Gertrude Lawrence [English actress], etc., but the sort of English that is always to be found more in the country than in London. Barbara and I kept on thinking of your possible reactions, and how you probably would write it all up or want to.

We arrived at Overton, a little country station, and there were several motor cars to take people up to the rectory about a mile off. We went along with some cousins of the Wells, and as we got off at the church, all the village was turned out, a nice little old village, incidentally, and a lovely old church, not one of the gems, but simple and old and nice. The village, as I said, was all turned out, prams and mothers, children and all lining the path to the church. The village church bells were pealing, and the daffodils and primroses were all out and it was *terribly* nice.

The church was cool, and with that particular damp smell of sanctity and ancientness that one gets in English churches, mixed with the lovely fragrance of spring flowers. The church looked beautiful, sprays of apple blossoms, lots of daffodils and narcissi, and great bowls and banks of primroses. All this had been arranged by the village, nothing set or fancy.

Then the people. All the men were bony and lean with the rather pronounced bones that Englishmen often have. The women nice and individual in the way you get them when an affair is not too fashionable or smart; lots of children, little boys in flannel suits and bare knees and little girls and school boys and school girls, the school boys all rather grown up in their black coats and grey trousers, etc.

The service was simple and quite nice: three hymns, one to come in to, one during the signing of the register and one sung, kneeling, by the congregation, and one psalm. Eddie Wells took the service, and the bridegroom's vicar gave the address, which was a bit on the line of Browning's "One Word More"; quite good.

Catherine looked so pretty, and radiant. Her husband looks nice, a solid young man with an attractive face and everyone seemed very happy. We walked back to the rectory, and Mother met all sorts of friends, some of whom had been at Dorothy Wells'[s] wedding 23 years ago, so it was all very "family." We all wandered about the garden and lawns and over the house to see the presents until the couple went off. Then we stayed with a few relations for a bit longer and then some cousins of the Wells, the Hudsons, who are great friends of ours, took us back to Basingstoke to catch our train.

It all made me feel more back in England than anything. The countryside, seeing so many old friends, the church, the rectory and everything, it all rather struck me of a heap. I really do think those sort of people as the Wells and their relations and friends are the salt of the earth: the old clerics, the old squires, the old K.C. barrister father-in-law, the avuncular colonial and imperial administrators, the tanned young empire-builders, home on leave, and their solid, comforting, maternal women folk, some of them rather like Gretta Harlow[1] or Juanita Piggott,[2] comforting, understanding, healthy and "unshrill" (I really revel in the voices—I haven't heard a shrill female's voice yet, thank God). I suppose they're fearfully unimaginative and all that, but somehow they are curiously reassuring.

I am sorry to dwell so much on all this. It is just a bit of concentrated England after three years' absence, and it rather struck Barbara the same way.

All my love—do miss you so—

Ursula

---

1. *Wife of Professor V. T. Harlow at Oxford.*   2. *Wife of General Piggott, a cousin of U.N.*

Union Theological Seminary
New York, NY
May 8, 1936

Dearest:

At last I got three letters today all in a heap. Nice letters too and reassuring. I am glad to know you are feeling a bit better with that flu bout, and have got hold of the nursemaid. Anxious to hear more about how she is doing.

Your reports of Tillich's visits were most interesting. But, I was quite jealous to have been left out of all that good company he was having. I got your letters just after closing my last class. So I stuck them in my pocket and ran for the subway where I read them on the way to East Orange where I had to speak.

Now I have just come back from the farewell dinner in honor of William Adams Brown.[1] That ends the two hardest days I have put in for many months. Since yesterday morning I have been going constantly, including a night trip to Harrisburg. Today I had a chapel talk, two lectures, a speech this afternoon, and this farewell business tonight.

The dinner was quite interesting. Everyone asked most solicitously about you, and about your mother. Mrs. [Ernest] Scott stayed long after to inquire how your mother was doing. Ernest came up to take her off, whereupon she said, "Go on home, Ernest, I am talking with Mr. Niebuhr." He was a little nonplussed and finally said, "Well, I think you ought to come pretty soon, too." Old William Adams Brown had a long series of reminiscences about the seminary; quite interesting. I was a little too tired to enjoy it. Tomorrow I am going to take the day off completely and not do a damn thing. On Sunday, I have to preach at Rutgers and Monday and Tuesday I have to speak for Kirby Page on his Peace Campaign.

I am still trying to get away on June 10th if I possibly can, but there is still no reservation on a boat. That is the earliest I can make it. My schedule is May 19th and 20th, the Conference of Radical Churchmen; May 25th and 26th, Conference of our Fellowship [of Socialist Christians] out of Pinebrook, NJ; May 28th, address in Philadelphia; and June 1st, visit to the [Delta] Cooperative Farm in Mississippi. On June 4th, Conference of Younger Churchmen; June 6th, Interracial Conference. This is the conference which is holding me up chiefly. On June 8th, the Negro Conference of the South begins and I could stay just one day there and leave on the 10th. I'll try to do that if at all possible. Of course, I haven't gone off for my passport. I'll do that next Wednesday.

Don't worry about arrangements here. Bridget comes weekly and does very well. I dust a little in between. No one uses the house, so it doesn't really get dirty. Jim Dombrowski, who was really very ill, is now doing better, and his faithful lady love looks after his room and what he needs. He is now getting up and insists on coming to the kitchen to join me for breakfast.

Human interest story: This morning, just before getting your letter, I heard a terrific wail out in the courtyard. On investigation, I found Hugh Van Dusen crying hysterically while John, his older brother, nonchalantly paraded up and down on his bicycle. I asked John what was the matter with his brother, and he mumbled something I could not understand. Hugh's cries got worse and worse. I finally discovered that the poor fellow had stuck his little finger in the little ringlet that holds the hook to the door. It was behind his back so I didn't see it at first. I finally pulled his badly swollen finger out and sent him up with Charles (the doorman) to his mother. John looked up, only mildly interested. These are the devils that crawl in their lack of comprehension.

Today, a whole package of *New Republics* arrived. I have the feeling that Bruce Bliven[2] discovered they had taken you off the list and he put you back on again. I didn't send in a subscription because he hasn't yet published my article and I need that. After all, I need a little extra cash. I will have $125 extra income in May which will have to go for overdue pledges for Jim Dombrowski and the Southern Churchmen, Howard Kester,[3] and Union Seminary's pension fund. I hope I'll get my passage in June as I will have some money coming in then. If Bruce ever publishes that article, then I'll have a little more than I mentioned. The *Nation* called me up today and asked for the identical article which I wrote for Bruce, and wanted to publish it immediately. At my suggestion they wired Paul Hutchinson in Chicago at the [*Christian*] *Century*. My article will be quite stale if they don't publish it this week. I haven't heard from the Blivens at all but then I haven't been in enough to hear from anyone.

News Notes: Mrs. Moffatt's eyes are not regaining their sight as quickly as was expected. Another operation may be necessary. This from Mrs. Scott, and may not be authentic. Professor Lyman and I are involved in a serious tangle between Dr. Coffin and [Harrison] Elliot on the problem of Mrs. Fahs'[4] dismissal. This little difficulty where one does not quite stand on one side or the other is trying. Big May Day demonstrations today. Preached a May Day sermon this morning, using George Lansbury's text. My sermon pleased both the radicals and Dr. Coffin, curiously enough.

Will write some more tomorrow as the *Europa* does not sail until midnight. I think I will go to bed, being about as tired as I have ever been.

This business of going to bed alone takes all the fun out of life. Bachelor existence is bearable only if you have never been used to anything else. Good night.

P.S. Sent you two copies of the *New Yorker* last week. They came back this week for insufficient postage. They're so badly chewed up I won't remail them, but I'll send you this week's issue, sorry. You forgot to have the *New Statesman* and the *Times* [Literary Supplement] sent to your English address, so they're still coming here and I don't have time to read them.

Next morning: Now for a day of complete relaxation. After extremely cold weather it has suddenly become unusually warm, 75° yesterday. You ask about the publication of my last book in England. I doubt whether it will be published there. I have asked the Harper editor, [Eugene] Exman, several times but he seemed vague. I doubt whether he intends to do anything about it. Wouldn't it be nice if I could just relax and be with you today. Life is so awfully stale if one has to do things alone. Here I am and I haven't the slightest idea about spending the day, and I must have some rest. But I can't think of what to do when you aren't here.

But I think I might talk to you a little more and I'll tell you about a little conversation I had with the Coffins last night after the farewell dinner for Brown. Dr. Coffin was bewailing the cares of an administrator. He said people did not recognize the necessity of organization and institutions. He said he thought I appreciated these problems more than I used to. I told him I had been, after all, a parson in charge of a parish for many years, and I knew something about holding things together, but I'd never be a natural institutionalist. He thought I was getting better at it and I told him I hoped not, and Mrs. Coffin intervened, "Now Henry, you were born a Yale politician and that is your life. Do not try to make Mr. Niebuhr something different that what he is." I thought that was rather good. Dr. Coffin looks rather darkly into the future. He says he can't find any good New Testament man for that department after Prof. Frame and Prof. Scott leave. He is equally pessimistic about the Old Testament.

About summer plans, I think your suggestion about a little travel in England in July and taking a cottage for August is good. Only we may have to leave before the end of August in time to get you back in case Sarah Lawrence wants you for interviews. Might it be better to turn it around and take a cottage in July and travel in August? Did I tell you I had an invitation for a three-day conference with the Archbishop of York [William Temple]? He wants four theologians from the Continent and four from England and a couple from here. If I can get the promise of an article to pay for our trip, I would like to take one of those excursions for a week to Germany.

Love to all your folks and to the old boy. How I wish I could set him on his pot in the morning and give him his orange juice for breakfast. Such affectionate longing for you.

Yours,

R.N.

1. *Professor at Union Seminary 1892–1930.*   2. *Editor of* New Republic.   3. *Kester was a Southern liberal who observed the race situation in the South for various organizations.* 4. *Mrs. Sophia Lyon Fahs, teacher of religious education at Union Seminary.*

Union Theological Seminary
New York, NY
Saturday, May 9, 1936

Dearest:

I got two nice letters from you today and am writing immediately so the letters get on the *Bremen* on the way back. You are obviously enjoying the familiar scene in England and it reminds me that you must be under an unconscious strain in having to live in this (to you) terrible country. Being myself habituated to its vices, only such reminders make me conscious of what you must suffer. So enjoy yourself fully before I come and spoil it with my American excuses and digs at England. . . .

Yesterday the temperature jumped suddenly to 87°, thus hurtling us from winter to summer without a spring. The Commencement will hardly be comfortable if it stays like this. I am leaving this afternoon for Wesleyan, where I will stay with the Cornelius Kruses.[1] They particularly invited you, and I wish you would be there. Am also enclosing a letter from Middleton Murry. I am writing him that I am leaving the matter completely in your hands. Will you decide what is to be done and write to him accordingly? I am disappointed that his affair[2] is in August. If it were in July, I wouldn't mind spending a week. Perhaps we might change things around and take a cottage for July and travel in August. I leave it all to you. Decide what you think best. I wouldn't like to miss his session entirely and imagine you would enjoy it too. But a week is a long time if we have a cottage rented for August. Still worse if we sail August 22nd, impossible, in fact, in that case.

You didn't say anything in your last letter about your mother. I hope she is managing to be fairly comfortable. Don't worry about me. I don't sleep too well but better than I did. A few days of rest will help a lot. Next week I must put in three days of travel. After that the engagements are intermittent 'til I make the trip down south.

I am really longing for you so very much. This is a truncated life and half the fun is taken out of everything because we can't do it together. But, I honestly believe that you need to have a right to your own vocational work. Sometimes you do beat against the bars and that ought to teach us both that we must find the greatest amount of happiness together if you can feel yourself a little more independent of me. Am I right to say I think you go through alternations of wanting to merge your work with mine and then perhaps protesting against that? And that is right and proper. You are too much a person in your own right and have to give of your own to allow you to be just my wife. Particularly since I am an egoistic soul. That is why I am anxious about the Sarah Lawrence matter. I do hope it comes through, if not immediately, then ultimately. I wouldn't mind if they said, "we will definitely take you on the following year"; that would allow us to have another year of preparation for your work. It might complicate the sabbatical year for me, but that would be a smaller price to pay than the loss of an infant for another year. If you could teach one year, you could always get off the following year for one semester. Have you written to Miss Warren?

I must go down now to get my passport. You asked about the *Radical Religion*. It will be out next week. There's an article in it by MacMurray. The rest of the number is pretty bad. Perfectly awful article by our friend Winnifred. It came in just before leaving town and I sent it to Harry Bone, asking that he either rewrite it or junk it. He rewrote it, but it isn't much better. Now it is in the proofs, so I am ashamed of it. Pretty bad running a publication with a board of editors and not one of them can write. It will cause more than one complication, I am afraid. I never thought Winnifred was quite as sophomoric as that article reveals her. By the way, will you do some of the reviews you spoke of for the summer number?

Much love and so many yearnings,

R.

---

1. *A fellow student from Illinois; became professor of classics at Wesleyan.* 2. *A conference that John Middleton Murry was arranging for congenial left-wing intellectuals.*

Union Theological Seminary
New York, NY
May 11, 1936

Dearest:

Got back late last night from Wesleyan and the Cornelius Kruses, who want to be remembered to you. Had a nice weekend with them. . . . I am getting so homesick that on Sunday night I wrote another letter asking to be excused from the Interracial Conference if at all possible. . . . I don't suppose they'll let me out of it as I could not truthfully make it preemptory. I just put it on their conscience. Also, I am regretting my decision to go to the Cooperative Farm in Mississippi. The whole visit would take so long and I am too tired to take a long hot trip to the southwest lasting 36 hours, because I would have to take most of it in the day coach, otherwise the cost would be too high. So, I am cancelling right and left.

The seminary is preparing for Commencement, with all the special guests for the Centenary. Charlie White [Union Seminary Comptroller] is working his head off and spending a lot of useless money getting the place spick and span for the guests. The other day they sandblasted the rotunda. I raised a big fuss about the waste of money. They might learn from England that dirt is really venerable; it has ceased to be dirt and belongs to the sanctities.

The American journals are offering a lot of useless advice to England. It seems that England is in a devil of a fix and advice is cheap. I can't for the life of me see how your Cabinet can do anything that is indubitably the right thing to do. Most of the criticisms, such as [those] of Tillich['s], for instance, do not take into consideration that England is not a nation but still an empire and has to think of the dominions. The Empire needs the League to survive and the damn League is falling apart. If you pull out of this hole, it will be political genius. . . .

Much love,

R.N.

P.S. Dr. Coffin has been up with all sorts of problems and we talked in my office for hours, putting my work back like the dickens. Jerome Davis[1] has been fired at Yale, so he told me all about that. Then, Rix Butler[2] came to him to report that he felt honor-bound to let him know that a communist cell of three members had been formed at Union, that he had been asked to join and thought the whole thing dishonorable, as the students took a vow of absolute obedience. We can't imagine who are these three students. In other years, that might not have been such a surprise. This year it is baffling. . . .

I am getting terribly homesick and am going to make a more preemptory demand to get out of engagements.

R.N.

1. *Well-known left-wing pacifist.*   2. *Student at Union Seminary.*

Union Theological Seminary
New York, NY
Friday, May 15, 1936

Dearest:

I would like to write you a long letter tonight and yet it will have to be fairly short. Today has been terribly hectic. I got back just in time to take my last chapel service. Term papers were piled high on my desk and the deadline for them was 5 P.M. I read papers all day, answered the telephone, and told students they could not come and see me, had luncheon with Prof. [Harry] Ward and the committee arranging the Radical Clergy Conference, went to the dentist, had dinner with the Coffins, dropped in on the missionaries who were having some final affair at which they insisted I must appear, and am now back in the office with five more papers to read and the communion service for Sunday to work out. Dr. Coffin insists he must have my Scripture passages for the service in the morning and Mrs. Britten in the Registrar's Office is waiting for the grades for the term papers. Yet—a boat leaves in the morning and I want to catch that with a letter to you. . . .

Your letters cheer me up to get and I am glad that you and the old boy are both well. I think I'll have to come over pretty quickly and make sure you will come back here. I *am* glad you are enjoying yourself, but I do feel that probably England makes you feel more relaxed and serene, which gives me a sharp reminder of the hazards of international marriages and the price the person has to pay who is the uprooted member of it. I am sorry I am not an Englishman. Maybe I'll have to find means to let you back every year for the purposes of relaxation, rejuvenation, and reinvigoration. I find our separation worse than ever before. So that evens up the score, if you are enjoying the separation a little. I haven't heard yet from Mississippi to know whether I can get out of the engagement.

Your letters are lovely, except for a little too much satisfaction with being in England. I hope I'll have another one in the morning. Lots of other things I want to write about, but I'll have to get to work.

All my love,

R.N.

Later [May 16]: Went to chapel and discovered all the professors were supposed to be in the procession. Had failed to look at instructions, therefore slipped in late. Dr. Coffin had the Centenary sermon with the typical Coffinesque text: "And Moses took the bones of Joseph with him . . ." [Exodus 13:19].

Just saw Harriet Harris [wife of a collaegue]. She has been in bed with a bad sinus infection for weeks. Didn't know anything about it. She looks wretched. Went over to Riverside Park for a walk, and seeing all the youngsters, I got homesick for the old boy. Glad he is having such a good time with your family.

I never wrote to you about those Donne poems. You gave the volume to me, and now I have read all of them and reread many. They are beautiful. Have taught me a few things, too. So I hope.

. . . The great battle has gone on over here about Charles Morgan's *Sparkenbroke*. Most of the critics, particularly Fadiman, have been much more critical of it than the English reviewers. Some of them pronounce the combination of mystical and romantic passion dishonest. Fadiman declared it to be a "clinch teaser" in mystical language and explained that clinch teaser is a trade name for erotic books which suggest more than they reveal.

Your plans for July and August seem just right. If we take a cottage just in the middle of our time, it will cause fewer complications. I am wondering what you did about Middleton Murry.

Now I'll have to get ready for the communion service. After a cool morning, it has just become scorchingly hot. Love to your parents and Barbara. The old boy will have forgotten me, so there is no use sending greetings to him, I expect.

With longing and love,

R.N.

P.S. Mrs. Fosdick has just called to invite me for supper. Fosdick, Counts,[1] and I are working on a big committee to "stop" Hearst. It may turn out to be quite a big thing. Some big money is interested, but we won't go ahead if they keep their contributions anonymous as they have asked. Afraid ulterior motives, financial, journalistic, may be hiding behind it. Charles A. Beard[2] wants to go ahead and take money for a big propaganda campaign against Hearst wherever the money may come from. Hatred of Hearst is now his religion.

1. *Professor at Teachers College, later Liberal Party candidate for U.S. Senate in 1952. He & R.N. served on Liberal Party Executive Committee as vice-chairmen.* 2. *Professor of American history at Columbia, resigned. Later president of the American Political Science Association.*

Union Theological Seminary
New York, NY
May 17, 1936

Dearest:

It is Sunday morning and I feel terribly lonely and wish I were with you. After variable weather, terrible heat, and then another turn of winter, the morning nice and cool and sunny.

Last night we had the opening of the seminary Centenary, with the Dickinson Choral Festival at Riverside Church. There were choirs of 1,500 voices and it was quite an affair, the program being made up of Bach, Palestrina, Liszt, and Handel. Really quite impressive. I think even you would have approved. . . . I have some old bird from some obscure seminary in Dayton, Ohio, coming to stay here with me tonight. The visitors for the celebrations have begun to arrive. About forty visiting academics were in the procession last night. There will be over two hundred of them on Tuesday. Charles White must have spent thousands of dollars, having everything painted up that needed painting and planting flowers in the courtyard garden. It does all look very pretty.

This afternoon I shall be conducting a communion service for the first time since I came here. I worked on it last night after the festival.

I have been trying to get out of some of those extra engagements that I accepted. But none of the committees or people will let me out of my promise to come. I am so tired that apart from wanting to come over to join you, I do not think I will be much good to anybody at these conferences.

My brother Walter still seems to have no job in prospect. He wishes, however, to stay in Tennessee as he thinks something might open up. He gives me the impression of desperately grasping after any kind of a job that will keep him and the family alive for the summer. I will give you their address so that you can send a card to them if you have a moment.

I am still not sure whether I am going to be able to break away and leave on June the 1st. I would like to so much. Life is stale and unprofitable and I yearn for you and Christopher so much that it hurts.

Last night I worked again on the translation of Tillich's book [*On The Boundary*]. Mrs. Tillich has transmitted an invitation from Dr. [Max] Horkheimer for dinner a week from today. He is head of the Institute of Social Research [moved in the Nazi period from Frankfurt to New York City] about which I told you. My going with Mrs. Tillich will square accounts with you looking after her husband in London. I think you and he get the best of the bargain!

Much love.

Still more love.

Yours,

R.

Union Theological Seminary
New York, NY
May 23, 1936

Sunday Evening

Dearest:

I have just finished my final chore with the translation of Tillich's book about which I must have spent about seventy hours since you left. Paul Tillich, of course, has no idea that I've done this, but the translation was too horrible for words. Bill Savage was an infant for having accepted it as it was.

I forgot to tell you that the theological conference with Archbishop Temple is from July 15th to the 18th. Since the 18th is the end of the week I hope this will not interfere with your arrangements for renting a cottage for four week?

I had a very pleasant visit with the Van Dusens and I was glad there was no academic gossip! They had become aware after all the celebrations and entertainments that they had to do that I was a lonely bachelor. Little Christopher Lehmann-Haupt was with them over the weekend, his mother Lettie—whom you know—casually parked him with them. Their son John confided to me in his gentle way, "This Christopher is a wee bit different from the Christopher who lives upstairs." But he would not divulge in what the difference consisted.

Now I am going to do term papers for the rest of the evening. All those for Teachers College of Columbia must be recorded tomorrow morning. That means I shall be finished with my work on the semester tonight. So I may have a little leisure. I took a long nap and a long walk out in the park today. I could not find anybody to walk with. . . . It's lonely, very lonely. But on the 18th I shall be with you I hope.

Yours always,

R.N.

Union Theological Seminary
New York, NY

Monday Evening
May 18, 1936

Dearest Ursula:

. . . Since the *Europa* doesn't sail until tomorrow, I am going to add a postscriptum on the Centenary. It is now almost midnight and I have been at it since 9 A.M., Executive Committee meeting, faculty meeting, luncheon with some of the recent alumni, Ivan Gould, etc., etc. This afternoon was a Centenary Service with about 100 visiting academics in the procession. This evening they had the dinner at the Hotel Roosevelt. Nicholas M. Butler [President of Columbia], Dean Sperry [of Harvard Divinity School], Dean Weigle [of Yale Divinity School], Dean Fosbrooke [of General Seminary], etc., and Dr. Fosdick spoke. It is what you would call "rather grim." We Americans cannot mix wit with wisdom in after-dinner speaking. The wit turns into story telling and the wisdom gets lost. I counted the evening pretty much of a loss. Not a really wise or challenging thing was said all the evening. Saw the Walter R. Bowies,[1] who send greetings, as lots of the recent graduates also did, but they are too many to remember. On the way back I met Betty Schinkman.[2] Luckily, I remembered she was Peggy Benn's niece, and we arranged for her to come over to get the baby scales next week when I get back from the conference.

I am getting frantic letters and wires from the south about my efforts to cancel my engagement. I am afraid it can't be done. The bird who is supposed to stay with me tonight hasn't shown up, and it is now midnight, so I suppose he won't come. Ran into Wilhemina today and found she has taken over her mother's work in the laundry for the missionaries. She is doing it so she can take care of all the children left motherless. I could only speak to her hurriedly, but I imagine this means she won't be able to come back to us. She says she will have to have a job which allows her to get the children off to school in the morning. The poor thing has the whole family burden thrust upon her.

I am hoping to hear from you in the morning and may have a chance to add a note before catching the boat with this letter. I am writing tonight because tomorrow is filled with further festivities of the Centenary. I feel almost an alien listening to all those clerical Presbyterians reminisce, and I imagine you would also.

Next morning, Tuesday: Two nice letters from you. You seem to be having such a good time with all sorts of other people that I am sure you can keep busy till I come on the 15th. But you arouse in me the ambition to come over as soon as possible, as it all sounds so nice and interesting. Tillich is dead right about the English, they are really quite wonderful, only of course they know it. But then they can hardly help it! You are right about the Empire though. The socialists haven't got a real idea of what to do with the Empire, and the Empire is beginning to crumble though it will hardly disappear in your lifetime. Political astuteness will probably save it for some time to come.

. . . I wish I were in Oxford with you now, particularly in that house where we spent our honeymoon! Will we have an invitation to go back there when I come?

. . . I am putting in extra hours on Tillich's manuscript. I finished the book proper some time ago. Am now doing the autobiography. The translation for that is as atrocious as the former. I am going to blow Bill Savage up when he arrives on Thursday. Such bad translations are beyond the pale, and he ought to have known better than to accept them. His excuse is that Tillich sanctioned them, but poor Tillich was only interested in seeing that his ideas were translated. He doesn't know that a Germanism is scattered in every line. Thus, for example, "Between my maternal and paternal influences, there was constant stressful conflict and the maternal could gain triumph only by a breakthrough. These breakthroughs occurred frequently." Horrible stuff.

Will try to find your Oxford cap and gown just as soon as the festivities are over. I have lost all pleasure in these damn conferences they want me to go to. This is an unnatural life and I would like to be quit of it.

Yours ever,

R.N.

1. *Rector of Grace Episcopal Church in Manhattan; a lecturer on homiletics at Union Seminary; joined its faculty in 1939 as a professor.*   2. *English wife of an American journalist, daughter of Sir Ernest Benn.*

Union Theological Seminary
New York, NY
May 20, 1936

Dearest:

I feel depressed and very much wanting you and the babe. I received your radiogram and wish that I could cable you that I am coming. I may still do it, but it does not seem probable. I suppose I would do it if I were absolutely hardboiled. But I have received so many letters and benedictions and petitions that I think I will have to stay until the 14th. Don't know how I can get out of it.

Today was devoted to our National Conference of Radical Christians and tomorrow will be devoted to the same cause. After that I have a few days of complete freedom, thank the Lord. I really feel a need of a rest. I am disgusted with this place, probably because I am so very tired. It is dreadful to be so critical of one's friends and colleagues.

. . . David Roberts[1] is back and will teach here next year. I think we will find [him and his wife] both a real asset. He is leaving tonight for California. He has not seen his wife since last August, nor his infant born two months ago. That was real deprivation for them.

. . . I am almost glad not to have to see or to talk to some of my colleagues here. I find H. Ward's sneering almost as difficult as some of the others' conventional remarks. How awful to have come to the place where I think I am the only one left who is right!

Paul Lehman suddenly turned up just before the Commencement exercises last night. He received his red hood, and this morning had a conference with Harpers, the publishers, on the possibility of his book being taken. I put him up for the night. Tonight I am putting up Scottie Cowan, a really fine Scotsman from Birmingham, AL, who came to represent the South in our conference. I am getting quite adept serving breakfast to guests, though I make them eat it in the kitchen just as we do when the maid is out. I have simplified matters by buying canned grapefruit juice because I don't like to have to squeeze oranges for many every morning. The rest is too simple for words. I think I can get breakfast in about eight minutes.

Tomorrow night I am having dinner with a Mr. Van Waren and wife, psychiatrists, who came to hear me preach recently and have invited me to dinner to meet Paul Mellon, son of the former Secretary of the Treasury, who is a patient of theirs and whom they think I can help in some way. I wonder what it is all about. . . . Incidentally, last night after the Commencement a nice looking old gentleman with an Irish brogue spoke to me and introduced himself as the Colonel of the Salvation Army downtown. He told me he always came to hear me preach. I was flattered by the approval of so orthodox a man.

I shouldn't send you so depressed and pressing a letter. I'm really perfectly all right, but merely cursing my luck that I cannot sail next week, and I am a little tired.

Much love and many yearnings,

Yours,

R.N.

1. A 1934 graduate of Union Seminary who completed his Ph.D. at the University of Edinburgh and was appointed instructor at Union Seminary.

Union Theological Seminary
New York, NY
May 27 & 28, 1936

Dearest:

Just back from the Fellowship Conference, one of the best we have ever had. We are really making progress and the journal is catching on in great shape.

I have written again tonight trying to extricate myself from my southern engagements without getting the committees absolutely angry. But it may not help me too much because the boat company insists it has no reservations. I'll go to the British Consulate tomorrow morning so as to be ready for anything. I haven't looked up your Oxford cap and gown yet but I will tomorrow. . . .

Wednesday, A.M.: I had the Mollegans[1] over for breakfast. They are leaving this afternoon. He gave a very brilliant talk at our conference. I shall miss them. The breakfast was simple. Just juice, coffee, toast, and eggs.

Next morning, Thursday: The whole of Wednesday was spent and wasted in taking care of odd details. In the evening I went with Mrs. Tillich to Dr. Horkheimer, the head of the Institute for Social Research. Four couples of the émigré colony were there. Interesting conversation. Horkheimer, whom I had not met before, although Tillich tried several times to arrange it, is a brilliant fellow. One of the men there was just back from England. He thinks there is a great deal of confusion in England but that the real rulers are not at all confused. Their policy is to avoid war at all costs and will therefore give Germany and Italy a great deal provided they do not demand something that would destroy the Empire or seriously impede it. He thinks it would be impossible to demand as much as a war would cause the demise of the Empire. Consequently, he expects Germany to encroach upon the Balkans via Austria with the uneasy connivance of England. He thinks the situation is such that all nations except Germany are so afraid of the consequences of war that Germany can get a great deal by threatening war like a desperado flourishing a gun which he does not have to shoot.

Sherwood Eddy stopped in briefly with reports of the [Delta] Cooperative Farm in Mississippi. It is going very well. Meanwhile the situation in

Arkansas is very bad. Howard Kester's strike is on, and there is much violence.

Today I have to make the last peace speech in Philadelphia. I expect news from the South today. But there is still a question of getting a sailing. I will cable you if I shall have the luck to clear myself from engagements and get a passage. . . . I saw your friend Mr. Walter Bell[2] yesterday at the British Consulate, and he gave me His Majesty's consent to set foot upon your tight little island so full of feudalism, sanity, snobbishness, political wisdom, and self-righteousness. . . .

Excuse this letter so disjointed and business-like. I've simply had time only for little notes during the last two days. I found your Oxford cap and gown. Still haven't heard from the South, but the problem will be to get a boat.

Much love,

R.N.

1. *Albert Mollegan was a Mississippi-born Episcopal priest who was completing his graduate work at Union Seminary.* 2. *British vice-consul in New York City.*

Four

1937
Memoir:
Oxford Conference and
Beyond Tragedy

A conference on Church, Community, and State was to be held at Oxford in the summer of 1937. Reinhold had been much involved in the preparatory work as had some of his colleagues. As a member of the commission on the church and its function in society, he had written a paper that had been translated and circulated among others preparing for the conference on "The Christian Faith and the Common Life."

Also that same summer, there was to be a conference for colonial administrators in Oxford. A fellow of my college, Margery Perham (later Dame Margery Perham), had helped the Colonial Office in the arrangements. My brother Robert Keppel-Compton was a District Commissioner in Nyasaland (now Malawi) and was planning to attend with his wife, Marjorie. They were going to be put up, as were Reinhold and I, in my college, St. Hugh's.

Hence, I was hoping to be able to go with Reinhold to England. But, could we afford it? Reinhold was not an official delegate and had to pay his own way. Luckily for us, our friend Sir Stafford Cripps[1] and his committee, which included Bishop Barnes of Birmingham, had invited Reinhold to give the Bishop Burge Memorial lecture that June in London. As compared with American fees, the fee for this was chicken feed, but Reinhold hoped that somehow it would manage to pay my way across the Atlantic. Unfortunately, we tried to get passage very, very late and all we could get was a dreadful cabin on an old German boat, the S.S. *Columbus*. This had been built for immigrant use after the First World War, and our very small and squalid cabin was in the old steerage, now called third class. Others a notch higher went tourist or second class.

Our cabin was a minute space under the engine, and so we lived with the vibration and heat of the engines morning, noon, and night. I found it very wearing and nausea making, worse than sea sickness. There were no public rooms except the dining room, and there were four sittings for each meal. As we stood about the little space on deck with a few benches at random places, or stood in line for the three meals, we understood how the immigrants were packed into these ships in the early twenties. We realized how people had to travel in those days to come to this land of hope and freedom.

Nevertheless, Reinhold, being Reinhold, worked. The draft of his book *Beyond Tragedy* was kept more or less together in this minute space of a cabin. Sometimes he would even try to find a corner on one of the benches to sit and type with the typewriter on his knees!

On the third day, a tall, efficient but pleasant German lady arrived in search of us. Some of the student groups on board in the tourist class had spotted Reinhold's name on the passenger list and had asked him to address them on such timely subjects as "War Clouds in Europe" and question-marked subjects such as "What Lies Ahead?" I think the fact his name was somewhat Wagnerian prompted the captain to send his secretary down to inquire if there was anything he could do for us. I was ready to say, "Yes, find us a better cabin." Reinhold, however, was always a Milquetoast compared to me, and would not ask for any privilege or favor. I, realizing this, waved his manuscript about and explained how difficult it was for him to work on his book. This struck home. The lady retired and fairly soon afterwards returned, suggesting we might like to use one of the private dining rooms in the first class where Reinhold might work at his manuscript in quiet and with more space. I was ready to ask for something more but no luck.

Thus, Reinhold would march to work with his folders under his arm. I followed, carrying the typewriter and thinking sardonically, That's the way Germans expect women to live, like the Arabs, carrying packages, and walking behind the men! Reinhold was amused but didn't seem to mind. We processed along long corridors and up stairs and down stairs to the most opulent, roomy, private dining room on one of the upper decks. We had the big room to ourselves, where obviously a party or a meal for forty or fifty people might be spread. Astonished waiters looked out at us and one of them came to remove the green baize covers from one of the tables for us to sit and work.

Reinhold had originally arranged to stay on the boat, which let off passengers for England by tender at Plymouth, so that he could continue to Bremerhaven. Through various friends in England, Bishop G. K. A. Bell[2] and Stafford Cripps and their contacts in Germany as well as Reinhold's own, and through people such as Paul Hagen,[3] Reinhold had news of the underground seminary (as it was called) that Dietrich Bonhoeffer[4] had gathered around him. Reinhold was hoping to get in touch with them and also to see Pastor Martin Niemoeller.

This was not to be. Before we could reach Plymouth, where I was going to leave the boat, we had cables from England warning Reinhold not to continue on to Germany. It was thought that his visit might endanger some of the friends he might try to reach.

Thus, Reinhold left the boat with me, and went up by the boat train to London. There he got in touch, as directed, with Cripps and others.

It was a very interesting three weeks. Reinhold's Bishop Burge Memorial Lecture, I thought, went off very well. He had, as usual, written and sent it ahead so that it might be printed. It was published by the Christian Student Movement Press with the title "Does the State, or the Nation, Belong to God or the Devil?" But, as always, at the podium he gave it very freely, and quite obviously the audience, which consisted of academics and VIPs of political and theological interest, received it very warmly. After the lecture, a tall, distinguished looking bishop, very elegant in his gaiters, came up to him and told him he was very interested in comparing the written text and the lecture given. He said, "I note a slight deviation from the written text in your lecture, but it was very effective the way you did it." Reinhold laughed and explained that it was awfully hard for him to read a lecture. The bishop, who was Bishop Barnes of Birmingham, agreed and was very friendly and said all sorts of nice things that I appreciated.

Bishop Barnes had been a hero of mine when I was a schoolgirl. He was a mathematician and a fellow of Trinity College at Cambridge. He also became a well-known preacher and was appointed as the Master of the Temple Church in London. Together with my Oxford tutor Canon Streeter and others, they had issued a volume critical of the more conventional, traditional understanding of Christology in theology. This at the time had created quite a stir among the more conventional churchmen.

Bishop Barnes and Reinhold were getting along famously when friends separated them, as we were all due elsewhere. Next morning, however, he had traced us to where we were staying, with my parents in East Moseley, which was less than five minutes from Hampton Court. When could we have lunch with him at his club, the Atheneum, a favorite haunt of clergy and academics? Or would Reinhold prefer coming to the House of Lords? For some reason or other we decided on the Atheneum. It was less than half an hour's trip by suburban railway to London for this engagement, so I briefed Reinhold on the Atheneum, noted for high thinking and low eating, or words to that effect. However, we had an excellent lunch. Scottish salmon had come in and fresh garden peas; I thought it was delicious. The bishop turned to me; "What would Reinhold like to drink with the salmon?" I did not like to tell him that Reinhold wouldn't mind anything, as his palate was not outstandingly particular. "I think a little Rhine wine. What about a hock?" I replied. With this, he called the wine steward. We had a splendid time.

Reinhold and the bishop discussed politics mostly, theology not as much. I had the feeling that the bishop had probably not read much of

Reinhold's theological stuff, which was not then too much published in England, although *Moral Man and Immoral Society* had been well received and much reviewed. But they got along so well as man to man. I found myself wondering at my own satisfaction. Was it the English part of me that was glad that my very American husband, with his indubitably midwestern voice, was "clicking" with these English folk? Naturally, I *expected* people to like Reinhold, but I was delighted when they did.

The next morning we had another telephone call from the bishop. "Would you like to see our ridiculous House of Lords?" The bishop was well known for his opinion that the House of Lords should be abolished. As that had not been accomplished, he was in duty bound, as one of the Lords Spiritual,[5] to do his turn at being a chaplain for the House of Lords when in session and by praying before their deliberations started. He used to do this during the summertime, and checking with his friends and family later, I had the impression that it was in the housekeeping interests of Mrs. Barnes to send him to the House of Lords and the Atheneum so that she could give the maids their holidays and thus be free to visit the family.

"We are inducting two peers the day after tomorrow, and I thought it might amuse you to see the whole kaboodle," said Bishop Barnes on the telephone. The date was free for us, so again we had a delightful lunch with him, this time at the House of Lords. We then observed the induction of the two peers, one of whom was Admiral Chatfield, who became First Sea Lord.[6]

The bishop placed Reinhold and me in a box upholstered in crimson leather. After the bishop had prayed, he came and stood in front of the box with his elbow on the barrier cushion in front of us. He looked magnificent in his bishop's robes and it somehow went with the whole set. In a low tone, he gave us a blow by blow explanation of the proceedings. I wish I could remember them more exactly. An example: "Perfectly ridiculous," he said. "The peers are all supposed to be cousins of the King." I think the word "coz" may have come into the proceedings. Anyhow, as Reinhold and I decided afterwards, it was not only the proceedings but also the bishop's sardonic stage asides that made the event quite delightful.

In spite of our stay in England being quite short, not quite four weeks, we managed to see many of our friends. Stafford Cripps asked us to have dinner with him at the House of Commons. Often we recalled that fascinating evening. Reinhold sat at Stafford's right and I on his left. There was a quiet man with a little moustache on the other side of Reinhold, and next to me was the famous George Lansbury, a trade union leader and a very important person in the Labour Party at that time. Ellen Wilkinson, the red-headed Member of Parliament, and James Griffiths, the trade union leader from Wales, and Stafford's son John completed the party. Stafford Cripps used the occasion to honor Lansbury's return from a trip to Europe.

Lansbury was a tremendous moral force in English political and Labour Party life. He was a pacifist and had journeyed into Italy and Germany to talk to the dictators. There had been pictures in the papers of Lansbury, the quintessential Cockney in a bowler hat, ascending or descending the steps in Italy surrounded by the operatic-looking forces of Mussolini's police and guards. He had also gone that previous April to have a conference with Hitler. Lansbury told us about this, and said, "When I approached Hitler, he immediately saw I had a gouty foot. And he said to his aide-de-camp, 'Get a stool for Mr. Lansbury so that he can put his foot on it to help his pain.' Now," said Lansbury, "a man as thoughtful as this cannot be as bad as some of you think he is."

Naturally, both Stafford and Reinhold, on the basis of what they knew coming out of Germany through the underground, reacted to this rather vehemently. Reinhold had been fighting this view in the U.S.A., and had been analyzing and attacking what he thought was lack of discrimination between individual virtue and collective virtue, and individual vice and collective vice. Before the discussion became too vehement, Stafford Cripps, instead of arguing with Lansbury, got up from his place at the table and came around and hugged him from behind, saying, "George, you know you are really rather foolish tonight." Stafford, who was a most accomplished lawyer as well as a politician, shifted the conversation around to trade unionism and put us all on safer ground. James Griffiths, who for many years was an important trade union leader, Ellen Wilkinson, and Lansbury all took part. There were many other aspects to that dinner I remember vividly. Cripps, who was a vegetarian, had an enormous bowl of salad brought in. The rest of us had saddle of mutton or something equally delicious, but I was sitting next to Stafford and he insisted on my having some of his special salad, so I did very well indeed.

When the members of Parliament returned to their job, for the House of Commons proceeded through the evening and night hours, John Cripps took charge of us and took us to Waterloo Station to get our train home. When John had deposited us, Reinhold asked me, "Who was the man who sat on the other side of me and never said a word?" I laughed and said, "Don't you know? That was [Prime Minister] Clement Attlee."

The star of the evening, however, had been Lansbury. We remembered that in his trade union life, Lansbury had not been simple or foolish, as Stafford had described him in his views about Hitler. He was quite shrewd.

After the Ramsay MacDonald debacle in the Labour Party,[7] Lansbury had become the new leader.

Did this mean, as Reinhold and I had so often discussed, that shrewdness in domestic politics does not necessarily mean that the issues of foreign politics are viewed with the same acumen and wisdom? Reinhold wondered whether it was not particularly the weakness of parties left of center to have a shrewd and realistic domestic policy but to be rather idealistic in foreign policy.

It may be that those who know the domestic scene do not know necessarily the facts of the situation that move politics abroad. We discussed this on the way home. Reinhold regarded Lansbury as a saintly character. Later, we remembered that Ernest Bevin, also a Labour Party leader and a shrewd functionary thereof (who later became Foreign Secretary) said, "I am tired of carting Lansbury's conscience around from Labour meeting to Labour meeting."

Reinhold was soon going to see Bishop Bell, whom he also regarded as saintly, and we compared George Bell and George Lansbury. Reinhold's thesis about the knowledge of the situation abroad was illustrated by the fact that George Bell did know about what was happening in Germany, as did Stafford Cripps, but Lansbury really did *not* know.

Lansbury rang us up at my parents' home the next morning. He had so enjoyed meeting Reinhold—could we not get together again? I explained that Reinhold had already left to see Bishop Bell. Lansbury and I had a delightful chat. He was very much the benign grandfather, and asked me about our family, which consisted then of only Christopher, not yet age three. He told me about his grandchildren, and both Reinhold and I were sad that we did not have another chance to see this benign Labour leader again. He did not live to learn about the Nazi horrors and the concentration camps.

A week or so later, the Oxford Conference on Church, Community, and State opened. This had been prepared for several years and, coming in the moment that the forces of evil under Hitler were intensifying, had particular impetus. Although Reinhold was not an official delegate of his church, he was, as were other theologians, a consultant. Friends of his on the Continent whom he had known since his earlier days in the World Student Christian Federation had been in touch with him in the preparatory years. In that decade, in the heyday of American liberalism, Reinhold was someone who understood European modes of theological thought and had read Karl Barth and Emil Brunner. The influence of Karl Barth had made itself felt more generally on the Continent than in the States. Although neither Reinhold nor Paul Tillich (whom Reinhold had helped to come to Union Theological Seminary in 1933) was Barthian, their language in description of the human situation reflected the use of modes of thought that had been influenced by Barth. Many regarded Reinhold and Tillich as "neoorthodox." Therefore, many of the delegates from Holland, Germany, and Scandinavia, whether they were Barthian or in a more contemporary way of Barthian thought, felt that Reinhold understood them. Reinhold's thought was also generally congenial to Anglican theologians.

The conference itself was like many others, with the usual bureaucratic secretaries, the different commissions with their reports, and the bigwigs from different parts of the Christian Protestant world. Obviously and tragically, there were no representatives from Germany. The reports were issued later in several volumes, and the proceedings were well noted in the press and on the BBC. Naturally, feeling at home and rather possessive about Oxford, I had mixed feelings upon seeing some of the ecclesiastical bureaucrats buzzing in and out of well-known places. The open meetings were held in the Town Hall, and some of these I attended. Reinhold, of course, was busy with his own commission meetings. He gave a speech at one of the last big open sessions which was quite electrifying and characteristically stimulating and moving.[8]

One luncheon at my own college I remember with delight and amusement. Barbara Gwyer, the college principal, had asked if Reinhold and I would join her. She had also asked T. S. Eliot. He was a partner and editor in the publishing house of Faber and Faber (which many years before had been Gwyer and Faber). Lord Robert Cecil, who was an old, strong League of Nations supporter and president of the League of Nations Union, and an old friend of Miss Gwyer's, was also to be there, and she had asked me to ask Paul Tillich to come with us. Charles Taft from Cincinnati, also an old friend, was invited as well.

We ate in the Senior Common Room, and afterwards, drinking our coffee in this pleasant room looking out on the celebrated terrace of St. Hugh's College, there was an amusing discussion between Reinhold and Robert Cecil about hopes for international sanctions against Nazi Germany. I can see the scene now: Robert Cecil, with the tall frame of all the Cecils, sitting on a padded window seat by a large bay window; Miss Gwyer, also tall and narrow (many said she was like an elongated version of Whistler's Mother); Paul Tillich looking slightly puzzled, behind his thick spectacles, at the rapid idiomatic English exchanges; and Reinhold, hugely enjoying the to and fro of comment and discussion. Eliot, as so often, was rather quiet. "Do you think Mr. Eliot is all right?" one of the fellows of the college whispered in my ear. "You know, as he was being shown the new library he fell down some stairs. We were awfully worried, but he insisted he was all right." I watched him, but he did seem all right although quiet, but that was quite usual.

Window seats are comfortable for folk with shorter legs, quite comfortable, and I had often sat on these and looked out on the lovely college garden. Lord Robert Cecil, however, was tall, well over six feet, and quite large of limb. He kept on shifting his seat, and pushed what he thought was a cushion underneath his rump. "Robert," said Miss Gwyer, who was not exactly a fashion plate, "You are sitting on my hat." Lord Robert pulled out what he had been sitting on, and indeed it had once been a hat! Miss Gwyer looked at it without changing her expression, pushed up the crown, and laid it firmly on the table next to the after-lunch coffee cups.

As we were saying good-bye to some of the visitors in the hall, a tall figure approached, who had been paying off a taxicab by the college lodge. "Is Reinhold here?" he said. Heavens, it was a cousin of mine, Bernard Causton. Bernard, who was a rather wandering character with various journalistic assignments, had just come back from Berlin where he had been for some time. There he had been very impressed, and in fact converted, by Martin Niemoeller's courageous preaching while Hitler's strength increased. He had just flown back to England and come straight to Oxford to this ecumenical conference to bring news of and from Germany churchmen, especially from Pastor Niemoeller. Upon his entrance, Bernard, Tillich, and Reinhold went off to the principal's study to hear the latest news about the situation in Germany. In those times, pleasure was never very far from business, and the German situation overshadowed all social gatherings.

At the end of the conference, I left Reinhold and went to Birmingham, where I had been asked to preach. The Vicar of Birmingham, Canon Guy Rogers, was very interested in the whole question of women and their ordination and their recognition by the Church of England. His own wife had studied theology at Cambridge, and he thought as Reinhold did that the Christian churches should move to recognize the ministry of women. Canon Rogers, a chaplain to the King and a good preacher, had often been in the United States and was a friend of Walter Russell Bowie, the well-known rector of Grace Church in New York City. He was concerned that I was not justifying my existence as a student of theology, and said so to his American friends, swearing that the next time I was in England, I would preach in his church. He was able to get permission to do so, for his bishop was Bishop Barnes, already a friend, who also thought that women should be allowed to do such things. So I went off to preach at Birmingham, armed with my Oxford cap and gown.

Canon Rogers and his wife met me from the train, and were kindness themselves to me. I am quite sure I did not do a good job with that sermon. I had had no experience of doing anything like that. I was quite good at reading Scripture in academic chapels and lecturing, but I had never preached before. Like an idiot, I tried to put entirely too much into a sermon of fifteen or sixteen minutes. Rogers, however, who had taught theological students, was kind and encouraging. "You should do this sort of thing more often," he said. Both he and Mrs. Rogers promised to keep in touch to see if I was following their advice.

(Not all minds were so liberal as Canon Rogers's. Prodded by Canon Rogers or his good wife, Dr. Bowie earlier had asked me to go down to Grace Church in New York City and have a talk with him one morning. This I did, with interest and anticipation. Much to my surprise, when I got there he took me up to a room in the parish house where a group of ladies were sewing white calico! He introduced me to the leader of the group, who welcomed me and sat down. After the rector had left, she explained that these ladies gathered once a week or so to sew these garments which were supposed to be underwear for Eskimos in Alaska. I suppose they were to keep the animal skins they wore from tickling in the wintertime. I was not made use of at Grace Church in the way that Canon Rogers and I had hoped. Retelling the story to the Rogerses later, we all laughed and thought it somehow typical of the clerical mind.)

While I was in Birmingham, Reinhold was at Bishopsthorpe with Archbishop William Temple. We had arranged to meet in London and spend the night with our friends the Wedgewood Benns before going to the Crippses at their lovely place Goodfellows in the Cotswolds for our last weekend. But, we had promised to have dinner with a more recent friend, the famous former vicar of St. Martin's-in-the-Fields, "Dick" Sheppard.

Sheppard's name may not be so well known in these later days, but after the First World War and until his death, he was known everywhere. He had put the city church on the corner of Trafalgar Square on the map, not only for his preaching there but also for the many activities that his ministry had inspired and for the varied personages of all kinds who contributed to the activities taking place in the crypt of the church.

There were ongoing programs, discussions, forums, play readings, and music as well as opportunities for those perplexed by problems. There was also a journal, *St. Martin's Review,* to which I subscribed even before I went to Oxford, and this had contributors of talent and fame. Among many who were associated with the church were the playwright George Bernard Shaw and the actress Sybil Thorndike, who had played St. Joan in the middle twenties to tremendous acclaim.

Although always associated with St. Martin's, to which he was appointed in 1914 barely a month before the outbreak of the First World War, Sheppard's ministry was often interrupted by events and also by his own bad health. Upon the outbreak of war, he went to Flanders as a military chaplain. But he was invalided out and he returned to England to recuperate and later to resume his work at St. Martin's. The church became a haven and a place of refreshment, physical and spiritual, for many involved in wartime activities. The church remained open all night, so soldiers returning to London from the front might rest and be refreshed as well as those in other wartime jobs.

The pressure of work and of his own ill health, however, caused him to resign in 1926. That year, too, his book *The Impatience of a Parson* was published. This expressed his indignation at the conventionality of so much in the Church of England, which was indeed, as Maude Royden, a woman preacher, had said, the "Tory Party at prayer." The ever haunting possibility of war, social and political problems—was the Church and were the clergy and the churchgoers aware of these problems and were they tackling them?

The book and also his national reputation (his sermons at St. Martin's in 1924 were the first to have been broadcast by the BBC) meant more strain for this man who was a friend to so many. After a period of recuperation, he was offered the deanery of Canterbury, quite an ecclesiastical plum. But again ill health meant that he had to give up that job after two years.

In the early thirties, however, a new treatment for asthma had helped his health. His friend and successor at St. Martin's, Pat McCormick, persuaded him to return there. This was a great joy to him and following this he was offered a canonry at St. Paul's Cathedral in London. He also started the Peace Pledge Union.

It was in connection with this pacifist cause that Dick Sheppard had come to the United States, where Reinhold and I had met him. Reinhold and he had found each other congenial and sympathetic. This often happened, even when Reinhold and the other person held opposite views. Reinhold was never "ideological" in his personal relationships, even though he was often polemic in his writing. Often at functions, I would be asked, "Who is the friend chatting with your husband?" I would tell the inquirer, who then would say, "But he [or she] has been so critical . . . and your husband's reviews came down very hard on his [or her] position." "No matter, you see how friendly they are—laughing and enjoying each other?"

But we had promised to meet Dick Sheppard, which we did all very punctually, at a restaurant off Bond Street. Obviously he was well known at this place, and we were accorded attention at once. "If this were Reinhold's or your birthday, what would he and you like to eat?" He and the head waiter decided, and it was the start of a delightful evening.

Reinhold had left his suitcase at Victoria Station, which was not far from where the Benns lived on Milbank, next to the Tate Gallery. (Their house, next door to the house of Beatrice and Sidney Webb, later was destroyed in the Blitz.) So we left after dinner, to pick up his case.

Sheppard came with us in the taxi, and told us he would take it on, as he wanted to go to St. Martin's, which was open all night for those in need of solace, food, or shelter. While Reinhold was reclaiming his suitcase, Dick Sheppard turned to me. "I cannot tell you what it meant to me to have you two with me this evening. You are blessed with love of each other. You see, my wife has left me." Reinhold coming back, I knew not what to say. I hesitated, but Sheppard repeated what he had said to me. We sat together in that taxi in silence, Reinhold holding his hand. Then—"Now we must see you to your friends" and he drove us to No. 29 Milbank. We bade each other farewell with the blessing of the good Lord, and he went back to his church.

Somewhat shaken still, we passed on what he had told us to our hostess, Peggy Benn, who knew the Sheppards. Her husband was in Parliament and had not yet returned, as the House was still sitting. So we went upstairs to bed, haunted still by the evening: Dick Sheppard's charismatic liveliness and self-deprecating humor and delightful interest in and concern for others, and the sadness of his personal situation.

The next day, we met Stafford and Isobel Cripps and drove with them to Goodfellows. The countryside was lovely, their house as always not only beautiful but welcoming, and the gardens fragrant in full bloom. Reinhold and Stafford had talked politics on the way down. Stafford was interested in Reinhold's account of the Oxford Conference and also in Archbishop Temple, whom he did not know well, although Temple was a member of the Labour Party.

Next morning, after breakfast, Lady Cripps came to me as I was reading in the garden. "Dick Sheppard has just telephoned. He loved being with you and Reinhold and wants to know if he and his daughter might come later on this morning. You know, Stafford does not know him but we admire and respect him, and George Lansbury always was trying to get us together. So, I of course said 'Yes, do come.'—Was that all right?" I was delighted and told her a little of the evening we had with him. Sheppard's secretary was driving him from London, and the schoolgirl daughter who was at Down House in Newbury would also be with them. In England, everywhere seems very close, and in good time the Sheppards, father and daughter and secretary, arrived. Characteristically, he was out of the car almost before it stopped, laughing at himself, and in a curious self-deprecating way made us all glad to see him and ready to respond in the same immediate fashion, without gushing or overtalking.

He shed a kind of sympathetic spell, an electric aura, with his presence, such that Reinhold and Stafford, who were both so different, found him easy and congenial. Time passed quickly, and pleasantly. Later, we would often recall the magical quality of that day. We were not to see him again. He died in October 1937, and with many others, thousands, we mourned his loss. We thank the Lord for the quality of his life and love and witness.

We returned to the U.S.A. in somewhat better style than when we had crossed the Atlantic in the other direction. Somehow we achieved tourist passage on the *Queen Mary*. This was positively luxurious compared to the accommodations we had coming over. In addition, it was rather fun, for we would look through the bars at some of the church bureaucrats and bishops who had also been at the Oxford Conference and were now traveling in second or even first class. A couple of them, congenial and also more humorous, suggested that we should not only make faces at them, but pay daily visits to them and use that visit for a good long walk around the long space of the promenade decks, which were so much bigger than what we had access to. Thus, in the morning we would look through the bars and later we would make our allowed call on our friends in the upper class. These lucky promenades did us much good in every way, making our voyage quite pleasant. Unlike the S.S. *Columbus,* the *Queen* was a quick boat, only five days compared to nine coming over. With pleasant weather and comfortable accommodations, the voyage went almost too quickly for us to finish our job of sorting and finishing and tidying up *Beyond Tragedy.*

1. *A close friend, Minister of Aircraft Production, and Lord Privy Seal. Earlier he had served as ambassador in Moscow. Later, in 1947, he became Chancellor of the Exchequer.   2. Bishop of Chichester and ecumenical leader. Bell, the contact person for the underground Christian resistance (of Dietrich Bonhoeffer and others) to Hitler, was also well known for his interest in and encouragement of the arts.   3. Leader of German underground in the U.S.A.; his real name was Karl Frank.   4. German fellow at Union Seminary 1930–31; leader of German underground; later killed by Nazis.   5. Two archbishops, the bishops of London, Durham, and Winchester, and twenty-one senior bishops of the Church of England sit in the House of Lords as "Lords Spiritual."   6. Member of the War Cabinet and Minister for the Coordination of Defence. He resigned after the Narvik disasters in March 1940.   7. Ramsay MacDonald; Labour prime minister, accepted the King George V invitation to form a national government. He was expelled from the Labour Party.   8. "The Christian Church in a Secular Age" was later published in R.N.'s Christianity and Power Politics (1940) and in The Essential Reinhold Niebuhr (1986), edited by Robert McAfee Brown.*

Five

1938
At Heath:
Reinhold as Father

In June 1938, Reinhold traveled with his mother, Christopher, and our wonderful maid Ruth to Heath, Massachusetts. They stayed in the Manse, a pre-Revolution house, as guests of our close friend Ethel [Mrs. John F.] Moors. (Reinhold and I had stayed in this house a few years before, when Reinhold had his unfortunate encounter with the Lenox police and I was recovering from my first miscarriage.)

During his time at Heath, Reinhold worked on his Gifford Lectures, which were to be presented at the University of Edinburgh in 1939. He also attended to Christopher, who was nearly four years old. Having had several miscarriages, I stayed prone in New York with occasional help to give me food and attention. From my bed, I edited the prayers for "Hymns for Worship" and read for Reinhold.

The Manse
Heath, MA
June 1938

Dearest:

First of all a full report to the Generalissimo—on the expedition of her army! The car functioned perfectly. No trouble there. It was very hot all the way so that we changed Christopher immediately into his light clothes, but changed back after we arrived. It was hot in Heath yesterday but very cool after six o'clock in the evening.

We arrived at 5:15. I did not go through the village as there would have been no room to pick up anything from the post office or the store. Instead I took the rather steep mountain road and after dumping the family and packages went back to the village to get everything that was there.

Christopher is playing, throwing the ball against the wall here on the porch while I type this letter. It rained all night and is now raining though I think it will clear later. The old boy has been awfully nice. Every once in a while his ball falls into the bushes, and I must stop this letter to retrieve it. This has happened three times in the last few lines.

We stopped at the Gleasons [the neighboring farm; Mr. Gleason was caretaker for the Manse] and discovered that the beautiful child which we had admired in church is their three-year-old son. I had forgotten that. So I'll see that Christopher plays a lot with him and his friendly big dog. . . . This place is of course immaculate. The groceries you ordered have arrived and also the things that Mrs. Moors had stocked for us.

Last night I discovered that the bed in my room was too heavy to move by myself and not wanting to bother anyone I decided to put up the old boy's cot in the next room where the big four-poster bed is. I left the door open. At four o'clock I awoke and thought I'd see whether everything was all right. I discovered the old boy was on the floor with all the blankets wrapped around him. So without a peep from him I stuck him in my bed where we both slept the rest of the night, until 7:30. . . . This morning I have of course rearranged things and put his cot between my bed and the wall. He was tremendously impressed by all this and thought he was a very big boy sleeping in a big bed. He doesn't seem to remember anything about rolling out of it. He only knows that he woke up this morning in Daddy's bed!

This place is really the most gorgeous spot in the world. But I don't think I could stay here all the time. It seems to me against *Die Ordnung* to be here without you. To think of what this would mean to you and then remember you worried every hour of the day by your own inflictions spoils the fun a little. I think I would honestly enjoy life more at home. . . . The hills this morning are beautiful, all in mist. The old boy has just wandered all the way down the garden chasing his ball and is back to report that the sun is coming and I think he is probably right. . . . I am going to see whether I can put up a rope for him to have a swing from some of the lower branches of the tree. . . . Long interruption. Christopher persuaded me to throw the balls over the L [el] of the house and one of them got lost. He can't tell me what happened, but evidently he tried to throw the ball back and lost it in the woodpile. Long searchings but no results. A nice way to waste time. Looking for the ball, I found a nice low rafter in the woodshed for a swing. So I will get a little rope in the village for that purpose.

This letter is very disjointed, as is the morning. But it's nice and restful. I wonder how you are this morning. Seeing that the little imp which is bothering you belongs to both of us, I really ought to be on hand to help with any need. I think I must come back soon. Having asked Christopher for a message for you, he wished me to say that he will paint the moo cow, baa lamb, and piggy for Mommy.

Later—3:00 P.M.: Christopher is napping. He played from eleven to twelve with the little boy from the farm up the road. But the child was too shy to respond, but his older brother, seven years old, rose to the occasion and showed Christopher all his cars. There are no piggys! It is a perfect mild day. What a pity you aren't here.

Much love,

Yours always,

R.N.

Heath, MA
[June 1938]

Monday Morning

Dearest:

Report of the day's doings. I left the old boy at Heath and I took my mother to church. I brought back Louise and Flora White and we had a pleasant chicken dinner. They both send their love. I took them back to their homes, and then my mother and Christopher went to the Gleasons' farm where the older boy had collected all his trucks, fire engines, and so forth for Christopher to play with. He had a great time.

I slept ten hours last night for the first time and feel rested. Glorious feeling. I have just come in from the after-breakfast walk to view the moo cows with Christopher. That is now a ritual. Last night after going to bed, he would have melted your heart. He looked out the window and said, "Member Daddy, birds, and beasts, and flowers soon will be asleep" [line from an evening hymn we sang together]. He is over his secular mood and every evening he wants to sing what he calls Mommy's songs about the far land. Can you scribble the words for me? I don't think I know how they go beyond "tender shepherd of the sheep."

Everything is going well, I have been vegetating so far and have read rather generally and not too much in the end of the day, but I think I'll be able to do more soon. . . . I have meditated a lot about us, with a sense of peace creeping over me with gratitude for you and for Christopher and for the new one to be born and of the joy we've had with each other.

I hope the nausea is not too terrible. I'm going to telephone Tuesday night to see how things are going.

As ever and always yours.

R.N.

The Manse
Heath, MA
[June 1938]

Tuesday

Dearest:

I have decided to begin a little work this morning and work at least every morning. My sleep has been improving, though I still wake up in the middle of the night but am able to go back to sleep and I have been going to bed at ten. . . . I am afraid some of the things I have on my mind with which to close this chapter will become dissipated. . . . I have told Mrs. Meade[1] to give Dave Roberts one of the chapters which she is copying for me. Will you ask him to return it to you when he is finished with it?

I am getting down to a little physical discipline. I take three half-hour dog trots around the estate once a day and am beginning to feel the difference. I was supposed to walk with Howard Robbins[2] yesterday but he telephoned to say that Dr. Clothier of Harvard who is related somehow to Louise Robbins was there and would I come to them to talk. So I missed that walk. Clothier says that President Conant[3] is in very hot water because of the Raymond Walsh case. The faculty committee which investigated reported that Sweeney and Walsh should not only be reinstated but promoted because of their fine work.[4] This is a bloody blow.

The old boy is having the time of his life and it really is a nice sight to see his towhead bobbing about all over the place. . . . I've just been interrupted to take him down to see the cows who invited him.

I hope you really are as well as you say. I read your letter to the old boy, who said again, "Poor Mommy is sick."

I am getting pretty nervous when I think it will be July the 15th according to present schedule before I can be sure of having four introductory chapters completed. Then the real task must begin with only two months of the summer left to do it. Terrible. My reading on those themes of last summer will have to be brushed up very considerably too. I do hope that by August your nausea will be sufficiently gone so that you can help, and can read the church fathers for me.

Later: I wrote four pages on my chapter this morning. I will try to keep up a schedule of three hours each morning this week.

> *Yours with a few imaginary*
> *"embraces" as the newspapers say,*
>
> *R.N.*

---

1. R.N.'s secretary. 2. Howard and Louise Robbins were neighbors; he was a professor at General Seminary; formerly dean at St. John the Divine Cathedral. 3. James B. Conant of Harvard, 1933–53; noted chemist. 4. Sweeney and Walsh were Harvard instructors accused of being radicals.

Heath, MA
June 1938

Wednesday Noon

Dearest:

I tossed off a letter to you this morning and hurried to the mail. But my letter didn't make much sense. I'll write another letter and have something in the mail for the following day. I worked three solid hours this morning on romanticism and feel well repaid. I had a good night and believe this is the thing to do. Play for the rest of the day for a while and exercise, but work hard in the morning. Then the Giffords won't haunt my dreams. I've practically finished the chapter on romantic individuality this morning.

I enclose two works of art from Christopher, which I must admit reveal artistic deterioration since last winter. But he was terribly interested in doing [them] for you and suggested the subjects himself. The bird which got caught in the kitchen scared him and he wanted it to go back home. It is rainy and cold this morning after the heat of yesterday, but Christopher is playing on the large porch with a couple of sweaters over each other. His health is perfect. And he looks bright. Yesterday afternoon Christopher kept Ruth busy all the time as he wanted to throw the balls over the house. For some strange reason this seemed to be particular fun. He finds other things such as the sand in the driveway, the cows up the road at the farm, the water in the fountain, and then he makes what he calls a train with all his little cars put together. When this palls there's always the fun of rolling marbles all over the porch.

All love,

R.N.

Heath, MA
June 1938

Wednesday Evening

Dearest:

I wonder how you are today. I just dread to think of you alone in New York. . . . We went down the mountainside today to pick some laurel for you and I mailed it from Charlemont. I wonder if it will come through alright.

The old boy almost shed tears last night talking to me how Mommy was ill in bed. I have tried to explain to him that pregnancy isn't illness, not too successfully. But he hysterically continued that Mommy "cried" because she really wanted to be with us in the country! I thought all this sympathy passed for some action, so I suggested that we should come back to you in New York, but his reply was, "When Christmas time comes, Doctor will fix Mommy up and then she can come to the country!" So you see time and space do not quite apply here.

I reread Plato this morning, *Timaeus,* trying to get started in that fourth chapter which has me rather stymied.

Howard and Louise Robbins dropped over for a few minutes today. Louise is still very stiff from her lumbago. She sends her love. She asked me to bring Christopher over on Friday to see a new stock of goldfish in one of their ponds.

The old boy had a great time wading in the little pool here today. It was a new experience and he was delirious in his satisfaction, but before the experiment was over I had to change him completely as all his clothes were soaking. He has never looked a more perfect picture of health. He is growing in wisdom as well as in stature!

Much love.

I do hope things are a little easier for you.

Always yours,

R.N.

Heath, MA
June 1938

Friday Noon

Dearest:

I am taking Christopher to see the goldfish in the pond of the Robbins. This gives me a chance to take this mail so that you have an extra letter for Saturday. I will leave tomorrow at 4:00 for Boston.

It has been raining all the morning. The old boy has been very nice, but of course he's all over the place. In order to allow me leisure so that I could work on my new chapter, he has been kept busy in the two kitchens by Ruth and my mother. He succeeded in pulling his rocking horse up on the table where it's having a "ride on the bus." Also he's been painting profusely, which included a great big red apron and another on one of his bedcovers.

Yesterday mother took a movie of him being "kissed" by the cows. He had the idea of crowning one of the very tame cows with a crown of white clover which he had made with his hands. When crowned it took the crown and devoured it. I was afraid of Christopher's look of consternation and finally his tears are not in the picture, though they were real drama. It all happened too quickly for Mother to take a snapshot.

I will write from Mrs. Moors'[s] [house at Cohasset] on Sunday morning. Hope to have reassuring news from you this noon. At any rate I will telephone tonight. I always have an uneasy feeling in the back of my mind that you might have had a bad night last night and if I had been there I might have helped you.

The new chapter is in the process of formation. At least I have a start after the usual four or five important beginnings.

Love,

R.N.

c/o John I. Moors
Cohasset
[June 1938]

Dearest:

I had a succession of minor misfortunes, which made it difficult for me to telephone you last night. I threw the buckle of my belt on the bed and thereby broke the crystal of my watch and the hand. I left it in Greenfield to pick up today, so last night I was really without a time piece. This will explain why I did not telephone you from here. Was worried and had an uneasy conscience and was wondering whether I could ask Mrs. Moors if I could call you. Please forgive this thoughtlessness!

This place is hard to describe. It is about three times as big as their place in Brookline, a great stone palace in a marvelous setting right on the Sound. But I don't blame Ethel [Moors] for preferring Heath. Just had a visit with Mr. Moors and am now in a big room with a private bathroom almost as big as the bedrooms, already to rework my sermon. Mrs. Moors is as gay as ever. She told me she had a most cheering letter from you which she liked so much that she read me parts of it referring to the early times we had with her in Heath.

I took the photos along which you had suggested and others that Mother had sent her earlier. Also I took her some mountain laurel. That reminds me that the old boy is very proud of his new achievement in general concepts. He told me at lunch that the flowers that I had picked were mountain laurel, that we had just daisies which were also flowers and that Mommy had picked roses—"all flowers." The old boy has been his most charming self. This morning the Gleason boys came over, they had a great time, they took off their shoes and stockings and played in the pool. The only mishap—Christopher threw Earl Gleason's shoes into the water in a burst of exuberance.

I worked on my chapter from 8:00 to 11:30, so I am getting into it. But I lack important points [for] which I did not provide the right books. Never could do these lectures in Heath as [there are] other books I will need.

I took a train to Greenfield at 4:20 and arrived in Boston at 6:45 and got here after a long drive along the shore amidst Saturday traffic. I do hope we can come to the place together some time. It *is* beautiful. I have an idea though that the sea prompts my traces of melancholy, almost think I like the mountains better.

That dream of yours is a little disquieting. Obviously it points back to the old history as you say. Does that mean that my going away has aroused slumbering but not dead unconscious resentments? I do hope not. I have read so much of Freud this week that I don't know whether the conscious mind exists at all. Everything seems determined by the unconscious. Maybe it's just your body rebelling at its isolation. After all we have not had our usual marital times these days, though I can't tell you how nice the memory of having that short visit with you last Monday is and stays with me. Flesh and spirit belong together, as I say again and again in these Gifford Lectures and as we have proved in our life together. So I am not really worried.

The old boy thought I was going off to see you today and instructed me to say that you should come up to this country as he wanted to stay here until Christmas. That is quite an idea with him now. He repeats it again and again, in the same way he does that the sun will come out when it is raining! This morning it rained like the devil. He started this magic formula and said the sun will come out quite soon. By 10:00 the sun was bright. There seems to be something in this magic! Incidentally, I believe that Christopher has gained a pound or two. He devours what he calls his "chicky" dinners, vegetables and everything else, and considering his exertions from 8:00 to 12:30, it isn't surprising he has a good appetite. Louise Robbins was quite elated by his appearance and said she had never seen such a picture of childish health. That son of ours is really handsome. But there pride speaks—. Much love. Will be ready to go to the bottom of that dream soon. Also I will hold you again in my arms soon and until then, all love.

Yours,

R.N.

The Manse
Heath, MA
June 1938

Monday Morning

Dearest:

It's just after breakfast and I will write briefly and get to that fourth chapter as quickly as possible. The old boy was very entertaining at breakfast.

Mother and Ruth and he went to church yesterday morning with the Gleasons up the road and he told me all about it. He was thrilled with everything that went on, Mrs. Dixon playing the violin and Ruth singing his favorite hymn, "Fairest Lord Jesus."

I stopped at the Robbins last night on my way home and they were full of admiration for Christopher's behavior in church!

My trip to Boston was very nice. Mr. Moors took me on an inspection of his twenty-acre estate right on the gold coast of Cohasset. It has been in his family since 1860. He tried to prove to me it was just as rugged and had just as nice trees as Ethel's place at Heath. It is rugged, but the cars pass incessantly in front, foghorns blow all night, and his neighbors are all millionaires with General Grant mansions of unbelievable proportions. So I can understand his wife's preference for her house at Heath.

I took her some mountain laurel from here which Mother cut from her garden. I was a little embarrassed by this as they have a great garden in Cohasset, but Ethel is so sentimental about Heath that she appeared very grateful, but particularly since the bouquet contained some yellow lilies which she has at Heath but which she has none here on the coast.

But a terrible moment of embarrassment! I put the laurel in my practically empty suitcase, with heavy paper covering my clothes against the moisture of the flowers—all the heavy paper did was to color the moisture that drifted through an ugly brown. When I started to put on my shirt I found an ugly brown spot right in the V of the vest. I washed it frantically with an oversalt. I finally decided in desperation I would have to make my tie hide the stain, and it did! I don't think anyone suspected my blotch. If it had been half an inch bigger I would have been undone!

The baccalaureate at Radcliffe was quite nice.[1] I had lunch afterwards with Miss Comstock [the president], who is of course a good friend of Ethel Moors. She is going to spend the summer in Scotland. We talked among other things about the relative merits and demerits of British casualness and rudeness and American simpering gentility! She is a very homely and direct person and she had some good stories on the unequivocal speech of your countrymen and women. So it was all very jolly.

Much love,

Yours,

R.

1. *Reinhold gave the baccalaureate address at the Radcliffe commencement.*

The Manse
Heath, MA
June 21, 1938

Dearest:

I have just come from the telephone and will write you a long chronicle. I had merely forgotten about my birthday though I had remembered it last week. Mother and Christopher reminded me of it this morning. Tonight we had a cake with candles, the candle holders actually being among Mrs. Moors many effects for her friends who come here! . . . The chief joy of the candles was that Christopher assured me a dozen times that he had put the candles in the cake.

It has been the warmest day here so far. So I put only a sheet over the old boy. Result: he has been getting out of bed and prancing about upstairs. I have just gone up the third time to shoo him back and quiet him. His eyes are so heavy that he can't hold out much longer. He is as brown as an Indian. Earl Gleason comes over practically everyday now and they play beautifully together mostly around the pool. Today was the first day he could wear his sunsuit.

Christopher's passion for general concepts continues. I took him over to the Landstroms' farm to see the piggys again while my mother and Ruth both rested. He assured me that "white trees are birches. Not all trees are birches. Brown trees are not birches. Some brown trees are maples. White trees are birches" and so on and so on. Then he does the same with flowers.

I don't know about Mrs. Moors'[s] plan. I'm a little worried about leaving next week as late as Wednesday. I will await further word from you. I think I can get my chapter done with another extra day. I'm on page fifteen only, chiefly because I have rewritten all of those pages twice and some three times. Somehow or other I have had a difficult time making it jell.

It is hard to think it is my birthday. My only sensation is that fifty years is creeping awfully close. But I have no more fear of the years as I once had. To be happily married and life is too nice. . . . Another week has passed since I have seen you. At any rate I will see you on Friday. I am awfully glad that that dreadful nausea is abating a little for you.

This afternoon I took some exercise by weeding the flower bed. But my chief exercise is a long walk and other forms of exercise each evening from 9:30 to 10:15. I am always in bed by 10:30. I regret to report I still can't work at night and sleep. I tried it once and failed. I may have to keep up this regimen for some time to come. Of course I can get in a good deal of work in the morning and in the afternoon. I have been working the past week from 8:30 to 12:30 and from 4:30 to 6:00. I do nothing at night.

I just went upstairs and found the old boy fast asleep at 8:30. Summer has certainly turned out grandly for him. After all, he will be in the city for only three weeks before he gets to what he calls "another country." Dulhagen on the Palisades [the Robbins' house in Piermont, NY] will be almost as good as this. Not quite so expensive but he doesn't need as much expense as this. I had difficulty in keeping him out of the sun today after he had played in it a little too long. So I kept him in the shade all the afternoon. First I played with him and then Ruth did.

Now I must close. It is 9:00 P.M. and I have about five official letters to write, answers to invitations, etc.

It is a happy birthday for me because you are a "worthwhile woman." What compliment could be more perfect although that word I know makes you laugh.

Yours,

R.N.

Six

1939
Memoir:
Edinburgh, Gifford Lectures,
and the Outbreak of War

In 1939 we crossed the Atlantic again. Reinhold had been asked to give the Gifford Lectures at the University of Edinburgh. This was a great honor, totally unexpected and altogether exciting.

The Gifford Lectures had been established by Lord Gifford. They were supposed to present arguments for natural religion, but in the case of Reinhold, this rubric had to be interpreted rather broadly. The lectures, two series of eight lectures each, were given at each of the four Scottish universities: Aberdeen, Glasgow, Edinburgh, and St. Andrews. At the time Reinhold was invited, the only American who had given the lectures at Edinburgh was William James (*The Varieties of Religious Experience*).

But the times were very critical. The threat of war hung over the international scene, after the surrender at Munich when Neville Chamberlain waved the umbrella of capitulation. We wondered whether the lectures would happen. Reinhold had been granted the second semester off from his teaching at Union Seminary, which would enable us to leave in February.

There was, however, another complication, not public but private. After several miscarriages, I was again pregnant. I had to spend many months in bed, and we hoped the baby would arrive soon after Christmas 1938. The academic committee in Edinburgh that was making arrangements for the lectureship was extremely thoughtful and flexible. A letter from our friend John Baillie, who was a professor at New College and afterwards its principal, wrote and told us that the academic senate would have a meeting to decide on the date as soon as they knew the Niebuhr baby had arrived safely, and that all was well with the Niebuhr family. All worked well; Elisabeth arrived on January 13 in a snowstorm. The University of Edinburgh Senate arranged, with approval from my doctor, that the lectures would be given in April. This meant that we could travel across the Atlantic a couple of weeks earlier and see my family in England—and also Dietrich Bonhoeffer, whom Bishop Bell was arranging to come to England for this meeting—before we should travel to Edinburgh.

Reinhold was working furiously—not only on his lectures, which were distilled from academic lectures he had been giving at Union Seminary, but also on all sorts of other projects, helping some of the refugees from Germany and writing about the threat of Hitler. He even managed in the late summer of 1938 to have his appendix out after an exploratory operation was suggested after an attack of diverticulitis. Our son, Christopher, a four-year-old with platinum curls and pink cheeks, announced to all and sundry, "Yes, Mummy is going to have the baby, but Daddy's gone to the hospital."

We crossed the Atlantic on the S.S. *Queen Mary,* a wonderful ship, and a splendid voyage! Elisabeth, not much more than two months old, behaved like the perfect lady that she always was, and ate and slept as a perfect baby should. The people in the next cabin to us were surprised when they saw us disembark with the baby in the carrying basket. "Did you have that baby with you in the cabin?" During the day, she slept on deck in a little traveling pram, and was admired by all who discovered her in a nice protected corner.

Our dear friends Eddie and Dorothy Wells met us at Southampton. Eddie had left his large parish of Eastleigh, a railway town near Southampton, for a smaller country parish, Overton, on the River Test. I can see them now, dear Eddie Wells, a saintly, humorous cleric, running along the dock carefully carrying Elisabeth in her baby basket, rather like a big shopping basket. We were to take a train, and connections were close. So my mind's eye sees Reinhold's tall form with Christopher, and Dorothy Wells and me bringing up the rear, while porters pushed a cart with our suitcases and trunk.

Our destination was Cooden Beach, a suburban extension of Bexhill-on-Sea in Sussex, where my parents were living. My mother, very fortunately, had rented a small cottage nearby for us to park in for the week or so before Scotland and also had a Swiss children's nurse ready on hand to help. I remember being rather annoyed, and am ashamed to admit it now, to find out that Bonhoeffer was being driven over from Chichester where he was staying with Bishop Bell later that very evening! But in times of crisis, it is odd how minor details of convenience and comfort interpose themselves when matters of great import are looming. I can see Bonhoeffer now, in that funny little cottage, sitting on a very inartistic sofa talking to Reinhold about the situation in Germany. Reinhold suggested that he could get Bonhoeffer invited to the United States, as Dietrich would be allowed to leave Germany if he had an authentic invitation to teach from America. So Reinhold cabled Dr. Coffin, president of Union Seminary, the next day to arrange for this invitation. Dr. Coffin complied. Dietrich was invited to teach in the summer school at Union Seminary in 1939.

We had arrived at the beginning of Holy Week, and I remember how Reinhold wanted to buy dyes to paint Easter eggs for Christopher. But this was not so usual in England, and Reinhold's errand to find paint in Bexhill was fruitless!

Cooden, where we were staying, was quite an attractive section of Sussex. My parents had moved from Hampton Court where they had been living to a much more convenient but smaller house in this pleasant part of the South Coast. The prospect of war hung over us all so much in those days. My parents had an attractive small garden, where my father, as always, cultivated roses. A bomb shelter had been built in the middle of the rose garden. Many notices for ARP (Air Raid Precaution), for everyone to take part, were plastered on boards and walls. Later, of course, this was to be regarded as the invasion coast, and my mother, after my father's death and before the fall of France, had to be evacuated to a safer area.

After a fortnight or so, we went to Edinburgh by The Flying Scotsman, a fabulous train, which thrilled Christopher as well as us. It ran smoothly. After a few short hours from London, we rolled into the Edinburgh Station on Princes Street.

Our friends John and Jewel Baillie had kindly taken a house for us quite near their own abode in a very pleasant part of Edinburgh. Jewel had been impressed by the signs of central heating, for springtime in Edinburgh is very chilly. But this house was extraordinarily chilly and the central heating did *not* exist. Jewel had been deceived by a grille in the hall that was decorative and not functional! Otherwise the house was quite pleasant, though the dining room, even with the gas fire on all day, only rose to 58 degrees! So we ate in the kitchen, and Reinhold and I had a pleasant bedroom that we used as a bed-sitting room, as it had a fireplace *and* an electric stove. We kept quiet, of course, about the arctic temperature when our friends inquired. The Baillies, after living in the United States, had installed a completely modern central heating system in their own home, which they displayed to all who visited them with pride and satisfaction.

The weeks we spent in Edinburgh were delightful in many ways. We had, or perhaps more particularly I had, several friends from the past living there. For Reinhold the companionship and close neighborliness of John and Jewel Baillie meant much to him, as it did to me. My friends included the famous Old Testament scholar Adam C. Welch and his wife and daughters, Flora and Ann. I had first met these friends in the summer of 1925, before I went up to Oxford, when I was reading for the first part of the London B.A. degree. I was spending a delightful summer holiday in Brittany with our friends the Wellses and some of their cousins. Many hours I spent reading sixteenth- and seventeenth-century history, sitting on the rocks of St. Jacquet, looking out on the sea and the fishermen's fleet. One day a distinguished gentleman with the resonant voice of a public speaker and a rather primly attired bespectacled lady, and obviously their two daughters, passed by my secluded spot. We exchanged greetings, and spoke of the view and the pleasant weather. In a friendly way, they sat down and noticed my books, and within minutes we were discussing the writings of Calvin and Luther. Part of my reading assignment for this summer included the documents of the Reformation period. The gentleman was obviously very interested, and they asked where I was studying. In the snobbish way that comes naturally to anyone who had been accepted at Oxford, I slid over the fact that I was marking time at Southampton University College, and said I was going to Oxford the next year on a history scholarship. Thereupon, they were quite excited, as the older of their girls had been accepted also at St. Hugh's College and was "going up" that autumn. Naturally, after this encounter we saw much of each other. The Wellses and their cousins were most interested to hear about the Welchs, and soon we had many theological walks and talks.

My friendship with the Welchs continued over the years. Flora, in her first year at Oxford, had taken a Geography Diploma before starting her history school, the same term that I came up. As freshmen in history, we shared the same history tutor, Evelyn Procter, afterward principal of St. Hugh's. After our first term, our academic paths diverged, but she and her family were always enormously interested and kind especially when, after my first year, I deserted the study of history for the study of theology.

Whenever Adam Welch came to Oxford for high-level biblical deliberations, I would see him, and soon my reputation with the Hebrew and Old Testament scholars at Oxford was somewhat enhanced because I knew A. C. Welch! When I took my finals, for the Honour School of Theology, which culminated in the viva voce exam, the Regius Professor of Hebrew led the questions on the documents comprising the book of Deuteronomy. I discovered afterwards this was because they knew I had seen some of the correspondence between A. C. Welch and the German Old Testament scholar Hölscher in the German biblical journal Z.A.W. Welch's writings and what he taught me by the way he talked about the documents and the language of the Hebrew Scriptures made a tremendous impression on my academic work and upon my own thinking.

Adam Welch also had been very prominent in the deliberations of the Church of Scotland, the union of the United Free Churches with the Church of Scotland. This union, completed in the late twenties while I was up at Oxford, was regarded as an ecumenical triumph. Those of the Free Churches that did not join were thereafter known as "Wee Frees."

Another close friend living in Edinburgh was a philosopher named Sinclair, always known as Angus, who had come as a postgraduate student to

Oxford and later was at Harvard as a Commonwealth Fellow studying with A. N. Whitehead the same year that I held a fellowship at Union Seminary. Often he came down to New York from Boston to see me, and I took him to hear Reinhold's lectures just about the time that Reinhold and I were getting, as they say, "involved." Angus was intrigued and impressed and a little questioning in a somewhat academic fashion. However, he gave us his brotherly approval when we got engaged and later married. At the time we came to Edinburgh in 1939, he was a member of the Department of Philosophy as a junior associate to the great Kantian scholar Norman Kemp Smith. Professor Kemp Smith took to Reinhold almost as soon as he met him, and, living not far from where we were staying, was a very friendly neighbor. He was a widower and, we thought, a little lonely. He often asked us around to tea and suggested we would bring Christopher. His wonderful housekeeper-cook made special scones and little sponge cakes for us, telling us that the latter were not too rich for a wee laddie.

Reinhold made many friends at Edinburgh. He discovered that his writing had become quite well known, and that people found it exciting and relevant. Many of John Baillie's colleagues were friendly and responsive. Also, residing at Edinburgh were several retired theologians—two had been principals of theological colleges. D. S. Cairns, who had been from Aberdeen, came to call upon us the very first evening we were there. A tall, big man, he was friendliness itself, and Reinhold saw a lot of him. I remember a delightful dinner at his house hosted by his daughter (for Dr. Cairns was a widower), who had been abroad working for the League of Nations. Another elder theologian was Principal Martin, to whom Reinhold became especially devoted. Then there was Professor Macaulay, who had daughters who had been at Oxford, two members of my own college. One married Professor Ogilvy, and later became principal of St. Anne's at Oxford after her husband, who for a short time was head of the BBC in England, died. But all this was later than our stay in Edinburgh.

Often, listening to Reinhold talking with these Scottish divines, I sensed that he seemed to be more at home with them than with some of his American colleagues. I wondered if it was that he was away from his home base, and although working very hard on the lectures—for the second series was to be given that autumn, so he spent many hours writing and rewriting not only those he was giving but those he was preparing for—yet he was separated from all the various other things that he did in the States. He was *not* spending every weekend in a university, speaking formally and informally, lecturing and preaching. He was not combining a busy existence in New York with political committee meetings, organizational wrangles, and all the extra jobs that came to him as an academic. I realized that in a sense he was having a vacation from all those other jobs, and able to relax and talk with his peers in a more leisurely fashion than perhaps he was able to at home. Nonetheless, he *did* feel at home with these scholars in Edinburgh. John Baillie, particularly, was probably one of the closest theological friends that Reinhold possessed. They had been colleagues at Union Theological Seminary before John and his wife Jewel and son Ian went back to Scotland. The call of his homeland had been somehow too strong to be ignored, and, as so often with others who have worked abroad, he and his wife wanted their son Ian to finish his education in Scotland.

Many were the walks and talks Reinhold and John and I had during those weeks in Edinburgh. John would call for us on the afternoons when the lectures were to be given, at five o'clock in New College on the historic castle hill in Edinburgh City, and we would walk a couple of miles through pleasant streets and parkland to the hall together. John's musical Highland voice somehow made that walk both stimulating and relaxing. I was apprehensive lest Reinhold be too geared up for the lecture he was about to give, and on which he had been working, polishing and repolishing up to the last. But John's wonderful understanding made the walks a splendid prelude to the lecture, and unless we were going on to dinner elsewhere, we would walk, or perhaps take a tram part of the way, back home with him.

Reinhold's delivery of the lectures was to many most astonishing. I was used to his delivery, and to his incredible facility for mastery of his material, but even for me what he did in Edinburgh was quite fantastic. He had written out the text of this first series, and a synopsis of the lectures was handed out at each session. His Edinburgh friends had more than hinted to him that attendance had fallen off at the previous Edinburgh Gifford Lectures, a couple of years earlier, which had been given by the English physiologist Lord Sherrington. Lord Sherrington, still a name to conjure with, was not only one of the great men in the medical world, but also a poet, and his written word was a delight to read. But, so we heard, his delivery was not good or interesting. And, although Edinburgh's preeminence in the medical world still held, he had lost much of his audience. I was rather shocked when I heard this, for I revered Lord Sherrington. (When I was at Oxford, there had been only three advanced medical postgraduates working with him, two of them American. One of them was the late Dr. John Fulton, afterwards professor of Neurology at Yale Medical School and then its dean, and the other was David Riock, who for many years was the head of the Neuropsychiatric Unit of the Walter Reed Hospital in Washington, DC. I did not know these men when I was at Oxford but had the pleasure of meeting both of them in America.) However, as John Baillie relayed to Reinhold, "Reinie, we are all hoping you will pull out the stops!"

Reinhold did what he always did. I doubt if Baillie's suggestion really made any difference. Apparently he had memorized the text of the lectures, which actually were a little longer than appropriate for the hour time span, and he gave them freely, adding his own characteristic touches and flashes of humor and wit. As most people are often lulled, if not bored by the reading of the written word, this free delivery was quite unexpected and hugely appreciated. Baillie sometimes disappeared before the lecture to do some academic chore or pick up his letters, and I would sit by myself, and as the place filled up I would not necessarily be near a friend or someone who knew me. So I was able to enjoy audience reaction. Reinhold himself managed to maintain an incredible modesty about his own performances. This was because he knew he was, as he said, a "spouter." He was too aware of the temptation to glory in one's gifts, but for him the whole point about the Christian faith was to give God the glory for those gifts. The very analysis that he was making of human nature and destiny in these lectures dealt with the human tendency to obscure the fact that we are all led by grace. Grace, in most languages, means a gift. *Charis, gratia,* and all the words thereby derived—gratis, gratuity, gratitude—remind us that what we have is given to us and that we should return them to the Lord who gives us these gifts. So Reinhold, naturally enjoying the appreciation of his friends at Edinburgh, did not glory unduly in their praise. Also, he was concerned about the second series upon which he was working.

The time therefore in Edinburgh was intense and pleasant. Old friends and new friends were hospitable. I remember vividly the dinner party the principal of the university, Sir Thomas Holland, and Lady Holland gave for us. This was a pleasant and interesting evening, with official guests, a couple of law lords[1] and, I think, their ladies, as well as academics. The food was good and the conversation was interesting.

After dinner, when the gentlemen joined the ladies in the drawing room, and the conversation became more general, Sir Thomas rose and walked over to the fireplace and bestrode the hearth rug. The conversation lessened. I remember wondering if he was going to make a pronouncement. Instead, he looked quite cheerfully at Reinhold, and said something like this, "You know, the Gifford Lectureship is the best paid in the British Isles. In fact, the fee is so generous that we are thinking of reducing it." This statement created a curious still. I looked at Reinhold, who obviously would have to make some sort of rejoinder. He did, speaking much more gently than he usually did, and I thought most humanely and kindly. His reply was something like this: "I appreciate very much the generosity of the fee, Sir Thomas. It has made it possible for me to come to give these lectures. After all, not living in the British Isles, as other Gifford lecturers have—Archbishop Temple, for example, told me he came and went in a day and a half, returning on the night train to York—I had to ask for academic leave of absence. And, not being due for a sabbatical, I am without an academic income from my institution for a whole academic year, this term and the next autumn term. Furthermore, having a British wife," and with a nice grin in my direction, "I had to bring her and our two small children. Furthermore, you know better than I how high your income tax is in this country, and I shall have to pay double income tax."

"Double income tax?" Lady Holland, a charming rather delicate lady who had won my heart, spoke in astonishment, "How *dreadful!* Thomas, does that happen in any other of the colonies?"

The conversation at this point became rather general, and I think it was the effort of everyone to cover up the gaffe of dear Lady Holland and ease the embarrassment of some of the others there about Sir Thomas's somewhat gauche comments about the Gifford Lectures fee. Anyhow, all was very pleasant, but as we went home with the Baillies, they were both most apologetic. Sir Thomas was not an academic. He had qualifications as a geographer and an administrator and had been in the Indian Civil Service in the period of the British Raj. So John tried to excuse him. I was rather put out, and glad he was a Scot and not an Englishman!

But even Sir Thomas in the end won my heart. I was asked to tea by Lady Holland a couple of days later. She was anxious for me to meet her widowed daughter, Mrs. Shea, and wouldn't I bring our little boy and the baby too if I wanted to? As Elisabeth was only three months or so, I left her in the capable care of my Swiss nanny. Elisabeth spent most of her time asleep in her pram outside in the garden of our house, which abutted on a cemetery. Some of our friends were worried lest the ghosts that might walk would affect her infant consciousness, but I have never noticed any dire results. Christopher and I sailed off to tea with Lady Holland and her daughter. We had the nicest afternoon, Sir Thomas joining us, and he and Christopher sat in the bay window of the drawing room, which overlooked the valley through which the trains went. I am not sure who had the greatest fun, Sir Thomas or Christopher. They were absolutely glued to the windows. Then Sir Thomas took Christopher out and showed him all the excitements of the garden, I have now forgotten what they were, but after such kindness and imagination with a small boy, who would not be melted? But Lady Holland's comment about the other "colonies" tempted us to keep a list of remarks such as that, which in the later thirties often were being made by quite well-educated people. The United States with its enormous area, its combinations of culture, had not really entered the consciousness of many, particularly of the older generation, in the Britain of that time.

Another occasion I remember vividly. The reigning dowagers of Edinburgh, the ladies of the law lords, were at some function to which we had been bidden to come, and one of them was being kind in a somewhat condescending way to me, whom they assumed was a small-town American visiting Edinburgh for the first time. Reinhold perhaps gave people this impression, as often he introduced himself as a small-town hick from the Middle West.

"I suppose this is the first time you have been in Edinburgh, Mrs. Niebuhr," said this kind dowager to me.

"Oh no," I replied, "I have been in Edinburgh several times before."

"Oh, really! Where did you stay?"

"In the castle"—slight pause—"of course."

When I was able to evade this kind lady, Reinhold who had overheard this exchange, said to me with a delighted grin, "You damned snob."

I replied, "Darling, it is *they* who are the damned snobs."

It had been great fun staying at the castle, which is a wonderful place in a magnificent position. The old town, a collection of very old houses and narrow alleys, leads up to where the great castle stands, as the guidebooks say, "brooding on its rocky crag." There was a wonderful view from the castle, overlooking various hills surrounding the city.

A good friend of mine at Oxford was June Kempthorne. Her army father had been stationed in the Northern Command,[2] and his residence was the Governor's House in the castle enclave. (Afterwards, I believe this same house was made more habitable for a Bowes-Lyon relation of Queen Elizabeth, wife of George VI.) When the Kempthornes were there, the winds of heaven swept in under the front door and in through the windows. I remember that even in August or September they put sandbags to prevent the wind blowing under the historic old front door. I also remember the marvelous view from an upstairs bedroom overlooking Edinburgh. When one drove with the Kempthornes in very old and battered Morris Cowley car, not quite as vintage as a "tin lizzie" but not at all grand, one would sweep up to the entrance to the castle, be halted by the sentries on guard, then be recognized. I for a brief moment felt like royalty.

So it *was* rather nice to be able to say where I had stayed before. Alas, the Kempthornes were no longer there in 1939, so I had to content myself with seeing other friends in very pleasant places—Regency terrace houses or comfortable country houses with gardens—but at the time I wished the castle was more than a memory.

Our time, however, was drawing to a close. We had to be moving south. Reinhold had engagements at Oxford, in London, and elsewhere, and we had to settle into a house we had rented in Sussex. Our children's nurse, Mlle Schwartz, was very apprehensive about the situation in Europe and wanted to return to Switzerland. Luckily I had heard of an English nanny who sounded suitable, so these various domestic details had to be settled.

Our time was up, and we had to leave our friends new and old, the long walks about the splendid city, the functions, and the wonderful Scottish baking that Reinhold so enjoyed.

By some unhappy chance, our tickets on The Flying Scotsman, that wonderful train, were for the very day when the General Assembly of the Church of Scotland met. This was most unfortunate, most undiplomatic, but alas it had to be. Reinhold had an engagement that made it imperative for this date to happen. The Assembly is not merely ecclesiastical but *national!* The representative of the king is there to assist, and the delegates all foregather. I remember the day before having seen many black-coated clerics in various places.

Much to our surprise, some of our friends, arrayed indeed in clerical collars and black clerical garb, came to wave us off. To my English-cum-American eyes, they all looked as though they were going to a funeral. But they did not behave as if they were, for the General Assembly was a gala affair, and they were delightfully cheery in bidding us farewell and au revoir. At that time, of course, we expected that we should be returning for the second series of lectures. But the good Lord and Mr. Hitler decreed otherwise, and plans were changed.

From Edinburgh we went straight to the Moat House, Wivlesfield, in Sussex. I had been lucky enough to find this house soon after our arrival in England. It was conveniently close to Hayward's Heath, where quick trains to London were frequent, and also not too far from my family on the coast. Here Reinhold and his typewriter were ensconced, also the children and our new English nanny, who was as good as she had sounded.

The summer passed very quickly. It was an incredibly beautiful summer for England, cloudless days and cloudless nights. The prospect of war somehow made this all the more poignantly beautiful, as we found ourselves looking at the clear sky and wondering if bombs soon would be falling from it.

Reinhold had promised to speak to a theological group in Cambridge. We spent a few days with our dear friends Harold [C. H.] and Phyllis Dodd. At a delightful dinner party, one of the guests, a theologian named Noel Davey, spoke of going to Thaxted, in Essex, for the service the next day, Trinity Sunday, and asked if I would like to go with him. Reinhold and

Dodd, both stalwart "nonconformists," were planning to hear a Presbyterian divine[3] preach in Cambridge.

I shall never forget that early morning drive across the flat, but to me beautiful, countryside of East Anglia. Reinhold and Harold were missing the beauty of a June morning, with the gardens bright with flowers—roses, poppies, and lilies—and the smell and sound of a somewhat sleepy part of England. But while we might be feeling so, we would pass an airfield, and there were the planes all ready for immediate takeoff. This was June 1939, and our talk and thoughts were of the imminence of war.

The church at Thaxted was a beautiful old church, cleared of much of the impedimenta of the Victorian age and of later enthusiastic restorers, with pews cleared out and simple chairs, as are found in cathedrals, placed facing the altar.

The service was a sung Eucharist, and the sermon from the rector, Conrad Noel, was a rather simple social gospel homily. It would have been very similar to a good Methodist social gospel sermon in the U.S.A. But the priest who preached was an interesting English character. Noel was a Christian socialist and was often regarded as "red." He was associated with a High Church group in the Church of England known as the "Christendom Group." He had written a somewhat simple *Life of Jesus,* which although I doubt he had ever read Marx was regarded as Marxist, especially by his critics. The Christendom Group, which issued a journal by that name, included people such as Maurice Reckitt (who inherited the wealth from the firm that made Reckitt's "blue" for the laundry). Canon Demant and others from time to time supported it, including T. S. Eliot, who was *not,* however, of their political persuasion.

I remember being amused by the span of interest expressed in the church notices given out by Noel. The Friends of the Soviet Republic would meet in the parish hall on such and such a night; there would be Morris dancing on the village green another night; and so on. The old traditions of English country life mingled with the outreach of Noel's radicalism.

With visits to and from friends, the weeks passed all too quickly. Reinhold worked very, very hard. There was a comfortable and pleasant little study where his typewriter was constantly working, and characteristically he would emerge for a break and for me to look at some of the pages. I think I did less critical work on the second series than I did on the first. I was very preoccupied with the children and being cook and general factotum, and seeing many of my own friends and family, so did not have the same time that I had had to attend to the first series. In the garden, which was a delight for all of us, there was a small pool. Christopher was happily engaged for much of the day in sailing toy boats on this pool, which was shallow and absolutely safe. But the coastline for his toy boats was quite hazardous. Although Nanny and I were on hand to rescue the vessels from disaster— and they were named variously the *Queen Mary* or the *Mauritania*—quite properly Christopher felt that his father was par excellence the prime rescuer. So, often Reinhold would be fetched from his work to rescue the *Queen Mary* which had run aground on the pebbled shore or the mud bank of this small pool. Reinhold, however, always worked in bits and snatches and interrupted himself as much as he was interrupted. I found this very intriguing, as I was quite the opposite. Many of his friends marveled at his ability to jump up and then go back and resume his writing and his arguments, and envied him. So did I, but it was just one of the things that belonged to his psyche and to the way he worked.

Another weekend we spent with the Crippses in the Cotswolds. Stafford had been involved with Lord Halifax (then foreign secretary) in the drafting of an important speech. The political situation at this juncture was so critical that we thought and talked of nothing else, yet were grateful to be reminded of the necessary jobs of everyday life.

Stafford also had been in touch with Winston Churchill, neither of them being in the government at that time. Stafford had approached Churchill to urge the formation of what he called an "All-in Government." Churchill reported that he could not do anything, but Mr. Oliver Stanley, president of the Board of Trade, was deeply moved and wrote to Neville Chamberlain, the prime minister, on June 30 to urge the "formation now of the sort of government which inevitable we should form at the outbreak of war. It would be a dramatic confirmation of the national unity and determination, and would, I imagine, not only have a great effect in Germany but also in the United States." Chamberlain merely acknowledged this letter but made no such move.

Meanwhile, the newspapers and general opinion were reflecting what Churchill described as "this surge of opinion." Churchill was speaking on the threat in Germany constantly in the House of Commons, and it intrigued us at the time to realize that he and Cripps, such different personalities and of such different policies, were both aware of the danger when the official leader of the country seemed if not oblivious to at least unheeding of the national will.

A visit to Bishop and Mrs. Bell at Chichester also remains very vividly in my mind. Again, it was a glorious summer day and we happily journeyed there by train through the pleasant Sussex countryside, arriving at the interesting old town of Chichester, shadowed by the beautiful cathedral (always described as the smallest cathedral in England). The palace where the Bells lived was also beautiful and interesting with a lovely garden. Reinhold and George Bell naturally had much to talk about, particularly with regard to the situation in Germany.

Sitting out in the garden with after-lunch coffee, they asked if we minded—the Dodds were staying nearby and wanted to come over for tea. We laughed at this delightfully English understatement. We told them we had been staying with the Dodds earlier in Cambridge, that he had been my examiner in Greek at Oxford only nine years earlier and that, apart from that academic connection, his wife had been a good friend to me also. As we moved our deck chairs out of the sun, Bishop Bell picked up a book he wanted to show me. It was *Journey to a War* by W. H. Auden and Christopher Isherwood, which Faber & Faber had recently brought out. This was a collection of poems, "The Sonnet Sequence" and "A Travel Diary," made from the separate diaries of both. Glancing through it, my eye caught a description of an afternoon tea in Canton. The two travelers had been having tea with some good friends of mine, Madeline and Geoffrey Allen. Geoffrey was head of an Anglican theological college in Canton. He had been vice principal of Ripon Hall, a theological college at Oxford, in my day, and later became principal of that place and afterwards had many important positions culminating in being bishop of Ripon. His wife, Madeline, was one of my oldest friends from Southampton days. She had driven Reinhold and me to the station after the reception following our marriage in Winchester Cathedral in 1931. Auden's and Isherwood's description of tea in Canton in 1938 was delightful, and Bishop Bell and I read it together. Canton was being bombed by the Japanese at that time. As Madeline Allen poured tea, the noise of shelling disturbed the visitors. Madeline remarked that it always started at teatime and continued pouring. The etchings of Oxford on the wall, the English chat about Oxford, and the contrast between the shelling and the drawing room calmness struck the visitors. (Commenting on this much later, in 1980, Madeline Allen, living with her husband in a beautiful old house near Oxford, remarked, "I shall never forget their visit. I recall a bat got into the drawing room, and Auden offered to catch it and leaped about on our rather fragile Chinese furniture with a tennis racket trying to catch the bat." This detail about Wystan's acrobatic chase has not been noted in the various biographies of Auden.) But the tangled loom of time connects our memories: the cloudless day and that beautiful garden of the bishop's palace at Chichester, the book about the Sino-Japanese War, the various ways our friends and their lives had intercrossed. As we were reading this book, the Dodds arrived and conversation became, naturally, more general. I have never forgotten that afternoon in 1939.

As the month of August drew to a close, there were mounting threats of imminent movement, no doubt reflecting the Nazi-Soviet pact. On

August 25, the British government proclaimed a formal treaty with Poland. It was hoped, so the historians tell us, that this would give the best chance for a settlement between Poland and Germany. But as we know, it was a futile hope, and Poland was attacked early on September 1 by Germany. Even we, in the country village of Wivlesfield, knew that the crisis was upon us. Plans for evacuation of children from city centers, particularly London, had been made during the summer. There was a garden house in our garden and plans had been made for mattresses and toilet facilities for a dozen children or more in our house and in this garden house. Yet it was somehow useful that we had to go on feeding our own children and doing the chores while this cloud of imminence hung about us.

On Sunday morning, September 3, Nanny and Christopher went across the fields to church. It was announced that the prime minister would speak on the radio at 11:15, so Reinhold and I stayed at home. The broadcast told the nation that we were already at war, and as soon as the short message had been made, there was a prolonged wail of an air-raid siren. Nanny and Christopher burst into the house from across the fields. The vicar had brought a radio into the church and they had heard the declaration of war and the air-raid siren go off. We were told to go into the trench that had been dug in the garden and to take our gas masks. After a few minutes, there was another sound, this time not wailing up and down but on a single note, the "all clear." Apparently it was all a mistake, we learned afterwards. Nanny, however, was very bothered that we had not got a gas mask for the baby. It was a relief to decide that we might as well have lunch after this was all over.

The next morning, however, news came on the radio that the S.S. *Athenia,* a passenger liner, had been torpedoed, and had sunk with a loss of over one hundred passengers, a couple of dozen of them being American citizens. This brought the reality of war home. There were no reports of movements of armies, but U-boats were already operating. Two days later, other boats were sunk off the coast of Spain, all of them important vessels. American citizens were notified they should leave England by the American liner S.S. *George Washington,* which was to sail from Southampton on September 12. So, we packed up and got ready to leave.

The University of Edinburgh, however, was anxious for Reinhold to deliver the second series of lectures. The American Embassy in London concurred, noting that it was good policy to continue and fulfill academic commitments, but that I should return with the two children to the U.S.A.

Accordingly, we went with our baggage to Southampton to await the sailing date. The army vehicles on the road and the troop trains took me back to my childhood and the war of 1914–18 when my family lived in that seaport. But the enormous barrage balloons constructed on the theory that they would obstruct invading airplanes were strange and new.

The children and I and a shipload of American citizens—the Kennedy clan, Hollywood stars, the Thomas Mann family, and hundreds of others—departed with all lights on the ship, to show it was a neutral vessel.

Reinhold returned to Edinburgh. His lectures were moved forward both in date and in time of day, for they had to begin early for reasons of the blackout. One afternoon he noticed that his audience was restless. He sought to add emphasis and interest. Later, he learned that German warplanes had been bombing the bridge over the Firth of Forth, trying to shut up or possibly destroy the part of the British fleet there stationed. This provided somewhat of an apocalyptic finale to his lectures on "The Nature and Destiny of Man."

1. *The legal system of Scotland is not the same as England's. When England and Scotland were united in 1707, Scotland retained its own religion and its own law, which is based on Roman law.* 2. *North Britain (Scotland).* 3. *Norris-Hulse; professor of divinity at Cambridge University; formerly at Manchester and at Oxford, where he had been examiner in the Greek New Testament for U.N.*

Part II

Letters from
Ecumenical Travels

Letters from
Ecumenical Travels

Seven

1943
Wartime Britain

Reinhold had been active in his writing and speaking for the support of Britain against the onslaught of Hitler and the threat this meant to the rest of the world.

At this time, many of the Christian churches in both England and the United States were pacifist, as was the American periodical *Christian Century,* for example. And there was much isolationism in the United States, generally as represented by the America First Movement. To offset this, Reinhold and his friends started a bi-weekly journal, *Christianity and Crisis.*

Reinhold's writings, both theological and political, had been published in England (from *Moral Man and Immoral Society* on). Also, his Gifford Lectures, published as *The Nature and Destiny of Man,* had been well reviewed and much read. Therefore, he had many invitations from church groups, universities, and journals in Britain as well as from sympathetic personages in church and state.

S.S. *Queen Mary*
En route to England
May 1, 1943

Dearest:

It is the tenth day of the journey. I have frequently written you longhand but upon rereading the stuff I found it illegible even to me. Meanwhile I found ways of using the typewriter occasionally, partly in the hour before breakfast, when the lounge is not overcrowded, partly in the cabin, sitting on my suitcase and sometimes when the weather is nice and the people are outside. In this way I have in the past five days prepared quite a few of my speeches. Written my BBC talk out completely at least in provisional form.

It is of course a tedious journey but surprisingly comfortable. Each cabin has three instead of two bunks. But only two in our cabin are occupied, the other by a young flight lieutenant who goes to bed earlier than I and sleeps later so that I make my toilet as if I had a cabin to myself. I have played endless games of Chinese checkers and will be prepared to spring all the new tricks I have learned on the old boy. Have had quite good reading picked up from various sources. Just finished the autobiography of [Henry Wood] Nevinson. Quite interesting.

The company is full of variety. There are Belgian and Polish diplomats, Dutch naval men, British civil servants of every description, American servicemen of many varieties, and quite a number of American wives of British airmen who are allowed to return upon the promise of entering one of the women's services in Britain. One of them is a Mrs. Darymple, just married to an English naval man, daughter of one of Suter's[1] families by the name of Harper. Most of the American wives are from Georgia or some other southern state where the British air-training stations are. They strike me as rather a dismal lot.

My table is composed of young Mr. Donelly, vice-consul in Chicago and friend of the Gilkeys[2] at whose dinner table I first met him, Ross-Smith, a gay blade of an Australian, and Jack Jones, the Welsh miner-novelist and playwright. The latter is about the most interesting man on board, a person of deep feeling, imagination, and wisdom. I have had many long talks with him. Malcolm MacDonald's [British High Commissioner in Canada] assistant in Canada with his wife and two children (the only children) are also in the company. The children, a 4-year-old girl and a boy of two, are naturally much desired and the mother has the help of many soldier nursemaids. They do make me homesick for ours. I suffer a good deal from melancholy and loneliness on trips like this. I keep on thinking of the things I ought to have done and did not do, not only in the immediate hours before departure but in the days and years before. But your letters are a constant source of cheer to me. The sort of the love and understanding at which we have arrived and the beauty of the most intimate relations with each other being all mixed up with our life in the children is a marvelous kind of solace as one thinks of past, future, and eternity.

I can't say much about the trip as almost anything one might say is censorable. But it is all quite interesting and the indications are that we will land within the two weeks and that I will miss only one engagement. I will begin with the Congressional Union[3] on May 10th. My health is fine. In recent days we have had much sunshine and everyone is browned. We have had three days of high wind, but I felt no ill effects. The greatest trial is stuffy air in the cabins because nothing can be open.

Second Tuesday [on board]: The eleventh day is past and the last days prove themselves the hardest just out of sheer boredom. I have more time, for the use of the typewriter but haven't got much to write. My mind has become too dulled by routine, though I imagine this fortnight of rest will do as much as anything to help me through the next months.

We have had several scares but nothing ever amounted to anything, though the course was sometimes changed. It is too bad that people back home have to worry. While one is in it there seems so little to worry about.

I have been worrying about you, particularly your ability to get through the next two months without complete exhaustion. I hope you will try to get to bed on time without me to serve as your conscience about bedtime. You do have an inclination to work through half the night if I am not about. Please don't do it and wear yourself to a frazzle. I wonder what kind of help you have secured. If you see Alicia [the Niebuhrs' cook and household assistant], please express my regards and thanks to her, for I am sorry that I missed her before going. It is so important that you get the right kind of help. I do hope you succeed.

Am reading a varied number of second-rate novels to beguile the time. But I do spend some time each day with my lectures. Have been eating too much on board and will be a good thing to do a little fasting when I get to Britain. Outside of Jack Jones none of the companions on board are particularly interesting though many are pleasant and nice. The chaplain on board is a conventional fellow with few ideas. The young officers spend most of their time playing cards.

I have toyed about with an outline for my book on war and peace but have about decided to give it up as I could not finish it this summer without forced labor.

Thursday: We are within a day of finishing the journey. It has been physically pleasant beyond all expectations. The slow speed means very little pitching even in a high sea. The boredom is the only drawback. I thought of a lot of things I would like to do but could not find a chance to do them. Funny how lonely one can be in a crowd. I have prepared quite a few talks including a possible BBC address. But I haven't felt particularly inspired by any bright ideas. I do think you are a good sport to let me go on this journey with so little fuss when it would have meant so much to you. I hope when the war is over we can come over for the summer pretty soon. I find that I can send a cable announcing safe arrival without difficulty. I'm glad that I can do this immediately because the anxiety on your end is so much more than for the one who is in it. After a few days one has little feeling that there is any danger and a constant reminder of all the precautions which are taken.

Give my love to the old boy and the old girl and tell them how much I miss them. How stale life becomes when one is accustomed to something richer than living alone. I wouldn't even mind arbitrating a morning spat right now.

With much love,

R.N.

1. *The Rev. Suter; rector of the Church of the Epiphany in New York. Later he became a canon at Washington Cathedral.*   2. *The Rev. Charles Gilkey; dean of the chapel at the University of Chicago.*   3. *Governing body of the English Congregational Church.*

London
May 9, 1943

Dearest:

This is a postscriptum to the foregoing letter. I have just arrived after an all-day journey, standing up most of the time, from an unnamed port. But it is nice to have arrived. I called Hugh Martin[1] on reaching Paddington and found that they had "booked" a room for me at the Waldorf. This place seems a little beyond my standards and I shall tell them so tomorrow. But the comfort for the first night will be nice.

Martin promised to cable Cockburn in the morning and ask him to inform you. We decided that this would be the quickest way since anything I might send would be subject to censorship delay for possibly several days, no matter what the message.

I saw the pretty English countryside today through your eyes and the familiar sights of London through your feelings, always wishing that you could be here to share it. London's scars are obvious but detract remarkably little from past views of her. It's essentially the same town. I have seen of course only the things to be seen coming in on the train and in the taxi ride.

We have been safe now for three days, and I have longed to send word to you, knowing that you would be anxious for days beyond the necessity of anxiety. But there was nothing to be done about that.

I must close now as it is late, and I must collect my thoughts for my first address tomorrow night. The day will have to be spent in red tape details of all kinds. Incidentally, fearing the prices here I went to a little restaurant around the corner for a belated evening snack before sitting down for this letter and had a delightful meal. So I don't worry about that detail.

With much love and rather too hurriedly for all the things I would like to say,

Yours,

R.N.

Am sending the children a letter each by regular mail. Give them a kiss for me.

1. *Staff member of the Religion Division in the U.K. Ministry of Information. Prior to World War II, he had been secretary of the Student Christian Movement.*

London, England
May 13, 1943

Dear Christopher and Elisabeth,

Daddy is having a busy time in England and Scotland. Look these places up on the map. I will go to them. Edinburgh, Glasgow, Newcastle, Birmingham. Now I am in London.

Hope you will enjoy Heath.

Daddy

London, England
Thursday, May 13, 1943

Dearest:

I am leaving this evening for Edinburgh and send you this short note together with a diary[1] of three days to show you what I have been doing. The note on the first day closes as it does because I intended to keep it for myself and put down my speeches to prevent repetition. But I thought I might better send the stuff to you leaf by leaf. This does not contain my visit with Wedgewood and Peggy [Benn]. Had most affectionate conversations with them on the phone. I have put in three very hard days and have been constantly on the go. I am actually so tired at the moment that I can't think, but I won't keep up this pace.

In digging around my suitcase I am constantly amazed and grateful for your thoughtfulness about so many things. You anticipated about every possible need of the traveller. You are a dear.

Eliot promised me air priority today for around July 15th. Of course, that does not guarantee my passage, but I put it at that date because my engagements here close on July 12th and I do want to be back before August 1st.

Everything has been grand so far. The Tunisian victories have of course bucked up the people greatly, as they undoubtedly have at home. [The German army surrendered in Tunisia on 12 May 1943.] Kingsley Martin[2] says I would not recognize the nation as the same of six months ago, when he returned.

The bank reported to me today that we have a balance of 184 pounds, which means that your mother must have returned 150 instead of 100 pounds. At any rate I am sorry I brought any money along. There is plenty here.

Much love,

R.N.

The lonely nights in the hotel are the only bad part of this trip. Perfectly ghastly!! Kiss the kiddies. How I miss them and you.

1. *Reinhold in 1943 and other times in his letters from Britain used the format of a notebook which had been used in his early book,* Leaves from the Notebook of a Tamed Cynic, *published in 1929. The reason was wartime censorship. Many persons in the U.S.A. had received letters from England with punched out statements, as you were forbidden to refer to future events. Reinhold wrote these leaves, then sent them home two or three weeks after the events to give me and the children a flavor of his schedule while in Britain.*
2. *Editor of* The New Statesman and Nation.

London, England 1943
May 10

First day spent in interviews at MOI and British Council, registration, and rationing bureau. Rationing card complicated by fact that I had a card in the national registration of September 1939 which must be found before I get another. Does not make too much difference as rationing applies only if one stays longer than 5 days at a hotel and my schedule does not permit that.

Driving rain all day. Soaked. Addressed the Congregational Assembly practically without preparation, going to Westminster Hall directly from the rationing board in Claxton Street, a lucky juxtaposition.

Had press conference at 2:30 with representatives of *Manchester Guardian, Evening Standard,* and The Press Assc. Very interesting.

Volumes of mail and telephone calls. Will have to work far into the night to answer urgent letters.

Congregational address: (a) Where Christian faith is irrelevant to problem of community; (b) Its points of relevance. Insights: (1) The universal character of moral obligation. (2) Recognition of the limits set by sin and creatureliness. (3) Contrite recognition of the grace which overrules the pride of nations. (4) Pity.

May 11

Luncheon with Lawson-Reece. Very nice. Talked with him after luncheon at the Saville Club. Then to Stafford's [Cripps] and an hour's talk in his imposing office. Looking very fit. Arranged to spend a Sunday with him and Isobel end of month. Letters and messages piling up. Made arrangements at BBC for "Postscript" on June 13th. Also a North American broadcast soon. They will also broadcast my address to the assembly. Lots of work. Dinner at the Atheneum with John Whale.[1] Very pleased with your review of his book. The "Londoners Diary" carries a note about my visit today, dwelling mainly upon my non-clerical clothes and my interest in politics. Can't get a copy because one has to buy a paper early to get one at all. Can't get half the visits in I want to.

May 12

A full day of interviews. Arranged at the BBC for a North American broadcast on May 23rd. Then to Paton's[2] office to talk about feeding the children. Then luncheon with Alan Richardson,[3] the new canon of Durham. Then an hour with Tom Eliot at the American Embassy. They will give me a per diem allowance for the whole visit. Then two hours with Kingsley Martin also correcting proofs on my article to appear immediately. Saw the really devastated areas for the first time. Around St. Paul's whole blocks are gone. Dinner tonight at the Atheneum with [J. H.] Oldham. Very nice. But the same story in a different form. I am now the key man for the Christian Frontier group.[4] Back completely exhausted from a most taxing day. Ready tomorrow for Scotland.

May 13

Written in advance. Reserved the day to try to work out speeches which are piling up. Particularly important the one before Chatham House.[5] Luncheon with Wedgewood and Peggy in the House of Lords.

May 15

In Glasgow today. Spoke to the S.C.M. [Student Christian Movement] secretaries and student leaders of Scotland. Had tea with Prof. and Mrs. Fordyce. Very nice. Dinner with Rev. Davidson of the cathedral, Profs MacGregor, Riddle, and Principal Hetherington of university. Interesting conversation mostly about whether intelligence is compatible with sainthood.

May 16

Preached in the Glasgow Cathedral in the morning and in the Wellington Church in the evening. Cathedral beautiful. Enjoyed both services very much. Back to E[dinburgh] on evening train.

May 17

Spoke to the Scottish branch of the World Alliance [to Promote International Friendship through the Churches] this evening. [World Alliance later became World Council of Churches.]

May 18

Assembly opened by the Lord High Commissioner. John Baillie elected moderator. Impressive service. Breakfast with Christian of Nisbets.[6]

May 19

Breakfast with Overseas Division of Assembly. Dinner at New College. Spoke to the Assembly this evening.

May 20

Dinner tonight at the [Holyrood] Palace. Luncheon with Rev. Walton. Walton gathered James Black, Slater of Toronto, McIntyre, etc., together for discussion. Discussion was a debate between the rest of us and Slater on post-war problems, the Toronto man being the Vansittartist. Was nervous about the dinner at the palace. But once in the swim everything was alright. The Lord Advocate was on one side with me and Churchill's parliamentary secretary on the other. Long talk with the editor of the *Glasgow Herald* on my article in the *New Statesman*. The bishop of Bradford (Blunt) was also there. He is to represent the Church of England in address today. Spoke to me with real imagination on the need of combining spontaneity with form in the worship of the church approving of the kind of thing Dearmer[7] and Studdert-Kennedy had done. The dinner lasted till 11:15.

May 21

Luncheon today with Prof. Thomas Taylor,[8] with whom I stayed four years ago at Aberdeen. He made a deep impression on the assembly yesterday with his report for the Foreign Board. One of the most impressive "ecclesiastical laymen" I have ever met. Last night the high commissioner asked me about him because he was so impressed by the address.

May 22

Luncheon today with Principal Curtis. Boring as usual. Dinner with Miss Sargeaunt[9] and Sir Herbert Grierson.[10] The latter an unrepentant liberal. Getting ready for my two sermons tomorrow. Rehearsal at the BBC for the broadcast tomorrow. Have tried to persuade the Baillies to no avail to let me go to the hotel because I have to get up at 1:20 A.M. for the broadcast.

May 25

Returned from Scotland. Saw Tom Eliot and all ties are out with the OWI [Office of War Information.] May have some difficulty with air priority but the MOI [Ministry of Information] will probably provide. [Hugh] Martin does everything.

May 26

Luncheon with [William] Paton and talk about church affairs. Tea with Craig at British Council of Churches. Dinner with *New English Weekly*[11] crowd. Liked them much better than their sheet. Very good dinner. Demant there. Arranged for a public lecture at St. Paul's. On July 2nd. Will probably stop all engagements on July 7th and use last week for writing.

May 27

Luncheon meeting of the Royal Inst. at Chatham House. Quite distinguished audience. Sir Fr. Whyte in the chair. Very good discussion. Talked on (a) the necessity of organizing preponderant power, (b) the difficulty of doing so, and (c) the danger of using it. Last question of a lively discussion: "Don't you think it is foolish to be concerned about the justice of our use of power? All the continental nations expect us to keep order on the continent and they know that we will be just to them." I answered: "Madam, you may be good but not that good. No nation is in fact so good as to be above suspicion in its use of power." Had a good hand. Gen. Piggott[12] was there and most affectionate. Wants me to come out. Have had so many invitations to the country that I could do nothing else. Wedgewood and Peggy also there. Also Zimmern[13] who wants me to meet with his FO com. [Foreign Office Committee]. Also Norman Bentwich[14] with whose com. I will also meet. Also Walter Bell.[15] A Mrs. Sheepshanks wants to be remembered particularly to Barbara. Also arranged to meet with Midvani.

The BBC called up; don't like my manuscript for the "Postscript." Say it is too abstract. May also object on other grounds.

May 28

Trip to Cambridge. Had tea with the S.C.M. staff and student committee. After tea went to see the [C. H.] Dodds. Both very nice. He quite restored. She very solicitous about you. Children very much grown up. Back to dinner at Westminster College with whole Cambridge Theol. faculty. Dodd and I walked back to it together. Big student meeting in the evening. 300 students present despite beginning of Tripos[16] next morning. Very good discussion. Afterward another hour of discussion with theologues. Slept at the Elmslies',[17] in principal's lodge. Very luxurious. Tea in bed for the first time over here.

May 29

Luncheon with some of the staff of the BBC. They are afraid my stuff is too philosophical for the "Postscript" hour, which has the largest audience in Britain. Am not sure whether that is their objection or whether my stuff is too critical. In any event they want me for several of their "intellectual" hours and I'll probably do that. Most of the "Postscript" hours are action stories by soldiers. They say I would have to dramatize myself and put myself into the story and I tell them there is nothing to dramatize. So that is a washout but nothing lost.

May 30

Spent the day with Stafford and Isobel in the country at her sister's very beautiful home. Walked about talking much as at Goodfellows. Stafford is through with the LP [Labour Party]. Hopes for a complete new alignment. Happy in his job, which is fairly non-political. Our car about the only on the road. He runs all the airplane factories in Britain and loves it. Isobel arranging an evening meeting to have Barbara Ward[18] in with me. Worried about the romance. The young woman more deeply in love than the man.

May 31

Luncheon with Canon Guy Rogers.[19] Most affectionate. Awfully anxious to know what his daughter looked like. Mother very homesick for the daughter. Afterward spoke to the joint meeting of free church ministers. Dinner with Angus Sinclair[20] who has given up BBC and is major in war office working on psychological experiments. Sends greetings.

June 1

Luncheon with Peggy and Wedgewood and son David in House of Lords. David very bright. 4 P.M. address to British Council of Churches. Representative gathering. About 150. Very good. Made arrangements with Temple's chaplain for my weekend visit at Canterbury.

June 2

Meeting with Peace Aims group with Temple in chair. Good discussion. Afterward a small crowd was asked to stay to talk with me on Jewish problem. Britain not inclined to do anything about Palestine. Some wish we could come into the Middle East and carry some of that responsibility. Moslem problem too complicated for GB to deal with it alone, just as I thought.

Dinner with Norman Bentwich, formerly secy. to British high commissioner in Palestine. Victor Gollancz[21] at dinner also. Very vital and slightly crude.

June 3

Meeting with Christian Frontier. Very representative of Christian businessmen. Luncheon with Wilson Harris [editor, *The Spectator*]. Wrote two articles for him for *Spectator,* both of which were set in print immediately.

Letter from Oxford informing me that I am to receive D.D. degree on July 1st. Cabled.

June 4

All day to be spent at MOI with three different committees. June 5th travel to Newcastle. 6th to 8th Newcastle. 9th with Leslie Hunter[22] in Sheffield. 10th University of London. 11th S.C.M. conference of leaders. 12th meeting with Gordon Walker.[23] 13th preach for Marcus Spencer.[24] Afternoon read Scripture in Westminster Abbey United Christian Service. 14th *New Statesman* luncheon. 15th munition factory. Evening with Stafford, Barbara Ward, and Geoffrey.[25] Afternoon with [U.S.] Ambassador [to Great Britain] Winant. 16th free. 17th Oxford Address to theological society in afternoon and students in evening. 18-20th the "Moot"[26] in Haslemere. 21th with Sir Alfred Zimmern's group. Evening *New Statesmen* dinner. 23-30th tour of army camps. 30th English-Speaking Union address. July 1st to Oxford for degree. Rest of July undated with about 24 invitations to fit into 10 days.

Dearest:

I write this short note under my schedule. I don't know whether there is much use writing to you again as I will probably beat anything home. Nevertheless will try one or more. Not a word from you yet. I am homesick and longing for news. Nobody has been getting mail. Knowing full well that you have sent some airmail this six weeks wait is inexplicable. Sorry to be in such a hurry with this letter. Have to write a BBC script within the next hour for use on June 14th. My correspondance is terrific. Takes hours out of my day. I do hope you are all well and that you are getting some relaxation in the country. Love to the children.

Yours,

R.N.

1. *Congregationalist theologian.* 2. *William Paton; ecumenical statesman and secretary of the International Missionary Council.* 3. *Anglican theologian; one of the first to read and review work of R.N.; later became dean of York Minster.* 4. *Christian Frontier group: Published the* Christian Newsletter, *concerned with religious issues of the war; 1939–45, published pamphlet "Spiritual Issue."* 5. *Office of the Royal Institute for International Affairs. Many of the research staff had been evacuated to Oxford because of the bombing of London.* 6. *Nisbets; the British publisher of R.N.'s Gifford Lectures.* 7. *Anglican liturgist and hymn writer.* 8. *Professor of law at Aberdeen; leading layman of the Church of Scotland.* 9. *Warden of women's residences at Edinburgh. She had known U.N. at Oxford, where they were both members of St. Hugh's College.* 10. *Famous literary scholar and professor at University of Edinburgh.* 11. *A literary & cultural journal famous for first publishing T. S. Eliot's "Dry Salvages."* 12. *Major General F. S. G. (Roy) Piggott; U.N.'s cousin. Long active in Japanese affairs.* 13. *Sir Alfred Zimmern; Foreign Office official. He chaired committees on international cooperation and the League of Nations.* 14. *London lawyer. Formerly he was the Secretary of the Mandate in Palestine.* 15. *A friend who had worked in the British Consulate in New York.* 16. *Cambridge final exams.* 17. *Former principal of Westminster College, Cambridge.* 18. *An editor of* The Economist; *noted Catholic speaker & writer (later Lady Jackson).* 19. *Rector of Birmingham. He had invited U.N. to preach in his church in 1937.* 20. *Philosopher at Edinburgh and friend of U.N.'s from Oxford days.* 21. *Publisher, founder of The Left Book Club.* 22. *Bishop of Sheffield. He advocated the disestablishment of the Church of England.* 23. *Labour member of the House of Commons.* 24. *Pastor of the Scottish Church in London.* 25. *Geoffrey Wilson; London barrister; close associate of Stafford Cripps; attaché at British Embassy at Moscow; a British representative at the World Bank.* 26. *An informal discussion group, also known as Oldham's Moot. Members included John Baillie, T. S. Eliot, Alec Vidler [canon of St. George's, Windsor], Archbishop Temple, and R.N. whenever he was in England.*

England 1943
June 4

Dinner with the Soviet section of the MOI Prompted by my *Nation* articles. Best discussion of any of my visit. Very illuminating. Came back and made a *Nation* article out of it because it crystalized many ideas about the B-A-R [British-American-Russian] triumvirate which must rule after the war.

June 5

Travel to Newcastle. Civic reception for Temple and the rest of us thrown in. Evening Lord Mayor gave dinner for Temple. I also spoke briefly.

June 6

Sermon in Jesmond Presbyterian Church, Empire broadcast. Evening sermon in the Newcastle Cathedral. Very nice service though a little long.

June 7

Temple spoke to the clergy. At his best. I spoke at a factory meeting, had dinner with the directors, and then went to Sunderland to speak to the parsons. In the evening Temple spoke to 3,000. Remarkable how he held the crowd with very simple yet profound stuff.

June 8

Spoke to the parsons of Newcastle in the morning with the bishop presiding. Evening addressed the multitude about 2,000.

June 9

Travel to Sheffield. Met with a very fine group of clergymen in the afternoon, gathered by Oliver Tomkins. Also saw Dorothy Emmet who came over especially to see me.[1] Evening spoke to a gathering of about 800 in the city hall. Leslie Hunter, the bishop of Sheffield, presiding. Afterward home with him. Very beautiful home and wonderful gardens almost too nice for a radical bishop. Both he and his wife very nice. Greatly enjoyed the visit.

June 10

Travel to London. Afternoon meeting with the London U[niversity] Labor Club. Lots of young radicals. Good discussion. Dinner with Russell Clinchy who had just arrived for consultation with Congregationalists. Pretty weary for the first time. Too many evening meetings.

June 11

All day meeting with the S.C.M.

June 12

Luncheon with Gordon Walker. Rehearsal at BBC.

London, England
[June 12]

Dearest:

Above is a very abbreviated diary. I have to write dozens of accumulated letters tonight so this will be brief. Your cable arrived in Newcastle and [I] feel much better. I am absent almost 7 weeks now and yet not a single letter. This is fantastic. I know you have written but am afraid you were eager and sent it airmail. No airmail has arrived here for weeks. Other letters have arrived. Letter from Leslie [Cross] about my stay in Oxford. Bless the children. I am homesick for them and worse than that for you. Wish I knew how things are in Heath.

Much love,

R.N.

1. *Oliver Tomkins; a good and old friend active in ecumenical affairs; later bishop of Bristol. Dorothy Emmet; professor of philosophy at [Victoria] University of Manchester.*

Edinburgh, Scotland
May 14, 1943

Dearest:

Just arrived at Edinburgh. John and Jewel in fine form, all ready for Assembly.[1] I will speak to the assembly on Wednesday. Tomorrow S.C.M. Glasgow and two services Sunday. Address before Royal Institute of National Affairs on May 27th and public meeting in Caxton Hall on June 14th. Travelled in great luxury to Edinburgh. First class sleeper arranged by MOI. What comfort. Do hope you have adequate help this month. MOI provides plane about July 15th. Peggy and Wedgewood were great. Really affectionate souls. Gave Peggy two of the lipsticks. Gave John the other cigarette lighter. My love to C & E. How I miss you and them. Everything nice here but evenings, nights, and mornings.

Yours,

R.N.

1. *The General Assembly of the Church of Scotland, held every May in Edinburgh. John Baillie was to be inducted as moderator.*

Glasgow, Scotland
May 16, 1943

[Post card]

Dearest:

This is a part of the diary.

May 16

Came to Glasgow yesterday. Met in afternoon with S.C.M. leaders of Scotland. Had tea with Prof. and Mrs. Fordyce, whom you will remember from Swanwick. They were most affectionate and interested particularly in you. Mrs. Fordyce insists that we must stay with them on our next visit over. Last night had delightful discussion with Prof. MacGregor, Principal Sir S. Hetherington, and Rev. Davidson of the cathedral. Preach in the cathedral this morning and at Wellington Church in the evening. Tomorrow World Alliance [of Reformed Churches] address in Edinburgh. *N.Y. Times* correspondent has been nasty, trying to embarrass OWI because of my activities in the U.S.A. I may go on my own to maintain my freedom.

R.N.

Western Union Cablegram
Edinburgh, Scotland
May 16, 1943

Ursula Niebuhr:

Permanent address Kingsley Hotel Bloomsbury Way   American broadcast twentythird at eight   Tell Savage send four books   Love

Reinhold Niebuhr.

Edinburgh, Scotland
May 18, 1943

Dearest:

I have just returned from the opening of the Assembly and saw John inducted as moderator with all the pomp and circumstance. Your nice cable awaited me. It made me feel much easier. I didn't seriously worry. Nevertheless it was nice to have the word. I do get terribly homesick for you and the children.

Reinhold Niebuhr

Reinhold and Ursula after their wedding in Winchester Cathedral,
December 1932.

Ursula with Christopher and Elisabeth, 1939.

Reinhold and Ursula with Christopher at Nettlebed, near Oxford, Summer 1936.

Reinhold with Christopher at Heath, 1938.

Mrs. Guy Rogers, Ursula, and Canon Guy Rogers at St. Martin's Church, Birmingham, 1937.

At Bishopsthorpe, ca. 1937, *front row, center,* William Temple, then Archbishop of York; *to Temple's left,* W. A. Visser't Hooft, Reinhold. *Back row, center,* Michael Ramsey, future Archbishop of Canterbury.

From left, Stanley Isaacs, borough president of Manhattan, Reinhold, and Harold Laski at a public meeting at The New School for Social Research, New York City, ca. 1938.

Reinhold, Union Theological Seminary, ca. 1940.

Reinhold with Elisabeth and Christopher in New York, ca. 1943.

Reinhold lecturing at Union Theological Seminary, ca. 1940s.

Reinhold with Arthur Schlesinger, Jr., Muhlenberg College, 1950.

The cover of *Time*'s twenty-fifth anniversary issue, March 8, 1948.

Reinhold, 1952, photo by Alfred Eisenstadt.

W. H. Auden, Winnie (named after Winston Churchill), and Ursula at Barnard College, 1956.

Ursula Niebuhr, ca. 1979.

Reinhold, ca. 1960.

It was nice to meet so many old friends today and I haven't enough meals to eat with all the people who have invited me. Will dine with Joan Sargeaunt on Sat. Had breadfast this morning with Christian who came up for the Assembly. The advance sales on my book [*The Nature and Destiny of Man*] are 900, as many as in U.S.A. and Christian is so enthusiastic about it that I begin to feel as if there might be something in it. The other volume has now sold 2,000 and he is expecting this one to sell 2,000 in six weeks.

I don't know whether the *NY Times* carried anything about me, but Raymond Daniels, their man here, was very nasty about my article in the N S and N [*New Statesman and Nation*] which he called New Deal propaganda. He challenged my official relations and I thereupon told Tom Eliot that I had better resign. It was a mistake to make that quasi-official connection to begin with. He is loath to have me do it, but I have just written a letter insisting. I think there is a value in being a completely private individual. We have a balance over here of 184 pounds. Christian is sending me 35 pounds royalty next week. So you see I can more than carry myself. I wish I had never gone into the thing. I called you about my broadcast. I will do the "Postscript" on June 13th, but that is not for overseas.

I must close now and return to the Assembly. Much love. Hope you are as well as your cable suggests and that you are not fooling me.

Yours,

R.N.

London, England
May 22, 1943

Dearest:

My visit here is coming to an end. Enclosed is a bit of diary. Will do the broadcast tomorrow night about which I cabled you and leave here on Monday. Have a letter from Tom Eliot accepting my resignation and will be on my own henceforth. Incidentally am getting enough fees so that I need hardly cut into our reserves here. Should never have made that arrangement. A letter from Mrs. Laski this morning asking me to come out, and a letter from Temple inviting me to stay with him at either Canterbury or Lambeth for two days. That will be nice. Also a note from Sir Archibald Sinclair [leader of the Liberal Party] asking me to have tea with him at the ministry, and a note from Andre Phillip who was here and left a note asking to meet with his crowd. That will be illuminating. The invitations are piling up to such a degree that it is nice to be free of some of the rather insignificant things I would have to do for the OWI. I won't be able to see all the people you had on your list, though I have already seen some. But so many other invitations have come in that I can only accept about half of the personal engagements which come along.

Jewel and John have been extremely kind despite the business of their household in Assembly week. The week has been most profitable. Incidentally your bishop of Bradford spoke yesterday to the Assembly and made a remarkably good speech, though he had the usual Catholic apologetic for Christianity according to which secularism is a way of satisfying self-interest.

Will go to Cambridge on Friday of the coming week and spend the weekend with Stafford and Isobel. Stafford was booed yesterday at an aircraft plant. I don't know why. You were really awfully thoughtful in getting everything in my bag, including the paper I am writing on. Everything you provided, except the lead pencils, are hard to come by here. I haven't used the pills however because I have been eating extremely well. Nothing is lacking except fruit. Have even had two eggs here at the Baillies during the week. That is unusual.

Had a talk with the American chaplains visiting the General Assembly (3 of them) and the five Canadian chaplains, two of which I knew in Canadian S.C.M. They have been away from their families so long that I felt ashamed of being so homesick after so short a time. They tell me that this separation is the worst of their privations. Much love to you and the children. Wrote Mother and Sis a postcard yesterday.

Bless you.

R.N.

Kingsley Hotel
London, England
May 26, 1943

Dearest:

I haven't received a single letter from you yet. As I am sure that you have sent some of them airmail and as I have been away from home for over a month, I realize that airmail doesn't help much. I am sure something will come through soon. I do wish I knew whether you are alright as far as health and domestic service is concerned. By the time this reaches you you will probably be in Heath. I will send this one more letter to NYC and after that to Heath.

Yesterday I had a talk with Tom Eliot. The article I wrote for Kingsley Martin spoke of "the sorry debates of the present congress." The *NY Times* correspondent wanted to make an issue of this but they succeeded in getting his story squashed in the U.S.A. I was a fool ever to go into that arrangement. But the curious thing is that the embarassment came not from what I expected, namely possible criticisms which I might make of home policy, but because I was regarded as a "New Deal propagandist." I am getting enough in fees (including 31 pounds for six months royalty on my book) so that I don't even have to touch our balance here.

Tomorrow is my biggest engagement with Chatham House. The *New Statesman* has arranged a luncheon and a dinner later in the month. I am dining with the *New English Weekly* group. I don't look forward to it because they are hipped on monetary reform about which I know nothing. Demant has arranged a public lecture at St. Paul's. The S.C.M. is providing me with extra help with an idea of writing down ten of my sermons for publication. I will probably spend the last week editing that. Hope to leave about July 15th. Since I am no longer with the OWI, I may have difficulty in getting priorities, so anything can happen. I will cable you about that when I know. Have arranged to stay with Temple on July 3–5 and to speak at a public meeting in Brighton on the evening of the 6th. Will visit British troops under YMCA auspices for the last week in June.

The kindness I receive on every hand is really very touching. The General Assembly was impressive. Last Sunday I preached to about 2,200 people in St. Cuthbert's. Too bad we never went there when we were over because you would have found that service more to your liking than any in Scotland. It was really a great experience, that congregation. To speak proudly I realize over here that my influence on this side is very considerably greater than on the other side. There is so much more history behind the things that I believe in over here.

The porter has just come in to take me to a bigger room. Since I have to work here for a month, I asked for a better room and have secured it. This is a little cramped. At the Baillies' I required no supplementary rations. The food was remarkably good and plentiful. But the stuff you so thoughtfully provided is a boon here. I am not starving but a hot cup of the stuff you put in my case tasted very good last night. The heater worked perfectly.

I won't have a chance to write the folks much of a letter for some time. Will you let them know how things are. I go to Cambridge for a public lecture tomorrow. Will try to get off some postcards to the kiddies.

Hurriedly but with much love,

Yours,

R.N.

Postal Telegram
June 4, 1943

Ursula Niebuhr:

Oxford granting degree July first   Wedgewood bringing news   No letters   love   good health   good program.

Reinhold Niebuhr

London, England
June 11, 1943

Dear Christopher,

I have just returned from Newcastle and Sheffield. Perhaps you can find them on your map. Will speak again on the radio on June 14th, but you will not be able to hear it. How is the garden? Give my regards to Uncle Howard and Auntie Lou.

A kiss for Elisabeth.

Daddy

London, England
June 12, 1943

Dearest:

I am always writing you the last letter. But I think this will have a chance of beating me home. Yesterday I received your first letter dated May 10th. Everything previous seems to have been lost. It made life much brighter. One forgets just what the children are like and would like to know. Your description of their foibles, of Christopher having his second supper in bed, completely satisfied, etc., was therefore a great boon.

Am a little tired for the first time due to a strenuous week of travel. Must rush off in a minute for a rehearsal at the BBC for a broadcast next Monday. The BBC supports me. Tomorrow I preach for Marcus Spencer and participate in the service on Christian reunion in the [Westminster] Abbey. Am completely pessimistic about this reunion business. Your old church, despite its many great virtues, insists on an essentially Catholic interpretation of church and sacraments, and reunion will never come on that basis. Tomorrow night I am having dinner with Geoffrey Wilson, just back from three months in Russia. He is a trusted Russian specialist in the Foreign Office. Will have dinner and spend the evening with Stafford and Isobel on Tuesday. Speak at Oxford Thursday, go to Oldham's "Moot" on Friday and Saturday and back to Oxford to preach in St. Mary's on the final Sunday in term just as four years ago. Following week my army engagements begin. Will see Ambassador Winant on this Monday and hope that priority will be arranged. Hope there will be no trouble.

I have practically no meal unscheduled until the close of my engagements on July 10th. Taking nothing after that, though I probably won't leave until 15th or 16th. May go to Roy Piggott's during that time. The Moberlys also want me to come. Trying to write out ten sermons for publication despite the hectic schedule but am afraid I will fail on that. Schedule too heavy. Will have meeting with Zimmern's Foreign Office group end of the month.

Wish I could visualize your life in Heath, particularly the quality of the new house! Hope I will land in NYC no later than July 20th. Preach at Harvard on 25th. Hope you can meet me in Boston on 24th.

My love to the children, and to Howard and Louise, and all the rest. Longing for you very intense.

Yours,

R.N.

London, England
June 14, 1943

Dearest:

I always think I have written you for the last time and then decide to try again, hoping that the letter will beat me home. I am convinced that airmail letters are no good at all but I will try one more of this kind. Incidentally, I left my license application with Mrs. Meade and told her to send my license plates to the Brophy's Garage with the license. But I should have asked her to send the license to you. Will you ask her for it and then use it to make application for gas allowance with Dana or whoever has charge of the board now? Then we can pick up the car in Shelburne Falls on July 25th. I have just been at the embassy and it seems fairly certain that I will get passage sometime between the 15th and 18th. I will see Winant tomorrow and make assurance double sure. Have still had only one letter from you. I hate to think that I am only a little over the half-way mark and have another month to go. But the time is so busy that it goes fairly fast. If it weren't for the lonely nights, it wouldn't be so bad. Here is my diary since last I wrote.

June 12

Luncheon with Gordon Walker. One of the best discussions on politics I have had. He is busy with propaganda to Germany but in close touch with everything and remarkably penetrating in his judgments. Asked me to spend a night with him because "my wife who is religious and I am not would like to have a talk with you about the combination of your interests." I promised to arrange it if possible though I don't see how.

June 13

Went for the night with the Marcus Spencers. She is daughter of Johnston Ross.[1] [She] dragged her husband (American) over here because she couldn't stand America! They are both very nice. Was prepared to dislike her from what I have heard, but she is very intelligent. Dislikes her native Scotland almost as much as America so it isn't just prejudice. They have one of the best Presbyterian churches in London. Preached in the morning. Principal Elmslie of Westminster College, Cambridge, in whom I discovered a kindred spirit on my last visit also there. So some good conversation. In the afternoon we went to the big service in Westminster Abbey where I read the lesson. I am getting fed up with Anglicanism. Beyond the great personal kindness to me I resent the official pretension. No non-Anglican was allowed in the sanctuary. All sat with the congregation. What was meant as a "witness of the unity of Christians" turned into an Anglican show with a Norwegian pastor and me reading the lesson. This thing is not going to work. Resentment growing on every hand.

I went from Westminster to Downing Street and met Geoffrey Wilson. Took a long walk together and then had dinner with his brother in a Quaker hostel. Brother coming to America shortly. Geoffrey full of interesting facts and interpretations about Russia. Very profitable. Will devote his life to this cause which the brother regards as anathema. Talked about Barbara Ward whom I will see tomorrow at Staffords.

June 14

Had a long talk with the chief of chaplains at headquarters who asked me at the service to come and see him. He is a Southern Baptist, priding himself upon having learned to be scrupulously fair in the army to all denominations and evidently is. Not a great light but a kindly soul, worried because the chaplains are inclined not to "preach the gospel" but to talk drivel. Wants to be relieved and sent somewhere else because he doesn't like the spiritual climate here, which is understandable.

Luncheon with Kingsley Martin and J. B. Priestley and his wife. Very good conversation. After long talk about politics Martin said, "Reinhold, we are all intrigued about your religious message. That is why I invited Priestley. We know all the modern stuff has broken down, but we don't think you can reconstruct the old and we would like to know how you do it." Good discussion with Priestley; much more understanding than Martin, partly because of pious wife, partly because less intellectualistic. Finally broke up on discussion of original sin and promise to read my new volume. Will have dinner with Martin and Tawney[2] next Monday. John MacMurray[2] called to ask for a luncheon and I could not give him a single date before July 10th. Schedule absolutely full. So many people I want to see whom I can not.

My love to the children. Longing for more news about them and you.

Always,

R.N.

1. *A Scottish professor who had taught at Union Seminary in the twenties.*
2. *R. H. Tawney, professor of economic history at the University of London and author of* Religion and Rise of Capitalism *(1926).   3. Professor of philosophy at University of Edinburgh. Later, in 1946, R.N. stayed with MacMurray and his artist wife in Edinburgh.*

London, England
June 21, 1943

Dearest:

Just received your cable on my return to London. The operation for Elisabeth gives me some concern because I don't know what it is about though I assume it is her adenoids. I hope I will hear soon. Your letters are coming through well now. Your mistake was to send any to Edinburgh. They all took weeks to catch up with me. I was so pessimistic about airmail that I am afraid I sent too many ordinary mail. The fact that Pit got my report before you got further letters proves this. As it is my birthday I will only say I am lonely and homesick for you on this birthday but grateful for the past joys we have had together and for the prospect of our future bliss. I understand some things about you from this visit and value them as never before. I have been tremendously impressed by the prayer side of the church over here, though more put off by its passion for "regularity" than ever. Just had another personal note from Temple today telling me what trains to take for Canterbury on the 3rd. Will see Winant again tomorrow. Also SK, who will come to see me in the morning because I have no other free time. Must go off in a moment for a dinner with Kingsley Martin and Tawney. My only chance with Tawney. I wrote you a postal about my visit to Oxford. Talked to the theological society with sixty present and in the evening to the S.C.M. The dean of Christ Church was most affable. Everyone was very kind. They made a good deal of my degree, and so I told them that I was pleased and particularly so because you would be. Spent the weekend with the Moot at Hasle-mere and returned to preach at St. Mary's last night. Didn't do very well. A little too fatigued. Spent the night with Lightfoot[1] who was delightful. Want-ed me to be sure to tell you about the garden which he has developed on the roof of New College. He is both so wise and so childlike. Really delight-ful. Didn't call Leslie [Cross] because he would have insisted on my going out there. Stayed with them on Thursday night. They were very affectionate. He is going to look up regulations about my gown. Told him I would not buy one until after the war. They both said you wouldn't like that and this morning your letter came with your wishes. So I'll try to bring it along. Costs frightfully much but I have a lot of money over here. Haven't spent a cent of our balance yet as I have made enough for all expenses. Leslie thinks it's 30 pounds. Will know definitely. Lady Ross was in church last night. I begin my army tour on Wednesday. That trip worries me.

This will really be my last letter. Winant's secretary assured me that they would get me over between the 12th and the 18th. My engagements completed on the 10th. Will give the promised lectures in the summer school from the 19th to the 23rd. Hope to meet you in Boston on Satur-day, preach at Harvard and come back to Heath with you on Sunday the 25th. I wrote you previously about getting gas rationing. Mrs. Meade is taking care of license, etc. I am afraid you must be completely worn out. I do hope things are restful now. Terribly disappointed about the house. That puts an added strain on you.

Give my love to Howard and Louise and to Mother if she is up there though I imagine she has probably gone back by now. Tell the old boy and the old girl that I can hardly wait to see them.

Yours always,

R.N.

1. R. H. Lightfoot; fellow of New College, Oxford, and New Testament scholar. He had been one of U.N.'s tutors and had stayed with the Niebuhrs when he was a visiting professor at Bowdoin College in the thirties.

London, England
June 22, 1943

[addendum to June 21 letter]
Next Morning

Spent last night with Kingsley Martin, Tawney, MacMurray, Geoffrey Wilson, and Koeppler, a German Fellow at Magdalen, Oxford, and now Dick Crossman's[1] assistant. Best conversation of my whole visit. Martin very much worried about religion so the conversation varied from religion to politics. At least it guaranteed that NS and N will review my book.

This morning an airmail letter arrived from you written on May 19th when yesterday one came written on June 5th. It is rather funny. In it you tell of a very hectic day with the old boy and Elisabeth. I'm afraid you are going to be completely worn out. Both of the children sound very entrancing. You seem to worry that I won't stay long enough. I am staying a week beyond all engagements made for me. I just couldn't stay any longer. Incidentally my health wouldn't permit either. I am bearing up but grow a little more fatigued each day. I have never had such a schedule in my whole life for months on end. Have preached 8 times, lectured 32 times thus far, and written thousands of words and attended 20 small conferences besides. SK is coming in a moment and then I must see Winant who wants a minute or two with me for something, I don't know what.

R.N.

1. *Richard Crossman; Labour member of Parliament; Oxford philosopher; wrote in liberal journals, especially* New Statesman and Nation.

London, England
July 2, 1943

Dearest:

The airmail is so much quicker now (I get recent letters from you together with ones a month old) that I will risk another letter. I received your letter of June 23rd today and also a cable which has been following me around. After hearing about Elisabeth's operation on June 21st and not having any further word I became more and more worried. You made the only mistake by not adding a single word like minor operation. Successful operation might mean anything, particularly since nothing was previously mentioned about any sickness. So I became more and more worried and wasted a lot of money on my army trip calling up London every night to see if any cable had arrived. But no matter. It's alright and I am glad my worries, probably induced by my fatigue, were foolish. Give the old girl a hug from me and also the old boy. I trust that Topsey is restored to him. Sorry to think of all the details you have had to manage.

Now about Oxford, which I must report to you.[1] The day was perfect, like the nicest kind of a June day. Arrived at 11 and went to the clothier with whom Leslie [Cross] had arranged for a second-hand outfit, not for the ceremony but to take home. No new outfit allowed, also too expensive, and also not exportable. Therefore a very good second-hand outfit fits the bill all round and will, I think, give both you and the old boy pleasure. Also the new outfit costs the terrible sum of forty pounds. This costs 22. I would not have bought everything—"habit," "scard," etc., etc. But since it was cheap I bought it all though I may never use more than the robe and hood. Met Lady Ross on the street who directed me to the place where I was to address the conference of refugee parsons. Then luncheon at Oriel with the Rosses. Her daughter from Northampton [is] back. All very chummy. Then marched through the streets in costume. Only thing missing was your presence. I thought of you a great deal all during the ceremony. The public orator made a most gracious concluding reference which ran something like this: Having had the temerity to marry a member of St. Hugh's College who took a First in Theology there is nothing for us to do but admit him also into the Oxford family. Rough translation. Everyone very pleased about that. The people all acted as if it were a family proposition—I mean Lightfoot, Crosses, Micklems (with whom I had tea afterward) and the dean of Christ Church who has been particularly friendly. Incidentally everyone says he is making a great success. Stayed with the Crosses again and arrived this morning.

Gave a public lecture at St. Paul's this noon, had luncheon with Demant and Matthews [dean of St. Paul's Cathedral, London], then to the MIO and now this letter before meeting with the Society of Social Workers for dinner. So it goes. Tomorrow to Canterbury, then to Chichester and then back here for about three engagements per day before my leaving. I couldn't keep this up another week. But it has been worth it. Still hope to be home some time in the week of the 12th.

Much love. Can hardly wait for the reunion. If Mother is up there give her my love. I haven't written for some time to her. A hug for the kiddies.

Yours,

R.N.

1. *The honorary doctor of divinity degree was conferred on R.N. on July 1, 1943. In his oration, the public orator's deputy, Mr. J. G. Barrington-Ward, described R.N. as one who "held and cogently preached that the principles of Christ should not only be meditated on in the cloister but also direct the affairs of the workaday world."*

Eight

1946
On Postwar Government Missions

In early 1946, an Anglo-American Commission on Palestine was convened with American and British members. Reinhold was invited to the last day of hearings, January 25, in Washington, DC. The Anglo-American Commission proposed a binational state, both Jewish and Arab, with the admission of 100,000 displaced Jews from Europe into Palestine. Britain and the United States accepted the idea of a binational state, but the British government rejected the admission of the Jewish émigrés. Foreign Secretary Bevin stated that the reason the American government supported Jewish immigration to Palestine was that it did not want more Jews in New York City, a comment that brought still more American support for a Jewish state.

Richard Crossman became the one British commissioner to support the American position; he was also, incidentally, the only one to have read Reinhold's work. He therefore took particular interest in questioning Reinhold at the Commission hearings.

Reinhold was well known in the United States for his longtime interest in foreign affairs. Most importantly, ever since his first visits to Europe in 1923, he had read and written about Germany and its problems. Important for the group known as American Friends for German Freedom, he had written extensively on the possible future for a democratic Germany. Also, he had supported the "underground seminary" as inspired and led by his former student Dietrich Bonhoeffer, who in 1944 was associated with the plot against Hitler and was executed by the Nazis.

Reinhold naturally spoke German (with a very Midwestern accent), which was much appreciated by Germans with whom he met, including Theodor Heuss who later became president of West Germany. His postwar work included meetings in England and on the Continent with German pastors and politicians concerning the future of Germany, and his participation in a fact-finding trip for the U. S. Commission on Cultural Affairs in Occupied Territories.

Washington, DC
January 25, 1946

Mr. Crossman: I want to ask you a question which perhaps has its foundation in the book, *Moral Man and Immoral Society*. That book really impresses me because of a certain basic theory in it of the innate selfishness of an organization. . . . Do you feel that, in your study of Zionism, any of the dangers pointed to in that book are apparent in the movement.

Mr. Niebuhr: Mr. Crossman. I would approach it this way. I regard every group, as you say, as selfish. I think there is a difference in the degree to which a group sets its own purposes under some general or universal scheme. I disagree with my Christian and Jewish friends who take an individualistic, liberalistic attitude and say Jewish nationalism is egotistic. This seems to me to be very unrealistic an approach. A group has as much right to live as an individual has. Through its survival impulse, perhaps it is morally neutral, but it gets to be selfish. The will to power develops out of the survival impulse, but I don't think that a group that is established can very well say to a culture which lives in a very precarious position, that is, a nation without a base, it is very difficult to say to them, "It is a selfish thing for you to want to be established."

Mr. Crossman: Your view would be to go ahead on the establishment of the Jewish home and then the mandatory power must see to it that they do not exceed their powers and rights over and against the other group of the state?

Mr. Niebuhr: That is right. I would make one criticism, I think, of some of the propaganda and the work that the Jews have begun. They have insisted that to give them justice in Palestine would not infringe upon Arab justice. I can see why they say that, because the introduction of a democratic technical society has produced benefits, and they have rightly emphasized that point. But I think they should be realistic and say, "Even if you give economic benefits to the Arab world, and you subtract political inheritance from it, that is at least, say from their perspective unjust." In other words, I would proceed upon the assumption that there are no perfectly just solutions for any of these problems where there are great conflicts of right. We mustn't say that our solution is absolutely a just solution for the other person, but try to make it as near perfect as possible.

Mr. Crossman: We have heard testimony in which the terms "Jewish state" and "Jewish commonwealth" are not used very clearly. . . . I was anxious to show there were three possibilities: one, a Palestinian state; one [sic], a binational state; and the third, a Jewish national state with an Arab majority.

Mr. Niebuhr: Yes. I would take the first.

London, England
July 30, 1946

Dearest:

It's 4.00 P.M. Had a needed nap and am going to tackle a heap of correspondence. First, a report to you. Arrived here yesterday at 2:30. Held up in Newfoundland for four hours by weather. Trip very nice but little sleep as there was only two hours of darkness. The meeting was held at 7:00.[1] Big crowd. The archbishop [Canterbury] very cordial, not very interesting but a modest man. He spoke of Temple with great affection. Also had a nice talk with B., who is one of those unknown friends. Went to Stafford and Isobel's after the meeting and am going there again tomorrow night. They leave on Thursday or Friday for Switzerland for a month. Stafford is very tired. He was most interesting. Not very anti-Zionist. But he thinks we are too irresponsible in refusing military aid [to Greece, Turkey, and Palestine]. Very close at the moment to the bishop of Coventry, who is coming down to meet me at their apartment. Put out with [Prime Minister Clement] Attlee because the latter has appointed 15 bishops in a year without consulting the interested members of the Cabinet, simply following [Archbishop] Fisher's advice. Stafford thinks the archbishop is not putting anyone in who is at heart with Labour.[2]

Peggy and the two boys were at the meeting last night, and I am having dinner with them tonight. She is sending the car. The rest of the week's program is as follows: Wednesday, at S.C.M. for luncheon; [J. H.] Oldham for tea; religious staff of the BBC for dinner and then Stafford [and Isobel] and the Bishop of Coventry. Thursday luncheon with Geoffrey [Wilson]. House of Commons in afternoon. Friday, luncheon at Tom W.,[3] etc., arranged by American Section of Foreign Office and U.S.A. Evening with Christian Frontier. Saturday, to Cambridge.

Geoffrey and Judy Wilson are leaving for a holiday on Friday. Just had a telephone call from Kingsley Martin, who is also leaving. Martin is as confusedly anti-American as our left is anti-British and for the same reason. Talks of uniting with Russia to build a socialist Europe, our loan debts, of course, make everyone pretty touchy. The Foreign Office people [are] very cordial because they don't agree with the Labour press or liberals on this issue.

Lovingly,

R.

1. *The founding meeting of the British Council of Christians and Jews, held at the Friends'
Meeting Hall on Euston Road, London. Many remarked on R.N.'s speech, including Alan
Paton: ". . . The big address was given by Dr. Reinhold Niebuhr. . . . He was speaking . . .
on one of his favorite themes, moral man and immoral society. . . . I had never before heard
a speaker who spoke with such apparent ease, who moved his argument forward with every
sentence that he spoke, who used language that could be understood by any nontheologian,
who could be witty and grave in one short sentence, who in fact held his hearers in the
hollow of his hand." (Alan Paton,* Towards the Mountain *[New York: Charles Scribner,
1980], 259–61.)   2. A secretary to the prime minister recommended to the prime minister
the bishops, suffragans, and church officials dependent on Crown endowments; then the king
or queen appointed church officials. In 1976 the procedure was changed and the duties of
the ecclesiastical secretary were abolished. Now the Church of England recommends a first
and second choice to the prime minister directly.   3. Tom Williams; Labour member at the
House of Commons who worked in American affairs for the Foreign Office.*

London, England
July 31, 1946

Dearest:

This is written in the hopes that it reaches you on your birthday. I
hope I can bring along a belated birthday book, but more important I
want to say an affectionate word of gratitude for the fifteen years of your
life that you have shared with me; for the love and joy we have in one
another. . . .

Had a grand visit with Peggy and the two boys last night. [Wedge-
wood is now Viscount Stansgate and Minister for Air] and their flat on top
of the Air Ministry is lovely. Peggy was at her best, and the boys are both
very nice. Peggy is greatly exercised about the question of rights of women
in the Church of England. Says that Fisher, archbishop of Canterbury, attacked Wedgewood after the latter appointed a Congregational woman
minister as chaplain and asked that Anglicans be barred from her services
and that the Anglican priests would not be asked to associate with her.
Peggy is almost ready to quit the church. Incidentally, she says that R. O.
Hall[1] should never have given in in China on the ordination question, this
action having retarded the whole movement.

Wedgewood has been in Egypt since April except for a brief visit. Peggy has a very justified pride in his patient labors there. She is completely
out of accord with the policy in Palestine and feels as we do. The chief
mistake seems to have been the arrest of Jewish Agency moderates, particularly the important labor leader Shatak.[2] Peggy believes that British offi-
cialdom in the Near East ought to be replaced.

Today is heavy. Luncheon with S.C.M. Tea with Oldham. Dinner with the BBC Religious Section and afterwards the Bp. [Bishop] of Coventry at the Cripps.

With much love,

R.N.

1. *Bishop R. O. Hall of Hong Kong had been in close contact with the Niebuhrs. On January 25, 1944, Hall ordained deaconess Lei Tim Oi as priest. He wrote the Niebuhrs in April 1944 with the news of the ordination: "I want you to know that you had a share in this, perhaps also a share in your prayers." In 1947 his ordination of Lei Tim Oi was repudiated by the Synod of Chinese Bishops.   2. Moshe Shatak; head of the Political Department of the Jewish Agency.*

London, England
August 1, 1946

Dearest:

Today is my easiest day. Had luncheon with Geoffrey and Judy before they went off on a holiday to Ireland. Last night I had dinner with the BBC crowd and promised to do the 1:15 broadcast on Sunday 11th. I had just finished writing the speech, which I fear they may not use again as three years ago because it is too heavy. Last night after I went to Stafford and Isobel's where the Bp. of Coventry came, Isobel said to meet me, but obviously it was really because he wanted to consult Stafford about a great perplexity. He does not want to build the new cathedral, which has been advertised all over the world, because Coventry does not need it. He would rather build a great religious and community center, make an open-air cathedral out of the ruins, and use a big unused church for the cathedral. The dean opposes the scheme. It was finally decided that he should appoint a national committee to advise him.[1] The discussion was interesting in one way and also boring because I knew of none of the personalities involved. Stafford orates at me about Palestine. I can't come to grips with him about it. Crossman[1] is the leader of the opposition to the Cabinet and seems to me he is taking the best line.[2] Unfortunately, he won't be be at my luncheon tomorrow. He is leaving tonight for Germany. I am missing a lot of good people because of the summer holidays starting, but I don't want to stay longer. Most of them are gone for the whole of August. . . .

Love,

Reinhold

---

1. Coventry Cathedral was destroyed by Nazi bombers on November 14, 1940. A cathedral, designed by Sir Basil Spence, was consecrated in 1962, with the blackened ruins of the old cathedral as an approach. A community center is part of the new cathedral.   2. On July 22, the Irgun had blown up the King David Hotel, center of British administration in Palestine. On July 23 the British Cabinet, including Cripps, had decided to take no action in response.

Girton College
Cambridge, England
Sunday, August 14, 1946

Dearest:

This will be my last letter. We had our final meeting this morning and I opened our discussion on the Nature and Limits of the Church's Task in International Relations. Girton is a very beautiful place. One gets lost in endless corridors or cloisters, but it is a perfect place for a conference. Reinhold von Thadden[1] of Germany is here. The British government wouldn't allow [Martin] Niemoeller to come, nor would our government permit him in America. The argument is that so noted a figure might give people the idea that many Germans are like that. The pride of victors is still a horrible thing. Many interesting characters are here, about which more on arrival. . . . The luncheon with our section was a washout in that it was meant to do me honor and no serious discussion was undertaken. . . . In the evening I had the best discussions so far with a group gathered by Oldham including a few MPs and Lord Hinchingbrooke [member, Tory Reform Committee]. We really clarified our thoughts on Russia and the West. I have arranged with Visser t'Hooft,[2] who sends his love, to spend till June 15th on the Continent next year.

. . . Have just called the [C. H.] Dodds and will go there tomorrow. . . . Will see Peggy and the boys before departing. . . . Am writing an article on Palestine for the *Spectator* between sessions.

Had a delightful letter from Christopher, the best he has done. Asks me for some British coins and thinks E. would also like a few. The old boy at his best, bless him. Very homesick, and feel very guilty being here without you.

Yours,

R.N.

1. German theologian and leader of post-war German Evangelical Church.
2. General secretary of the World Council of Churches; prominent Dutch theologian.

Washington, DC
Wednesday, August 21, [1946]

[R.N. was in Washington to prepare for traveling with the U.S. Commission on Cultural Affairs in Occupied Territories.]

Dearest:

I didn't get a chance to write more than a card yesterday but today is better. I missed most of the sessions yesterday wandering around the Pentagon building. They accepted my doctor's certificate but demanded lung X rays, blood analysis, and urine analysis in addition. All this took time. Assistant Secretary [of State William] Benton gave us a luncheon yesterday, and today we had luncheon in the War Department. Heard a lot from the men in charge of German affairs and it was most interesting. One has the feeling that a lot of people are right on the German issue here in official positions. But the general trend is too much against them. One thing they just obviously hope from us is influence on public and congressional opinion in favor of more help to Germany. Miss White[1] sends her regards. She is first rate. The committee is not as strong as our original one. Zuck, the chairman, is only fair. T. V. Smith and Dean McGrath of Iowa are good. The Catholic father, Pike, is very conventional and not too intelligent. The rest so-so. This morning we saw one of the British pictures on Germany which Benton is using to help people understand the magnitude of the problem. We can't do it because Congress ordained other government agencies to make films only for export.

Tomorrow we meet in the morning. I have luncheon with Secretary Benton privately and then we go off in the afternoon via Newfoundland, Azores, Paris, quite a different route.

John Tucker of the U.D.A.[2] [Union for Democratic Action] has just come in. Must close. Will try to write tomorrow. Thank you again for everything, for bed and board, for love and life, etc., etc.

Yours,

R.N.

1. *Professor Helen White from Wisconsin was the one woman member of the U.S. Commission and a friend of U.N.* 2. *The Union for Democratic Action, a liberal lobbying group that R. M. had helped to found; a forerunner of Americans for Democratic Action.*

Washington, DC
Thursday, August 22, 1946

Dearest:

I am writing this while waiting to go to the airport to be checked in. That does not mean departure as we return for luncheon and don't go out until the afternoon. I have already purchased extra coffee, chocolate, etc., for the Bonhoeffers.

Last night I had dinner with Benton. Had a good time with him, his loyalty to Hutchins[1] is absolute and also includes me now as a friend because of this. He is looking for the right man to head UNESCO, who is by agreement to be American. This probably will be Winant. Ruml[2] and Hutchins had suggested me for the job but Benton said he assumed I would not want to spend my life in administration. He tried to get Henry Wallace, but Wallace would, of course, not consider. We talked over all sorts of things and he apologized for the commission not being as strong as it should be as Day and Graham[3] had turned him down. Perhaps I should have done so too. This month in the country would have been very nice. And you are right. I ought to do it. So good-bye. The return will be sweet. Hope you can find the right help. Love to your sister and to Elisabeth.

With every love,

Yours,

R.N.

1. *Robert Hutchins; president, University of Chicago; later director of the Fund for the Republic.   2. Beardsley Ruml; economist; known for his suggestion that U.S. government withhold taxes from a person's salary, adopted in 1943.   3. Frank Graham; president, University of North Carolina.*

Dahlem [an area of Berlin], Germany
Sunday, August 25, 1946

Dearest:

Now for the first report. We arrived in Berlin last night at 6:00 after taking off in Washington at 2:00 A.M. Friday morning, being delayed until 8:30 Thursday by a storm. We travelled via Newfoundland and Azores and Paris. Yesterday a group of officers met us in Paris and brought us to Berlin. Before landing at Templehof we were given an air view of Berlin by circling it, a ghastly sight, with thousands of buildings standing like empty honeycombs. Fire, I gather, was worse than bombs. Four million people live in these shambles. They still walk as if in a dream.

We are living in the beautiful guest house of the former Kaiser Wilhelm Institute for Scientific Research. It is only a few blocks from the headquarters of the military government which is ensconced in the former Air Corps headquarters, a beautiful set of buildings. Our meals are taken in a new dining headquarters called Truman House!, which is the place where the whole American colony eats, about a thousand officers at each meal. This whole place is like a dream land of luxury amidst destruction. The difference between conqueror and conquered does not change through the whole of history.

As I write, the American military church service is being held in the theater of this guest house. I went to the Jesus Christus Kïrche, Niemoeller's old church, for the 10 A.M. service and have just returned. The sermon was the purest other-worldly version of Christianity I have ever heard, understandable in the present circumstances but nevertheless pathetic. This is surely a place of the dead and the kind of Lutheranism I heard this morning was pretty pure escape.

This afternoon we make a tour of the city and start our meetings this evening. I have not gotten in contact with anyone. In fact I went to bed right after supper last night to recover from two nights on the airplane. I feel all restored after 10½ of sleep. The trip was strenuous.

The party is only so-so. Quite a few specialists or special types of education. T. V. Smith and I will have to hold up the university end. Larry Roper of the C.I.O. [Congress of Industrial Organizations], an old friend, is on for workers' education. Paul Limbert, for teacher training, etc. The Catholic priest, Fr. Pike, is very conventional.

It is time for luncheon and for more registration before we go on the trip. I will write more fully tomorrow when I get the feel of the whole thing a little more.

Hope the old boy enjoys being home after camp. Give both of them my love and also to our friends.

Love, Yours

R.N.

Berlin, Germany
Monday, August 26, 1946

Dearest:

Yesterday after I wrote you we took a tour of the city and saw the destruction at close hand. The inner city of Berlin is a city of the dead. Not a building stands. We stopped at the new imperial chancery which Hitler built and which was destroyed almost completely. The long and high reception rooms of this palace are fantastic in their pretensiouness. I picked off a piece of mosaic from Hitler's great reception hall to take back to the old boy.

I am writing this while Dr. Taylor[1] is giving a general report on education. This morning we had interviews with Gen. Clay[2] and then with a whole series of officials on political life. Denazification, economics, etc., etc. We are accumulating vast amounts of material. Tomorrow I go to see Dibelius,[3] Dilschneider[4] (the translator of my book), and the Bonhoeffers. Will write more fully when I have seen them.

I am not enough of an artist to describe the destruction but I am sure world history has not seen its like before. The people walk about in a daze.

Had luncheon today with Kurt Mendeshausen, formerly of Bennington [College] and now on the economic staff. Tonight I am having dinner with Kurt Schmidt, the socialist leader, so I [am] getting light on the political situation. On the whole one is impressed by the goodness and intelligence of the officials and by the way the whole thing is frustrated by the general situation, particularly the intransigence of the Russians and French.

We are leaving Wednesday night for Frankfurt and will there be travelling until the final week when we'll come back here for writing the report. We will go to Marburg, Heidelberg, Wiesbaden, Munich, and Frankfurt, mostly by car.

We naturally live in great comfort, not to say luxury. One man said: "The occupation authorities are divided between those who have no conscience about their comfort and those whose consciences [are] so uneasy, that they become too sentimental to do their work."

This must stop as the lecturer is speaking. Hope the old boy is back safe and sound and happy and that the old girl is her happy self.

Much love.

R.N.

1. *Political officer for the Army of Occupation.*   2. *General Lucius Clay; General of U.S. Army's occupation, later American high commissioner in Germany.*   3. *Bishop Otto Dibelius; Bishop of Berlin, a diocese that included eastern and western sectors of Berlin, as well as territories in the Soviet zone that became East Germany.*   4. *Translated* Nature and Destiny of Man *into German.*

Berlin, Germany
Tuesday, August 27, 1946

Dearest:

Had lunch with Dr. Delschneider this forenoon to talk over the translation of my book and the affairs of the Confessional Synod Theological

Seminary. The theological faculty and all faculties in the University of Berlin are being slowly strangled. Every professor must submit outlines of his lectures and lists of all books to which he refers. The Germans all insist that communist supervision is more absolute than were the Nazis'.

After spending the day listening to reports on control of radio, newspapers, etc., I went to see Bishop Dibelius at 5. His diocese is in Russian-occupied territory. "After facing one dictatorship for twelve years and now being forced to submit to another," Dibelius declared, "we Christians in Germany can think only eschatologically. Man has reached the limit of evil and there is not enough substantative strength in Christian culture to overcome the evils to which we are exposed."

Dibelius, as almost all sophisticated Germans, believes that a war with Russia is both inevitable and desirable. He thinks however that, as in the case of Hitler, the democracies will not bring themselves to such a war for ten years. I had dinner last night with the editor of the largest Berlin paper. When I asked him why the Germans, who had suffered so much, preferred war to Russian domination he said: "We anti-Nazis have lived for 12 years in the consistent preference of death to tyranny. Death has no terror for us and tyranny has."

Dibelius declares that eight of his pastors were forced to turn informers through the simple process of offering them the alternative between death or a contract in which they undertook to inform the NKVD[1] weekly on all happenings in the church. The pastors are now weighted down with an evil conscience and try to escape from the Russian Zone. He has told them that if they do not risk death in the first encounter they'll be lost.

The Germans seem genuinely convinced that the communists' terror is worse than the Nazi[s']. They are also convinced that the factories which we are delivering for reparations are being set up again, not in Russia, but in the Russian Zone of Germany and are manufacturing war materials. They are practically all quite hopeless about the future.

Yours—all love,

R.N.

---

1. *Russian secret police.*

Berlin, Germany
August 27, 1946

Dearest:

The pace has been so swift that I can't find time to write a letter. I sent you a short two pages yesterday after two interviews. Last night I had a touching visit with the whole Bonhoeffer family. I'll have to wait to tell you about it. Now we are packing to push off to Frankfurt. Decided this morning to quit in time to get home on Tuesday, September 24th; will you let Pit and Mrs. Meade know when you return to NYC? No hurry. Have not had any letters yet. They'll probably be coming soon. Sorry to be so brief. Trying to see Tillich's sister before it's time to leave.

Love,

R.N.

Wiesbaden, Germany
August 29, 1946

Dearest:

Just before leaving Berlin last night I received your first letter with the enclosure of Christopher's card. Today he has arrived back in Heath and I hope he is a new source of joy in the family circle. I just wonder how camp has affected him. I do wish I could be with you and the children in the coming September days. I don't know whether I wrote you that we decided to come back about September 24th. I am glad for any reasons including the fact that pressure on time is such that it is quite foolish to think that I could have worked on my courses. Every minute is taken.

Last night we took the train for Frankfurt and this morning drove by auto to this state capital of Hesse, which was also the center of the universal bath tourist business. There is nothing but hotels in this town. It is only one-third destroyed, which is unusual. The military of course occupies all intact hotels. We live in one called Schwarzen Bock Hotel which means Black Goat Hotel. Had a sumptuous luncheon at noon by the military commander of the state in a sumptuous villa. The ceremonial gorging in a hungry country is nice weight upon the conscience. All day we listened to education reports. We are gaining much more material than we ever can embody in a report.

Tomorrow Miss White and I will speak at the University of Frankfurt and on Sunday and Monday at the University of Marburg. On Saturday we spend the day on a Rhine excursion boat and have our meetings on it, partly to give an outing, partly to find a way whereby we can talk freely with invited German officials. There is no other way for Germans and us to eat together though we meet them all the time.

We will visit the other two German states of our zone, Bavaria and Württemberg-Baden, with capitals in Munich and Stuttgart in turn, and then return to Berlin to write our report. The sense of tension with Russia is much less here than in Berlin where it is all-engrossing. The health of the people is also better because the country is nearer and almost everyone gets something from relatives in the country. Also the headquarters of the American Air Force is here and I gather that more of the pilots and mechanics live in commonlaw marriage[s] with some German women, whose relatives they help to support. This is at least better than the widespread promiscuity of earlier days. The British are now going to regularize this relationship by allowing marriage. Our people are still holding out for some reason. The whole ethics of occupation is of course a cockeyed part of our tragic world. I have to write an editorial tonight for *Christianity & Crisis* and will put into it what I have otherwise written you about the religious situation. Hope to write the old boy a birthday letter over the weekend. Give my love to Howard and Louise and the old boy and the old girlie. I say again God bless you!! and am surprised that this blessing should arouse so much speculation and theology, but it is my faith. Anyway I live by faith and memory and anticipation.

Yours,

R.N.

Berlin, Germany
September 3, 1946

Dearest:

We have finished our visit in this state and I write this as we wait to go to the commandant for a farewell dinner which will probably be terrific. Last night I spent the evening with Niemoeller and Fricke. The former drove down especially to see me and we had a great time together. This noon I had luncheon with the commandant of a neighboring town, a Jewish refugee professor of mathematics at Columbia. He is a friend of Eberhard Schulz,[1] who was there with three journalist friends. Schulz sends his regards. He has not changed in fifteen years. He is more resentful of the injustices than anyone I have met, and the luncheon was a terrific debate between him and the captain, the latter defending our policies too simply and Eberhard attacking them too emotionally. I was almost a neutral observer. This world is completely cockeyed. We all went off to our meeting an hour ago to get our week's ration: a carton of cigarettes, a box of Hersheys and in addition what we actually needed. I spent $2.20 and carried off stuff the value of half a year's wage of a skilled laborer. Outside stood hungry German children to whom we distributed candy. It's really quite unbelievable.

One trouble about me writing more fully to you is that I have promised so many articles and have so little time that I sit into the night writing articles. By way of excuse I wonder whether that is not one of the reasons that my letters are so uninteresting generally. I pour all but the most personal things in the endless stream of journalistic junk I write.

The Lord's blessing to you,

R.N.

1. *Former German Fellow at Union Seminary and a journalist.*

Stuttgart, Germany
September 6, 1946

Dearest:

Last night I received Helmut's letter informing me of Walter's death.[1] I was sorry I could not be there to help. Otherwise I must confess to a sense of relief, for his tragic life would have become more and more a burden to himself and those near to him. Of course I had a revival of my memories of a genial childhood and of his great kindness to me in early years and he matured earlier than I, and then of the tragic subsequent years. Living in a situation at the moment when a whole nation writhes in agony I am able to bear the easier the thought of this sadly confused life. I am sorry that I cannot help Mother. I am sure she feels no different but with even longer thoughts about his future.

I had a lovely letter from Christopher which I greatly enjoyed. The high period today was Secretary Byrnes'[s][2] address to which we were invited. It was the best thing yet done for this sad nation. I met with Bp. Wurm[3] this morning and then looked at the great Protestant relief work. Met with a group of theologians this evening. Please forgive these brief notes. I have been pushed the last few days and haven't had time to think or write. We intend to begin next week with two days' rest in the Bavarian Alps. Will also visit Berchtesgaden and inspect Hitler's Alpine nest. I enclose a picture which may interest the old boy. Had dinner with a nice young captain, Wright, who is in civil life a master at the Choate School. He said, "For goodness sake don't send a sensitive boy to a boarding school for the 9th and 10th year, but only for the 11th and 12th." The first years, he insisted, are too difficult for such boys.

I have too many impressions of this many-sided tragedy to write intelligently. I wish I were with you. Would like to share this all with you, and miss you physically and spiritually. Love to the old boy and give all love to yourself. This will be the last letter I will send to Heath. I don't know when you will be leaving or how long these letters take to cross, so I'll play safe.

All love,

R.N.

1. *Walter Niebuhr, elder brother of R.N., died suddenly of heart failure. His health had not been good. U.N. and her sister Barbara attended the funeral in New York.   2. James Byrnes; secretary of state. In his address at Stuttgart, Byrnes asked Germany to partici- pate in its own recovery.   3. Bishop Theophil Wurm of Württemberg (1868-1953); leader of a church not taken over by the Nazis during World War II.*

Stuttgart, Germany
September 8, 1946

Dearest:

Yesterday, I received your nice letter written on August 27th and telling me about Elisabeth's discovery of how chickens are killed. It was long in reaching me because it was re-addressed in Berlin. I had Helmut's letter about Walter's death two days earlier. I had just written you a hasty note as I was overtired. Now I am rested up, having had both a nap and a long sleep.

Yesterday we went into the French Zone to visit Tübingen University only 20 miles from here. We went there because we heard that the French, despite their harsh general policy, are anxious to out-do us and Britain in the institutions of higher learning and we feel this to be true. The beautiful old university is intact and gets as much special consideration as possible. Hans Stroh, who is university chaplain, was in Switzerland attending a "group's" meeting.[1] Buchman is going strong by the way, having bought a big place there and in London.. . . I saw other friends on the faculty and also the editor of the largest publishing firm who can get proper rations to publish the translation of *Nature and Destiny,* which is not to be had in the U.S. Zone. However *Children of Light* and *Beyond Tragedy* will be published in the U.S. Zone. The publisher had a letter from a professor of classics who wrote that my Giffords were the most important volume on the English works to be published, which pleased me.

In the afternoon, I had a meeting with the leaders of the new Christian Democratic Union, a party which has had the same mushroom growth as the MRP [Mouvement Républicaine Populaire] in France and which contains about as many political elements, being held together by religious convictions. What is new is that it is Catholics and Protestants that are united in it.

This morning we went to church in St. Mark's, the only intact church of Stuttgart. The professor of systematics, Prof. [Helmut] Thielicke of Tübingen, preached. He is the outstanding young theologian of whole nation and as gifted as a preacher as he is as a theologian. sermon was really quite tremendous and as the liturgy of the Lutheran church here is much simpler than in the north and the sermon is very central, I find myself arguing with you in absentia on this old point of debate.

In a few minutes our party is driving to Bad Boll[2] where I visited in 1930. It is a church retreat thirty miles from here founded by the father and son Blumanhardt, two men who were my father's favorites; the father was a faith healer and the son was the first genuine Christian socialist of Germany. Both influenced the piety of this region strongly. We are going to a meeting on "Christianity and Literature" called by the theologians and younger poets. There is life here in every direction.

I gave my week's rations of Hershey bars to Eideln who studied with us in 1930 and who is now Bp. Wurm's coadjutor. He has 4 children. I eagerly await every letter. Will be home in a little over two weeks. Three weeks ago today we had those nice days in Heath.

Lovingly,

R.

1. *A group meeting concerned with the Moral Rearmament movement, a somewhat peculiar evangelical movement that originated in Princeton with Frank Buchman, an evangelical. He was asked to leave Princeton because of his strategy of using personal relations and forced confessions in Moral Rearmament activities.* 2. *Bad Boll in 1945 was the first Evangelical Academy organized on the site of an old retreat center which had been founded by Blumanhardt.*

[Appended letter to Elisabeth]

Dear Elisabeth:

I wrote Christopher a birthday letter but have not written you. But you haven't written either. Maybe a letter from you is on the way. The children here are all hungry. They do not have enough to eat. Almost all the buildings were destroyed by bombs. We must pray for these children and help them.

With love,

Daddy

Tegernsee, Germany
September 10, 1946

Dearest:

I am writing this in Himmler's drawing room while educational officers of military government are writing their report. We drove here from

Stuttgart yesterday and instead of stopping at Munich went on to the lakeside resort of Tegernsee, where all the big Nazis had summer homes. Himmler's home, where we are staying, is now an officer's club. Wherever a nice hotel or home is you can trust the Army to grab it, and across the lake a big hotel is a rest home for the Air Force. It is in the hotel where Hitler killed Röhm and 70 members of his staff. We took a little trip on the lake this morning before beginning our meetings. When we finish this noon we go to Munich for three days and to Erlangen, the only Protestant university in Bavaria. As I write our commission is listening with amazement at the report of what a real clerical state is like. I look at Helen White occasionally wondering what she is thinking. Bavaria is better off than the other states because it is agrarian. But not much better off because of the million refugees from Silesia and Czechoslovakia. All American officials feel that this refugee business is the worst injustice we are doing.

Before leaving Stuttgart I had a long affectionate letter from Hans Stroh, whom I missed in Tübingen. Sunday I attended a crowded service in Stuttgart.

I have had only two letters from you. The rest are heaping up in Berlin and I will not get there until Friday.

At this point I had to stop because I was being called upon for an opinion. We have since come up to Munich, I lost my pen, we had a long afternoon meeting with the Educational Ministry and heard all the problems of the clerical Catholic educational system. I had dinner with the general.

I had a whole batch of letters from you, all about Walter's death, Elisabeth's broken arm, etc., etc. I am sorry to be away through all these trials. Had letters from Hulda and Helmut today. I think the funeral helped Beulah. She chose the "Lead Kindly Light" hymn because Walter hummed it so much. Her willingness to forget all the suffering Walter caused and remember only his faithfulness to her is quite touching. . . .

I write this ensconced in a two-room suite of rooms in a big Munich hotel where we will be for three nights. We go to Erlangen, Nürnberg, and then Berlin. I will try to see Gerhard's[1] sister, but so far I have seen only the Bonhoeffers. I may have difficulty in seeing both Paul Tillich's and Gerhard's sisters. The program is so heavy and transportation is so difficult that one never quite knows how to get everything in. I'll do my best. Bonhoeffer inquired after Gerhard and was delighted to hear the news.

I wanted to send the old boy a message by cable today for him to read on his birthday but government nowhere has a cable officer. I'll send it tomorrow though it may be late. Tell the old girl I sympathize with her and hope she will be all well by school time. But I must write on our report before it is too late. The hours are too long, the food too rich, the exercise too minimal, yet I am in fair health and hope to come back not too tired. I hope you will excuse distracted letters. I can't seem to get my mind on anything.

Love to the old boy, the old girl, and my grateful love to you.

R.N.

P.S. I loved your letters although they were about domestic trage-dies, major and minor, and had to read them while the Bavarian school system was being explained. It made me feel less homesick to have them.

1. *Gerhard Witt, a psychiatrist who had been a pupil, an assistant, and a junior colleague of Dr. Karl Bonhoeffer, professor of pathology and neurology at Berlin University and Dietrich's father. Witt met Barbara Keppel-Compton in England, and later the two were married in New York. He died in the late 1940s.*

Berlin, Germany
September 14, 1946

Dearest:

We have just arrived from Munich by plane and I find your two nice letters of September 6th and 9th with the account of the party with Sydney and Bob,[1] etc. Ever since I wrote you last we have been all over Bavaria. We drove 500 miles by car in two days. We visited schools in Garmisch and Oberammergau. We stopped at the famous Monastery School at Etal close to Oberammergau and at the latter place looked in briefly at the Passion Play Theater before visiting the woodcarvers' school where the young men are trained to keep up the great wood carving tradi-tion of Bavaria. We have seen beautiful scenery for two days, thousands of ox carts and hay ricks—no horses, always oxen. We lunched in a terrific mountainside inn, etc. That was Thursday. Yesterday we went to a second-ary school where I made my first and last speech in German for Teachers Training Section of a large school. Then we went on to the Czech border to observe the human misery pouring across the border, where Sudenten Germans on the one hand and Polish Jews on the other are pouring across the border at the rate of 1,000 every day into an already overcrowded Germany. What a mass of misery. Can't stop to describe it. We stopped for the night at Nürnberg, and early this morning to see the ruins of the old city and the courthouse at Nürnberg. Then we drove on for a two-hour's visit with the faculty at Erlangen University and caught a plane at 2 P.M. for Berlin. Here we are back for the final week's meetings. I am pretty spent but will rest all day tomorrow. . . .

Yours,

R.

1. *Sydney and Robert MacAfee Brown; summer neighbors at Heath. Brown edited the Es-sential Reinhold Niebuhr; he is professor emeritus of theology and ethics at Pacific School of Religion, Berkeley, California.*

Berlin, Germany
Sunday, September 15, 1946

Dearest:

It's Sunday morning. After a sleep of nine hours the weariness of days of constant travel is gone. I am sitting at my desk at the office assigned to us where I have a large desk, as big as a house. This building, with typical army profligacy, was cleared for us and each of us given a desk though we will use it only this week and has been standing vacant while we travelled. I will be glad when this awful contrast does not daily weigh upon the conscience. The British have just evicted 18,000 families in Hamburg to make room for English families and we are doing it at the same rate. Germans live on an average of two and a half per room. An apartment like ours would have to house 16. Five German families have to be evicted to make room for one French or English one. It's really a cockeyed world.

I think I'll get rested this week of freedom from travel and [of] regular hours. Last week was terrific.

I'll call you from Washington as soon as I get in. That will be any time between a week from tonight, Sept. 27, or two weeks from tonight. I hope it won't be later than Wednesday.

I am getting terribly homesick, spiritually, physically. Longing for you and for the children in different dimensions of my existence. I want to give the old boy some real time if possible. I have a little wood cart from Oberammergau for his birthday. Now I must try to find something comparable for the old girl.

Love,

Yours,

R.N.

Nine

1947
Teaching and Preaching in the
Churches and Universities
of Northern Europe

After the war, Reinhold was bombarded with invitations from European universities, theological colleges, church groups, and political groups to speak and to meet with their representatives and leaders. Such invitations came from England, Scotland, Holland, Switzerland, the Netherlands, Denmark, and Sweden, where he was supposed to have given the Olaf Petri Lectures in September 1939, but the outbreak of war, of course, cancelled that occasion. They were held in the spring of 1947.

Edinburgh, Scotland
Saturday, February 1, 1947

Dearest:

I am writing this from the guest room of Rev. Walton where I came yesterday because they expected me here in Edinburgh for the weekend. I am to preach at St. Cuthbert's tomorrow. My lectures begin at Glasgow on Tuesday and will run until the 11th. I will get the degree on Feb. 27th in a special convocation. Better not speak about that in the old boy's presence because I don't want him to talk about it around the seminary.—Had an uneventful trip. A strong tail wind brought us to Newfoundland in 3½ hours and so we waited there for almost three hours in order not to arrive in Scotland too early. We did arrive at Prestwick at 7 and by 10:30 I was here in Edinburgh. My address in Glasgow till Feb. 11th will be Belhaven Hotel. After that the Aberdeen address.

I am trying to reconstruct my schedule so that I can be back by April 22nd. I don't think I need miss anything essential except the Cambridge lecture. I don't feel like staying away so long for many reasons some relating only to me and some to you and me. I still think I would like to be with you—although I bother you I am sure when I am at home—so that we could have more unhurried time together. Life is so nice with each other, and time as we so frequently have had, last summer for instance. But more of that later.

I bless you for all the preparations you made for the journey. The woolen underwear for instance and the socks are a great help because the houses are still cold. Had luncheon with the Baillies. They received your package and were tremendously pleased. It was a big package. Love to E and C. Will write more fully to you and them Monday.

> *I think of you constantly with love and contrition. Yours,*
>
> *R.N.*

Glasgow, Scotland
Wednesday, February 4, 1947

Dearest:

I am just about to go to Principal Hetherington's for dinner after taking a bath. I mention the bath because one has to steel oneself to take it. I knew the bathrooms were cold, but had forgotten how cold. All the things you acquired for me are remembered with gratitude every time I put them on. I wear the sweater all the time. I go to bed with woolen socks on and that helps a lot. With the warm clothes one manages, though it is cold. It has snowed ever since I have arrived.

Today I gave my second lecture and I think they are well received. The people are extraordinarily kind. Yesterday the monthly meeting of the Glasgow Presbytery gave me an official welcome and asked me to make a speech. Everywhere people ask about Dr. Coffin[1] who is certainly a great favorite here. I was deeply touched by the fact that the Union alumni are giving me a lunch on the 27th when I get a degree and are presenting me with a D.D. hood which I am afraid is much too much for them. I think by the way I will be content with the hood and forget about the gown. The hood is, you will remember, scarlet and white.

I have a fair amount of time to study if only I could do so without distraction of the cold. Tomorrow I will write an article for the *Spectator* on the American political situation.

I give my last lecture this week tomorrow and then come back here Monday and Tuesday for the final two. I have rewritten all of them and think I have improved them. Soon I have to start on my big chapter for the book of the Assembly of the World Council which must be completed in April. That is my main job in writing.

Have cabled to Holland asking them if I could come March 4th to 11th. I have that time free. My new schedule cuts down my stay in London somewhat but otherwise cuts down no engagements except possibly Cambridge. This allows me to get back about April 22nd. I just can't stay until May 10th. It's too long. You may not want me back earlier, but I think I would like to be and I won't have such a heavy schedule, which worries you. I would like to do some leisurely studying for a month if possible. I hope you won't mind. Wrote to the children yesterday.

I think of you constantly with love and longing.

Yours,

R.N.

1. *Henry Sloane Coffin had not only studied but also served in a church in Edinburgh. He had also preached in Glasgow and had received an honorary doctor of divinity degree from the University of Glasgow.*

Edinburgh, Scotland
Saturday, February 8, 1947

Dearest:

I finally got some lighter paper for my work so I can write longer letters. I am sitting in a suite of rooms at Prof. MacMurray's, beautifully appointed and warmer than anything I have enjoyed since arriving here. I have to work on two sermons for tomorrow morning, one at [the Reverand] Walton's and one at Morningside Church. But I'll write a little to you first.

Have received no word from you yet because the schedule was wrong. They started me in Glasgow instead of Edinburgh and your letters have gone there. I don't know whether I wrote you, but the schedule now is Feb. 10–12, Glasgow; Feb. 13–14, St. Andrews; Feb. 15–22, Aberdeen; Feb. 23–26, Edinburgh; Feb. 27 [receive] degree, etc. . . . On March 3rd I go to Holland till the 11th, March 12–21 will be London, then Switzerland, Denmark, and Sweden. I have a straight passage from Sweden to NYC April 21. This cuts out the Cambridge University lecture, but I am not willing to sacrifice three weeks away from home for that lecture.

I am with Prof. and Mrs. MacMurray for the weekend, leaving tomorrow night for Glasgow again. They have been most charming. She is an artist and I think the suite I am in is her studio. Most remarkable hospitality with everything thought of. . . .

This afternoon they had a large tea; among others Miss Cairns was there who wants to be remembered to you. . . .

Had luncheon today with Prof. Tindall of New College who was Montgomery's[1] chaplain. He brought along a very fine young colonel who was Monty's aide. They gave me some interesting sidelights on the war.

Now I must get to my sermons. I'll finish this before sending.

Sunday, Feb. 9, 1947: I've preached my sermon this morning in Walton's church and came back here for dinner with the MacMurrays who have as guests Professor Kemp Smith's successor [in the philosophy department] and Mrs. Ritchie and Kemp Smith himself. The latter sends his love to you. He is as nice as ever. I have had an hour's rest and have worked on a new sermon for tonight on the text, "And when he came unto himself" (Luke 15:17).

I have a slight cold but nothing serious. The MacMurray house has been so nice, I hate to leave.

Am looking forward to a pile of letters stored up from you. Am anxious to know how the old boy's remedial reading goes and whether the children are reasonably cooperative with their jobs and how you are. I do find these absences trying. Life was not meant to be lived in isolation. I'll try to be less isolated and preoccupied.

Much Love,

R.N.

1. *Viscount Montgomery of Alamein.*

Edinburgh, Scotland
February 13, 1947

Dearest:

I am writing almost every day. Today I write to express my joy over your letter of yesterday telling me about Christopher's reaction of relief about his language situation. I didn't realize how much the old boy's problem weighed on my mind until I received that letter and felt that his relaxation was an indication that the root of the problem has perhaps been reached, however much time it may take. I wrote him yesterday in that vein. I am sitting in Jewel Baillie's drawing room writing. Leave this afternoon for St. Andrews. Last night they had the big mass meeting on Germany but I was not good. My voice was almost gone. I have had a slight cold but it suddenly reached my vocal chords. The BBC was going to broadcast the speech but probably did not after the first sentences. Jewel has been medicating me, and Adam Burnett of St. Cuthbert's was quite touching in his solicitude. He arrived with an inhaling machine which did me a world of good. I slept all night without coughing and am fine today.

This noon I am meeting the London representative of *Time* for luncheon before going on to St. Andrews. He writes, "I have an urgent cable from my home office asking that I secure an interview with you for a 'cover story' to appear in the March 10 issue." I thought that idea was buried in view of their small story. Don't say a word to the old boy about it as I don't want him to hawk it around the student dormitories. The editor writes: "It will be a general story with the theme that mankind is entering a kind of lenten age and realizing its intense need of more compelling spiritual values."

One more thing. If enough money has come in, could you write out a check for C.A.R.E. for $30 and send it to Mrs. Meade and ask her to order three monthly packages for Dr. Dilschneider, my translator. I have just heard of his great need and my package to him ordered via Denmark did not arrive. Mrs. Meade will have all addresses. Tell Mrs. Meade to inform Dilschneider of the order. I'll write next from Aberdeen.

Much love as always,

R.

Aberdeen, Scotland
Monday, February 17, 1947

Dearest:

This is beginning my third week. I am surer than ever that it was good to cut the visit to April 20th. To have a chance to work in the library without pressure and to be home again is a kind of heaven to look forward to. I miss only the Oxford and Cambridge lectures and I have done those before and can do them again. I will lose none of the continental engagements.

I wrote from the Baillies. Since then I spoke twice at St. Andrews and then came up here on Saturday. Preached in the chapel of the university yesterday and begin my lectures this afternoon. I am staying with Prof. Taylor and his wife, who is as you may remember, a physician. They have adopted two little children, now two and four. It is a delightful family. He is the greatest expert in Scotland on the Roman basis of Scottish law and combines legal with classical and theological learning, all borne with the diffidence and modesty of a child. Quite a remarkable person who conforms better than anyone I know to the scriptural description of the harmless dove and the guile of the serpent. . . .

Tell Henry[1] I had a nice visit with his father at St. Andrews. We talked about the funny British and agreed that they had more moral and political wisdom than any other people, but it was too bad they had not learned that a stove is better than a fireplace to keep you warm. Brunner was really quite funny about it, having a sense of mission about converting his hosts, which I have long since given up. . . .

If you see Pit, you might tell him that I send greetings. My hosts are good friends of his. I have not yet called Betty Van Dusen's sister at Elgin,

---

which is some thirty miles from here. I hope to phone her some time this week.

Love,

R.N.

1. Henry Brunner; Swiss pastor studying at Union Seminary; guest at Niebuhr's apartment; son of the Swiss theologian Emil Brunner.

Aberdeen, Scotland
February 19, 1947

Dearest:

Just received your letter about Dr. Orton's examination of the old boy. . . . I find your report most interesting and on the whole encouraging. We were right about our general feeling of his lopsided development and am glad that we [are] at least on the way to correction though I suppose it will be a long process. I wonder whether Ben Bradford[1] really has the time to help with him, though it would be grand if he could.

I have a fairly easy time here, spending each morning on my typewriter. Have just had a most terrific schedule sent me from Holland, providing for two addresses at each of the universities of Leyden, Utrecht, Groningen, and Amsterdam. And a minister's conference. Most terrific. This place is not interesting and very much out of the way. But my host makes up for it. He is tremendous fellow; law professor, judge of the court of appeals, and expert on Roman law and civilization. Have already learned at lot from him.

Am having a bad time with *Time*. They are probably not consciously angling my interviews because they are so anxious to get them right, but they write as if I were a Christian "liberal." Today I had to spend hours correcting copy to send back to the young man in London. I hope the stuff won't come out too badly, but I am apprehensive.[2]

Excuse the brevity. Have to write some stuff for Ehrenstrom[3] and the World Council before I leave.

Love to the children. I hope I can find time to write them over the weekend.

Love yours,

R.N.

1. A divinity student who helped Christopher Niebuhr with his reading and writing; formerly assistant drama critic of the New York Times.   2. The cover story, written by Whittaker Chambers, was published in March 1948.   3. Nils Ehrenstrom; director of Research Office of the World Council of Churches in Geneva; author, Christian Faith and the Modern State.

Aberdeen, Scotland
February 21, 1947

Dearest:

Here it is only three weeks since I left home and it seems ages. I am really not meant for this barnstorming and already count the days to the return, though I have just two months more to go. This place is of course out of the way and the theological people are about the level of some university in Texas. But the university is very good and my host is really one of the most interesting and fine spirits I have ever met.

Had a letter from Barbara Ward. She is going to U.S.A. next week and will be in NYC beginning April 18. I told her to get in touch with you. Letter from Bishop Leslie Hunter this morning wanting me to stop off with him. Incidentally, my London address March 12–21 will be the Bonnington Hotel.

Your reports on Christopher are most interesting. Sorry I am not there to see how the new regime will work. But it probably will not show immediate results. I judge, however, from your reports that he is on the whole better than he was during the winter and has had a certain amount of release from the knowledge of what's wrong.

My cold is completely cured and I am feeling very fit. One can get used to everything and I now feel almost completely acclimatized.

Tell the old boy I liked his letter very much and also that I hope for another and one from Elisabeth. I will be most interested in hearing reports on Christopher's work. I do hope Ben Bradford is not loading up too much with this, though it is very nice if he can do it.

Your old country is in some respects in a bad way. The discipline and sense of community is marvelous. But a million men have left productive industry and almost a hundred thousand are employed in betting pools, etc., alone. The deficit in the export-import quota is considerable even with the American loan. There is fear that after the loan is exhausted living standards will sink catastrophically. The impoverishment from the war is terrific and one realizes that the Continent will not revive for decades because it is many levels below this level. U.S.A. is certainly in an enviable and spiritually unenviable position. Most of the students here simply assume that we are already a kind of fascist nation. Envy and justified criticism of our social policy are mingled in these judgments. Last night I had an interesting session with the Senate of this university and discussed all sorts of things, including our relations.

Yesterday was rather strenuous. Meeting with the divinity students at noon, my lecture at 3, the S.C.M. at 5, and the university Senate at 8. Today I have only the lecture and tomorrow morning I go to Edinburgh.

Three lectures there, two sermons on Sunday, the degree at Glasgow on the 27th, two sermons in Glasgow on March 2 and my visit is done.

Must write the children soon.
Love to them,

R.N.

Edinburgh, Scotland
February 24, 1947

Dearest:

Your letter written on the 18th arrived here Saturday the 22nd. That's pretty good. I couldn't answer because I arrived from Aberdeen and had to prepare for two sermons, one at St. George's in the morning and then at the university last night. Had a thousand students out, several hundred in a discussion period afterward. Was tired for the first time since my trip started. I am free of my cold completely and have felt very rested. Somehow the schedule is less strenuous than a regular round at home. Saturday night John [Baillie] had five professors in, one of them Prof. [Richard] Pares, the son of Sir Bernard. He was in the civil service during the war with Oliver Frank.[1] Learned much from him on how a planned economy works and what are the pitfalls. He takes a rather grim view of the future, believing that neither we nor Britain have the right answer.

Your report on Christopher is most cheering. I feel very thankful that Ben Bradford can take him on. . . . Do hope life is not too strenuous for you. Those extra affairs you have had sound rather strenuous. Had a letter from SK [Ratcliffe]. He is coming to the States on March 15. I shall miss him. I return to London on the 13th. Oldham has arranged a meeting with members of Parliament. Don't know what I ought to talk about. Just now I have to prepare an address for the Senatus of Glasgow when I receive my degree. Sir Hector Hetherington wants me to make an extended address.

Have just received my Swiss-Danish schedule. It is as follows: March 21–27, Ecumenical Institute [at Bossey]. March 28, University of Lausanne. March 28–30, Geneva University. March 31–April 1, Zurich. April 2–3, U. of Basle. April 5, U. of Copenhagen. April 8, U. of Aarhus. April 10, Sweden. How glad I am this barnstorming will be over April 21. Will have spoken in 15 European universities.

Must write the children soon.

Love,

R.N.

1. *Oxford philosopher; later British ambassador to the United States.*

Edinburgh, Scotland
February 26, 1947

Dearest:

I wrote only two days ago but this is my last day with the Baillies and I may not be able to write the next few days. They have been very kind to me and it has been nice to be with them. This afternoon I give my last lecture here and then go to Glasgow for the degree. Had a nice luncheon with Union alumni, Ebor Roberts and his wife, Bill Tyree, and Henry Pettit.

Now for some details and chores: The dean of Manchester, Dr. Garfield Williams, is anxious to come to America possibly next fall or winter in order to visit the parents of a GI who is engaged to his daughter, a doctor and his wife in Cortland, NY. He is a good friend of John Baillie's and John suggested to him that if he could take six weeks off he might get enough preaching engagements to pay his way, which is an important item. He is a former medical missionary who went into the ministry or, as is more proper to say, took Holy Orders. John says he is a first class preacher and belongs to the evangelical wing. I wonder whether you could let Miss Pratt know or even possibly Bishop Gilbert[1] directly because I am sure that he and Pit Van Dusen could make very good use of such a visitor in various places.

John will be speaking in our summer conference the last week of July. I have invited him to stay with us. He is hesitant and says that Pit will offer the "prophet's chamber,"[2] but will you put that down on our calendar? We may not be there but probably will if we stick to studying as usual in NYC in July. Also, Adam Burnett will be in NYC the first week in August and I would like to offer him a room even if we are absent. Is that all right?

Last night Canon V. A. Demant expounded my *Nature and Destiny* for 15 minutes on the BBC in a series of five talks on modern theology. It was done with real distinction. I wouldn't have known about it, but several people at my lecture called my attention to the BBC announcement. Incidentally, Demant must have been in touch with Wystan Auden for he described me as looking like a benevolent eagle.

My letter was broken off because a man came to interview me and right after I had to go downtown for a luncheon, then the final lecture at 2:30, tea with the Union students, back to John and Jewel's, supper, and a taxi ride through a terrific blizzard to the station which required 35 minutes; the trip to Glasgow, another long fight for a taxi, and finally arrived the hotel at 11:30. After a good night's sleep, I feel very well. I have the luxury of a heated room though the temperature is only about 50°. But that is a great boon. The public rooms on the other hand are cold because they are heated with electricity.

The cable from you, Christopher, and Elisabeth just arrived [celebrating the honorary degree]. It is very good of you to remember me today. I won't be able to finish this letter now because I must go off for lunch, then the degree, and then dinner with the faculty.

Here is the final installment. Met with the Union alumni at 12 for a cup of tea. At 1, they presented me with the hood at the luncheon of the entire student body of the divinity school. I met again with them from 2 to 3. The degree ceremony was at 3:30, very nice and formal and then informal, ending with a tea party. Then a dinner with the divinity faculty. I have just arrived home at 8:30, having left at 12:30. Ralph Barton Perry from Harvard was specially invited, the only outsider. Otherwise the whole thing was in camera with only the University Senate present. I haven't been at the Fordyces', but she sends special regards. This finishes my engagements except for two sermons here on Sunday, one in the morning in the university chapel and in the evening at the Wellington Church. I fly to Holland at 8 A.M. on Monday, leaving here at 6 A.M. and have to be in Prestwick on time for that.

Except for the cold, the four weeks have been enjoyable. I have many good friends here and they have all been most kind. I have not suffered too much from the cold thanks to your forethought. Right now I am writing this in a tolerably warm hotel room. The blizzard which started yesterday morning was no more than a very heavy snow of the kind we often have. It was heavy. I had twice to help my taxi last night to get out of a drift. But I am in excellent health. I am really tired for the first time due to two evening meetings in Edinburgh which left me sleepless but I will sleep long tonight.

Your two letters of the 20th and 22nd awaited me on my arrival here and I read them even before taking off my overcoat. It was good to have them and know that on the whole things are well. I got the old girlie's letter just before I sent her a postcard which probably won't arrive for weeks. It was a nice letter and I was glad to hear about the splendid movie of the dog.

Ralph Barton Perry has almost an obsession about the heatless character of British homes. To hear him talk you would think he is on an arctic expedition, and he never takes off his scarf. Have had some interesting talks with various faculty people in economics, etc., and I gather that the future here is pretty grim. Everyone is only gradually recognizing that the nation is really greatly impoverished. Living standards at the moment are being maintained by the American loan and no one knows quite what will happen when the payments cease. What is a bagatelle to us is a matter of life and death here. I am sure that Geoffrey Wilson is right and Patrick Gordon Walker is wrong. The people here don't want to bear the burdens of empire any longer. They have become too heavy. They will not quite become a Sweden because the Dominion commitments are important. But they are anxious to live comfortably without too many imperial harassments. Meanwhile, Prof. Pares says that British industry has allowed plants to run down for 30 years and this partly the fault of the unions which have never allowed a two-shift day, which is common in U.S.A., and which alone makes expensive new machinery viable.

But no more of this. It was really very nice to get the cable. Much love to you and the two. How glad I am that it is only two more months. But that is a long time. I don't know why I ever thought I could stay until June.

Would you ask Mrs. Meade to send the Freedom of the Press Commission Report on the Moving Pictures to: George Singleton, Esq., The Anchorage, Upper Bourtree Drive, Burnside, Rutherglen, Scotland. The copies are paperbound and there are about six of them stuck away on one of the shelves. He is the movie magnet who invited me to his home here on my last visit.

Also would she write to Jim Loeb[3] to let David Williams in London know that I will arrive in London March 12 and that my address will be Bonnington Hotel, Southampton Row. I thought I had Williams'[s] address and told Jim so but I do not have it and he must know when I will be in London.

I will have tomorrow and Saturday to work on my World Council chapter which is all the serious work I have done.

This must go.

R.N.

1. Bishop Charles K. Gilbert; suffragan bishop, later Episcopal of New York; a summer neighbor in Heath. Miss Pratt was his secretary.   2. Union Seminary's guest rooms.
3. James Loeb was executive secretary of the Americans for Democratic Action, a liberal lobby group that he and R.N. and others helped to found.

Glasgow, Scotland

Saturday Night
March 1, 1947

Dearest:

This is my last letter from Scotland. As I won't have a chance to write tomorrow I'll send this word today. Tomorrow I preach at the university in the morning, have dinner with Principal Hetherington and then in the evening at Wellington, and supper after the service with the Rev. and Mrs. Jarvis. I will come straight back after that and go to bed as I leave at 6:30 in the morning for Prestwick and Holland.

I have just come up from a long after dinner talk with Ralph Barton Perry who is very good company. We sit together at the dining table. I spent the day writing stuff for Religious News Service and the *British Weekly* and getting started on my World Council chapter. I had hoped to finish this during my Scottish visit but have only just started it. This is the only place which has been warm enough to make work in a room possible.

Of all the really funny things in Britain the cold bathrooms are the worst. This hotel for instance is heated but not the bathroom, the one room where one is completely exposed. Funny, Perry never quite gets over this. Refers to the incongruity again and again.

Yesterday the students of divinity called me and asked whether I would spend the afternoon with them as they had assumed I was scheduled to do only to find that the Presbytery had scheduled me for March 28th instead of February 28th. I do not know who made the mistake by one month but instead of meeting the large group of parsons and students, I met the students alone and had a very good time. The theological teaching here with the exception of Edinburgh seems uninspired and fairly irrelevant, and the students are more eager and on the mark than the professors. At least that seemed true at Aberdeen and Glasgow.

Had a nice note from Peggy Benn today re my degree. Will be with them on March 17th. I sent Elisabeth's letter on to Jewel and John because John had told Jewel so much about the old girl. I hope Christopher continues in good spirits. I will write Ben Bradford shortly, but I hope you can tell him that I share your gratitude for taking this on.

I am over here just 30 days and 50 more days to go. It is a long time. I dread to think that even after the Holland engagement I am only halfway through. But all things come to an end and the homecoming will be a great joy.

Much love and paternal greetings to the children. I sent each a card today.

Yours,

R.N.

Utrecht, Holland
March 5, 1947

Dearest:

This is written in a hotel in Utrecht after finishing speaking to the theological students and before my general lecture. I haven't been able to sit down for even a word to you since leaving Glasgow. On Monday we tried to land at Amsterdam but there was fog and we went to Brussels. We tried again in the afternoon and returned to Brussels for the night. We left again at 9 on Tuesday, landed at Amsterdam at 10:30, took a train to Leyden at 11:30. I spoke to the S.C.M. at 12:30, to the university at 8, stayed with Dr. Kraemer[1] for the night and came on here this morning, arriving at 12:30 and speaking again at 2. I have this two addresses a day for all four universities, but they had about three other small engagements a day and I rebelled. Mrs. [Ellen] Flesseman is travelling with me for the week as interpreter, guide, and secretary. She makes all arrangements and that is a great help. She also insisted on cutting the schedule and I will be all right. But the week will be strenuous at best.

Holland is very formal. Everywhere I am met by the student executive committee in frock coats and with badges of office something like an English Lord Mayor. Then in the evening the whole University Senate is present in wing collar, etc. Very formal introductions and very formal everything. They are very friendly, however, and treat me as a sort of VIP. The religion seems to me an extraordinarily straight-laced Calvinism, but there are some very fine spirits among students and professors. It's really quite an experience. I dread to think of similar proprieties in Switzerland, Denmark, and Sweden. I probably appear like a middle-western yahoo to them. —Here I was interrupted by a radio man who wanted me to speak ten minutes on the radio. So I lost my chance to finish the letter. Then I went to give the university lecture. Before speaking I had to shake hands with 15 presidents of the various student organizations, all bedecked with their badges of office and also the deans of the various faculties who made a deep bow. It was really quite an experience. I gave my lecture and afterwards had to confer with the young man who is translating *Nature and Destiny* into Dutch. The last two books *Children of Light* and *Discerning the Signs* are completed and will be published this month. So for the moment I make a peculiar stir here. Dutch Calvinism seems to be on the level of 17th century legalistic Puritanism and I gather that one of my tasks is to challenge this legalism for people like Kraemer and Banning. I did that with a vengeance tonight.

I still haven't had a chance to write to Ben. I will do so in the morning if I possibly can find a moment. I am sorry my letters have lacked marginal stuff. But the schedule has become terrific. I do so feel encouraged by your reports on the old boy. He seems to have already profited greatly, whatever the further outcome for him.

I can't tell you how lonely I get and how I count the days. When I finish this week I will be half-through. That's something. Give my love to the children. I am sending them a card from here. Leave by car in the morning for a four-hour drive to Groningen. Saturday night I meet some of the Dutch cabinet at dinner. And so it goes.

Much love,

R.N.

1. *Dr. Hendrick Kraemer; well-known Dutch theologian, expert on Christian work in the Third World.*

Utrecht, Holland
March 6, 1947

Dearest:

Have just a moment before we push off to Groningen. It is very good of you to get those food parcels for my hosts and the children's things for the Thomas Taylors in Aberdeen. It wouldn't have been necessary to get the parcels as I did buy extra fruit for them as I went along. That is now plentiful at a price, most of it coming from South Africa. But it will be nice for them to have it. . . .

I like the old girl's long view of things. She sounds like Prof. Shapley of Harvard with whom I once debated at Town Hall. He was supposed to be the optimist and I the pessimist but it turned out that he agreed with me for the next ten thousand years but had astronomical years to console him for his optimism afterwards. [Elisabeth was studying at school what was called "Life on the Planet" and she asked rather charmingly, "Have you studied life?" and she also carried with this quite a critical view of some Bible stories; we were intrigued with her picture of biblical criticism and astronomical time in point of view of "life."]

Do you think it might be possible without too much expense or bother to send me two cartons of cigarettes airmail to Switzerland? They ought not to go to the World Council but to the Institute at Bossey where I will be the first week from March 21st on. Cigarettes are very expensive here and are useful to give away. . . .

I must tell you again how all the clothes you bought have helped. I haven't been without the sweater a single day since arriving. Holland is warmer than Britain. Coal is short but is put in stoves rather than fireplaces so there is a little warmth in every room heated. But I do need the clothes. I needed an extra pair of underwear because laundries require two weeks to do the work. Jewel kindly gave me a pair of John's which he never uses. He sticks stoically to BVDs.

These lonely hotel rooms are a trial. I keep on wanting to talk things over with you and I don't want to sleep alone. I won't make a trip like this again for a very, very long time.

All my love,

R.N.

Amsterdam, Holland
March 8, 1947

Dearest:

I have had a good night's sleep in a nice hotel here and feel very good. I have finished my tour of the universities. This morning I must talk to the ministers of Amsterdam and then this evening go for the weekend to a ministers' conference. Sunday night I meet the politicos in The Hague. Last night I gave the university lecture at the University of Amsterdam to the largest audience, about a thousand people. The strain of adjusting oneself to these new audiences each day is considerable. Yesterday besides, I drove 6 hours from the University of Groningen to get to my appointments here. I had foolishly neglected to tell them that I wanted to stay in hotels and they had me dated each night at a different professor's house. If it hadn't been for Mrs. Flesseman, I don't know what I would have done. She insisted that these private appointments be cancelled and made reservations at hotels. I suppose some hard feelings were left, but at least I survived. She also insisted on the cancellation of innumerable tea, etc., engagements sandwiched in with my two lectures. They really have given me a strenuous week and for that matter there are four days still to go.

Last night I had dinner at the Flessemans'. He has reestablished his private law practice. But he has no confidence in Europe and is thinking of coming to America. He is coming on a visit next week and you may see him as he wants to bring Elisabeth a pair of wooden Dutch shoes. If he brings them, tell Christopher that this is my present for Elisabeth and that I will bring him his special present from Sweden. I don't know of anything particular to get for him here.

I am grateful that I am almost halfway through my schedule. I almost dread to go back to cold Britain now. It is cold here too, but the hotels are warm. But I did adjust myself quickly enough in Britain and will do so again.

The Dutch religious life is interesting. The pastors are exceedingly well trained, very theological, and either Barthian or strictly Calvinist. Barthianism is actually a very good leaven against the strict Puritanism of Calvinism which exists here in a much more rigorous and I should say more arid form than in Scotland. Yet in a way it is more profound than Scottish theology, which seems to me more sentimental. It is rather a shock however to see the beautiful medieval churches taken over and made into Calvinist meeting houses. In Scotland the cathedrals are still cathedrals but not here. The choir here, which is sometimes very beautiful, is shut off and used as a separate room, mostly for communion services. The remaining church is very bare.

My visit here has been rather curious because three of my books appeared here in translation during the month. So that the visit was accompanied with a kind of fanfare.

> *Give my love to the children. I think of you and them with gratitude, love, and longing.*
>
> R.N.

Amsterdam, Holland
March 11, 1947

Dearest:

I have forgotten when I wrote you last because I have been on such a terrific schedule. Today I was to be at Twente for my final day. But yesterday I spoke to the ministers of The Hague in the morning, to a very plushy group of businessmen at noon, and to the ministers of Rotterdam in the evening. I was exhausted. I suddenly said to myself, why should I kill myself in this way? I have weeks to go. So I simply told them that I was too fatigued to finish my final day. Mrs. Flesseman, who has tried to save me as much as possible, rather added spice by upbraiding the officials for my too heavy schedule. This was rather unnecessary though justified enough. At any rate, I have had the day free here in a nice hotel in Amsterdam. I arrived at 11, had luncheon, and then slept till 3:30. Now I had a little walk and will do letters till supper. I fly to Britain tomorrow at noon. But this almost two days of rest will be a great help.

I am sorry for a slightly sour note at the end because the trip has been most interesting and instructive. I wrote about the universities, I think. I think I also wrote about the large meeting in Amsterdam. Then I spent a weekend with the strict Calvinists who had a retreat in a beautiful mission school. They were very nice. I was expected to shock them out of their literalism, being invited by a few of their theologians who would like to move away from literalism but find it difficult. Of course, the discussion was fairly abstruse, dealing very much with whether the perfection before the fall was a period in history.

My most interesting meeting thus far was on Sunday night with the leaders of the Labor Party. It was a grand meeting of genuine proletarians and church leaders which promises something really new. Kraemer has been one of the organizers of the party. He is really a great man. I enclose a note to Jim Loeb about it. Would [you] have Mrs. Meade send it on to Jim? I also enclose a self-explanatory note for Bill Savage.

After Sunday night, I had that difficult Monday I reported above and here I am at the end of the tour. If all the other national visits are a little less strenuous and as profitable, the whole trip will be very much worthwhile. One does get an insight into the continental situation. The reason for my large crowds is quite sobering. I am being used as an alternative to Karl Barth by those who do not want Barth's transcendentalism. Brunner's political ethic is too bourgeois for them and that is where I seem to come in. I talked to the ministers of Amsterdam, The Hague, and Rotterdam and in each case began purely theologically with a final ethical application, attacking Calvinist legalism and the idea of Christian political parties. The one here is as old as the Catholic ones and has the same philosophy behind it. Though 75% of the ministers belong to the party and only the leaders have joined the new Labor Party, I was received with great friendliness and the questions were friendly and searching. It was good fun.

I'll probably not send this letter until I arrive in London tomorrow and have had a chance to read your mail there.

[R.N.]

London, England
March 13, 1947

Dearest:

I arrived last night and found your three letters awaiting me and I hardly took off my coat before reading them. I do hope you are getting hold of some help, for you are obviously doing much too much with your job and the problem of the children and visitors. I do feel rather mean being away when I might be of some help if I were at home, though I am not really sure if I am very good at that. Your report of the Toynbees is most interesting. I knew there was something wrong about the religion of his former wife. Her action is a complete expression of St. John of the Cross'[s] ideas. I am sorry I miss him here.

Arrived yesterday in a driving rain and had a nice evening with the bishop of Sheffield[1] at the Atheneum. Told him about Will Scarlett because he wanted to know which of our bishops would be most congenial to his interests.—Incidentally, I had a long cable from Cliff Stanley, saying that the Virginia Episcopal Seminary would like to conduct a big campaign for expansion and needs the help of the Diocese of NY. He wants me to write to Bishop Gilbert, asking for his cooperation. I feel it would be quite pretentious for me to do that, mixing in these Episcopal matters and making demands on Bishop Gilbert. Perhaps you could talk with Miss Pratt and ask what could be done. I would gladly express my conviction that Virginia Seminary is the most vital one in the church, at this time.

Today I have had a flood of letters and telephone calls. Tonight I speak to a non-partisan meeting of the House of Commons with R. A. Butler[2] in the chair. It will be a difficult meeting. What can I say that would be profitable? Tomorrow I spend the day with the S.C.M. and the evening with the Christian Frontier. Saturday I have dinner with your cousin Bernard. On Monday with Wedgwood and Peggy. Tuesday and Wednesday I go to the World Council. Thursday night I have dinner with Dick Crossman who just telephoned. I can't get to see half the people I would like to. I don't know what to do about Stafford Cripps, but he is so busy that it mightn't be possible. His star is rising, incidentally, as he has gained great prestige during the [shortage of food and fuel] crisis. Harold Nicholson has joined the Labour Party. Halifax, after defeating the Tory motion of censure on India, is also a possible recruit for the party, so Bishop Hunter tells me.

After two good nights of sleep, I am restored from the exhaustion of my Dutch trip. This hotel is warm and comfortable though the rooms are very small. Incidentally, the cold seems over. This morning spring is in the air and everyone is breathing a relieved sigh. It has been a winter for these poor people.—Glad you provided me with so much laundry. Here in London, the laundry takes three weeks. If Jewel had not taken care of me in Scotland and Mrs. Flesseman's maid in Holland, I would be out. The Flessemans incidentally were most kind. Are thinking of coming back to America if he can find the right kind of a job. He is a lawyer in Holland but in America would have to help her uncle's business affairs. The uncle [a Van Leer] incidentally is one of the richest men in Holland and departed yesterday just before my plane in a private plane to inspect his factories all over the world. I met the group in the London Airport again, eight crew members in all. Very pretentious.

I didn't have a chance to write about the dinner at the Flessemans' house but it deserves mention. At the head of the table was her old Jewish father, a very nice man who has become converted I suppose from her influence, though his brother, the millionaire, is a Zionist. Next to me was the most prominent Barthian clergyman of Holland, a really nice man with a merry twinkle in his eye with whom I was a complete ally because we both oppose Calvinist legalism and he felt that I had aided them in their battle on it. The conversation switched between theology, politics, and Jewish affairs. Her husband is much abler than I had known and has a large law firm here of seven partners.

I am skipping about in this letter I know, running from one thing to another. It's just that one wants to share large and small impressions and the written word is never quite adequate. How much the two become one in marriage so that all of this would be so much more fun if shared. We'll do it that way next summer.

From London: I have been to the House [of Commons] and made my speech. About 20 MPs showed up, mostly conservatives though the invitation was signed by Tom Driberg, a fellow-travelling Anglo-Catholic, and John Edwards, who has just been made junior minister. Had a discussion which was quite good and R. A. Butler was, as last summer, extravagant in his generous remarks. He and his wife are coming to America in May, and he wants to come and see us. I don't think the meeting was really worth much.

Will have to try to do another 3rd Program broadcast as per enclosed invitation. I'll have to devote Sunday to it. That is my only chance. I note that this letter is terribly incoherent, jumping from one thing to another, but that may be symbolic of this kind of incoherent life. My speech finished any set speeches until I start in Geneva ten days hence. All the rest is committee work here and personal interviews. Sorry I won't get to Oxford and Cambridge, but we can do that the next summer together.

Please tell the old boy that I greatly appreciated his letter. On second thought I had better add word for him and I might encourage Elisabeth to write also. Tell her I would be willing to put up even with a strident voice to be back in the family bosom. Her threat of divorce is a marvelous new strategy, impotent defiance, and shows just what the spiritual problems of weak against the strong is. They hope to divide the strong. My love and best wishes to friends who may inquire, especially Paul and Lila Scherer, the Muilenbergs, etc.[3] Have just written to John, also to Pit from Scotland.

Here I am through the sixth week with only five to go. This will be the last long separation.

I long for you when separated.

R.N.

1. *Bishop Leslie Hunter of Sheffield had established a program of industrial chaplains. Bishop Scarlett had participated in labor negotiations and bargaining sessions.* 2. *Tory member of the House of Commons who had been minister of education. After the Conservatives rejected him as leader he became Lord Butler of Saffron Walden.* 3. *Colleagues and friends at Union Seminary.*

Bonnington Hotel
London, England
March 18, 1947

Dearest:

I wrote you a rather stupid letter on Sunday. I was down with a cold and stayed in bed all day. Geoffrey Wilson was awfully nice. He came in the afternoon with grapes, oranges, etc., more than I could use and dropped in again yesterday morning to make sure I was all right. The day in bed cured me and I am all right. I was almost bound to come down after the Holland trip. He and I are having luncheon with Stafford and Isobel this noon. Last night I spent with the Benns. It was, as usual, delightful. Anthony [Benn] came down from Oxford especially for the evening. He has just become president of the Oxford Union and also chairman of the debating team. He is as fine a youngster as you could find anywhere. He would like to come to America and is trying to arrange a tour of his Oxford team in American colleges this summer. I don't know whether enough good colleges are open to make that possible. Would also like to come over and study for a year. He thinks he isn't good enough for a Commonwealth Fellowship and I will try when I get back to see whether some kind of scholarship can be wangled. We spent the first part of the evening talking about Peggy's almost consuming concern about the place of women in the church. She informs me that Bishop Hall did not acquiesce in the resignation of the Chinese woman preacher [Lei Tim Oi], that it was forced upon her by the SPG [Society for Propagation of the Gospel], which threatened to cut off aid if she did not resign and that Bishop Hall intends to do it all over again.[1] Peggy is very determined and is becoming the center of the whole movement over here. She was in Scotland, while I was there, at a woman's conference and I heard repercussions of her visit everywhere in the university communities where [those] like Mrs. Forrester, the wife of one of the St. Andrews professors, sang her praises.

The final hours of the evening were spent on international politics with Anthony and I taking an identical line against David [Benn] and Wedgewood. Wedgewood thinks Wallace's doctrine[2] is just about right. We had a terrific debate lasting for hours. Anthony actually argues with much greater sophistication than his father, or so it seemed to me, probably because I agreed with him. It is really about the nicest family anywhere.

On Thursday morning I am doing a long third program broadcast again on "A Foreigner's Appreciation of Britain's Contribution to Current Political Thought and Life." Have just about finished it.

The rest of my program is: Tomorrow luncheon with Kenneth Lindsay who is now National Labor MP and interested in Germany, tea with Wilson Harris [editor of the *Spectator*], and dinner with a crowd gathered by Christian [R.N.'s London publisher]. Thursday BBC broadcast in the morning, luncheon with Canon Demant, tea with Christian Frontier, and dinner in the House of Commons with Dick Crossman.

I do get terribly homesick. Yesterday I had an awful sense of being separated from you and reliving in memory the experiences we had together over here. . . . Do you do things like that? Not much more than four weeks to go. I was a fool for signing up for as much as this. Haven't see the *Time* people so I don't know anything about their chucking me. But I am just as well pleased because I didn't like the stuff they showed me. It was angled.

Much love,

R.N.

Tuesday afternoon: Just back from luncheon with Stafford and Isobel. Stafford was very nice, more relaxed than on my last visit. Didn't orate but talked very quietly. He's conscious of his great responsibilities [as chancellor of the exchequer] and is a little worried. Asked many questions about American leaders including Wallace, whom he rightly estimates though personally fond of him. Isobel is unfortunately drawn in a little into the Oxford Group business [Buchmanism]. Tried to convince me that the play they are putting on here is significant. Geoffrey and I were amused. She is bitter about the church, saying there is no leadership since William Temple's death. Spoke of how Beaver, Attlee's ecclesiastical secretary, makes bad appointments of bishops because no one has time to consider the matter and she and Stafford intervened only once to assure the appointment of a good bishop. Geoffrey and I walking through to my Strand bank afterwards indulged our non-conformist ire over a church which makes so many pretensions about the episcopacy but allows establishment in which this important office is determined by a minor clerk in the Cabinet. Geoffrey will begin his Cabinet work next week. [He was appointed secretary to the Cabinet.]

Do try to take things a little easier which means you must get more help even if it means trying to find a full-time person. What shall it profit if you have a job you enjoy but kill yourself in the doing of it?

Must now get to work upon my course at the Bossey Ecumenical Institute. The address, incidentally, though you probably have it now is: Institute Oecuminique, Chateau de Bossey, par Celigny, Switzerland. I'll be there until April 1st.

Incidentally, Stafford sends special greetings to Christopher and of course both the Stansgates and the Cripps send love to you. Stafford wanted to know: "How is my part of the Niebuhr family?" [meaning Elisabeth, his goddaughter.] I gave him a good account of the old boy. Isobel thinks it would be foolish to try to find a house over here next year. Thinks we ought to have freedom to move and suggests spending a month at a comfortable hotel at the seaside. I think we must come alone and not try to bring the family.

Love,

R.N.

1. *Lei Tim Oi withdrew as a priest in Macao and resumed her diaconal duties.*
2. *Secretary of Commerce Henry A. Wallace was regarded by many as too sympathetic with the Soviet Union.*

London, England
March 20, 1947

Dearest:

My typewriter ribbon is used up and I must wait to get a new one in Switzerland. I did my broadcast this morning and have just waved Oldham and Bliss[1] off after a final session on our document [for the World Council of Churches]. Now I only have to see Crossman for dinner and tomorrow morning I'm off.

Yesterday I had a sort of revulsion against this whole trip and wondered why I ever made it. I have not too many years left for scholarly work and from that standpoint these months are wasted.

Thinking like this I went to Christian's dinner and there met Dean Smyth, just come from Cambridge to be dean of Westminster Abbey. He is one of those friends one has never met.[2] Walking home together he said:

"Would you mind a word of advice? I don't think you ought to do these kinds of trips too often. We are expecting you to do a few things for us which can't be done while you use up your energies like this."

It fitted in so much with my own day's reflection that it deepened my gloom. He was incidentally extremely good, and Canon Demant tells me he is one of the most intelligent men in the church. I discovered though at the dinner that Christian was going to bring out my *Leaves* having asked Demant to write an introduction. This made me angry and I wrote today forbidding it, though Smyth was strongly in favor and had written the opinion on it for Christian. I don't think it should be done, do you not agree with me?

Your letter just arrived. So glad to hear about Ed Cherbonnier.[3] One gets attached to some people so much that it feels almost as if one's son had carried off an honor, and I feel this about him. Glad the children are still giving such a good account of themselves. Could you possibly, if you haven't done so, drop Mother and Hulda a line telling them about how the children are. I think it would mean a lot to them.

The man from *Time* called up to say that the cover story would appear for Easter, but don't say anything about it because it may not. It wasn't Arnold Toynbee, incidentally, who displaced me but General Marshall, that was the issue. The office here put days on the story. But I don't trust the quality too much.

So glad John [Bennett] asked you to write for *Christianity & Crisis*. I wish I could have heard your sermon, and I hope this will start a new era of preaching for you.

> My love to the children and my
> longing for you. Four weeks to go.
>
> R.N.

1. *Kathleen Bliss; editor of* Christian Newsletter. 2. *U.N. had met Dean Smyth earlier at Cambridge and had liked him. R.N. did not always know her acquaintances, friends, and relatives.* 3. *Edmund Cherbonnier; a Union Seminary student from St. Louis, MO; won the traveling fellowship for 1947–48.*

New York, [NY]
Lent, 1947

Sunday Night

Dearest:

I hope your journey was not too bumpy? I do find your disappearings just as bad as ever. The tension between—

"They who one another keepe
alive, ne'er parted bee."

And—

"When I dyed last, and, deare, I dye
as often as from thee I goe."

Goes on even though we do hope to "keepe one another alive."

And it's so queer to have our family reduced to Elisabeth and me—too.

Elisabeth and I went to Evensong. She was out in the Quadrangle in overalls and jacket playing football with the boys and a couple of students happily—and I called her in just after 3:30. She was annoyed and "foul of mouth," which I paid no attention to, and we took a bus to 112th Street in silence.

She popped out of the bus happily and put her hand in mine, and sat good and wrapt, and followed the service carefully. The music was, as ever, pure and lovely, and young Canon West read the lessons clearly, and we could hear service and lessons. Then we skipped home, a little chilly and had tea—supper by the fire.

She was all agog to learn the Catechism, and we had a couple of hours' instruction—on the Hebrew law, and its relation to Egyptian ethics and religion and Babylon. She is *frightfully* quick and quite saw the contrast between the earlier polytheism of Egypt and Hebrew henotheism and ethical relationship. (The monotheism of Iknaton too.)

Then she got down to the Catechism, and lapped it up. She was convulsed over my explanation of "the devil, and all his works and pomps and vanities," and "the lust of the flesh"—the latter which I interpreted as egoism and selfishness, which made her liable to be taken in by pomps, vanities, etc.

After our discussion on that, she said, "But that was all done at my baptism—let's get on to where I am now!" She discovered she was to know the Articles of Religion, "but I've got four or five years for that!" She loves the Creed. . . . So you might know I don't neglect her education.

Love as ever. Your own,

Ursula

**Ecumenical Institute
Bossey, Switzerland
March 23, 1947**

Dearest:

I am writing this on Sunday morning, immediately after Anglican communion with continental Lutheran trimmings. Very nice. After two

days of rain, the sun is out and the place is beautiful. From my window I
see the lake and beyond the snow-covered Alps. I have to speak only once
a day so will get a lot of rest. Virginia Markham sends her love. Her young
man, Howard Johnson, studying Kierkegaard in Denmark, is here for a
week. The student body numbers 37 and represents 15 nationalities. My
first address was pretty much a failure I think but the next will be more
en rapport with the students, for I have since met many of them. They are
a fine lot. Ten are German. The cigarettes arrived and I have a bad conscience for bothering you and for the expense because they certainly cost
a lot to transport. So loved your letter and that of the old girl's. It is so
nice to know that both she and Christopher are making progress in every
way. It will be such fun to get back and see their development.

I had a most interesting session on Thursday night in the House of
Commons with Crossman and Michael Foot[1] and a group they invited.
We talked international affairs and I went after Crossman for the new left-
ist isolationism of the *New Statesman* and *Nation*. He was most amiable but
not altogether honest I think because his line with me is different than his
line in the paper. The relations between us and Britain are going to be
difficult at best because the shock in Britain in the gradual discovery of
the economic plight of the country is producing a great deal of resentment
against us even when not merited. On this issue I find Geoffrey Wilson
more understanding than anyone. Incidentally, I gave Geoffrey my tan
shoes and sent some of my winter underwear to Prof. Taylor after washing
it out myself after a fashion. Even so I was much overweight as continental
air limit is 45 pounds. I am sending my winter overcoat back via Visser
t'Hooft. This whole crowd is leaving for America on April 2nd and this
makes me homesick.

My schedule is: Here at the Institute until March 27th; Lausanne,
March 28th; Geneva, March 29–30th; Zurich, March 31st; Basle, April 2–
3rd; April 4th, free day; April 5th, Copenhagen; April 6th, Easter with
Prof. Skysgaard[2] at Copenhagen. April 7th, public lecture in Copenhagen;
April 8th, university lecture in Aarhus at 4 P.M. and public lecture at 8.

Back to Copenhagen and university lecture there on April 9th. Sweden, public lecture at Lund University on April 10th. University lecture at
Uppsala begins on April 11th. Have only six lectures in ten days. That
will be an easy close. Incidentally, haven't spent any money of my own but
this Swiss trip will cost a lot as they seem to think I am doing this all for
my health. But that won't be too bad. Had a nice letter from Henry Brunner in which he made references to your having helped to get him back
to civilized society after bachelor existence. He says he enjoys Christopher
very much. I do think that between Bradford and a little help from Brun-

ner the old boy has had better male companionship than from his father. Hope to hear soon that you have help for yourself. You must not so consistently overwork. Have bought Martin D'Arcy's *Mind and Heart of Love* and am studying it carefully evenings, my first chance to study since I came on this trip. Hope to stay put for a week.

Much love to you all,

R.N.

1. *Labour Member of Parliament, later their Parliamentary leader.*   2. *Leader of the new Labor Party in Parliament and also a publisher.*

Ecumenical Institute
Bossey, Switzerland
March 26, 1947

Dearest:

I got your letter with the report of the Toynbee cocktail party and Elisabeth's very nice letter to her hard-working mother. I have the feeling from your letter that the children are really easier than in past months and this is nice to know. Evidentally both are developing. I am now getting into my fourth week before the close. The weeks become longer however as I become more anxious. Have given my third lecture here today. Tomorrow (Wednesday) many of the students are leaving and I don't know whether the Thursday lecture will be given or not. I came in just at the end. It's a most interesting group once you get to know them. I have talked particularly with the 10 German students, including Bishop Dibelius'[s] assistant, several pastors who were in the Resistance, and Christopher Dehn, the son of a well-known Barthian resister, Gunter Dehn, who was in the Nazi Party against his father's wishes and now is trying to find himself. I find the Germans nice and eager but difficult. They're so full of biblical lore, biblicist literalism, refined theological distinctions, etc., that they can't see the wood for the trees. All the ability and pathos of German scholarship is apparent in them. One could almost long for an old-fashioned liberal, if he had imagination. Liberals do not have imagination, of course. But the imagination is lacking here in another way. Every total view of biblical truth seems to escape them, and every synoptic conception is foreign. Above all they empty the Scripture of meaning because they consider only the ultimate issue. Lutheranism is really not a good version of the Christian faith. Young Howard Johnson who is here from Denmark tells me that the Scandinavians are almost as bad.

Last night we had dinner with the Mackies in Geneva [Robert Mackie was secretary of the World Student Christian Federation] and a committee meeting afterwards. Tomorrow I go to Geneva again to meet with the Study Commission. On Friday I will speak in Zurich at a public meeting arranged by Brunner. Will you tell Henry if I have not said anything about it before how much I appreciate his letter? I think you pulled the pedagogical stunt off with him very well. He seems in very good spirits. Visser t'Hooft and the whole lot are off next week to New York City. T'Hooft is bringing my winter overcoat so that I won't have to drag it all over Scandinavia. Will you give him the article in the *Nation* on the Dutch Labor Party which King Gordon [editor of *The Nation*] promised to publish in a letter I had from him today. T'Hooft was disappointed that I didn't mention it in my *Christianity & Crisis* report, but I did not want to duplicate. If I have time at the end of the week, I will write an article for the *Nation* on British-American relations, which will be critical for a long while because the shift in power has been great. I have never felt that political wisdom and the technical backwardness of Britain so much. Stafford Cripps made a speech the other day and said there would be no coal crisis if Britain had discovered in time that fireplaces waste 85% of the coal! The discovery comes too late, however, because the money for reconversion is not there. It is all really rather sad. . . . Virginia Markham has been very good to me, plying me with extra cups of coffee in the middle of the morning, chocolates, etc. She is leaving for Italy and returning for the next course in June.

I have finally had my laundry done here, the first in four weeks. Everything but shirts I have done myself. I am afraid I lost one shirt, either lost or stolen in the hotel. It was good you gave me so much linen.

Give the children an extra hug for me. Your letters have been of great help.

> *For these and all other mercies, my loving thanks.*
>
> *R.N.*

Hotel Residence
Geneva, Switzerland
March 30, 1947

Dearest:

I am writing after a long nap which helped me to recuperate from a strenuous week. I finished my week at Chateau Bossey on Thursday, went to Lausanne and spoke to the faculties at Lausanne University on Friday, and came back to speak to the Society for Christianity and Economic Life on Saturday morning. Then last night t'Hooft had all the secretaries of the World Council and all the so-called denominational ambassadors, and I answered questions for two and a half hours. It was an exciting evening at least for me, but it was hard to sleep after the long conversation.

Yesterday noon I had lunch with the t'Hooft family without his wife, however, who is in the hospital for a gland operation. He has two boys and a girl ranging between 14 and 18. Very nice young people who speak four languages. The whole crowd are leaving here tonight or tomorrow and sailing for the U.S.A. on the *Queen*. It makes me feel very homesick. I have three weeks to go alas but that will go fairly quickly since eight weeks are behind me. T'Hooft will give some lectures at Princeton and then come on to NYC I assume about April 15th and stay in the "prophet's chamber." He is sending my overcoat up through Ehrenstrom, whom you will find a very charming Swedish gentleman. If you want to invite t'Hooft up for a meal, you can reach him through John MacKay.[1] I told him you could not invite him to stay because Henry Brunner was occupying the guest chamber.

This morning I went to a reformed church confirmation service, conducted very much as I used to conduct them. But the service left me unsatisfied. It was so barren and unimaginative and the sermons—there were two—so dull and commonplace. The Swiss are not strong on poetry or on any of the graces of the spiritual life. They are terribly earnest and realistic and dull, or so it seems to me.

I am taking things easy today and tomorrow, and on Tuesday I speak at a student conference at Neufchatel and then go on to see Barth first and then Brunner. So I have only one speaking engagement for the week which ought to put me in good shape for the strenuous final two weeks.

Have called your cousin Mme Charles Bufil several times, but she seems to be out of town for the weekend. She left word for me through Dr. Cockburn that she would like to see me. Cockburn says that she has two very charming children, but I will report on her later. I only have a vague remembrance of you telling me about her.

Have been reading Barth's third volume of *Dogmatics,* a strange book on the Christian doctrine of creation. It is all exposition of the early chapters of Genesis in which he finds, partly by poetic intuition and partly by literalistic interpretation, some strange and some very profound ideas. The exposition of "male and female created he them" arrive at conclusions long familiar to the "liberal world" but very revolutionary on the Continent. On

ole he is becoming a democrat and a liberal in social policy, all on
sis of some very complicated biblical exegesis, or so at least he sup-
poses. One has the feeling that he has arrived at some of these conclusions under the pressure of world events and brings in a whole scenery of
interpretation in order to justify his position.

I have a little more sense of the value of this trip when I note the
importance of continental and Anglo-Saxon understanding and how American Christian liberalism draws a complete curtain between us. They almost fall into one's arms when they hear a familiar biblical accent. Last
night's discussion was interesting with people like Bishop Larned, Francis
House and his wife (he will become Religious Director of BBC after the
Conference at Oslo), Ehrenstrom, Michael Eilder, the Lutheran representative, etc., etc. But whatever the value there are two things to do to justify
such trips. Next summer we will come over and you can make the round
of trips to friends and we will do a few together and go to Amsterdam
together, but I'll study as much as possible. I have so many ideas for
which I have inadequate scholarly foundation that I would like to
work on.

Am longing for the next letter. It will probably come tomorrow. Am
sending a few lines to the children, enclosed.

With love and longing,

R.N.

1. *President of Princeton Theological Seminary.*

Basle, Switzerland
April 2, 1947

Dearest:

Two of your letters forwarded from Geneva were handed to me by
Karl Barth on my arrival here. He came down to the station and I have
just had four hours with him from luncheon through tea. I'll report on
that first.

He is, of course, a very charming man but also very honest, and we
had some very searching discussions the upshot of which was that he criticized me for trying to make a new wisdom out of the foolishness of the
Gospel and I accused him of forgetting that the Gospel was really the
wisdom as well as the power to them that believe. This involved the
whole question of the relation of faith to philosophy on the one hand and
to ethics and politics on the other. I found it most stimulating and helpful. I told him I was too much of a preacher not to look for points of

contact between the truth of the Gospel and the despair of the ↘ was surprised that I preached, and I told him that you accused me ↙ preaching like Schleiermacher on religion to its intellectual despisers. 11. pleased him very much and he repeated, "Did she say that, really?"

He, like all the Swiss and all the continental Calvinists, has no sense for liturgy and was indifferent toward my criticism of the barren confirmation service I attended on Sunday. He depends upon the sermon to maintain faith. I do not think that is enough though it is just as good as a liturgical service with no real sermon. That is I suppose a kind of dividing line between us as it is between England and the Continent. I am continental of heart and faith but not so (after being corrupted by you) that I could stand these services long. Another thing about Karl Barth. He has developed curious sectarian tendencies having thrown the church in an uproar here by his criticism of infant baptism. Now he is on the Congregational tack, insisting that the real church is only in the simple community of faith in the congregation and that theologians, bishops, secretaries imagine they are the church. I went after him on these issues pretty hard though I must grant he is right in regard to the emphasis that faith, hope, and love in the life of believers are the real substance of the church and that all else is superstructure.

I am staying here tonight and going on tomorrow to Zurich and will spend Thursday and Friday with the Brunners. Had a very nice letter from Henry today saying how happy he was about his decision to stay in America though it was hard on his mother. Emil Brunner is becoming a good friend. Barth told me several times that he recognized that Brunner and I were closer together than I to him or than Brunner to him, and I acknowledged this. Then he said, "But in reading your books, I can see you have read me and learned some things from me, or, of course, it is just possible that you have rediscovered the Reformation as I did." Then he added slyly that he thought I was in my spiritual development where he was when he wrote the commentary on Romans. "I thought," he said, "that I had to beat the people over the head with divine judgment. Now I know they do not repent unless they know the divine grace."

In regard to the Toynbees, I am delighted to know I will get to see them before they leave. I fly from Stockholm at 1:30 noon [on Monday] the 21st and arrive at LaGuardia at 11:45 but don't come down. You couldn't anyway on Tuesday but besides that, the plane may be late. It is only 2½ weeks now but it will be long. Next week won't be because I will be terribly busy. But the following week I have only one lecture a day. I close on Friday and then have to wait until Monday. The lectures are in the evening. I do wish they had made them a day shorter.

I have [been] cheered by your reports on the children. I do hope that things continue to go well. But you make no report about getting extra help, and I am sure you are consistently overworking and you mustn't. Do try to find more help.

Much love and gratitude,
R.N.

Copenhagen, Denmark
April 5, 1947

Dearest:

It was very nice on arrival here to have Mr. Soerenson hand me a letter from you. You do not say how you got his address and I am mystified because I did not have it myself until Wednesday; I simply couldn't get my Danish addresses and until I received a cable on Wednesday; I was at sea. I have a very free weekend so that my vacation will extend now to a full week. Tomorrow I go out to the suburbs for a meeting with the Labor Party leaders at Mr. Soerenson's home, and on Monday I have a meeting with the parsons at noon and then the public lecture in the evening. Then I go on to Aarhus for two lectures and return here. I gather my university lecture is off here because of the Easter holidays. So I go to Lund on Thursday.

Had two most delightful days with the Brunners. I stayed in a downtown hotel in Zurich, but immediately on arrival Emil Brunner came to take me out for tea, and then I went home with him and had dinner and afterwards we went to the City Theater and heard Goethe's *Ephigenia*. It was a perfect performance of Goethe's greatest play. On Good Friday I went to a service alone and then Henry's brother got me and took me to a beautiful mountain hotel where I had dinner with the whole family. We went back for tea to which they had invited various members of the faculty, two old Union students, Sonderegge and Sutz, and also Dr. Max Huber, one of the most distinguished jurists of Switzerland who was long on The Hague court and also active in ecumenical affairs. We had a long discussion on world affairs, and after dinner alone with the Brunners I went to the hotel to prepare for an early departure this morning. The Brunners were charming and it was really one of the nicest parts of my continental visit, partly of course because one felt so completely at home.

Had an uneventful four-hour journey today from Zurich to Copenhagen and was met at the airport by Mr. Soerenson who is the leader of the Labor Party here and is one of those fellow spirits whom one is glad to meet. He evidently regards my stuff as important for the formation of thought in his party and has translated some of it. I am not yet aware of what he is. Will be here alone for the rest of the day though I have just called him to let him know that I left my briefcase at the airport and I may have to waste some time finding it. I am staying in one of those "alcohol-free" hotels which religious organizations run all over the Continent and Mr. Soerenson was apologetic about it saying that one of the theological professors had picked it for me. But there are no causes for apologies. It is the most perfectly appointed hotel room I have been in on this trip and the cost is $1.25 per day! My host informs me, "The hotel in which you are staying is run by the Pietistic Movement which began 100 years ago. They are very otherworldly but they know how to run hotels. The Gruntwig Movement which is much more this-worldly also runs hotels but they are no good."

With regard to your letter. I really don't understand your peeve about something I have said in regard to making a "career" in theology. The difference between vocational and avocational pursuits is quite obvious and clear and the Holy Spirit has nothing to do with this difference. I don't remember ever having used the word "career." I like the old boy's letter with his nice combination of sport news and questions. You might tell him that I did not see any Alp resorts in Switzerland. When I arrived in Zurich on Thursday the whole of the town seemed to be at the station carrying skis and moving to the mountains for the Easter holidays. Here too everything is very dead. The Continent does not move anything in Easter Week and it is of course the same in Britain. But fewer people are in church than with us. The attendance in Zurich yesterday was very bad. It is a little bother not to be able to speak the language and not to be able to converse with anyone. This is my first experience in thus being cut off except for the one day in French Switzerland.

You are right about the Scots and Swiss and Dutch in general. But you must not call it Protestant. It is Calvinist. The Scandinavians, as all Lutherans, are full of the joy of life for instance and full of imagination. This town is supposed to have the lightness and gaiety of Paris. The Swiss of course are not pure Calvinists but Zwinglists which is less forbidding. But they are all imaginatively deficient and the services are very bare.

Copenhagen, April 6, 1947 (Sunday): I broke off this letter yesterday when I suddenly discovered that I did not have my briefcase. Fortunately my lecture notes were out of it, but a well-marked copy of *The Mind and Heart of Love* which I had been studying with great care was. Mr. Soerenson has been trying to get it reclaimed at the airport but so far no success. It is a great lack not to know the language and get into a taxi and go out to find it. One feels very helpless. The morning is cold and cheerless, rain pouring down. Will go to church in an hour and then this afternoon to Soerenson's house. It is not too nice spending Easter like this in a hotel room. This is a day to be in the bosom of the family. Celebrated Easter by having my first egg for breakfast since leaving home. Back in the land of butter and eggs. You write about taking a half year off. I am not sanguine. The pressure of students at Union makes that difficult. We will have to be very firm about summers. That is where my salvation will lie. I must guard them and work resolutely. If we have the money, we ought to extend the house just because you and I need working room in the summer, a real library. My worry is the summer after next when we ought to go to Europe. Perhaps you will have to go alone and we will be together just for Amsterdam. I don't know, I dread to think that I won't be able to work after the summer until 1950. The years slip by when one's work is not done.

You still don't write about having any new help. The children seem to me by your account a good deal easier than they were. It will take a lot of conversation to help me catch up on their development. Just wrote Cliff Stanley. I completely forgot to answer his cable after writing to you to get in touch with Miss Pratt or the Bishop.

Have just come from the cathedral, famous because of Thorwaldsen's statues of the twelve apostles. The cathedral is of Baroque architecture and as in the whole of Scandinavia, altar, etc., and liturgy, are closer to the Catholic than any other form of Protestantism. The liturgy was beautiful and the difference in the bare Calvinism of Holland and Switzerland is striking. . . .

Copenhagen, Easter Monday, April 7, 1947: I couldn't mail this letter yesterday because everything was closed. Yesterday afternoon I went to Mr. Soerenson's suburban home, and your nice Easter letter with the old boy's photo awaited me. I showed the photo and my hosts' parents invited their four boys, all blond like Christopher, in and they might have been his brothers. The mystery of my hosts cleared. He is the leader of the new Labor Party in Parliament and also a publisher and is bringing out four of my books for all three Scandinavian countries. In the evening he had the Party leaders in and we had a discussion until midnight. The Party is oriented like the Dutch party and in both cases an effort is made to overcome the Marxist-Christianity conflict. Language difficulties made the discussion less profitable than in Holland where they speak so much English. All these people are sad about Britain's decline. The Liberal-Labor forces of the Continent rightly feel they can count less on us than on Britain.

About that request to Mrs. Meade about Western dates, she has already turned down dates requiring more than one talk. I told her to make a single date in May out of pure penuriousness. I felt that in any event, since I wouldn't see Mother and Hulda during the summer, I should pay a brief visit sometime there [in Chicago] in May and I wanted to cover expenses. So you better let it stand.

I still feel that the *Leaves* ought not to be published. The more I think of it the more I think the British public should not be burdened with such a book that can only be interesting from the standpoint of interest in me and that makes the book presumptious. Don't you think? I would defer decision until we can talk it over but I am rather set even though you originally seemed opposed but now less so.

Would you by the way ask Mrs. Meade to send the *Nation* article on the Dutch Labor Party to Prof. Banning? It is two weeks from today that I can come home, glory be.

Love to you all,

R.N.

New York, NY
April 8, 1947

Dearest:

I seem to write letters to you while listening to lectures. Bp. Aulén[1] is lecturing for the Hewitt Series, his first; John Bennett, Henry Brunner, and I are sitting together and getting one word in five. [Bp. Aulén had a curious problem in speech delivery, whether due to some throat constriction or a mere manner of speaking; one listener said it reminded him of a sea lion!] (Wretched 207, frightful room, too many people, too many squeaking chairs, too many people coming in late; when they have special lecturers, why aren't professors asked to close their classes a little early? So rude!)

I hope they [the lectures] will be published. I hope *your* lectures in Denmark, Norway, and Sweden may be heard—and, understood. Anyhow, if not heard, you are fun to watch for the faces [you make] and the show is worth keeping awake for. I wish I might have a magic carpet, and pop over and sit under you, instead of being here! But three weeks today you will be back.

I wrote hastily last night. I had dinner with the Bennetts; very nice; Oliver Tomkins[2] was easy and casually interesting about his travels with

Edward Hardy and Bp. Brillioth,[3] etc., to the Greek Church, Syria, and Egypt. And the Dutch gent, from Utrecht, something Sprinkle [?] was very anxious to know your reactions and impressions about Holland, so I got your letter, and edited, omitted, and paraphrased some of your Dutch letters, and I told them about your conversations with Karl Barth, which interested them all vastly.

. . . It was a relief to start on "the common round and daily tasks," and to get the children off to school.

Two days later, Thursday, April 10th: It is 11 P.M. and only time for a couple of lines. Am very weary. I have paid $50.00 deposit on the camp in Maine for Christopher in order to reserve a place. I think it is the best thing, and now we must find a place for Elisabeth for July. Plans for the school must wait until you come back. Christopher is very active at the moment; walked to and from the school, played tennis with the boys of his class at 94th Street, took things for me to the post office, and then played baseball with some of the students in the park. He gets rather fagged looking but goes to bed early and reads resting on his bed.

Ben Bradford is "off" this week; his wife has been laid up after having wisdom teeth taken out, and he is a bit done up after Easter jobs and term papers, so as the weather has been fairly good, Christopher has been out a lot. So has Elisabeth, who seems over her little cold and the upset of Good Friday.

I saw and spoke to the Auléns yesterday; they are coming to tea on Saturday. No word or sign from Visser t'Hooft or Ehrenstrom yet, although I believe the latter is somewhere about. Saw Oliver Tomkins again briefly at the tea for the Auléns yesterday. He wants to see Wystan [Auden] and de Rougement,[4] so we are hoping to get together next week sometime. . . .

Wystan and I have been through your *Cynic* again. He feels as I do that in certain places, particularly your F.O.R. [Fellowship of Reconciliation]-ish liberal spots, and your Protestant anti-sacramental places you should have a little footnote, or else cut the latter out. I feel more strongly about the latter too, also, as some of the remarks seem too naive for you (e.g., "capsule Christianity" and so forth), but the former reflect an authentic stage in your theological and political development, while the latter ones *might* strike a reader just as bad taste. I'm sending a list to Mr. Christian of places that need slight notes. Wystan likes them as much as I do, and thinks you ought to do another such—up-to-date—now. Awfully keen about it, and *I* think it's a good idea! . . .

Longing for you in the flesh,

U.M.

---

1. Bishop Gustaf Aulén, Swedish theologian and author of Christus Victor.   2. An English cleric active in the World Council of Churches, later bishop of Bristol.   3. Hardy was a former professor of Church history at General Seminary; he and the Swedish Bishop Brillioth were both active in the W.C.C.   4. Denis de Rougemont; Swiss author of Love in the Western World.

Hotel Royal
Aarhus, Denmark
April 9, 1947

Dearest:

I am out of ink and my typewriter is in Copenhagen, but I have time to write. Your letter with the *Christianity & Crisis* article was here awaiting me. It is first rate and quite thrilled me. Now that the ice is broken in my absence I can ask you for more. Pit wrote me of your chapel talk and said that it had been greatly appreciated by everyone. So I am glad and proud. I think we can manage the old boy's camp without worry. I am writing an article now for the *Atlantic*.

Would it be possible to let Elisabeth and Hulda and Mother stay together for July? That would save us her camp. We ought to keep the place for the whole of August, I think. We can talk that over however when I return.

This is a provincial town with a new university built in a modern style and nice. I came here yesterday by plane 40 minutes but must return by train on a tedious eight-hour trip. You can see on the map that I have to go around a big bay. Dean Prenter, the dean of the faculty, is one of the best theologians on the Continent. I talked twice here yesterday and then sat up until midnight talking with his faculty. It was strenuous but worthwhile to make this contact with Scandinavian Lutheranism, which is so much more balanced than the German. I suppose that it is my combination of Lutheranism and prophetism which established my affinity with their thought. At any rate I was welcomed as an old friend and all the students had my *Nature and Destiny*.

I arrive in Copenhagen at 8:00 tonight and go early tomorrow morning by air to Malmö which is only ten miles from Lund. There I speak twice and then to Uppsala. Have the weekend to rest up and then the final week. Somehow the weeks seem longer as the trip draws to a close. I do so long to get back.

Had a letter from Roger Shinn[1] asking me to speak to a student Fellowship of Socialist Christians' meeting in late April. Will you give him a date in the last week of April or even the Friday after my return which will be April 25th, that or 28th? I would like to make a general report so this is as good an occasion as any.

To come back to your article. You may have been hurried when you wrote it, but it has the real fire of the Gospel in it and put in a very telling way. It is really very good. I have lost my very notated *Heart and Mind of Love* with my briefcase, which is a great loss. It means going over the whole again to find what was particularly important to me. Going to the station now for that long trek back to Copenhagen.

> *My love to you and to the old boy and old girl.*
>
> R.N.

The trip took 10½ hours instead of eight. It's 11:00 and I leave at 6:00 in the evening for Sweden.

> *So, love,*

1. Graduate student and later professor at Union Seminary.

Lund, Sweden
April 10, 1947

Dearest:

Last night I sent off a letter hastily scribbled in Aarhus and a note attached in Copenhagen. After a delightful day with the faculty and students at the new university at Aarhus, I spent a miserable day in over-crowded trains getting back to Copenhagen. The trip of 150 miles made by air in 40 minutes required 10½ hours. I got back at 11:00 pretty tired and arose this morning at 6:00. The bus left at 8:00 and the plane at 8:00. But lo and behold the plane trip was exactly eight minutes long to Malmö and the university town of Lund is a half hour from Malmö, so that by 9:00 I was having breakfast in this lovely hotel and am now en-sconced in a comfortable room waiting for the faculty lunch at 1:00. Then I will give my lecture at 3:00 at the university. I have worked out a new lecture first used in Amsterdam and then here on "The Foolishness of God and the Wisdom of the World" in which I try to come to terms with Barthianism over here. I work out in what sense the Gospel is a contradiction and in what sense a fulfillment of (a) wisdom, (b) virtue, (c) security as it exists in the world. The lecture is really better than my prepared stuff for over here, and I have had a very interesting newspaper article from

Holland, in which a Barthian pastor, a very fine man with whom I had long discussions, deals at great length with my thesis and expresses himself satisfied that it is a necessary corrective to continental thought. I say I had the paper, but it was lost with my briefcase, which I do not expect to find again. I asked for it at the airport again this morning but no trace. I probably can't send this letter as I am without money. They wouldn't change my Danish money this morning, and I will have to wait until tonight when the university pays me 125 krone for the lecture, which is probably about $30. Incidentally, you will be getting checks from England to the extent of $300 from BBC broadcasts and my article for *Leverhulm's Magazine* which we can salt down for a part of the expense for the old boy's camp.

I had a cable today from Dr. William Talley, Maxwell School of Citizenship, Syracuse, NY, asking whether I would speak on the occasion of the inauguration of Paul Appleby as president on May 17th. The fee, which is $250, would complete the old boy's camp fee, but I don't know whether I should take it. I will leave it to you. Will you wire him as from me whatever you decide, saying Mr. Niebuhr regrets delay and can, or cannot, accept your kind invitation, etc., etc.

Will finish this letter tonight or tomorrow. I take the night train to Stockholm and then for the final pull. It is only 10 days now until I return. What a relief. I think you are right, the trip was worth it particularly this contact with very vital Lutheran and Calvinistic theologians who are breaking the old forms and stereotypes. I do feel the necessity of serious study all the more however after the contact because I feel I must come to terms with this thought or allow it to fructify my own in detail and not merely in general terms like this lecture today.

I am now back from the lecture. Had a nice luncheon with the theological faculty with all the Swedish pickled fish, etc., as first course and then a sumptuous second course. These Scandinavians do live well. Have visited the 11th-century cathedral built, of course, in (pre-) Gothic Romanesque style. Now I have 1½ hours before a general faculty dinner. I wanted to sleep but am a little too tired for that. Will have to wait for tomorrow and the relaxation of the weekend. But I am all right. At these public functions they make you [introduce yourself with] a little speech in a very formal way. Had such speeches in Copenhagen, Aarhus, and now here.

I am sitting in a rather ornate hotel room with the afternoon sun streaming in the window. Spring has arrived but there is a nip in the air. This is quite a new world and I am glad to make this contact with it. My sense of frustration is over and I admit you are right about the trip as you usually are. Maybe it is so nice because so close to home.

Love,

R.N.

Uppsala, Sweden
Saturday, April 13[?], 1947

Dearest:

Your two nice letters written on Easter Day and before arrived this morning. It was so nice to have them and to hear about the old girl's for instance dramatizing herself as a beggar. How well I remember such fantasies of impotent childhood trying to gain moral superiority over the parent. I feel like a renegade when I think how hard you have worked and how easy I have it now. I sit in the lap of luxury. Beautiful hotel rooms with bath. Unbelievable meals. The first course of assorted pickled fish, cheese, etc., is so big that it takes away one's appetite for the entree. The living standards here exceed the American's. There is a particular grace about the hospitality too. Yesterday I had my first lecture. Today Prof. [Sigfrid von] Engeström had a faculty luncheon and next Saturday will be an official university farewell dinner. My expenses at the hotel are paid to the last cent. At each dinner the host delivers a little speech to which you respond. What they say about me makes me feel like a big fraud who might be found out before he gets away ahead of the sheriff. The knowledge of English is not as good as in Holland as German was the second language. They asked whether I could deliver my lecture in German, but I had to beg off. As it is I am rewriting my lecture totally because I speak very slowly and get through only about a half.

This afternoon after the luncheon I was taken by my host to the induction of a new professor in the Aula. The affair was similar to such an event at Oxford with perhaps a little more pomp, trumpeters heading the procession, then the King's messenger, the Royal Ukase,[1] and then the rector and the faculty. The new professor then gave a formal address. Instead of academic gowns and hoods, the formal dress is a special adaptation of tails with special ornamentation. After the performance, Archbishop Eidem stopped me and took me about to see the various historic relics, etc., in the main university building. Tomorrow I will go to church in the cathedral and then will be driven by my host to Old Uppsala. The whole spirit of the place is more like Oxford than any other, except that the university buildings are of too many styles, the medieval ones having been wood and destroyed, or rather it is a combination of Oxford and Canterbury because the cathedral is in the center of the university and the archbishop is the sovereign of the place. The Stockholm and the Uppsala papers have stories about me this morning, but I couldn't make out a word. One of them carried a caricature about like that picture from the Advertising Council. My schedule is a holiday compared to the past months. I speak at 7:00 each day, Monday and Tuesday here, Wednesday before the ministers of Stockholm, and again Thursday and Friday here. If only I could take a plane on Saturday. Have to stay over the weekend however because the plane leaves on Friday at 1:00 and my lecture is at 7:00. That means I have to stick to the Monday plane, the 21st. I had hoped that I could gain a little time when I found I had only six lectures in ten days. But they are paying me $400 and all expenses so I must not make demands. In any event, the lectures are widely advertised for the appointed days.

I have made some purchases, a Lapland knife with caribou casing for the old boy, some Swedish linen, a Swedish sweater, and a few other things still to get. Prices of course are very high and I'll get only what seems unique.

I hope you will get this letter on the Monday plane. If you don't, I will beat it home. It will be such a joy. You have been great in the way you have managed work and children. I am afraid I have had a holiday compared with what you have been doing. Sorry my letters have seemed dull. I am just not very good at expressing my gratitude and love to you but I hope to prove it. Love to the children. I will miss making reports to you for the rest of the week because I don't enjoy things without reporting them. I'll call you up from the airport while waiting for the customs, which is always about an hour. Even if on time I won't be home much before 1:30 so don't make any plans for meeting me, etc. Also the plane may be hours late.

R.N.

1. Royal proclamation of the new academic rank.

Ten

1948
Conferences at
Oslo and Amsterdam

Reinhold spent a good part of the summer of 1949 at two important international conferences in Europe. The first was held in Oslo—the assembly of the World Student Christian Federation. The second was the founding assembly of the World Council of Churches; Reinhold was a member of the American delegation to it.

After Reinhold's Departure—July 19, 1948

Reinhold left this afternoon by air for Norway. Clifford Stanley came with us, to see him off at La Guardia Field, and as usual we chatted about the accidents that had happened lately, and lightly debated the law of averages, with the same old refrain recurring in our minds and on our lips, "but, of course, you never know . . ." But the Lord knows, or does he? As we stood watching the various aircraft being prepared, Constellations and Douglasses, "Yes," we heard our unspoken thoughts drifting on the air from a group of waiting passengers and attendant friends, "We used to say that the Constellations were risky, and we felt safer going on a Douglas, but all these last accidents have been Douglasses, which shows . . ." Which shows what? one wondered. Which shows again that "you never know." Only the Lord knows. Generally or specifically? Does he know that this ship is going to crash, and that So-and-So, that you, that I, may perish in the crash? "Who hath measured the waters in the hollow of his hand, and metered out heaven with the span, and comprehended the dust of the earth in a measure, and weighed the mountains in scales, and the hills in a balance." Lord, Almighty God, who knowest our necessities before we ask, please measure the runway with a span, and make sure it is long enough for the load of the plane. A voice to the left of us observed, "They say that the crash here at the field in May was because the pilot chose too short a runway." Lord, please measure it. Another voice, equally meditative, replied, "And they say that the crash in Maryland was because the wind shifted as the plane was going over the mountains." Lord, if thou weighest the mountains and the hills also are in thy balance, keep the winds as they should be.

"Let's go down to the waiting room," my husband turned to me, "We can get some orange juice there."

Back in the waiting room, the passengers familiar as types, somehow were reassuring. The young mother with a baby, the businessmen, the talkative departing relative much surrounded by family and burdened with messages, and the glamorous presumable actress, yes, we travelled with them before, their familiarity was in itself a comfort. Why, I found myself wondering, for after all in every crash there seems to be a young mother and a baby. Perhaps it is just the feeling that there is safety in numbers. Oh, Lord, let me not die alone. But death is solitary. Isn't that why people fear death? The jump into infinity—even though there are a thousand beside me, and ten thousand at my right hand—has to be made alone. The solitariness of the soul—Christ in the garden and on the cross: "My God, my God, why hast thou forsaken me?" Why does that cry hold our faith and our lack of it? Was Christ doubting his own reading of God's plan for himself? Did he question God's ultimate power and goodness, or was he feeling just dreadfully alone? Naked I came into the world, and naked I go out, clothed in nothing save myself. Naked and alone, as removed from the fellowship of family and friends as when one is wheeled, doped, antiseptic and anonymous, into an operating room. But even then, or before, during the preoperation ritual of cleansing and anointing (if one flickered out during the operation, of course, one would want to assure the authorities, "she hath done what she could, she hath anointed my body afore hand for the burying"), the self receives a final baptism of individuality. As the hypodermic starts to work, and the ordinary reactions of the body slacken, the Isness of the I and the I-ness of my being increases and intensifies. How often have I wanted to expound, philosophically and vividly, on the freedom of the personality, as my acquiescent form is wheeled down the corridor to the operating room. Would the orderlies and the chaperoning nurse enjoy a lecture on "the transcendent self," I wonder? But as I move my head to make the introductory clearing of the throat, the nurse looks down, and pulls up the covering blanket. Her movement seems to belong to a world of long ago, when Mother or Nanny soothed, "Ssh, Baby go bye-bye." The trip to the operating room is a return to the world of childhood and babyhood—a return to the womb or tomb—but also "another shall gird thee and carry thee whither thou wouldest not." My transcendent self seems to have ebbed; perhaps the lecture can wait. . . . I feel sleepy. . . . I would like to hold Reinhold's hand, but he isn't here. . . . My God, my God, why hast thou forsaken me?

"My wife and I," I heard my husband's voice explaining to an acquaintance also waiting at the bar for orange juice, "have decided never to fly together; other couples we know do that, and we think it's a good idea because of the children." But I would far rather die with you, darling; we belong together in eternity. The children are ours in history, but I would like to start the life everlasting with you. Yes, I know, we agreed, and of course, it *is* better for the children. But I wish you didn't sound so cheery about it.

"Have some orange juice at last," my husband handed me a super Dixie cup, "with the compliments of the airline." His gesture bestowing it upon me, suddenly seemed priestly and sacramental. . . . "Preserve thy body and soul unto everlasting life." As I drank, the woman behind me spoke, "I always say that orange juice is so healthful." "Yes," her equally typical companion agreed, "they say it has all the vitamins necessary for life." Orange juice with its vitamins, is that our viaticum? . . . Hear us, O merciful Father, we most humbly beseech thee, and with thy Holy and Life-giving Spirit vouchsafe to bless and sanctify both us and these thy gifts, that they may be unto us thy Body and Blood of thy Son, our Saviour, Jesus Christ, to the end that we, receiving the same, may be strengthened and refreshed both in body and soul. . . . "All passengers for transatlantic flight 46, this way, please," the call came.

"Good-bye." Almighty God, have compassion upon our infirmities; and those things, which for our unworthiness we dare not, and for our blindness we cannot ask, vouchsafe to give us, for the worthiness of Thy Son Jesus Christ, our Lord. Amen.

Oslo, Norway
Tuesday, July 20, 1948

Dearest:

I've just had breakfast with the Niemoellers, who send their love. This is quite a gathering of the clan. Others who have inquired about you and send greetings are t'Hooft, Mackie, Oliver Tomkins. I spent most of yesterday writing out my address for the translators. Last night a group of us met with the German delegation at a home some ten miles out of Oslo and overlooking the harbor. It was about the most beautiful vista I can remember. The meeting was fairly interesting but not too much so. The conference begins this afternoon and tonight Bishop Berggrav[1] preaches at the opening service.

The American delegation of youngsters are having a difficult time because the Asiatics are very vocal and terribly anti-American and the Continentals scarcely less so. There was much talk in the preparatory conference of leaders on the tail end of which I heard several discussions. Our youngsters scarcely know what has hit them and some of them are a

---

little bewildered. Visser t'Hooft is meeting this morning with the Indonesian delegation who are of course violently anti-Dutch and asked him for a conference to explain the course of Holland to them. He does not relish the prospect as he is deeply disturbed.

Can't tell you how nice it is to live in the glow and memory of our past two weeks together. It does make a difference to every level of consciousness. Can't always be as nice as that amidst the cares of life but still one hopes for some of it.

Am sending both children cards. Give John Baillie my love. Back a week from today at about 11:00 A.M.

With love, gratitude, and longing,

R.N.

1. *Eivind Berggrav; bishop of Oslo. During World War II, the Nazis had kept him under house arrest.*

London, England
Friday, August 14, 1948

Dearest:

I met Barbara this morning and we had coffee together at the Picadilly and then went together to the Toynbees' for luncheon. Barbara had an engagement with them and they asked me to come if I could. We spent till 4 P.M. there and had a very good time as you can imagine. Came back to the Wilson's to rest and will take Geoffrey and Judy out to dinner tonight.

Will arrive home by air on September 5th. Tell you how it happened. I spent the whole of yesterday frantically running from steamship to airlines. The *Cunard* held out no hope for a passage on September 2nd in tourist. I might have got a passage in cabin but it would cost an extra $100 and there would be no certainty that I could get it even then. The waiting list was smaller and that was all. Thereupon I made the rounds of the airlines and the American Overseas had a passage for September 4th. In addition they were willing to take English money. The fare is only $90 more than I would have had to pay for cabin class on the *Queen* and I save the $160 which I have already spent.

Incidentally, I didn't get much work done on the *Queen* coming over. I save a whole ten days coming back in this way, and some of it I may be able to apply in getting my final chapters written. At any rate I am very happy that I can come back for many reasons including the chance to spend a final week with you and the children in the country. I will arrive about 6 P.M. on Sunday the 5th. Will take the early morning train on

Labor Day. Wish now that I had taken that special key for the seminary, which is closed, but a hotel will do.

Am doing the broadcast recording tomorrow morning and then having luncheon with Ronald Preston.[1] Leaving Sunday morning by air for Holland. I realize now why the Geneva people were so shocked that I was coming late. I thought I was no longer chairman of the Commission III. Actually I am until the Assembly meets when Patijn[2] takes over. I would have missed two days of meetings which I am supposed to chair and in addition two days of the International Commission meeting. As it is I will spend a full week in preliminary meetings in Holland. The Assembly begins on the 22nd.

Toynbee and his wife have been reading Iremonger's life of Temple[3] and were thrilled by it. They say it is an extraordinarily good job. I will buy the book tomorrow. Have given the [Henry] James *The Princess Casamassima* to Geoffrey and Judy as a present as she likes James. I thought we could easily replace it, and it hasn't come out here as yet. I greatly enjoyed it. It was the only thing I read on the boat.

Hope things go well with you and that you have been able to get on with the job. I would like to think that the old boy continues to do haying but even that has to stop some time. Will write next from Holland.

Love to the old boy, and love to you,

R.N.

1. *Professor of theology at Manchester; had done graduate work at Union Seminary.*
2. *C. L. Patijn; a lawyer and counselor to the Dutch Ministry of Economic Affairs.*
3. *Archbishop William Temple had been provisional chairman of the World Council of Churches until his death in October 1944 at the age of 63.*

Amsterdam, Holland
Monday, August 17, 1948

Dearest:

I flew over from London yesterday, arriving here late in the afternoon. Spent this morning with the Dutch publisher who is putting out my books and drew enough money from him for my Dutch stay. Now I am on my way to Woudshoten where the preliminary meetings will go on until next Sunday. I do feel badly about you not being here for the women's meeting.[1] It is being held at Baarn. T'Hooft is driving over there this afternoon for the close. Peggy Benn is evidently very much in evidence, though I understand is being criticized somewhat for placing too much emphasis on the ordination of women, rather than the wider problems of women in the church. Incidentally, some Anglican dean has just stirred matters in Britain by the announcement that the ordination of women is contrary to the "nature" of God since God is male. Had luncheon on Saturday with Ronald Preston who tells me that Billy Greer [bishop of Manchester] was very disappointed with Lambeth. Says absolutely nothing happened. A majority favored being in communion with South India but a minority strongly opposed, and so the matter was merely recorded. Nothing indeed can be done without complete consensus as the conference has no particular legal status.[2]

Geoffrey and Judy were very nice to me and begged me to come back. But as Judy is very busy with the infant, one has the feeling a little of adding to work too much. At any rate I have made arrangements at the Bonnington for the night of the 3rd.

The clans are beginning to gather. One meets people from everywhere. My health is good except that the cough persists as it was three weeks ago. Have accomplished a little but not too much on my manuscript.

Much love,

R.N.

1. *U.N. had worked with its preparatory commission, under the chairmanship of Mrs. Samuel Cavert. However, the demands of her academic work, care of their children, and the, she felt, unnecessary expense of the journey kept her from attending.* 2. *Every ten years the bishops of the Anglican Communion meet in conference at Lambeth, the London residence of the archbishop of Canterbury. In 1947 the Church of South India was formed of all the Protestant denominations in South India. Their bishops were received at Lambeth in 1948.*

Amsterdam, Holland
Tuesday, August 18, 1948

Dearest:

I have just received your letter with Elisabeth's nice enclosure. I am due at the conference so I will write hurriedly the most important news. Yesterday, Pit and I had tea with the Dodds. He is coming to give lectures at Princeton in 1950. Pit offered him an apartment and $3,000 for a semester's seminar and he and Mrs. Dodd accepted on the spot without taking it under advisement, etc. She sends her love to you and says that she looks forward to being our neighbors. [Karl] Barth and Dodd had the opening speeches yesterday in the presence of royalty. Dodd was superb on the Bible and the church. Barth was brilliant and irresponsible as usual.

The Sunday formal opening was a sad washout. John R. Mott[1] spoiled the opening service with banal reminiscences, and in the evening meeting, which was foolishly devoted to "Our Heritage," Boegner,[2] Chichester [Bishop Bell], John Mackay, Eidem, etc., foolishly revelled in further nostalgia. It was boring and disappointing. Bill Pauck[3] and I beguiled the tedium by checking Dulles'[s] German translation of his speech to be delivered today.[4] Dulles has become almost a pacifist in insisting that there must be no war, but there is little relation between his Christian affirmation and his political prognostications for he is very pessimistic. So is everyone else. People over here are talking about war in a month. This is probably foolish but the situation is serious.

Incidentally, the Flessemans are coming over for ten days to renew their exit permits so as not to lose their status. They arrive Oct. 10. I tentatively invited them to have our guest room as they have practically no American money. I told them how we live. I hope this is all right. It seemed impossible not to. She runs a taxi service for me to get to and from meetings and in every respect looks after my comfort. I am quite well after a rather too strenuous preparatory week. Today my work with the message committee begins. Yesterday I rewrote my speech to make it an answer to Barth's otherworldliness. But I am not on for a week. T'Hooft is put out because my address cooked up in Heath is all translated and mimeographed. But it was dead as if it was produced in a vacuum.

Billy Greer was disgusted with Lambeth but Angus Dun [bishop of Washington, DC] is inclined to be defensive. Everyone thinks the section on women in the church is indefensible. Dictated altogether by fear of losing caste with Eastern Orthodoxy. Angus did say that the conference gave him the impression of a lot of old men clutching at familiar things in a world of perdition.

We are not due to arrive in New York City until 6 P.M. Sunday so I will probably have to take the morning train. But I will call you.

The old boy seems to be have an awfully good time. Do hope you don't lose all the hours set aside for study. Must run.

Love,

R.N.

1. *Co-winner of 1946 Nobel Peace Prize; American church statesman; chairman of YMCA and other church organizations.* 2. *Marc Boegner; pastor of the leading Reformed Church in Paris; well-known for resistance to Nazis and helping Jewish children flee France; president of the French Protestant Federation.* 3. *At this time, exchange professor at the University of Frankfurt and professor of church history at University of Chicago.* 4. *John Foster Dulles; delegate of the Presbyterian church and foreign policy advisor to Governor Dewey, then Republican candidate for president.*

Woudschoten, Holland
Thursday, August 20, 1948

Dearest:

We are in the second day of our commission meetings after having finished two days of the international affairs committee. It's fairly strenuous but so far I am surviving. The actual Assembly will not be so strenuous as I will have no responsibilities for chairing our section. I have however just been elected to the message committee of the Assembly. Berggrav is chairman. Angus Dun and I represent U.S.A. Barth also is on [the committee], etc. It will be an interesting group. Everybody that one has ever met is here. We live in the YMCA camp, beautiful place but real camp conditions. Bishop Brillioth, and a Hungarian professor, and I share a bedroom. The Hungarian is most interesting in describing conditions in his country.

Peggy Benn arrived from the women's conference yesterday. The Lambeth Conference seems to have been hopeless on the women['s] question. Angus says one could not even raise the issue significantly. C. S. Lewis has come to the support in *Time and Tide*[1] of an Anglican dean who declares that women as priests are impossible because both God the Father and Christ are masculine, and the priest must represent them. The little Dutch baroness who is chairman of the International YWCA is as worked up as Peggy. . . .

Last night we went to a nearby pub and Barth, Bishop Neil,[2] t'Hooft, Pierre Maury, and Bill Pauck and I had some beer. Bill reports that [Paul] Tillich has had indeed a triumph in Germany and is enjoying himself hugely.

I hope you are having the time to do the work you set out to do. I have had to stop all work on my chapter. No chance any more. I would like to pick up the special summer key for the seminary. It would be easier than going to a hotel. Excuse this hurried note.

Love,

R.N.

---

1. *An English weekly journal.* 2. *Stephen Neil; assistant to the archbishop of Canterbury and assigned to the World Council.*

Amstlevenn, Holland
Saturday, August 22, 1948

Dearest:

For the first time since coming to Europe I feel at leisure for a real letter. This morning we finished the week of preliminary meetings at Woudschoten, and Ellen Flesseman came over to get me in time for a later luncheon. Then I had a rest and we went to Amsterdam, which is only ten minutes by car, and I went through registration, etc., etc. Now I have the evening free. Tomorrow afternoon the ceremonial opening takes place. While I feel some responsibilities for the sectional meetings, the real reason why Vim [Visser t'Hooft] wanted me here was for these preparatory meetings so I'm glad I was not late. Incidentally, I have the usual difficulty with my address. The thing I cooked up at Heath to send off seems dead as a dodo when I read it now. I could do a great deal better after being in the give and take of ecumenical discussion for a week and hearing the problems of India and Hungary, etc., etc. But my address is in print and in double translation. I think I will disregard it nevertheless though Vim was quite angry when I told him I would.

What you write about the ecumenical movement is quite correct. When one thinks of the people who make it up one realizes how inadequate we all are. Yet there will be moments when one cannot be too critical. I realize that the only time the church is really sufferable is when it is at prayer. When it talks, it claims too much for itself. The evening devotions at Woudschoten led by Chichester, Lilje, Kraemer, Florovsky, etc., were really the true church.[1]

We met in four sections as you know. John Baillie reported that a cynic had said: "Sections 2 and 4 are in great confusion. Sections 1 and 3 are not sectional meetings at all but seminars by Barth and Niebuhr and are proceeding in perfect order."[2] Barth charms everyone. His section has certainly not been a seminar but a lively debate between his position and that of Ramsey[3] for Anglo-Catholicism and Florovsky for Orthodoxy. Ramsey has become much more intransigent than when I used to see him before the Oxford Conference. Incidentally, what I find simply impossible about his position is precisely the claims he makes for the church when you think of the realities of history. Part of the debate: Ramsey: "I am glad the Roman Church is not represented at Amsterdam. That will remind us that we are merely fragments and not the true church." Barth: "I am also glad that Rome is not here because it is a pseudo-church which worships itself."

It was so nice to get four of your letters, the first I had because Mrs. Flesseman was afraid they might miss me if sent on. I gather you are

---

having rather too much social life for your liking even though you enjoy each particular instance. What you write about Charlie Packard and the building is very encouraging. I am glad that I am coming back just to be able to be in on the final plans as well of course for other reasons.

I have had some difficulty in sleeping after evening committee work, which makes me realize that the margin of health I have is fairly thin. I am going to take next week easier than last if I can, though if the message committee should make heavy demands I must meet those. Incidentally, both Barbara and Peggy Benn say that the summer has been so miserable in Britain that it was good we did not come. I has rained all summer except for one week of quite excessive heat. Did I tell you that I will have dinner with Barbara, [and] Bob and Marjorie [Keppel-Compton] on my one evening in London. I am so glad I could make this connection. At least I hope that Barbara can arrange it as she hopes. I do feel badly about your not being here not only because you miss Bob and Marjorie but also because it would be so much more fun to do this assembly together. It might even be the occasion for resolving many a theological debate between us for there is a certain power in these ecumenical discussions. I see that what I am writing on the backside of the page is illegible so I had better close. My stamp is only good for one piece of paper and the post offices are closed until Monday. I'll continue on Monday.

I hope you don't mind my flying back. I rather like the idea of getting back so early and having a few days with you at Heath. Christopher sounds very happy and occupied. So glad the [Felix] Frankfurters are there. I wonder if they will be gone when I arrive. It would be nice to see them again.

Much love,

R.N.

1. The evening devotions were led by an Anglican, Bishop G. K. A. Bell of Chichester; a Lutheran, Bishop Hans Lilje of Hannover; a Dutch Reformed, Professor Hendrik Kraemer; and a Russian Orthodox, George Florovsky. Florovsky was dean of St. Vladimir's Seminary, a Russian Orthodox seminary that moved in 1947 to Morningside Heights adjacent to Union Theological Seminary. 2. The sections discussed "The Universal Church in God's Design." 3. Michael Ramsey; archbishop of Canterbury.

Amstlevenn, Holland
Friday, August 27, 1948

Dearest:

Just received your letter with your news about the trip to Arden [music and dance summer school where Elisabeth was]. I loved the letter from Elisabeth. So very typical.

The conference is now well under way. Last night John Baillie, Pierre Maury, and Niemoeller spoke. John is very solid and sound, though of course not as moving as Niemoeller. One did realize that there is a difference in the accents of Anglo-Saxon and Continental religious thought which can hardly be bridged. John spoke in a form of thought we all found acceptable while both Niemoeller and the young Frenchman were so eschatological and so contemptuous of any natural theology as to leave many of us uneasy.

Peggy and Mrs. Cavert[1] report interesting debates between Barth and the Anglo-Catholics on the place of women in the church. Barth challenges them to produce Scriptural evidence that women should be excluded from the priesthood, which they cannot. He on the other hand constantly warns the women that they must take Scriptural authority more seriously which means Paul's admonition that the man is the head of the woman as Christ is head of the church. This has some deep significance for him and he distinguishes it from the "time-bound" admonitions of St. Paul. Peggy says we are delivered from tradition into Scriptural literalism by this debate.

Today I have to spend all afternoon on the drafting committee in my section and tomorrow all afternoon on the drafting committee of the message committee. The bishop of London asked yesterday that Demant introduce me to him and he told me he desired it not only because he wanted to meet me but also because he had once been your teacher.[2] I gulped and pretended that you had often spoken about him which was partly the truth because I did remember some connection at Oxford. After that, conversation was difficult. We had so little to go on.

—At this point I stopped this morning. Spent the morning discussing Christianity and communism and the afternoon on a drafting committee. Had luncheon with the young Norwegian pastor who chaired the Oslo meeting and French chaplain in Berlin whom I also met in Oslo. After lunch had a talk with Robert Mackie who is being asked to become associate General Secretary of the Council and wanted to know whether it was a good idea.

The conference is at the point where little has jelled except the decision to come into being. In various sections there is still much confusion upon most issues. Difficulties of language and theology are both great. Thus if a continental Protestant declares that the church should repent of this or that he is always challenged by an Orthodox or Anglo-Catholic who declares that the church as such does not repent. Then they are off on that issue rather than the one under discussion.

Last night I had dinner with John Collins of Oriel College, now the new canon at St. Paul's. Told me about his Christian Action movement which is pretty much an adjunct of Stafford's. Just had a note from the Dodds. Will have dinner with them on September 1. Must now work on a draft for a committee tomorrow. Am working a little more than I should but it is hard not to. I do however get to bed by 10:30 and sleep till 8. So I am well. Wish we were doing this together. It would be so much more fun to share it. But much of the experience is frustrating rather than creative.

Love,

R.N.

1. Mrs. Samuel Cavert; chair of commission on women's work. 2. Bishop Wand had been dean of Oriel College, Oxford. U.N. attended some of his lectures on church history, but she found them dull and did not continue going to them.

Eleven

1949
Paris:
Delegate to UNESCO

A major question before the United Nations Educational Scientific and Cultural Organization (UNESCO), founded in London in 1945 and headquartered in Paris, was local versus national control of education. Since Reinhold had been a member of the U.S. Commission on Cultural Affairs in Occupied Territories, and had toured Germany in previous years, he was suggested as a person who could speak on the issue of West German education in the debate scheduled for the 1949 meeting of UNESCO.

The American delegation to the Conference in Paris included Assistant Secretary of State George V. Allen and the president of the U.S. National Commission on UNESCO, Milton Eisenhower, who was then president of Kansas State University. The three other delegates were Luther Evans, librarian of Congress, who later became director general of UNESCO, Reinhold Niebuhr, and Martha Lucas, president of Sweet Briar College in Virginia. In addition, the delegation contained various advisers from Congress; also Myrna Loy, an American actress who had been observing Italian schools for UNESCO that summer.

Poland and Czechoslovakia were members but Russia was not and did not welcome UNESCO staff to East Germany. The U.S., Britain, and France, however, had welcomed UNESCO to observe schools in West Germany, which were under the supervision of their Länder (states). The West German Constitution, adopted in 1949, declared, "The entire educational system shall be under the supervision of the State. The parents entitled to bring up a child shall have the right to decide whether it shall receive religious instruction."

Paris, France
September 7, 1949

Friday, 10 P.M.

Dearest:

This is my first chance to write as we have been rushed from one thing to another. We arrived yesterday at 3 after a smooth trip. As I didn't sleep much on the plane I thought I would get a nap before going to the embassy for a reception at 6. But newspaper interviews, etc., kept us going until we had dinner at 9 and I piled into bed at 10 for a real long sleep. Feel fine today. Am ensconced in a fabulous old hotel. My room, dressing room, and bath are big enough to make a sizable NYC apartment. UNESCO is across the street. Its building is the old Majestic Hotel where the German army had its headquarters. Hitler, when he came to Paris, stayed at this hotel, and, I am told, in my room, the "suite royale." I doubt this however as the other rooms seem just as pretentious as mine.

We have met all day, then went to a cocktail party at the home of Chet Holland, the permanent U.S. delegate to UNESCO and the young man who as a student ran that student meeting in Washington in 1933 during the holidays where Henry Wallace spoke, etc. Remember? There are cocktail parties practically every night. Tomorrow night at the home of the deputy director. Had luncheon today with John Maud[1] who sends his love. His position in the English delegation corresponds to that of [George] Allen with us, and he is very much liked.

For one who is accustomed to church, rather than governmental conferences, this whole thing seems fantastic. We have a secretarial staff of 24 people. Besides the five regular delegates there are 15 consultants from various walks of life in U.S.A. There are mountains of mimeographed paper which makes the stuff I got in Washington seem like an airmail letter. I just don't understand why so much paper is necessary. On the other hand, there is real work to do and the hours are long. Allen is an intelligent, suave, and kind director of operations. Every position taken by our government is fully discussed though I suspect that not many positions could be changed by our discussion. But I'll learn more about that later.

Right now, I have to read a book of "position papers" containing 220 pages before going to bed. These represent the position the department takes on various issues to come before the conference. John Maud tells me that they have asked [Bertrand] Russell merely to come over and make his speech, and now he is worried that what he has to say may appear to be completely irrelevant because he is not a member of their delegation. If I was going to do this at all, I am glad to go through with the whole of it.

The speeches come on the 27th, 28th, and 29th. I don't know yet when mine comes. I understand they are to be broadcast on a world hookup.

I think of you often with a feeling of uneasiness about these days with Elisabeth in bed and Christopher to be gotten ready for school. I hope you won't be completely wrecked. Love to the old boy and girlie.

With anticipatory joy of return and reunion.

R.N.

1. Oxford scholar; later Lord Redcliffe-Maud; master of University College at Oxford.

Paris, France
September 16, 1949

Monday, 8 P.M.

Dearest:

It is now 3 P.M. in NYC which means that you are just about saying good-bye to the old boy. [Christopher was leaving for boarding school.] I hope you haven't been wrecked in the past two days with the two kids. At any rate you did a grand job the past summer with the two and I wished I had matched you. I also hope you will have a little more time to get into your work and not feel too frustrated.

I have just come from the second plenary session. We heard tepid oratory all day. The director general and the chairman of the board made their reports and members from Greece, Iraq, Afghanistan, etc., told what they liked and didn't like about UNESCO. Also, credentials committee reported, etc. Not too interesting except that our crowd of young men in the State Department give various members of our delegation assignments and make engagements for us to meet members of other delegations. I sat next to [Georges] Bidault all day, the head of the French delegation. [Bidault was appointed prime minister the following month.]

Tonight is the first soup and fish affair. Have to put on "black tie" for the reception at the house of the director general. Have gone to three cocktail parties already and stood about until I thought I couldn't stand any more. The plan for enlarged work in Germany has been passed by the steering committee, and it is one of the two projects with which I am entrusted to present to the plenary session. Every step we take is carefully debated in our delegation and unanimous decision striven for. All this makes for a lot of talk, more talk than I have heard in years. I won't get a thing accomplished on my courses as I expected. I will do well to be able to rewrite my speech by snatching about an hour a day on it. As the reception does not begin until 10 P.M. I will work a little on it now.

Hope to hear from you soon though I wouldn't blame you if you didn't find time to write. Incidentally, the address, rather than the embassy, is Hotel Raphael, 17 Avenue Kléber. Will have dinner with Charles Bohlen, counsellor of the embassy on Thursday. They can't change my ticket so I must fly to London on Saturday, Oct. 1st and arrive home about 4 or 5 A.M. on Sunday morning.

Much love,

R.N.

Paris, France
Wednesday, September 18, 1949

Dearest:

Received your second letter today and am happy that the children were reasonably nice though still not physically well. [Both children had allergic reactions in September just as they had had the previous spring. This meant they started school with sniffles and wheezles.] I do wish I could help you a little more. You are right. The September season is terrible for you. We must find some better scheme than the present one.

We move from day to day in what is at once an interesting and a boring experience. Boring because it's endless committee work. Let me suggest my schedule today.

9 A.M.–Delegation meeting. Assignments given out. I am etc. liason person for U.K. delegation.

10:30 A.M.–Plenary session. Endless speeches on the general report.

1:00 P.M.–Luncheon with Sir Ronald Adam, a nice old boy of the British Council. We discuss differences and common convictions of two delegations.

2:00 P.M.–Drafting committee on my section.

3:00 P.M.–Meeting to discuss outline of broadcast for U. of C[hicago] Roundtable with Stoddard, Laves, Eisenhower and others.

3:30 P.M.–Plenary session. More speeches. I can't leave even for a moment because I am secretary for the day and take down the relevant points in the speeches. Polish delegate makes fierce attack on U.S.A. and UNESCO. Iraq, Israel, Turkey, South Africa, Liberia, etc., etc., speak.

6:30 P.M.–Steering committee of delegation meets.

9:00 P.M.–Dinner with George Allen.

10:00 P.M.–Subdrafting committee meets for an hour.

11:00 P.M.–The present hour. I am exhausted. It's not uninteresting but so full of procedure, budget, and details that I could stand no more than two weeks of this. Happy that I served notice about coming home on Oct. 1. Look forward to it but it's a long way off.

With love and longing,

R.N.

Paris, France
Wednesday, September 18, 1949

Dearest:

It has been impossible to get another ticket for Friday or Saturday, so I am definitely coming home leaving early Saturday morning, spending four hours in the London airport and arriving home Sunday morning at about 3 A.M.

Made my "big" speech last night and it was well received. Allen at the delegation meeting this morning made a very gracious report on it. The evening was terrible with eight speakers saying the usual things about the rights of man, humanity, etc., etc. Bidault was fair. I had quite a nice time with him.

From now on life will not be quite so strenuous. The work is now in subcommittee phase and the inner circle of our delegation does that work, meaning Allen, Eisenhower, and Luther Evans. We just have returned from a dinner given by the Indian delegation to five other delegations. It was a large ornate affair. Beg pardon, not dinner but luncheon. All of us wondered how we could possibly eat again today. I will pick up a sandwich tonight so that I won't feel as loggy as I do now. These official affairs are really something. The only other one I have is on Thursday at the British Embassy. One is always completely finished after the fish course, which is much too large, and then wonders how to get through the next. Sat next to the Canadian minister to Russia today who regaled me with stories of his experiences. Yesterday I lunched with a Hungarian diplomat who was second in command to the condemned Rajk[1] and who escaped from his diplomatic post in Vienna when a telephone conversation asking him to return to Budapest for consultations tipped him off to danger. He used to be head of I.S.S. [International Students Service] work in Europe after the first world war and is a friend of Walter Kotschnig.[2] He gets almost daily telephone calls from his mother in Budapest asking him to come back which he feels certain are prompted by the police. He is in great stress because he believes that his resolve to escape will cost the life of his father and mother.

All in all I suppose this has been worthwhile though I sometimes wonder. At any rate I am glad that it is coming to a close and that there are only two more full days before I go. I had hoped to pick up some little knickknacks of some kind for the children but I haven't had a chance yet to get within a mile of a shopping district. Perhaps I will go on Friday. Friday night I will make a speech to an American colony group.

Much love,

R.N.

1. *Lazlo Rajk, the Communist Foreign Minister of Hungary, had been arrested in June, setting off a purge of officials accused of deviating from pro-Soviet policies.* 2. *Also connected with ISS; later a professor at Smith College.*

Paris, France
September 20, 1949

Friday Evening

Dearest:

I have just received your letter telling about Christopher's departure. I do hope things are beginning to straighten out for you a little. My heart went out to the old boy as I read your letter. I should have taken him to school. It would have been a wonderful opportunity. But he was undoubtedly happy with Richard. [Christopher's cousin, Richard Niebuhr, took him for his first term to boarding school.]

Today we had a 2½ hour discussion on how to organize our debate on the great theme. The conference expected nine speakers but had to invite every delegation to present a speaker. 27 responded. So we spent hours on how to choose 3 or 6 or 9 to make the principal addresses. Hardman of the British delegation was a little sticky by insisting that Russell would have to have at least 45 minutes to develop his theme. The delegate from New Zealand wanted a debate between Russell and myself. After hours of discussion the matter was referred to a subcommittee. I was supposed to serve, but the committee meets in the morning at the same hour when I have been designated to present the delegation position on the German question. You will probably find something on that in the papers. I will have to fight with the Pole and Czech. Today I spent the good part of the day lining up the Swiss, Dutch, and Norwegian delegation[s] so that we would not take the lead. John Maud had unfortunately not returned, and so I have to look up the British delegation tonight after this letter to see how they stand. Vim t'Hooft and Bishop [Stephen] Neil suddenly appeared this evening at dinner time. They have arrived for a high level discussion with the Catholic theologians on Saturday and Sunday. Invited me. I hope I can go on Sunday at least. Have to cancel a trip to Chartres to which I was invited. So it goes. I really will be glad when this is over.

A week from tonight I will speak on American foreign policy at a meeting organized by a group of Americans. You ask about Myrna Loy. Last night she was at the dinner given by Counsellor of Embassy [Charles] Bohlen. Took me and Congressman McDermott and his wife home in her car. She is quite intelligent and naive. Has spent the whole summer on UNESCO business in Italy.

Most of the evening discussion was between Bohlen's diplomatic realism and my Christian realism, and Miss Loy's [and] young Arthur Compton['s][1] (who is like his father) and the congressman's utopianism. Everyone but Bohlen, who has read my stuff prodded by Art[hur] Schlesinger [Jr.], thought it impossible for a theologian to be anything but what they called idealistic. Quite a discussion. The delegation asked me to preach and conduct a little service for the delegation next Sunday morning. But I understand Allen has vetoed it for fear of embarrassing someone. Allen is a first-rate fellow however.

I must get on the political beat. Counting the days for the reunion.

Love,

R.N.

1. *Co-winner of 1926 Nobel Prize for physics; chancellor, Washington University, St. Louis, MO.*

Paris, France
Monday, September 23, 1949

Dearest:

Just received your letter. There must be some mistake about the old boy's galoshes. They were size 13 and we took his largest pair of shoes to fit them on. I am afraid he hasn't gone to the bottom of his trunk. So glad you are getting back to normal. I never wrote about my cold as you asked. It is gradually wearing off but has taken a long time.

Have had hectic days. Saturday I had to represent us in the struggle about Germany and had a real tangle with the Poles and Czechs, which I enjoyed. The "debate" comes off beginning tomorrow. I speak on Tuesday with Bidault, and Russell is on Thursday. There are three speeches and innumerable smaller discourses on each evening.

Yesterday I had expected to go to Chartres, but I think I told you that t'Hooft and Neil arrived all primed for a conference with the Roman Catholics. I spent Sunday that way. The conference didn't get very far and my French isn't good enough to follow. Leonard Hodgson and Oliver Tomkins also were there. The discussion was within narrow limits, but the priests present represented some of the most vital intellectual elements in French and Belgian Catholicism and it was fun to speak with them informally.

Today Allen gave a luncheon to the director general and tonight for the English delegation. So I have to eat an awful lot. Tomorrow I must boil my speech down to 20 minutes and then deliver it. This morning we recorded a Chicago University Roundtable discussion on UNESCO with myself as moderator and Eisenhower, Stoddard, and Laves.

One goes round and round and I haven't even looked into my brief-case and taken out my notes. This may be the last letter. I am scheduled to leave early Saturday morning, fly via England and arrive at about 3 A.M. Sunday morning. But they are trying to get a plane for me for midnight Friday, which would get me in Saturday afternoon. So if I don't arrive by about 6 P.M. Saturday, you needn't expect me till the middle of the night.

Hodgson, of course, sends all kinds of messages. Oliver Tomkins had some extra hours and spent them with me at the hotel. We had particularly good time with a robust young professor of theology at the Dominican seminary in Brussels. Here I am back on the previous proposition. I am getting woozy, I imagine. You can't imagine how dull and uninteresting the evenings and nights and mornings are. During the day one is in a whirl. But in the evening one longs for the bosom of intimacy. So—

Love to the old girlie and
Vicky [our poodle],

R.N.

Selected Letters
from Correspondence with Friends

Part III

Selected Letters
from Correspondence with Friends

Letters from friends speak for themselves. They often express more fully than conversation the quality of the shared interests of the correspondents. Often they may be written to inquire about an enterprise or matter of mutual concern.

Yet many good friends with whom interests are shared do not write letters. Nowadays, the telephone rather than the pen, is the medium of communication. There are many who do not write letters, many others seem not to know how to write letters.

Reinhold and I, however, were rich and lucky, for many of our friends wrote letters. (Other friends, colleagues of one or the other of us who shared participation in academic, theological, or political organizations where meetings or journeying to meetings provided opportunities for conversation, of course had no need for correspondence, and little with them exists.) Limitations of time and space require me to exclude here many wonderful letters that, I hope, may enrich later generations who will find them in archives and other sources.

Twelve

W. H. Auden

Wystan Auden was a close and dear friend to Reinhold, me, and our children. He was always kind, interested, and generous; we, as did other friends of his, gave him a family setting.

He and I had shared the same sort of English and Edwardian childhood. We both had doctor fathers; both of us had devout mothers. As children we had read many of the same books. Born the same year, we had been at Oxford for much of the same time. Although we had not known each other there, we had known some of the same people.

Anglican liturgy also had influenced us both. Reinhold would call us "d——d Anglicans" and Wystan would call him a "Prot."

His range of interest and reading meant much to both of us. The imagery and mythology of theology fascinated him, and fed his own imagination. He was much more theological than many academic theologians.

We had got to know him in the early forties, after our return from England and Scotland and the outbreak of war in Europe. He had come to this country about the same time. He had described his coming to the U.S.A. as "one of the most significant experiences of my life," and further enlarged on the characteristics of an open society and its demands and dangers.

His theological interest meanwhile was showing itself. In a review of Kafka, he described Kafka's hero as being "in constant danger of denying the Necessary he cannot understand, of losing his Faith, and to lose Faith is to be damned."

Influenced by Søren Kierkegaard, as also were we, he wrote of the "leap of faith": "It reminds us that we cannot live without faith in something, and when that faith which [people] have breaks down, when the ground crumbles under their feet, they have to leap even into uncertainty if they are to avoid certain destruction."

Both he and Reinhold made use of Kierkegaard's concept of irony. Thus, Don Quixote was not a tragic or comic hero but an ironic hero, who uses "the language of the feudal knight, but his behavior is that of the Suffering Servant" . . . and he "reveals himself to us as the Knight of Fate, whose kingdom is not of this world."

Reinhold, preparing some lectures on the interpretation of history for publication, used the concept of irony as a framework. This is expressed in the first and last chapters of *The Irony of American History*.

But this ironic imagination was to be used not only in an analysis of history or of literature, but existentially, in judgment upon oneself. The poet and the teacher both were very aware of the peculiar temptations of their callings. Thus, Auden's poem, "At the Grave of Henry James," according to his letter of July 28, 1941, owed much to Reinhold:

All will be judged, Master of nuance and scruple,
Pray for me and for all writers living or dead; . . .
For the treason of all clerks.

Reinhold likewise often repeated in prayers he used, and in addresses to clergy or theological students, his warning against spiritual pride, a special hazard to the "professional."

"Nothing is more insufferable than a professional holy man in the pulpit who pretends to all the Christian virtues. He is a pathetic sinner, this fellow: He may have entered the ministry because he is an exhibitionist at heart. . . . The more successful you are, the more you will be judged to various temptations of pride and exhibitionism."

We cherished this friend, his imagination, and what he saw and taught us about life, not only about the human situation but also about a certain vision of glory.

Ann Arbor, MI
December 19, 1941

Dear Mrs. Niebuhr,

Thank you ever so much for your letter though you sound very overdone. I hope that the Christian Dynamo Reinhold will give you two or three days' rest at Christmas, or rather that you will very firmly put him to bed and keep him there. How I laughed over your story about him not getting anything DONE. I'm sure if Lutherans had father confessors, Reinhold's would say "Now, my son, as a penance for being an ecclesiastical Orson Welles, you shall sit in an arm chair for 48 hours with NO RADIO and just twiddle your thumbs." In Purgatory, while you and I are picking Oakum, Reinhold will be condemned to a rocking chair.

After the shock of the first twenty-four hours, the war has fallen into being part of the natural climate. Until I am wanted for anything, I shall carry on with my daily routine. As it had to come, I suppose it couldn't of come in a better way as far as American opinion is concerned, though it makes me a little sad to realize that there is more indignation over the Japs than the Germans, because they are "little and yellow." The Hearst Publisher editorial the next day in the *Detroit Times* might have been written by Goebbels. It even mentioned Castor Oil. . . . The news from Malaya is grim, isn't it? But enough of that. I think one ought to make a rule with oneself never to talk about the war except when there is something practical to be done.

I am pegging slowly away at my *Christmas Oratorio*, which will be immensely lay, and very theological. . . . Vacations begin today and I leave at noon (it is now 8 A.M.) for California. Some of my students are coming along nicely. There are many theories about me. One party believes that I am a starry-eyed idealist, another that I am a crass materialist. One professor who is a fanatical Aristotelian met another professor in the corridor and said: "I don't like to say anything malicious about another human being, but I hear that Auden is a Platonist"!

The class is very shocked at the moment because I have told them that for their exam at the end of the semester all they have to do is to learn six cantos of the *Divine Comedy* by heart and write them out. They think this cannot be done, so I have promised them that if I can't learn the whole assignment in the train between Chicago and Los Angeles, I'll reduce it.

Have you and Reinhold found that American students are not used to having their work criticized severely? They seem to imagine that it can only proceed from a personal dislike. . . . Now when WE were undergraduates.

By the way, have you ever read Arthur Waley's *The Way and the Power,* the translation of the Quietist Tao Te Ching? Seems to be wonderful stuff in it.

I must stop and start packing and distributing the leavings of the icebox to neighbors.

> *Much love to you and to Reinhold*
> *and to the Family and a happy*
> *"Ivory Tower" (God, how I hate*
> *that term) Christmas.*

> *Wystan*

Swarthmore, PA
June 2, 1944

Dear Mrs. Niebuhr,

Thank you so much for your letter. I'm glad that you liked the Kierkegaard piece.[1] I have just finished an article-review of Cochrane's book

[*Christianity and Classic Culture*] after writing it four times. Trying to explain the doctrine of the Trinity to readers of the *New Republic* is not easy.

I would love to see you all again. I'm here teaching till June the 25th; then am one of the few lucky ones who get the summer off. I hope very much you will not have left for the country by then. I was up very near you the other day for a wedding at Riverside Church (an old pupil) but had to dash back here directly afterwards. What has American Protestantism come to? Do you know what the organist played before the wedding? The prelude to *Tristan!*

I've been pretty busy teaching, etc. I have a new book coming out in the fall consisting of the *Oratorio* (revised since you saw it) and another lay work based on the characters in Shakespeare's *Tempest,* which is really about the Christian conception of Art. A collected volume of my stuff was to have appeared last April, but Random House put the ms. in the safe and forgot it for four months. And now there is no paper, so it won't appear until next January.

If Reinhold ever has an hour to spare at Philadelphia on his way to or from Washington, I hope he'll let me know, and I'll come in. The political future is pretty black, don't you think? But we shouldn't, I suppose, be surprised.

Did you ever see a little book by Charles Williams on *The Forgiveness of Sins* which was published in England about two years ago? I thought it very good indeed. Hoping to see you soon.

Love,

Wystan Auden

1. *Auden reviewed the new translation of Kierkegaard's* Either/Or *for the* New Republic.

Swarthmore, PA
Sunday, October 1944

Dear Ursula,

Thank you for your letter. I rang you up twice while I was in New York, in August and beginning of September, but of course you were still away on vacation.

I hope the copy of my book [*For the Time Being*] you have was the one I asked Random House to send you. One bad misprint of page 128 line 3 (looked read locked).

I had a nice quiet summer, terribly hot but have managed to get some work done, though I shall never equal Reinhold, however hard I try.

I am glad you are taking a rest from Columbia and Barnard, but I can't believe a nunnery is the place for you to go to. You would keep imagining during mass that you heard the telephone ringing.

At *last*, the *New Republic* has printed my now months' old piece on Cochrane's book—they've cut it about a bit but I'm really quite pleased with it.

I shall certainly be in New York during the next month as until November, I only have a Bryn Mawr class to bother about, and I want to see you both very much.

Love, ever yours,

Wystan

Swarthmore, PA
1944

Dear Ursula,

Thank you so much for your letter. Terribly sorry to hear about the grippe and hope that the convalescent Blues which usually follow it won't be too bad.

It was such a pleasure to see Reinhold again, looking more of a benevolent eagle than ever. His *Destiny* [*The Nature and Destiny of Man,* Vol. II] is grand, I think, and is already on the required reading list for my seminar in romanticism which starts tomorrow. Poor things, they have no idea what they have let themselves in for—Kierkegaard's *Unscientific Post-script,* for instance. Seminars last from one-thirty to six, so I have to provide refreshments. Quakers or no Quakers, I shall serve bread and cheese and beer at four o'clock.

I enclose two examinations of mine for your bedside reading.

Get well soon and come down for a visit.

Love,

Wystan

New York, NY
February 14, 1946

Dear Ursula:

. . . It's not fair for me to judge Reinhold's preaching on a single hearing, but I was worried. Your comment was quite correct, that it sounded like a review of *Nature and Destiny,* and for that the occasion was wrong. Looking round at my fellow congregation, I felt the effect was to make them smug. "*We* are not like Dreiser." (How many of them have seen as clearly as Dreiser just how dreadful life is? If they haven't, they haven't earned the right to say he is wrong.) *We* are not like Aquinas (how many have used their reason enough to criticize him?), we *know* we see through a glass darkly, we know that hereafter we shall see face to face, we are good honest biblical protestants, we are . . .

It seems to me a sermon must attempt one of three things: to teach and explain doctrine, to call the sinner to repentance, or to refresh those that are heavy-laden, and that preaching to a church congregation now is very different from preaching in Union Square. Kierkegaard as usual put his finger on the sore spot when he said that the task of the preacher is to preach Christ the contemporary offense to Christians. We who profess ourselves Christians must not be allowed to forget how much justice there is in Nietzsche's assertion that as a whole we are a nastier lot than the pagans (one has after all to be pretty nasty to admit that one is in need of Grace).

But enough of this. Hope I'll see you soon.

Love to you both,

Wystan

New York, NY
June 29, 1946

Dear Ursula and Reinhold:

I sent off birthday presents yesterday. I hope that my choice will be satisfactory. The Henry James Prefaces [*The American Scene,* by Henry James, with an introduction by Auden, Scribner's, 1946] are the best stuff I know about the nature of the creative act.

All in a dither about tonight. [T. S. Eliot was coming to dinner.] It's the first real dinner party I've given. The menu is:
Watercress soup (Chinese style)
Cold salmon (Will the glazing go right?)
Hollandaise Sauce
New potatoes–Kidney bean salad
Zabaglione
Wisconsin Bleu Cheese (A favorite of T.S.E.'s)
And as much Chilean white wine as we can stand.
The rest is up to the Comforter.

I got back to find an invitation from the Guild of Episcopal Scholars.[1] (What a vision that conjures up!) To address them in December on

"Religion and the Artist"; people seem to have an insatiable appetite for that kind of thing, and I find the word Religion very suspect, but I suppose I must do what I can.

I hope that Elisabeth's injections were not too unpleasant, and that no one has had to leave the table for shouting under the Emergency Decree of last Monday.

I had a lovely weekend.

Love to all.

Wystan

1. *After Auden's death, the Guild of Episcopal Scholars, which meets every year at General Theological Seminary in New York, asked U.N. to read a paper to them on Auden and his interest in theology. She had great pleasure in quoting from this letter.*

Forio d'Ischia
Prov. di' Napoli, Italy
April 26, 1950

Dearest Ursula:

A happy Post-Easter. Wish you could have been with me for mass at our Santa Lucia's. Before it, the women have their Rosary and scream as if they were cursing the men. During the collection people ask for change, which I have never seen done before, and the responses during Benediction are an extraordinary mixture of Latin and Forian Italian. I'm having rather an embarrassing time with the Parocco[1] who will call just at dinner time and try to convert me. Went over on Good Friday to the next Island, Pioceda, where they have a procession of floats representing incidents in the Passion. The Last Supper looked *delicious,* lots of antipasto, but the oddest feature was the mourners following the dead Christ, little girls of 4 or 5 dressed up in blonde wigs and beaded costumes looking like midget whores.

The weather has been most unwoppy, quite lakedistricty in fact, which I fear may have killed the cucumber seeds. We are simply *deluged,* however, with broad beans to which I am very partial.

Was *just* getting into a museworthy condition when I got a wire to go to Naples, where I was presented with a two-page film script in German of *The Odyssey* and told to make a two-page English synopsis in ten days for Ingrid Bergman. The present suggestion is that I do the English dialogue. I'm hoping against hope that, as the producer is clearly a crook, he is going to balk at what my Agent asks for the job, but if he accepts I can't afford to miss the financial opportunity. Well, we shall see. Meanwhile I am back again at a poem I had started, and reading the new Peter

Quennell edition of Byron's letters. I find him so sympathetic except for his neurotic digestion. Why, he couldn't even eat bacon and eggs.

How do you like my Laity piece?[2]

Was very upset to hear about Matthiessen.[3] Who is going to look after his cats?

Much love to all,

Wystan

1. *Parish priest.* 2. *"The Things Which Are Caesar's," Theology, Nov.-Dec. 50.* 3. *F. O. Matthiessen; Harvard University English professor who committed suicide.*

Forio d'Ischia
Prov. di' Napoli, Italy
July 22, 1950

Dearest Ursula:

Your letter arrived rather opportunely as this morning I completed the book [*Nones*] I'm dedicating to you and R, with a poem entitled "Nones."

To Reinhold	and	Ursula Niebuhr
whose view it is		who knows that a real
that life is full of		Prot. will never kneel
moral ambiguities		but only squat

with love and admiration from Wystan
who is forty-four today
and still a sinner, I'm sorry to say

Really, Reinhold is disgraceful the way he won't stop. If I were his confessor I would forbid him to speak outside Union for a year and give him a rosary to use when he felt fidgety.

The presses are rolling at last on our Viking anthology but it will be years I fear before we pay off our debts for proof corrections.

Much love to all,

Wystan

Forio d'Ischia
Prov. di' Napoli, Italy
Corpus Christi, July 14, 1955

Dear Ursula:

I have to send you the enclosed [poem, "Clio"] because you were so much in mind while I was writing it, as the only person who will understand my Anglican problem: Can one write a poem to the B.V.M. without being "pi"? The Prots don't like Her and the Romans want bleeding hearts and sobbing tenors. So here is my attempt which I submit to your severe, theological and feminine, eye.

All is well here. It is getting hot. We had our first figs today at lunch. Leonora [the cat] has two hideous black kittens to which she is madly overdevoted. I went to mass this morning at a church where a "congregatione" of elderly gentlemen devoted to La Virgine di Loretto sang in turns a very long sequence in her honor; never in my life have I heard such a caterwauling: it was very touching but I hope the Virgin in question is tone-deaf.

How is Reinhold? and Christopher? and my precious, Elisabeth? I duly did my piece for Dean Pike.[1] I fear it is rather shy-making as all such pieces can hardly help being. Now comes a letter from the literature committee of The N.C.C. [National Council of Churches] asking me, if you please, to list twenty great books which would be suitable for "Christian" criticism. What do the Trinity say to each other about such folk?

Lots of love,

Wystan

1. *In* Modern Canterbury Pilgrims, *introduction by James Pike (New York, Morehouse-Gorham, 1956).*

Cherry Grove
via **Sayville**
Long Island, NY
June 7, 1956

Dear Ursula:

I was so sorry I didn't manage to get hold of you before I left. Are you at Heath or in N.Y. again? Really, Columbia is a funny place. I went to a publisher's lunch. Jacques Barzun was there and said "I'm glad we're going to hear you on June 2nd (it was on May 23rd). "What do you mean?" I asked. "You're reading the Phi Beta Kappa poem. The notices are printed." It appears that some Barnard girl suggested that I do it, but nobody took the trouble to ask me. I was furious but professional conceit wouldn't let me refuse lest it be thought I couldn't compose a poem in a week. I worked like a *beaver,* God was gracious, and the result was, I believe, not at all bad.

I am here all by myself, cooking breakfast and lunch but going to the hotel for dinner. Rather lonely at times but writing busily and finding it a great relief not to have to think about one's next lecture.

Have been reading the latest Wallace Stevens; some of it is very good, but he provoked me to the following little short:

Dear oh dear, More heresy to muzzle.
No sooner have we buried in peace
The flighty divinities of Greece
Than up there pops this barbarian with
An antimythological myth,
Calling the sun the sun, his mind *Puzzle*.

If you or Reinhold are either one in N.Y. for a time, I do hope you'll come out here for a night.

Love,

Wystan

Forio d'Ischia
Prov. di' Napoli, Italy
May 30 [1957]

Dearest Ursula:

Many thanks for your letter (undated) which I got last night when I returned from a three-week visit to England which was looking as lovely as ever. Pappa was well and much happier for his move to Repton [Parish Church, St. Wystan's] where he was born. My only worry is his habit of dropping off to sleep suddenly which might end in his setting himself on fire. Spent Whit weekend in Oxford which is *very* changed. Was very interested to see the new younger generation (also at the Slade School where there are a number of ex-pupils of mine). They're much nicer, more sensible and less neurotic than we were, but I wonder how they will age. Is it a good thing to have so few flings at 20–25, and such a practical attitude (even in the arts)? The younger generation in the U.S. seem much more like I remember myself.

Had dinner with Old Possum; apart from saying nice things about you, we talked almost exclusively of dentures, hernias, and piles. The *Time* piece and photo were typical of that revolting periodical; it's so much worse when they [are] trying to be nice.

India, at least the Congress, was pure Hell and quite useless. To begin with Bombay has total Prohibition and then I was overwhelmed with the decreative power of Public Life. (I wanted to write Reinhold a warning.) One can lecture to a large audience on a subject about which one knows and in which they have a genuine interest (i.e., in the truth not in the teacher) and one can talk to a small group of friends. Everything else, all "saying a few words" is vanity and vexation of spirit. I must, however, [admit] that I had flu at the time. Got over to Calcutta to see Brother, sister-in-law, and children who are enchanting. All are coming here for three weeks in July. John (my brother) has become an R.C., I think rightly, because the Anglican Church in India is impossibly tied up with the British.

Have been reading a lot, writing pensées, but have had too many distractions to write the poems I want to which I have to find my way into. My besetting sin is impatience, so I hope the delay is a good discipline.

Among other works have read Simone Weil's *La Pesanteur et La Grâce*. Have you? Wildly exasperating, I think, but very important. An exposition of the *Via Negativa* carried almost to heretical lengths, i.e., for her it is not the Cross that is the stumbling block, but the Incarnation, or rather any of the references in the Gospel to Christ enjoying himself. However, it is more honest than any modern work I know about the characteristic experience of God in a sceptical schizophrenic age like ours. By contrast am reading an account of his life by a manic-depressive which seems extremely untypical in its swing from thinking one is God to thinking one is Satan.

Lots of love to all,

Wystan

Christ Church
Oxford, England
May 27, 1958

Dearest Ursula:

Many thanks for your letter which I should have answered before but have waited till I finished my lectures. . . .

I had a letter from Christopher which I answered saying that, if he wished, I would try and get him a guest-room here but I daresay he will want to be with Elisabeth.[1] Am much looking forward to seeing them both. I ran into a young man who is acting at the Playhouse who told me that, in some Harvard circles at least, Elisabeth was the sensational freshman (woman?) of her year. It's nice to know that the young can have such good taste.

Have finished my side of the Creweian Oration:[2] I can't bear to see my beautiful Protestant English being turned into Catholic verbosity. Whoever started the astounding notion that Latin is a *concise* language? One of my farewell tributes is to Canon Hodgson.[3] Such a dear, don't you think and also, I suspect, saintly. As a whole the Christ Church canons are pleasant enough, but they don't strike one as exactly *unworldly*.

England has been lovely, so cold and wet. I hear from Chester that work on the kitchen in Ischia is proceeding smoothly. I shall fly out on June 26th.

The social whirl here is terrific. I receive undergraduates in the Cadena[4] at 11 A.M.–6 P.M. daily.

Have seen C. S. Lewis several times. I think it was very unkind of the Lord to give so good and brilliant a soul such an unprepossessing manner and voice. He should have been sent to a Finishing School.

We had two members of the Beat Generation here who created a great impression. Some thought them as wise as Socrates: others threw shoes. But at least they didn't take their clothes off in public as I understand they are apt to do.

The George[5] has closed. I feel very upset.

Much love to you all,

Wystan

1. *Christopher was on leave from his military service in Germany with the Seventh Army. Elisabeth was due to go abroad with a good friend. Both were planning to be in Oxford.* 2. *One of Auden's duties as professor of poetry at Oxford was to deliver the Creweian Oration every second year. The Latin text, which was printed on left-hand pages, was prepared by a classics scholar. Opposite the Latin text on the right-hand pages was Auden's English text.* 3. *Leonard Hodgson; canon of Christ Church and professor of theology.* 4. *Historic Oxford restaurant.* 5. *Oxford hotel.*

New York, NY
February 18, 1962

Dearest Ursula:

I miss you both, and want to see you. If I came to Cambridge in latter half of March, could you put me up?

Among other things, I need your ghostly counsels, in case I am going crazy, because I find myself being driven to the conclusion that the U.S. must unilaterally destroy all its bombs. They are only a deterrent if we are prepared to use them and I do not see how, if the worst happened and we were bombarded with 50 megaton bombs, we could have the moral right to retaliate, any more than it would have been right if, after 1945, the

Jews had taken six million gentiles and gassed them. But this might wait till I see you.

Much love to you both,

Wystan

Kirchstetten, Austria
May 11, 1962

Dearest Ursula:

When I came across the enclosed I knew I had to write to you.

After a few fine days at Easter the weather turned bitterly cold, but at last it is warm again and, belatedly, the fruit trees are blossoming, and our broad beans and peas beginning to sprout—we were afraid they were all dead. As I write, a cuckoo is carrying on in the wood just behind us and a maddening little bird—I wish I were a naturalist who knew all the names—who has nothing to say but itsky-bitsky-bitsk but is very fond of saying it.

I have written a longish poem in praise of the bathroom, and am now working on a commentary for a Canadian documentary about a seventeen-year-old runner who holds the record for the three miles—this I am finding very difficult: I want to find a modern equivalent to Pindar.

If you haven't read it, do get hold of Laurens Van der Post's book about the African Bushman, *The Lost World of the Kalahari* (it's in Penguin). They were, apparently the original inhabitants and I get the conviction that, until they met, first the later invading tribes and then the whites (who killed most of them) they were a pre-lapsarian people. It makes me wonder where exactly the Fall took place.

We are going to Vienna this evening to see Qualtinger, one of the world's great comedians, in *Herr Karl,* a monologue of a typical Viennese about the last forty years which has caused great offence with its home-truths.

We were reading some of Graves' recent love poems the other day and Chester remarked: "He seems to be hoist with his own Petrarch." Rather good, don't you think?

Much love to you both,

Wystan

Kirchstetten, Austria
June 10, 1965

Dearest Ursula:

I keep thinking and worrying about you both (and praying for you), as I fear you are having dark days.

Berlin was quite fun. More conscientious than most of my colleagues, though obliged to do nothing, I spoke to all sorts and conditions, including the wives of British officers. They were quite incredible: as if they were living in Ceylon and surrounded by natives.

All well here. Since the liturgical reform, it is impossible to tell a Roman Mass from a High Anglican one (except for the portion of the Gloria, where we are liturgically superior, I think).

I enclose two pieces. The Anthem was commissioned by the Dean of Christ Church from me and William Walton. The first performance was in the Cathedral on May 16th and sounded well I thought. I hope you will find the text O.K.: it's frightfully difficult to be contemporary without becoming South-Banky.

As for the Epithalamion, the Bridegroom, an old Choir boy, is very nice and intelligent. Unfortunately, they had to be married in a registry office. Rita[1] is an R.C. studying to become a doctor, and has decided she can't have children until she has qualified—so.

Much love,

Wystan

1. *Wystan's niece.*

Kirchstetten, Austria
Corpus Christi
July 14, 1971

Dearest Ursula:

As you can imagine, you are very much in my thoughts in these days.[1] I do hope the end came easily. As you know, I lost another friend this year, Stravinsky. I saw him a week before he died—he was only half conscious, but I think he recognized me.

I'm sure Reinhold would have appreciated my diary entry for June 2nd. (Naturally, I didn't hear the news for two days, late.)

> *Reinhold died.*
> *Home-made potato-chips with cocktails.*

Overleaf a poem ["Talking to Mice"] which, as a fellow Edwardian child, I hope will amuse you.

Bless you, dear. You know how much your friendship means to me.

Love,

Wystan

P.S. This month I get a D. Lit. from Oxford which is flattering. The Prime Minister is getting something too.

1. *Reinhold died June 1, 1971, in Stockbridge, MA.*

Kirchstetten, Austria
May 30, 1972

Dearest Ursula:

Delighted to get your letter.

I shan't be in Oxford till October, but am pleased that you won't be going to Israel until Feb., so we shall be able to see each other. So glad that you now feel like working. From my observations, I would say that, hard as it is for both, life is easier for widows than for widowers.

I was so ashamed the other day. We had a local blood-donation, so, naturally, off I went to do my neighborly duty, only to be told that I was too old.

Hope the poem overleaf will amuse you. ["Short Ode to the Cuckoo" was handwritten on back of letter.]

> *Much love,*
>
> *Wystan*

Kirchstetten, Austria
August 30, 1972

Dearest Ursula:

Many thanks for your letter. I expect to come to England on October 7th and to be staying with Stephen Spender. . . . We *must* see each other.

The story about the U.N. Anthem is true. You can imagine how difficult it was, since one must not offend anyone's religious or political convictions, to avoid the most appalling clichés. I hope I've managed. I'm a bit worried because my spies tell me that, as a composer, Casals is not very good.

I have, naturally, thought about writing something for Reinhold, but can't see my way. To write a successful elegy, one has to combine the personal theme with an impersonal. R. was a theologian, and the only theological bee in my bonnet is Liturgical Reform which wasn't his province. Did I tell you that, since my own parish church went mad, I am reduced to going to a Russian Orthodox Church?

I know exactly how you feel about America. Strictly *entre nous*, if it is financially possible I am thinking of retiring next year to Christ Church, Oxford.

I have just got back from Lake Ohrid in Macedonia where I was given a golden watch!

Chester sends greetings.

I can't wait to see you. Bless you.

Love,

Wystan

Thirteen

Felix Frankfurter

Felix and Marion, his beautiful wife, were very dear and important friends to both of us and to our children. I had met them first at the hospitable board of Mr. and Mrs. John Moors in Brookline. The Moorses and the Frankfurters had been good friends ever since they were associated in the defense of Sacco and Vanzetti in the early twenties.

At this first meeting, a Sunday lunch at the Moors', the Frankfurters had only recently come back from Oxford where he had been Eastman Professor. They had enjoyed Oxford, and I knew Oxford had enjoyed them. There was much to talk about, particularly as they and Mrs. Moors were Anglophiles.

The Frankfurters were anxious to meet Reinhold. As he was on the Board of Preachers at Harvard University—he came twice in the academic year to preach at the Memorial Church and to meet with various groups such as the Nieman Fellows or to speak to the Law School Forum—this was quite easily and soon achieved.

After Felix was appointed to the Supreme Court, Mrs. Moors lent them for three weeks her beautiful old house near Heath, Massachusetts, the village where we summered. It was the same house that she had kindly lent us first in 1933 for me to convalesce in and in 1938 for Reinhold and Christopher.

Having them nearby, our more occasional friendship became much closer. We often met for tea in the afternoon, for he, as we academics, observed strict working hours in the morning. Village life fascinated him and he enjoyed all the human and humorous aspects of party-line telephones and gossip relayed from the village store.

We were delighted when the Frankfurters asked us to help them find somewhere to rent regularly for the summer. Luckily, Bishop Gilbert of New York had a house available, as he and his son had restored and were living in the old red mill nearby. So the Frankfurters inhabited the Bishop's White House, often described to tourists or stray journalists as the "Bishop White's House." Thus Felix acquired the dubious identity of a Bishop White, which delighted him enormously. As he was interested not only in theology but ecclesiastical history, we used to tease him and tell him he belonged to the eighteenth or early nineteenth century and should have been an English bishop of that period.

He was enormously interested in religion and theological thought, which was lucky as many summer residents were theological professors from Cambridge and elsewhere. Also, there was another summer resident who would become bishop of Washington, Angus Dun, and both he and Mrs. Dun were friends of us all.

Felix became friends of everyone. He was quick to notice and draw out the interests of others, young and old. Their house was about a mile away from ours, down a hill in a little hamlet called Dell, where radio reception was not good. So our schoolboy son, Christopher, often went down the hill on a bicycle or telephoned Felix with up-to-date bulletins. I recall Felix receiving rather glumly the news of President Truman's appointment of Tom Clark to the Supreme Court. In return, Felix would provide us with news from the *Washington Post* and the *London Times,* which came to him regularly. I did not always relish having to listen to the proceedings of the House of Commons, duly recorded in the *London Times,* especially when Felix wanted to read them to me in the evening when I was preparing the family dinner, but all this was part and parcel of our friendship.

He partook enthusiastically of village activity. I remember, for example, his response to a wonderful couple, Bill and Mary Kirk, who with their three daughters came to Heath every summer as we did. They were active in both church and social work in St. Louis and later in New York. Gifted and practiced in community affairs, this couple added enormously to the common life of the whole village. Sometimes, however, an alluring prospect of an expedition or picnic planned by them would cut across our perfectly laid plans for our study time, the children's activities, and, of course, meals. Felix, always sensitive even to these domestic details, would notice my concern and would ask Reinhold if these sudden changes of plan were helpful. Reinhold, waving a hand cheerfully, would say "Oh, it works out all right. I just say 'Bill, take them off.' Then I tell Ursula that the children will be all right with Bill and Mary."

These summer weeks provided many occasions for long talks on politics and theology, and the Frankfurters shared their friends with us and were always interested in ours. Felix particularly enjoyed the amateur theatricals at the Village Hall or other social events, and occasionally attended the village church. With such a population of theologians, the pastor wisely took advantage of this plenitude and asked them in turn to take the Sunday service.

Although we saw them in New York, where Felix—if coming to a meeting—would stay with his old friend C. C. Burlingham, whom also we knew, or in Washington, it was the particular flavor of those days in the village of Heath that come to mind and memory. When Harvard University conferred an honorary doctorate on him in 1956, his friends honored him with a dinner the night before at the Somerset Club. An anonymous poem was read at that occasion, which had been written by our daughter Elisabeth. Only three or four of those present knew by whom it was written.

Washington, DC
December 24, 1941

My dear Niebuhr:

That the editors of the *Nation* and, more particularly, any Jew should be worried about publishing your two papers only proves to me the great need for doing so. Too many liberals, as you indicate, are still enslaved by their romantic illusions, and cannot face your clean, surgeon-like exposition of reality. I find your essays as refreshing as is cooling spring water to a parched throat. Agreeable to your suggestion, I showed the two papers to Isaiah Berlin[1] and we are of the same mind about them. He has one suggestion to make and I another. He will tell you his. Mine is a question of phrasing. I think you can convey the idea of "imposing" a settlement in a less startling phrase to people who have never faced these problems with ruthless honesty. Why not speak of it as "part of a world settlement, etc." or some such phrase to indicate that it is not brute force you are talking about, but accommodating the enforcement of global as against mere regional interests.[2]

But I do not think you should publish these papers in the *Nation*. There ought to be a much wider, a much more influential, vehicle for them. I should think you could make one effective article either for *Harper's* or the *Atlantic,* or even for such high-brow publications as *Foreign Affairs* or the *Yale Review,* which are influential through seepage.

I really want you to know how enthusiastic both my wife and I, as well as Isaiah Berlin, felt about your essay.

I assume that C. C. Burlingham told you that the State Department nonsense so far as you are concerned was all cleared up.[3] I am really glad the episode happened because it helped to illumine dark places.

Marion and I send you and your wife and Christopher all good wishes.

Very sincerely yours,

Felix Frankfurter

---

1. Oxford social and political philosopher then working for the British Embassy in Washington.   2. R.N. stated in the Nation on February 28, 1942: "The whole matter is so important that it should be explored by an International Commission consisting of both Jews and Gentiles, both Zionists and non-Zionists. The Jews were, as they have been, the chief victims of Nazi fury."   3. R.N. was appointed to a committee to clarify the "Four Freedoms" of Roosevelt in 1941, which brought him, as others, to be investigated by the FBI.

Washington, DC
October 3, 1951

Dear Reinie:

You will recall that I undertook to send you two items: (1) a quotation from Brandeis on "separation of powers," and (2) the reference to T. H. Huxley's prophetic remarks at the opening of Johns Hopkins on the difficulties that were bound to confront America, with the superb sentence "Size is not grandeur, and territory does not make a nation."

(1) These are the Brandeis observations:

> "The doctrine of the separation of powers was adopted by the Convention of 1787, not to promote efficiency but to preclude the exercise of arbitrary power. The purpose was, not to avoid friction, but, by means of the inevitable friction incident to the distribution of the governmental powers among three departments, to save the people from autocracy." Brandeis, Louis D., dissenting in *Myers* v. *United States*, 272 U.S. 52, 293.

(2) Huxley's remarks you will find in his *American Addresses* (1877, pp. 124–126). If you have any difficulty in putting your hand on this volume let me know and I shall send you the quotation, or you might get hold of a little book of mine called *The Public and Its Government,* published by the Yale Press, in which I quote the relevant portions, at page 164. Unfortunately I have no copy of this little book of mine, otherwise I would send it to you.

I hope that Ursula has thoroughly recovered from her silly conflict with the double-decker and that all is well with the rest of you.

As always, it was a great pleasure to have seen something—although too little—of both of you at Heath. And Christopher and Elisabeth also gave us delight.

Ever yours,

F.F.

Washington, DC
November 7, 1951

Dear Ursula and Reinie:

Being in need of some theological goods of course I turn to the distinguished firm of

Niebuhr & Niebuhr.

I need some enlightenment on what is deemed from time to time to be "sacrilegious" in the Roman and other churches, and the criteria for determining it. (If in the very way I put my questions I betray ignorance please remember that while judges are supposed to know the law—what hokum that is!—that merely means I should hope profane and not sacred law.)

Anyhow, will you be a good pair and refer me to a few books or authoritative article on the subject? Perhaps you should know the assumption of my inquiry. If that is wrong throw this in the wastebasket. It is that [the] concept of sacrilegious is not fixed, final and definite, but has its own history of changes and chances, of diversities and distinctions, of conflicts and controversies. (I hope you will not infer from this that I have reached that stage of senile juvenility where one again indulges in youthful excesses of alliteration.)

I hope the Niebuhrs, both at home and at school, are flourishing. I had a happy talk with Barbara Franks[1] about Familie Niebuhr the other night.

The royal pair managed to impose their easy, human ways even upon our snobbish democracy—at least in Washington.

Affectionately yours,

F.F.

1. *Wife of the British ambassador to the United States.*

Union Theological Seminary
New York, NY
November 10, 1951

Dear Felix:

Since you turn to the firm of Niebuhr & Niebuhr and do not specify the alleged head of the household, I will take the privilege of answering your letter.

I can give you the gory details about sacrilege fairly briefly. First of all in this, as in many matters, there has been no development of consequence in the theory since Thomas Aquinas, who fixed the definition in this *Summa* [*Theologica*] II, Question xcix. You will find his definitions nicely elaborated in Rickaby's *Moral Teaching of Thomas Aquinas,* also in Slater's *Manual of Moral Theology.*

I can give you the essential points. Sacrilege is defined as violation of a sacred object but also in the wider sense as "any transgression against the virtue of religion." Thomas distinguishes between real, personal, and local sacrilege: (*a*) Real sacrilege is defined as irreverence toward sacred things. The core of this seems always to be irreverence toward the Eucharist and the altar. Included here is the improper attitude by the priest. (*b*) Personal sacrilege is violation of a sacred person, meaning cleric or member of a religious order. This includes laying violent hands upon them, or upon a total religious community but also the violation of their vows. (*c*) Local sacrilege is defined as a violation of sacred places, including churches, cemeteries, hospitals, and anything that has been consecrated. This sacrilege includes theft from such places, committing a sin within them, which pollutes them, and desecrating them by improper use, such as turning a church into a stable.

This is perhaps too summary an account for your purpose, but it will give you the general idea.

I have finished my book [*The Irony of American History*] and will turn it into the publishers tomorrow. We are all well and send you our affectionate regards.

Yours,

Reinhold

Washington, DC
November 20, 1951

Dear Reinie:

Many thanks for your "sacrilegious" learning.

I am driven, not recalcitrantly, by you to the *Summa.* My Latin is so rusty that I am contenting myself with the recent translation by the Dominican Fathers.

You must be feeling good these days. There are few joys greater than to turn a manuscript over to one's publishers.

With warm regards,

Ever yours,

F. F.

Washington, DC
May 17, 1952

Dear Reinie:

1. It was most relieving and comforting to read a fortnight ago in *Christianity and Crisis,* that you are yourself again.[1] A lad with your terrific vitality also has the great defect of that great advantage—the limitations even of great vitality. But you are also a man of will and I am one of your friends who is not skeptical that you will have sufficient good sense and will to realize that not even you can root out the sinfulness of man's nature or even make him adequately aware of its existence, and that therefore you should leave some of your efforts to God and to other men. I look forward as a windfall for Marion and me that you will be giving to Heath this summer what during previous years you thought was meant for mankind.

2. The responses evoked by Stafford's death[2]—what a gallant fight he made for life, which he employed so gallantly—give new point to one's faith that the mass of men respond to high qualities of mind and character. It is one of the strangest aspects of political life that so many public men fall far below their own insight and consciousness of what is the right and wise thing to do on the assumption that their fellowmen are not equal to appreciating what is good and true. You may not have seen the unusual light that Dame Myra Hess's[3] appreciation shed on Stafford, the man.

3. I turn to you for some information that I should like to have, not to put you to any trouble about it but on the assumption that you can tell me, if you have not the information readily available, where I could turn for it. From time to time I have seen items by ecclesiastics or theologians of the Western World in regard to the functioning of the church in Russia. I should like to get any reports or statements dealing with the Russian church—and of course the contemporary Russian church—but I want the full texts of such statements and reports and not merely newspaper snippets. Tell me where to turn for this information,—is it the department of Research and Study of the National Council of the Churches of Christ?

4. May I whisper solely for your private ear how glad I am that the editorial note in the May 12th issue of *Christianity and Crisis* does not carry your initials.[4] I hope I need not say that I am not referring to the point of view expressed in that note. I do mean to say that to me it is a bit saddening that issues of such gravity, not merely on the merits of such issues, but also considerations of morality in the exercise of the judicial process, should receive such flimsy treatment. In the first place I think

your readers are entitled to be informed regarding the issues in contro-
versy and I do not see how that can be done without a fair precis of the
opinions that were written in that case for I assume that your readers,
scattered as they are probably all over the world, however few in mere
number, have not all had the benefit of reading and then remembering the
adequate account the *New York Times* gave of the four opinions in the
case. In the second place, and closely related to the first, your readers are
entitled to a consideration of the issues if *Christianity and Crisis* is to deal
with them at all. I am fully mindful, I hope, of the vast range of interests
of *C and C* and the very small space at its disposal. But you ought not to
be like *Time* and other periodicals of miseducation in disposing of far-
reaching and complicated issues by mutilating brevity. *Christianity and
Crisis* could either wait until it had adequate space for dealing with the
problem, or at least refer its readers to the controlling documents on the
basis of which alone fair judgment can be made. But then you are about
the last person on whom I need urge the awful consequences for a democratic society of assuming that its understanding of deep issues can be got
on the cheap—cheapness also in the time necessary for really understanding the nature of issues.

5. We hope to get to Heath much earlier than last year and therefore
stay much longer, and we are keenly looking forward to seeing all the
Niebuhrs.

Our love to you both,

Ever yours,

F.F.

1. R.N. had suffered his first stroke in February and had had to cancel his teaching and
preaching activities for several months.   2. Stafford Cripps died on April 21,
1952.   3. Famous pianist; she had performed luncheon concerts in London during the blitz
of World War II.   4. The editorial note addressed the issue of release time in public schools
to allow children to receive religious instruction in their own faith.

Washington, DC
February 20, 1953

Dear Reinie:

Many a letter is in my head unwritten to you. I have tapped every
potential source of news about you and I have derived great satisfaction
from seeing the "R.N." pieces in *Christianity and Crisis*. And that energetic
young man C. C. B. [Burlingham] of course anticipated you in telling me
of the visit he had with you and Ursula, and giving the good report which
you confirm. Thinking of all the talk I would like to do on paper, when

face-to-face is precluded, I wonder if ever Thomas Jefferson, had he my job and had he to carry it on in the circumstances of our times, would have been able to write the letters he wrote from the fecund seclusion of Monticello. I'd give some of Ursula's shortbread—which I haven't got but would like to have—for a good chin with you about everything and about nothing in particular.

By way of a generalization let me say that I am surprised at the silly prematureness with which otherwise sensible and informed people commit themselves to judgments on the new administration. And I find just as many uncritical judgments on the part of enthusiasts as I do on the part of the people who seem to think that the Government at Washington no longer lives. But all sorts of genii would come out of that bottle if I were to pull the cork.

A word about our old theme church and state. It ought not to surprise you if I tell you that I think Mr. Will Herberg is far from being lucid in his thinking or wise in his judgement.[1] I am not unaware of all your concern about Teachers College secularization stuff, but in sending you the enclosed I do so because I have reason to believe that it is a fair sample of what's going on to an extensive degree. I have reason to believe that because this is not an isolated letter that I have had. It is a recent good sample to bring to your notice.

One of the most interesting things published by *Christianity and Crisis* was Professor [Robert McAfee] Brown's "Confession of a Political Neophyte." I thought it so good that I bought half a dozen extra copies to send to some of my friends who are teaching what is usually called "Government." Every fellow who is dealing with politics in our college[s] and universities ought to use the "Confession" as part of the reading for the course. Professor Brown deserves gratitude for spelling out his belated and important education.

You will be delighted to hear that Christopher is happy at Harvard. (Incidentally the hope of what Jim Conant will do in Germany has not replaced my regret that he didn't remain here to lead the fight against the Veldes.[2])

I assume all is going well with Elisabeth.

> *With affectionate regards to both of you from Marion and me,*
>
> *Ever yours,*
>
> *Felix*

P.S. I had the good fortune to attend a dinner for Will Scarlett on the occasion of his retirement. There were something like ten speakers, each talking very briefly, every aspect of the life of a great city was present (except that there was no Catholic speaker). And I never attended a comparable function in which such good and true things were said about a man. Will's response was deeply moving and generously candid.[3]

1. Will Herberg was educational secretary of the International Ladies Garment Workers Union and interested in theology. Teachers College was known for enshrining the secular empiricism of John Dency.   2. In January 1953, President Eisenhower appointed Conant high commissioner to West Germany. Harold Veldes was chairman of U.S. House Committee on Un-American Activities.   3. Frankfurter had first met Will Scarlett, then dean of Christ Church Cathedral in Phoenix, AZ, when he was sent by the War Department to investigate the Bisbee deportations during World War I.

Union Theological Seminary
New York, NY
February 25, 1953

Dear Felix:

It was a pleasure to get your letter and the enclosures. Ursula and I paid a visit to C.C.B. yesterday. He lives across the street from my doctor so we try to see him about once a week. He was in good spirits as usual and was rather priding himself about holding his fire about the Eisenhower administration for two months. I agree with you that others ought to follow his example. Both the enthusiasts and the critics are making a lot of snap judgements. . . .

I am gaining strength every day. Next Tuesday I am going to give my first lecture. I'll have to sit down while lecturing but otherwise I will be as of old. I naturally find it very exciting to take up my work again bit by bit.

I am glad you liked Professor Brown's "Confession of a Political Neophyte." He is a former student of mine whom we are recalling here to the seminary from Macalester College.

> With affectionate regards to you and
> Marion from both of us,
>
> As ever,
>
> Reinhold

Union Theological Seminary
New York, NY
May 18, 1954

Dear Felix:

Together with the whole nation we were thrilled this morning with the unanimous decision of the Supreme Court on the segregation issue.[1] I was particularly thrilled not only because the decision was unanimous, but because it was so wise in the reasons given for the decision, and the time that it permitted most of the states to adjust themselves. I think that this proves that the Supreme Court is operating in terms of the best wisdom of the common law tradition, where both justice and liberty "broaden down from precedent to precedent."

I was also very pleased to get your address before the Philosophical Society at Philadelphia, which expounded the temper and mood which is the basis of such decisions.

I hope that we will see you soon at Heath. We are going up about June 12th.

> *With affectionate regards to you and Marion,*
>
> *Yours,*
>
> *Reinie*

1. *Brown v. Board of Education of Topeka was decided by a unanimous Supreme Court on May 17, 1954, a day before this letter was written.*

Washington, DC
December 28, 1956

Dear Reinie:

Increasingly I find satisfaction in the paragraph signed R.N. in recent issues of *Christianity and Crisis.* You give me the satisfaction that one derives from agreement, though you express our agreement on the gnarled issues of our time usually with more penetrating analysis than does my own thinking. But I find not merely this satisfaction in what you write, but the satisfaction of making me forget some of the dogmatism and self-righteousness of other contributors. You remember John Morley's remark about Carlyle that he preached the golden gospel of silence in thirty volumes. Am I censorious in finding some of the preachments on humility by some of the editors of *C. & C.* in cocksure and self-righteous tones.

We rejoice over the good news that we have about you and [that] your Stockbridge move is full of the promise of its evident wisdom.

With our affectionate regards,

Ever yours,

Felix

New York, NY
December 31, 1956

Dear Felix:

Not only I but the whole family rejoiced in your letter and I am going to answer it with many mistakes on my own typewriter, my secretary being on vacation. Christopher is on his way to Germany in uniform. He has been on his way since Christmas and calls up every day to say that they have been again delayed. They are going over on the transports which bring the Hungarian refugees over.

In regard to the substance of your very complimentary letter, Ursula rejoiced and said "You see other people also detect the self-righteousness," which she incidentally detects everywhere among religious people. I agree with you and with her, but I am defensive about my profession and maintain that piety only accentuates a common human frailty. We have a brilliant philosopher of science at Columbia who is insufferably self-righteous in the name of "reason." He used to maintain that "rational" Jews could not vote for a demagogue like La Guardia and did so only because they were prompted by "irrational" motives. You see you have touched on a favorite theme in this family in which we all have a common viewpoint, but I introduce a slight professional variation on your thesis and Ursula's.

I have an invitation from Oppenheimer to spend a year at the Institute for Advanced Study writing a book on political ethics or more precisely on "The Morality of Nations."[1] Have accepted. The prospect of doing this is both thrilling and frightening because I must elaborate an avocational interest into something which will not make the Institute look too silly.

We hope Marion's condition is improving and that you both have a very happy new year. It is so good to hear from you and I wish we could see you both more frequently. Too bad we missed you the other night. Christopher could not get a leave. I was at the Philosophy Club and Ursula had to wait for Elisabeth coming home from Radcliffe. She enjoys her studies and the swarms of young men, but I gather that she doesn't sleep very much, being both studious and social.

Our love to both of you.

Affectionately yours,

Reinie

1. J. Robert Oppenheimer; noted expert on atomic energy; director of the Institute of Advanced Study, Princeton, New Jersey.

Washington, DC
February 6, 1957

Dear Reinie:

If you have not seen this manifesto of the Richmond Ministers Association, you will want to. I know one swallow does not make a summer, but sometimes one swallow is a harbinger of others. I know hope rather than prophecy—particularly these days—is behind.

"If winter comes, can spring be far behind?" But at times it does turn out that way.

Of course, I take a serious view of the situation, but not a tragic one. Certainly, for myself, I am not expressing hindsight when I say that I did not anticipate a quicker or more comprehensive acceptance of the Supreme Court decision. Nor was violent resistance, here and there, unanticipated. What one had hoped for was the steady permeation of a conviction of inevitability and the displacement of old habits by the acquisition of new ones in the border states. Through them and some ferment within the deep South, one hoped, as I still hope, for an almost imperceptible change of habit by bowing to necessity in the communities having a large percentage of Negroes. Not remotely do I mean to sound complacent or happy about the situation. That is not the state of my feeling. I am merely trying to convey my own state of mind as of May 17, 1954.

Let me repeat on paper the great pleasure I conveyed to you over the phone about your forthcoming year at Princeton. I can hardly tell you how pleased I am about it, because I am confident that it will be a year of great satisfaction for you and Ursula. By the way, is she taking a year off from corrupting the young at Barnard?

What wouldn't I give for a chance to talk with you *de omnibus rebus et aliis*. One of my favorite notions is that laymen far outdo lawyers in the manipulation of legalisms, in its mischievous sense. The current behavior of the U.N. is a striking illustration of this. One would suppose that the problem with which the U.N. is dealing, by insisting on the immediate and unilateral withdrawal of the Israeli troops, began with Israeli "aggression." I need not tell you that one has to be alert all the time in this business of adjudicating not to mutilate a problem by isolating the so-called legal aspects. The U.N. is giving us a master demonstration of such a mutilation.

No doubt if you and Ursula were here I would let everything else go to the dogs and have a talk. As it is, I had better stop.

Affectionately yours,

Felix

P.S. Since I started to dictate this the Florida editorial has come. It is significant—as is Senator Smathers'[s] revised attitude.

F.F.

Union Theological Seminary
New York, NY
February 8, 1957

Dear Felix:

Thank you for your nice letter and for sending me the manifesto of the Richmond Ministers Association. We have been holding off with a statement from northern ministers because we were told that there was a conference of southern ministers from all over the South to make a statement on the race issue, and that anything from the North would seem like Yankee interference.

I was also asked by Martin Luther King to sign a statement to the president asking him to intervene in the situation down South, but I was advised that such a pressure would do more harm than good. A group of southern preachers are going to see the president privately to try to influence him to act. I confess that I don't know why a Republican president should be so hesitant on this matter. I agree with your analysis of the situation except that I think some of the evidence points to the fact that the hopeful parts of the South are advancing faster under the lash of your decision, while the recalcitrance of the deep South seems to be accentuated.

I wish I could talk with you about this and all other affairs. I wrote an article for the *New Republic,* but I unfortunately do not have an extra copy, on the title "Our Stake in the State of Israel." The legalistic way in which our State Department and the U.N. are handling this problem gets to be more and more fantastic.

You ask about Ursula during my year at Princeton—she is going to try to cut down her work so that she will only have to go to Barnard two days a week.

Incidentally, I promised the ADA [Americans for Democratic Action] to meet for a brief time with them on Saturday morning, March 30th. Perhaps we could drop in and see you and Marion Saturday afternoon. Would that be possible?

With affectionate regards
to you both,

Sincerely yours,

Reinie

Washington, DC
February 15, 1957

Dear Reinie:

1. That's rejoicing news—that you and Ursula are coming down here sometime in March. Of course Marion will want to see you. Why not arrange to lunch with me, the two of you, that is, and turn up, say, about noon for a visit with Marion before lunch. If your duties here preclude such an arrangement, indicate the time that is free for you.

2. No doubt the decision of the court had a powerful influence on the contending forces in the South. I did not remotely mean to imply otherwise. I was concerning myself with the influences that would, as a process, bring the Court decision to practical realization.

3. We have been having some accounts of your well-being, which greatly cheered both of us. It was something of a tonic for Marion. For myself, I should like to see you in that tweed jacket which you are sporting.

4. I wonder if our whole history in the conduct of foreign affairs there ever was anything to equal the pettifoggery and shortsighted maneuvering of which we have been witness during the last two weeks in dealing with Israeli withdrawal.

With affectionate regards
to both of you,

Ever yours,

Felix

Union Theological Seminary
New York, NY
February 19, 1957

Dear Felix:

Thank you so much for your letter. Since you have written the situation has gotten worse, and we have not only pettifoggery but a fantastic stupidity in handling all of the relationships between our allies. For the first time in many decades I feel seriously concerned about the future of this great country, because the two men who seem to be guiding its destiny seem both to be stupid. The one is amiable and the other not, but the stupidity is equal.

About our visit to you to which we look forward very much, I don't know whether we can come for lunch because actually the only time I have promised to speak to the ADA, which is the original purpose of my visit, is on Saturday morning, and I don't know whether I can put a simple terminus *ad quem* to it.

I am much intrigued by your clairvoyance, or who told you about my tweed jacket; and Ursula would like to know if the shortbreads, which she ordered for you for Christmas, and which have come to many of our friends very late, have finally reached you.

It will be so nice to see you and Marion again.

Affectionately,

Reinie

Stockbridge, MA
June 26, 1957

Dear Felix:

We thank you very much for sending those two memorable decisions, which are chapters in the Supreme Court's creative influence on the history of our time.

As I never was happy about the Smith Act[1] I rejoiced with many others that the court decision makes it quite explicit that it is necessary not only to advocate in the abstract but actually to incite to revolution, to run afoul of the law. I was also glad to see your dissent on the Dupont decision.[2] I don't know anything about it but it seemed to me that the decision was anachronistic.

It is certainly wonderful to see the founding fathers vindicated in having established that very "undemocratic" institution the court, to protect the liberties of democracy. But perhaps that was not so radical a step because an independent judicatory is by its nature "undemocratic," that is freed from popular and public pressures.

We had a nice visit at the Binghams with Prof. and Mrs. Goodhart,[3] and we talked half the time about you. We are ensconced in our new home in Stockbridge and only wished that you and Marion were once more in the neighborhood. What wonderful news about Sir Isaiah Berlin.[4]

> With affectionate regards
> to you and Marion,
>
> Yours,
>
> Reinie

1. In 1940, it made illegal any group which taught or advocated the overthrow of the U.S. government by force.   2. Justice Frankfurter dissented from the Supreme Court decision on anti-trust requiring Dupont to sell its shares in General Motors.   3. Arthur Goodhart; a New York–born attorney. Goodhart taught at Oxford University and was master of University College. R.N. met him at a joint birthday party given for June Bingham and R.N. in Loudonville, NY.   4. An announcement of his engagement to be married.

New York, NY
February 13, 1959

Dear Felix:

Our whole family was delighted with your letter for many reasons but first of all about the news of your returning health. These "episodes" or "incidents" as the doctors call them are means of saving our lives. I envy you because your episode was of the heart and not of the brain. I have a more serious reminder of unwillingness to admit my years because I have a permanent case of spastic paresis. And I never was quite as profligate with my energy as you have consistently been. But don't expect justice from the natural process, so I am content with the fact that my life has been prolonged by the shock I suffered. May a justice of the Supreme Court also learn wisdom and restrain his native dynamism.

We had a grand time in Princeton and for the first time in my life I spent a whole year on a book. I am anxious to send you a copy when it comes out in July. I think it will be called *Dominion in Nations and Empires: A Study of the Structures and Dilemmas of the Political Order* [published as *The Structure of Nations and Empires*]. The moot question among my friends and advisors is whether it should not contain some clue to the fact that I try to make the damned study relevant to the perplexities of our age. I agree with you as against the ineffable Salvemini[1] that I would like to see how the tragic drama unfolds. Incidentally I don't think you would like to know the end of the story "agnostic though I am." I should have thought that not having dogmatic preconceptions you would be the more anxious to know the details which the dogmatists, both religious and metaphysical, know in advance. I remember that after a service in the church at Heath we defined the differences between us as between a "believing unbeliever" and a "believer with unbelief." Incidentally there are many forms of agnosticism as there are of belief. I say this because Archie [MacLeish] was with you at the time. While I think his *JB* is a great work and particularly good theatre, I suspect he solves the problem of life rather more simply than you would. For he bases his play on the happy ending of the old prose part of Job and leaves out the profound pious impieties of the real poem, which give the book its real meaning.

I see by the morning paper that the whole court was present to hear [Carl] Sandburg's eulogy of Lincoln, who rightly becomes more and more our national symbol, I think for many reasons but mainly because he possessed the rare gift of a "tragic sense of life."

Give our love to Marion, and may your recovery give her new hope and strength.

Affectionately yours,

Reinie

1. *Gaetano Salvemini was a distinguished Italian scholar émigré.*

Washington, DC
May 24, 1960

My dear Reinie:

From time to time Marion charges me with being a romantic believer in reason. Like you she knows that evil is an inherent ingredient of man and has a strong belief that public men who do not adequately gauge its extent are dangerous. But when I read what you tell me of the recent report of the Committee on Race Relations of the Federal Council of Dutch Reformed Churches of South Africa, the limits of my credulity assert themselves. I say this, although I know enough of the history of South Africa to know that the social teachings of the Dutch Reformed churches have always been more obscurantist than that of other Protestant faiths. But to see it in black and white as you set it forth really stops me in my tracks—as does not quite as much but sufficiently so the announcement of the publication of *The Spiritual Heritage of John Foster Dulles.* I must believe that people who thus invoke "God" or "Christ" or "spiritual heritage" have not the remotest realization of their blasphemy.

I have to get this much off, though I feel deeply frustrated not to have talked with you. Not the least disturbing thing to me is the way all sorts of people are running to cover after the debacle at Paris,[1] full of demands that all the rest of us search our consciences and reexamine our thinking, without the slightest indication that their own thinking also calls for reexamination. Thus, Walter Lippmann tells everyone to beat his breast, but not a word about the geometric demonstrations he made on the very eve of the collapse that all the four leaders, and not least of all Khrushchev, were absolutely dependent on a detente. Even George Kennan, in his letter in Sunday's *New York Times,* wrote as one who implied that his own thinking during recent years was adequately searching and appropriately guiding. However, it is idle to indulge in these puny tidbits when the opportunity of real exchange of worries with you is not possible.

> *With affectionate regards*
> *to all of you.*
>
> *Ever yours,*
>
> *Felix*

1. *The summit meeting of Eisenhower and Khrushchev failed after the Soviet Union shot down a U.S. spy plane piloted by Francis Powers.*

New York, NY
May 26, 1960

Dear Felix:

We were so glad to receive your letter. It came on the same day when we had a visit from a mutual friend Will Scarlett. We talked much about you and I gave him proof sheet copy of your book of reminiscences.

In regard to your estimate of the Dulles book as full of blasphemy, I could not agree more heartily. The introduction to the book by the president of this seminary makes vivid all the concerns which Ursula and I have increasingly felt about the smugness of the current piety, as revealed in this seminary and indeed in the whole church. It has been reduced to triviality and smugness. You can imagine my state of mind after having devoted all these decades to the religious enterprise.

I am distressed as you and everyone about the summit meeting, but I don't agree that Khrushchev needed a detente or that this was his chief need. Pressed by the Chinese and his own military on the disarmament issue, and facing a solid front on the Berlin issue by the Western powers, he took the only way out by wrecking the conference. We should never have gotten into the position of going to a summit conference without previous successful negotiations. The president sounds very naive when he declares that the shift in Soviet policy is a mystery. We should have known about the internal pressures on the communist empire before the summit. Nobody has come out of that debacle with credit.

We are moving from the apt. where we have lived here for 15 years. It is quite a wrench despite everything.

Our love to you and Marion. I wish we could have a good talk.

Affectionately yours,

Reinie

Santa Barbara, CA
July 23, 1960

Dear Felix:

I talked so much about you in the past days, chiefly with Abe Chayes[1] and his wife; and heard so much political gossip from journalists returning from the conventions, mostly old hat to you, that I am inspired to write you a letter. First of all I promised to spend the summer here with the Fund for the Republic[2] people partly for economic reasons and partly because I like the moderate schedule of three hours of meeting per day and partly because people like Harry Ashmore, Prof. Harrison Brown, and the journalist Paul Jacobs working in various ways on the project are very interesting.[3] Chayes came here on the way back from the convention. I was surprised to find that he was the original academic Kennedy man in MA. Three liberal southern journalists, among them McGill of the *Atlanta Constitution,* also visited us. They were Stevenson men, who had however predicted Kennedy's nomination. Stevenson visited here a week ago. I was among the many academics who were really for Stevenson; but his indecisiveness was revealed in his ambiguous position in the convention, where he was and was not a candidate. I write to you to make a confession, that one who has preached a lifetime to Protestant purists that they must come to terms with the moral ambiguity of the political process, found it very difficult to swallow Kennedy, despite the persuasion of some of our mutual friends. Even now I probably would follow Grenville Clark's[4] example and not vote at all but for the imminent nomination of Nixon. I don't like papa Kennedy at all and the two brothers, Jack and Bob, are intelligent, shrewd and tough, also ruthless and unscrupulous. I know that great magician of politics, FDR, was not always too scrupulous, but he had a heart; and he never bought primaries as Kennedy did in Wisconsin and West Virginia. Yet a liberal journalist, who expects to support Kennedy, told me yesterday, that he knows of no man who has so whole-heartedly and shrewdly devoted himself to the pursuit of power. He nevertheless expects him to be a good president, counting on his cool common sense in this hour of crisis. Perhaps you have heard the story of Kennedy and Nixon: "Twin brothers are going to be in mortal combat in the election and one will murder the other." The point that Nixon will be murdered is probably good prophesy unless Rockefeller helps him out.

The fact that Johnson, who tried to be a bridge between north and south, could not be more than a southern candidate, while pathetic for Johnson, is probably an indication of how far we have traveled on the race issue since the famous decision of your court.

Incidentally, before closing this aimless confession of a bewildered man, who expects no reaction from one who has, in your phrase "taken the veil," I must report one more reaction to the moral ambiguity of the political process, at least as conducted in national conventions. A friend said to me, "I am critical of Galbraith and Schlesinger for deserting Stevenson for Kennedy before the latter's nomination. Intellectuals must accept a political *fait accompli* but they ought not to anticipate it." I thought that was a perfect definition of the irrelevance of the "intellectual" in the political order.

The climate here is wonderful, cool nights and two hours of warm weather each day, while Los Angeles sizzles just a hundred miles south. No one has explained this phenomenon adequately.

Ursula's and my love to you and Marion and our constant gratitude for your friendship. We do wish we could see you as frequently as we once did in Heath. Vain hopes but precious memories.

Affectionately,

Reinie

Postscript

Dearest Marion and Felix,

To bring our love and the fact of our constant thought and gossip to you:—and the news that:

1. Reinhold is "bouncy" now that he has left the HORROR of Union Seminary's last effort. (He was bait for the promotion dept., and they almost killed him in the process.) He seemed headed for another

depression, in fact seemed in it, BUT getting out and aloft, and seems to have brought him back to a very happy and proper le fruitful living.

2. This is a lovely place.

3. Elisabeth has a Fulbright in Paris.

4. Christopher has been accepted for a municipal govt. training programme at the Univ. of Penn.

Ursula

1. *Professor of law, Harvard Law School.* 2. *An organization funded by the Ford Foundation to study the American republic.* 3. *Harry Ashmore; Fund employee; formerly editor, Little Rock (AR) Gazette. Harrison Brown; consultant to Fund. Paul Jacobs; labor journalist and consultant on automation for the Fund.* 4. *Prominent lawyer; co-author of the Clark-Sohn plan for World Government. Clark had known both Frankfurter and R.N. as he was a senior member of the Harvard Corporation, the university's governing board. He drafted the Selective Service Act of 1940.*

Quincy House
Harvard University
Cambridge, MA
November 8, 1961

Dear Felix and Marion:

Your very great kindness to Elisabeth is the immediate occasion for this letter.[1] Ursula and I are so grateful that you should have taken her in, particularly when it cannot be convenient to either of you. We are more grateful than words can express. We do worry about the delay in the transport of her furniture, which must be worrisome to you and to her. We thought we had everything arranged for Friday and Saturday, but the state blue laws seem now to make this impossible.

Even without this immediate prompting of parental gratitude, we would have had to write to tell you something about our adventure at Harvard.[2] I find the pace here a little exacting for my limited energies, though I lecture only two hours a week. But we greatly enjoy it. Most of all we enjoy meeting our and your friends. At almost every dinner party the subject turns sooner or later to F.F. We had dinner the other night with Archie and Ada MacLeish. One of the guests was Merle Fainsod of the Russian Institute, a new acquaintance with whom the common bond was our admiration of you. At another dinner we met Mark Howe[3] and he gave an excellent presentation of your consistent judicial doctrines. We were enlightened and pleased.

Meanwhile our private woes and pleasures are engulfed in the tragic world situation, in which there seems no improvement. Or am I too pessimistic?

With affectionate regards from both of us to you both,

Yours always,

Reinie

1. *Elisabeth was staying with the Frankfurters in Washington while awaiting her furniture; she had moved to Washington to work in the State Department.* 2. *R.N. and U.N. were at Harvard, where R.N. was a visiting professor for the year 1961–62.* 3. *Professor of law, Harvard University.*

Quincy House
Harvard University
Cambridge, MA
January 2, 1962

Dear Marion and Felix:

Ursula and I were tremendously cheered, gratified, and complemented by your New Year's telegram to us. We answer more prosaically by letter to wish you both all good things for the new year; and for Marion particularly new health and vigor.

After suffering from a fall and resultant brain concussion, which seems to have aggravated my paralysis, I have more sympathy than ever for Marion's weakness. I hope she will find new strength in the new year. I hope for myself that I can fulfill my contract with Harvard in the second semester.

Elisabeth spent the holiday weekend with us and told us enthusiastically of your graciousness to her in her difficult beginning as government bureaucrat. She likes her boss tremendously, at which I am not surprised. Incidentally she owes to you, among many things, her first introduction to Mr. Isenberg[1] in Paris.

Most of all we want to thank you for the friendship of the past and for all the ways it has enriched our lives and that of our children.

Affectionately yours,

Reinie

1. *Max Isenberg, who had clerked for F.F., was Elisabeth's boss as Assistant Secretary of State for Educational and Cultural Affairs.*

Quincy House
Harvard University
Cambridge, MA
February 15, 1962

Dear Felix:

Your nice letter gave me great joy in two counts. In the first place it reiterates your consistent position, which I may say I understand rather more fully than some of your law critics, and which made me never doubt that you would understand my signature to the petition for clemency for Scales.[1]

In the second place both Ursula and I are so grateful for the way you and Marion have acted in *loco parentis* for our daughter and we are glad that you find the relationship not too onerous, as she enjoys it so much.

We are glad to hear all kinds of reports about Marion's improved health. Our love to her in our thanks for her really imaginative understanding of a young thing. I have only one peeve against our errant daughter, but I won't ask you and Marion to strive to correct it. She does not write the old folks frequent enough letters, though when she writes one forgives past sins easily.

We are enjoying life at Harvard very much. Just returned from a rather large class in "Govt 110" of about five hundred. One of my auditors is Mrs. Wyzanski. See the judge monthly at the Saturday club. Both of them are really rare spirits.[2]

With love to you both,

As ever,

Reinie

P.S. Our mutual friend, Will Scarlett has survived a prostrate operation at Mass[achusetts] Gen[eral Hospital] and returned to Maine. Glad to chew the rag with him.

1. *Scales had been convicted under the Smith Act.*   2. *Charles Wyzanski; a Federal district judge in Massachusetts.*

Princeton University
Princeton, NJ
December 5, 1962

Dear Felix:

Thank you for your gracious letter. I am glad that you approved of my interpretation of your doctrine of judicial review. I was flattered by the invitation from the *Law Review* to enter the holy of holies, reserved for lawyers, and wrote the article with a good deal of trepidation, being fearful of betraying my ignorance.

Therefore your kind letter is doubly welcome. I trust that you find retirement not too difficult though I admit it has its difficulties, which must be multiplied for a person with your vitality and exuberance. But just a few essays, after you have cast off the "veil" of which you often spoke, might cure the world of its confusions and might be a vent for your great talent as a guide of the nation.

We hope both you and Marion are in reasonably good health, which is all we old folks can ask. Just about finishing my teaching chores here as visiting professor.

With great affection,

Yours,

R. Niebuhr

Tribute to Felix Frankfurter

With thousands of his countrymen I regret the retirement of Felix Frankfurter from the Supreme Court. Both as a vital person and as a creative teacher and interpreter of the law he has left his mark on our generation.

It is difficult to do full justice to the kindling vitality of his mind and person, to the range of his intellectual interests, to his sympathy for all sorts and conditions of persons, and to his charismatic gift with young people. He never patronized them or talked down to them. His only weakness in this respect was that he did not suffer fools gladly and intelligent young people were the particular objects of his care and interest. Perhaps one could put down as another marked personal characteristic his fierce loyalty to his friends. In this loyalty his passionate nature was at tension with the cool objectivity to which he disciplined himself as teacher and as judge. Felix Frankfurter is, in sum, the most vital and creative person I have ever known; and this testimony is not unique but widely shared in my opinion.

Reinhold Niebuhr

Harvard Law Review 76 (November 1962): 20.

New York, NY
November 20, 1963

Dear Felix:

I appreciated so much your brief notes when I was at the hospital. I am now slowly recuperating but still very weak. I hope time will cure the weakness. Living in retirement and unable to do real work, my heart goes out to you who had so much more an active and significant life and have been forced into retirement by the frailties of the flesh. It must be difficult to read the decisions of the court without having a part in the decisions.

I wish I had some time for unhurried conversations with you as of old. I would ask you about the JFK administration, whether it is bogged down by the old Republican-southern coalition, or whether the president's lack of FDR's warm humanity makes it impossible for him to appeal to the people over the heads of Congress. His civil rights program seems to me courageous, the last chapter in making the South conform to the standards of the nation. How stubborn all racial prejudices are. They seem to dog mankind even in the highest stages of civilization.

Our love to you and Marion.

Affectionately yours,

Reinie

New York, NY
December 20, 1964

Dear Felix and Marion:

Instead of sending you a holiday greeting, Ursula and I thought we would write you a letter to say how much your friendship has meant to us through the years and express the hope that the infirmities of age are bearable for you. I have had a second stroke this summer and I am quite lame, so I can sympathize with Felix the more.

I hope Felix is satisfied with the course of events, particularly the smashing defeat of the absurd Goldwater movement. I confess that the millions who voted for this nostalgia leaves me concerned.

We hear rather regularly from Will Scarlett. He suffered because of the Goldwater movement.

Our affectionate greetings and gratitude for the years of your friendship.

Yours,

Reinhold and Ursula Niebuhr

Fourteen

Hans Christoph von Hase

We first met Hans Christoph von Hase in 1933. He had come to Union Theological Seminary as the German Fellow, three years after his cousin Dietrich Bonhoeffer had come on the same fellowship, when I had come as the English Fellow. Reinhold took to him at once. We found him pleasant and easy in manner, less theologically obsessed perhaps than his cousin Dietrich had been.

After his year in New York, he was going to stay with his cousin Dietrich in London, where the latter was in charge of the German Church. I suggested that he might like to visit my family, the Keppel-Comptons, who then were living a few minutes from Hampton Court Palace, and an easy journey from London. My mother and my sister Barbara, both of whom had studied in Germany and spoke the language well, enjoyed meeting him and noted that he had become very proficient in English.

Early in 1987 I discovered among our papers these two letters from von Hase. The first, very beautifully handwritten, was in English, the second in German. Realizing how important they were, I sent copies to him, the text of which he edited. More exchanges followed. The letters tell their own story. So, in our eighties, our friendship has been renewed over a span of fifty-four years. It was a momentous period of history.

Berlin, Germany
September 3, 1934

Dear Dr. Niebuhr:

The start of the next [student] generation for America will be a good occasion to realize what I had in mind to do since I arrived here: to thank you for all the interest which you took in my work and my person, and for the realistic and deep view of American life and theology which I was able to take home with me from your lectures and discussions with you.

Yesterday I met all the outgoing students at a meeting in Köpenik near Berlin and, at the illuminated table in the courtyard of the castle there, I remembered all the things of one year ago, a little bit sorry that it was all over. I think I will never lose my little love for America and Union Seminary, for the wide space of the country, for all the chances which it has for active and creative work and the friendliness and open-mindness of its people. I know your criticisms just concerning these points, and I myself also took a glance at the backside of these things, but passing the Liberty Statue on the sixth of June, I thought [that] you folks do not know what you still have in America. It is a bad theology of course which you have across the ocean, but it is a young one, which is to be developed, we have an old one, which has still its strength and will—as I hope—prove its strength again. However, your theological crisis arises on the basis of a peaceful culture not yet earnestly troubled (in spite of the crisis of the NRA [National Recovery Act, June 1933] and the big strikes), while our theology, hardly restored in the last decade from the destructive period of "Kulturprotestantism," has to stand a struggle for the very existence of Christianity itself.

You will find Protestant and Catholic ministers, "German Christian" and protesting ministers alike, saying that the "Volkskirche" in Germany is a thing of the past. I would not be worried about that, if I would know that a new voluntary church is ready to take its part: but this is what I cannot see, at least not here in the North and the East. It is quite different in western and southern Germany, where the pastors can rely on the piety of their communities. The church struggle has created there a kind of revival and Dr. Leiper[1] can tell you about it. I myself went up to Berlin and here you find German Christians and Opposition alike in the position of an army after a lost battle. Dr. [Paul] Tillich's famous sentence, that the proletariat of Berlin was the truly religious and Christian class, would be regarded by himself, could he see it today, as a romanticism without reality. The real danger of today is neither the pagan movement (being romantic itself) nor the changing polity of the state (which certainly does not want to destroy Christianity) nor even the present church government (which helps much to hamper the church in its efficiency and by the necessary struggle consumes much of the religious energy which is necessary to win the people back to the church), but simply the totalitarianism of political life today. The church has still enough freedom, despite all restrictions, but we have neither the Word of God nor its strength at hand, that we might use this little rest of freedom, . . . to win back the realm of life for it. We mourn that the political form of life covers everything—like snow covering everything outdoors—that activities, youth groups, clubs die (and the official church-government certainly helped this process) sometimes by a natural way, sometimes otherwise, but *not* for the reason of violence, but because these thinly constructed activities of the church, without much life behind them, are no more able to resist the vital claim of politics for totality. The church is at the present not able to send an army for the protection of its territory, and so it has to give it up.

I joined the confessing church, of course, but am quite conscious that the right weapon (not to speak about victory) is not yet found in our hands. We ministers deeply feel the lack of a new kind of pious, religious, ascetic life for ourselves. This would mean to withdraw from the political claim of life, to look for the way of God outside of the ways of the people. How can you do that? My cousin [Dietrich Bonhoeffer] in London intended to go to India and to stay with Gandhi in order to make the experience of his way of life (please take this as confidential) and you will find these ideas arising all over the theological youth. Maybe, that the new style of present political life requires men devoted to God in the same totalitarian way as politics are totalitarian—no more in the way of Luther's ethics: in the way of "inner-worldly" asceticism, but in a new kind of monasticism. The totality of life is occupied in all the important classes of men, in the life of youth up to the life of the men in their best years, not only practically by social and political activities, but by their spiritual attitude also. The new Weltanschauung and the directions for all realms of life leave simply no space for a religion having an authority of its own. Weltanschauung becomes in itself an authoritarian religion.

Now the very interesting fact is, that in the formerly communistic and proletarian districts this new religion is about to occupy the minds. Marxism is really replaced by this new view of the world. In those districts of Berlin you will find presbyteries of churches, the large majority of which are members of the new pagan movement! Lessons, training, and instruction about these ideas are given and accepted with great enthusiasm, while in the "bourgeois" quarters the National Socialism is regarded more as a form of politics. But you will find all over the country very few people, who would be willing to concede to religion a real *authority* of its own.

The former nationalists as well as the former socialists say equally: the church was formerly closely connected with the state, why should it now be otherwise. Among the people, who join the protesting groups, you find a type of real Christians. If you see them, your hope will be increased, but a large percentage, at least here in the eastern part of Germany, a type of religious people who, being not able to express their disapproval of the state and the conditions otherwise, take gladly this chance to criticize Muller,[2] to gossip about church politics, and to feel as a kind of martyrs. The movement of the confessing church of course, is neither born or carried on by these reactionaries, but its ranks are filled by it. And we younger ministers feel this to be a heavy burden. We need people who learn again to pray, and this is what we cannot do even ourselves as we ought to.

I never agreed with your opinion that behind National Socialism the "Reaction" was taking command of the state. My experience here is an absolutely different one. While of course egoism has not yet died here, a socialistic attitude has occupied the vast majority of all minds, and the spiritual and propagandistic manifestation of all Germans, together with a form of state, which actually gives and controls the work and earnings of everybody, has really made the social struggle—at least for the present period—a thing of the past. Nor will there be again—as I see it—a fight for political ideas. There are no more enough dissenters and less of their spirit left, to start an uprising. Perhaps there will be some more ambitious leaders using the discontented groups of the nation, who may start a "Putsch," but I do not think they will do any real harm to the present government. And people, abroad and at home, who are hoping for any improvement of the situation are entirely on a wrong way. The only thing they will achieve will be chaos and brutality in addition to the system of government which we have today. Thus we have a government, which establishes order, fights unemployment, and has the support (even the faith) of the large majority of the people. The one struggle which will become more and more deep and intensive, and which will decide about the spiritual future of Germany, will be a religious one. It will be Securalism (today Mythos—Weltanschauung against Christianity). And this will decide the social and political questions too. The political strength of the church at the present is about zero, but this is a necessary situation, because the church ought to rely on God alone. You will understand, however, that it is easier to say than to practice it, and the certainty that this kind of faith will have to be practiced is not an easy outlook.

Nevertheless, I am at the present time an assistant minister at one of the new churches in the southeast of Berlin. Three ministers and 5,000 members. This is very stimulating. I hope to get a smaller parish of my own pretty soon. The only thing is: I don't know whether it is now the time to go to the countryside, in order to try a real spiritual life in a religious parish or to stay here among the secularized masses, in order to win some of them for a Christian life. The 23rd of this month, I intend to get married. I hope this will be a real spiritual help at the present time, besides the rest of what it means in man's life.

I do not remember whether I wrote a letter to Dr. Coffin. I am afraid I did not. Please, will you tell him my regards, and also my thanks for the

---

year I could stay at the Seminary. I shall certainly write him a letter also, tell my best wishes also to Dr. Tillich, to whom I promised a letter too. Would you mind to give him this letter. I shall write him a new letter.

I wrote in English in order to keep up with the language. Thus you will have to excuse linguistic mistakes, because I do not have the time to be careful about style.

With many greetings to Mrs. Niebuhr and you.

Truly yours,

Hans Christoph

1. *Dr. Henry Smith Leiper; important ecumenical member of the Federal Council of Churches, U.S.A.* 2. *Ludwig Muller; nominated by Hitler as his delegate and plenipotentiary concerning Protestant churches; Muller was elected in July 1933 as Reichsbishof. The church he led was known as German Christians.*

Jüterbog, Germany
July 31, 1935

Dear Professor Niebuhr:

My reply to your friendly and very interesting letter is long overdue. It is so difficult for me to give a detailed account of our situation and to send it to the United States by mail that I am glad to use John Schaefer as my courier. He studied in Tübingen for one year and visited me here near Berlin. He will have to tell you most things personally; he has seen a great deal himself.

First I wish to congratulate you and your wife on the birth of your son. We have also been blessed with the arrival of a son, on July 10th, and I don't have to tell you how happy we are. He is both a visible and tangible sign that God, as well as his church, may remain with us in Germany a while longer.

John will tell you about my work. Only those of us who are young ministers among soldiers have the chance to bring young people between 20 and 30 years of age to Jesus Christ; virtually none of these young people have a live impression of Jesus Christ. In this age they are being alienated from Christianity by various organizations which persuade them of the fantasies of the new heathenism.

The circle of half- and full-fledged heathens in which I have endless discussions about Christianity and the church brings me into close contact with people whom our confessional church, unfortunately, knows only from a great distance. Those who still hold on to the entirety of the Bible firmly: Old Testament, Sin and Grace, Cross and Resurrection, comprise a very small group. And while they stand by their faith with admirable loyalty, thus leaving a stronger impression than anyone else on those . . . who suddenly realize that Christianity is not dead after all, more open-mindedness is urgently needed. Most young people are so removed from Christian thinking that they no longer understand what Christianity is all about, hard as they may try. That is why those who would like to put a quick end to the church as we know it, keep getting away with brutal political terror (concentration camps, deportation, arrests, etc.) without the average German ever regarding this as religious persecution. The masses always tend to buy the argument that the members of the church are reactionaries who threaten to disturb the peace. Such accusations resemble those made against early Christians perfectly.

We must face the fact that there is no one left in the [National Socialist] party leadership who will support the Gospel of the church. We are virtually without political help, and that is a good thing if we want the church to be a *communio sanctorum*. I recently heard Rosenberg ask what it was that we expected? After all, the church and its teachings had always complied with the demands of national movements and would doubtless do so now. The church's "legal advocate," Jäger, said: "In a national church the national principle will outweigh the Christian principle." German Christians are leaning more and more and more and more in this direction: they want a National Church, Catholics included, and are prepared to look at the Old Testament in an "elastic" fashion, i.e., to finally reject it. They often state that the death and resurrection of Christ has nothing to do with them. That marks them as total heathens in the eyes of resolute Christians, even though they . . . constantly talk about Jesus.

The interior development of the confessing church is very promising. There is a serious effort under way to renew faith in our time. The differences between the Reformed and the Lutherans shrink in the face of our joint task to profess the Christian faith. When Barth left Germany, . . . Bishop Wurm of Württemberg published a testimonial to him, thanking him for the service which he had rendered in the battles of the German church through his theological work. . . . But the road is a long one, and Hannover and Bavaria still harbor a lot of particularism. John is bringing you a report from the Augsburg synod that will demonstrate what I am talking about.

Their struggle against the political influence of the Catholic church is continued on all fronts. For the state it is a matter of breaking "political Catholicism," but for Catholics it is an article of faith that the Pope should have both swords in his hands, that he determine political direction and morality and decide whether a country is "Christian" or not. That is why Catholics view this general struggle against their church as an attack on the very essence of their faith, and no one can tell what the outcome of this conflict will be.

I understand better and better what dawned on me in the U.S., namely that the kernel of our decisive questions of faith are the same in the entire Protestant world, and that we need a more thorough exchange of theology. . . . It is about time that we start tackling the ecumenical task anew and from within. I am certain, partly because of John's remarks, that it will not be different in the U.S. once social and political movements have recognized their purely secular independence and once they have informed the church that it has no business interfering in socio-political matters. The churches in the U.S. should be proud of their achievements in the socio-political sector, but the fact remains that their work in the areas of brotherly love and rights of the unemployed was a necessary task to which they were called but which was not their only mission. . . .

I have to finish; John is waiting for this letter; he is on his way to Wittenberg to see Luther's house and grave. I guess he must have felt some of his spirit even while here with us. Please give my best wishes to your dear wife. My wife and I hope that your son may thrive. Will you honor us with a visit to Germany when you are on your sabbatical? It would be so good if we could meet.

Would you let Tillich read this letter too? I plan to write to him personally soon.

> *With heartfelt greetings, I remain*
>
> *Respectfully yours,*
>
> *Hans Christoph*

Fifteen

Lewis Mumford

Lewis was a special friend to Reinhold. There was no one Reinhold would have liked to see more often. Lewis always cheered and invigorated him, even when both of them may have been analyzing the sorry state of the world.

Reinhold not only enjoyed Lewis but admired him for his intellectual integrity. He belonged to no particular group or clique but pursued his independent path. He was an architectural critic, and he was also a critic of contemporary culture. As John Ruskin and the Pre-Raphaelite movement inspired by William Morris in England, Lewis was concerned with ethics, economics, and religion. Architecture after all was and is the expression of our society and its culture.

Reinhold had taken me to visit him and his wonderful wife Sophia at their house in Amenia, New York, not long after we were married. As a university undergraduate in England, I had been very interested in the William Morris tradition and had spent one summer holiday in Gloucestershire in the village where the architect Ernest Gimson and kindred spirits, builders and craftsmen, had lived and worked. So this first visit meant much to me.

In demand as a teacher, Lewis had taught at various universities, such as Stanford, the University of Pennsylvania, Dartmouth, and Harvard. But many people besides university students were educated by his writings, in journals and books, and especially his architectural reviews in the *New Yorker*.

His influence extended widely outside this country. As a minor example I recall how Oxford dons and especially the dean of Christ Church were delighted by his analysis of and the prescription for the traffic problem through Oxford, a problem, incidentally, which has existed since the thirteenth century and is not yet solved.

Reinhold always regarded Lewis as a very noble character. He was right. He was more than that; he was a prophet of his age and to his age.

Heath, MA
July 6, 1940

Dear Lewis:

I promised Ursula some days ago to answer your letter with its question about Hitler and Buchman.[1] I'm sorry that I didn't do it immediately,

---

but I neglected a pile of correspondence while living in a general state of torpor. The international situation is so desperately bad that I can hardly think or live. I have never recovered my health sufficiently to face it properly.

Now about Buchman. I wrote an article about his relation to fascism in the *Christian Century* in 1937, but I can't give you the issue without my files.[2] The article was based upon an interview published in the *World Telegram*. The idea of that interview was not that Hitler was all right or would be all right if he were in communion with God. The idea was better and worse. It was that the dictators, both Mussolini and Hitler, offered a marvelous opportunity to place the world under "God control." Since they had brought the world under their control and concentrated power in themselves it was necessary only to bring them under "God control" and thereby place all their power under God.

This impossible idea was not an aberration of the moment. The Buchmanites have always gone on the assumption that powerful men must be converted because their conversion would bring the whole system of power which they controlled under God. This was what prompted their cultivation of Henry Ford and also their perfectly impossible effort to convert Prince von Stahrenberg, who was, in the dim past, the dictator of Austria.

I don't think Buchman knows enough history to have been influenced by historical ideas, but there was a type of German pietism which had the same idea. It was called "das Christliche Kaisertum." The idea was that if the Kaiser was pious and sought to do God's will the whole empire would be controlled by God.

I don't know when we will come down to NYC, but we still hope to stop off and pay you a visit when we do come probably at the end of July. I desperately need the invigoration of your mind and heart. I'm constantly skirting the edges of despair.

Yours,

Reinhold

1. *Frank Buchman; founded the organization called Moral Rearmament.*   2. *This article was reprinted as chapter 12 of R.N.'s* Christianity and Power Politics.

Heath, MA
July 17, 1940

Dear Lewis:

Thank you for both of your too generous letters. I read the proceedings of our Atlantic City conference with great interest and will forward them to Bloch as soon as I get his address from you. I am wondering whether we will have that midsummer meeting. That may be the only chance of seeing you. It now seems that we will not go to NYC. Ursula has settled her business by correspondence and I must confess that after six weeks of rest an auto trip is still very tiring for me. In fact I am beginning to worry whether I will be restored before the summer is over. I garden and gather wood and saw it for a good part of the day, following your advice. I work only an hour a day revising my Giffords. If I do more than that I tire to such a degree that I can't sleep. The ever present nightmare of the international situation may be a contributing cause. I am deeply disappointed that the country seems to have sunk back into sleep after the collapse of France. Most disappointing of all is Roosevelt's and the democratic disavowal of their former position, for fear of being called a war party. I am afraid that the disease which is destroying democracy is further advanced here than even in France. The next month will probably tell the story of Britain and whether there is the soundness there to defy the Hitler mania. If Britain collapses one could hardly blame her since we hold out so little hope of ultimate help, and it is difficult to fight on without hope of final victory.

I look forward to your book. You are too generous in your estimate of my contribution to your thought. But it is a source of great happiness to me that we should have found each other, for I always regarded you as the most intelligent social analyst in this country.

I suppose the attack on Britain will begin any hour now. Ursula is trying to prepare herself for her courses at Barnard, her first venture in teaching. With family cares and worry about her family in England this is a difficult task, though of course work of this kind is a good antidote for the anxieties which might fill vacant hours.

How little any of us, even in our most pessimistic moods anticipated the possibility of the collapse of two great empires. To have allowed themselves to get into so precarious a position means of course that they really have no right to survive. But the alternative is so horrible that despite their corruption, they should have survived. Do you think France was as rotten internally as she proved to be? I knew France was sick but did not realize that she was as sick as that.

Do hope I'll have a chance some time during the summer of exchanging thoughts with you, even if the thoughts have to be gloomy.

Affectionate regards from both of us to both of you.

Yours,

Reinhold

Union Theological Seminary
New York, NY
November 14, 1940

Dear Lewis:

Thank you very much for your kind letter. Scribner's has just sent me the copy of an ad in which they used your generous blurb in my behalf [for *Christianity and Power Politics*]. It is very good of you to undertake that address for our conference[1] in January. I hesitated to encourage the young men to ask you since I know what time means to you when in the throes of production. But your book [*Faith for the Living*] has made a deep impression upon all of them and they were bound to ask you.

I wrote you on Sep 25th suggesting as a title for our talks at New London[2] either "Is Our Contemporary Culture Adequate for the Preservation of Democracy?" or merely "Democratic Civilization and Its Culture." I asked you at the time to send on the title in any way you cared to phrase it, and I think you wrote saying that you had sent on one of them unchanged, but I don't remember which one. I assume it was the last.

Since the college asked me for a synopsis I sat down this morning to work one out so that I might send you a copy. I will not send it to the college until I have had time to hear from you on possible alterations, etc.

Funny, what you say about Roosevelt was the topic of a conversation between myself and my brother at Yale over the weekend. I used the pessimistic arguments which you advance and he used the optimistic ones and wondered whether Roosevelt was any more the opportunist than Lincoln was. At that I think Lincoln possessed a degree of honesty which Roosevelt lacks. At any rate he is certainly infinitely superior to the crowd which opposes him.

Yours always,

Reinhold

P.S. If you sent in the title as "Democratic Civilization and Its Culture," we might use the two sub-titles:
Mumford: The Political and Economic Problems of Democratic Civilization.
Niebuhr: The Cultural Problems of Democratic Civilization.

---

1. *A group of friends interested in the condition of post-war Europe, including the American Friends of German Freedom, of which Thomas Mann as president.*   2. *Mumford and R.N. were to speak together at Connecticut College in New London.*

Christianity and Crisis
New York, NY
December 24, 1940

Dear Lewis:

Some of us have started a modest, bi-weekly journal of eight pages to counteract pacifist sentiment in the churches.[1] We are going to start publishing on February 7, 1941. Each issue is going to contain but one article of about 4,000 words and editorial notes. Our committee is terribly anxious to have you write one of the early articles, and they are counting on me to bring home the bacon. I know how immersed you are in your book and that I have no right to ask this of you, but I merely follow the tradition of many friends asking things of me that they ought not to ask.

What we would like would be some article that deals with the necessity of maintaining relative justice, even if it falls short of Utopia. In other words, we would like a little section out of your book. If it could be made to deal particularly with the disillusionment which followed the Treaty of Versailles because of the Utopian hopes that had been aroused during the World War, this would fit in particularly well with our schedule of articles. We wouldn't need the article until March first.

I shall quite understand if you do not feel it possible to do this. But Dr. Henry Sloane Coffin, who has been acting as a sales agent for your book wherever he goes, is particularly emphatic about the necessity of having you.

> *With affectionate regards and*
> *best wishes for the New Year,*
>
> *Sincerely yours,*
>
> *Reinhold Niebuhr,*
>
> *Chairman*

1. *This is one of many hundreds of letters written by R.N. to solicit articles for* Christianity and Crisis, *which he helped to run for many years.*

Union Theological Seminary
New York, NY
March 1941

Dear Lewis:

Your very generous words about my book [*Christianity and Power Politics*] are much too extravagant and yet they warm the heart for I would know of no one whose approval of my work I would desire more than yours. Denis de Rougemont has written an able review in the *Nation*. You must meet him incidentally. He is a brilliant Swiss journalist whose *Love in the Western World* is really a very profound study of the relation of the erotic to the tragic.

The new issue of our little sheet is just out and the office is sending you 6 extra copies. If you want more let us know. You have made a great contribution to our work with this article and we are deeply grateful to you.

About your statement that you prefer Aquinas to Luther I want to have a long talk with you sometime. My second volume of Giffords is an exposition of the proposition that neither Aquinas nor Luther, neither Catholicism nor Reformation are right. Catholicism makes grace the Kingdom of God, or whatever symbol is used, the completion of the imperfections of nature. Reformation theology declares that it is the negation of the goodness of nature. I solve the matter, perhaps too simply, by declaring that the highest possibility is both a completion and a negation of the natural. It is a completion in the sense that there is an original perfection in man which must be completed. It is a negation in the sense that all historic reality and truth contains an egotistic corruption of the essential reality and truth. Thus the ideal political possibility must always be a completion of what is genuine justice in the British Empire and a negation of what is imperialistic corruption in the British Empire.

I try to carry this pattern out in the various problems of philosophy and politics.

Come to see us soon.

Yours,

Reinhold

**Union Theological Seminary
New York, NY
April 1941**

Dear Lewis:

We have had a good fan mail on your article, one man suggesting that it ought to go into the *Reader's Digest* and another ordering many extra copies. I have asked our secretary to mail back the manuscript though I am afraid it is pretty dirty from much use and deletions, etc.

In regard to the questions you raise, I don't think Thomism is right in exempting reason from sin. There is no reason which is not tainted with self-interest but neither is the Reformation right in believing the total depravity of reason or any other thing. For this reason there can be an advance in truth, etc., and yet we never have universal truth but always truth from a perspective. On the other hand I am interested to have you use the word ecstacy because I think there can be essentially perfect acts which are even better than the mystic's idea of a moment of perfect contemplation. I have no question about the possibility of complete disinterestedness being possible in contemplation, but the mystic is inclined to remain in contemplation because he knows the action will not be perfect. While no one can jump out of his own skin and act with complete disinterestedness it is nevertheless important that there can be more perfect actions than lives just as there may be a perfect sonnet but no perfect epic poem. But these perfect acts must be regarded as symbolically perfect or perfect when viewed externally. The martyr himself would know if he could analyze his deed of martyrdom that it is possible "to give my body to be burned and have not love" [1 Cor. 12].

I am very interested that though the emphasis is different our minds seem still to be travelling along the same paths.

Yours,

Reinhold

Heath, MA
August 1942

Dear Lewis:

It was very nice to receive your letter, as I had often thought of you and regretted that I have had no personal contact with you this summer. Gas rationing is responsible for our failure to show up at all. We have gone to NYC only twice this summer for a day or two and each time of course by train. Meanwhile I have done what you have done. I have kept a closer schedule than ever before and as a result I am on my last chapter of the second volume of Gifford lectures. I expect to be finished by the middle of next week. It has been the longest ordeal of concentrated labor which I have ever undergone, as I do most of my work by fits and starts. I do wish we had a chance of seeing you, but it does not seem possible. We can't get back into our apt. in NYC until September 8th.

Incidentally there is a possibility that I will be at Stanford in January. I have been approached about a lectureship there which is to last for a week and for which I would fly out during our exam period. Had a letter about it last week saying that the final selection had not yet been made but would be shortly. It would be a great boon if I could see you out there. Meanwhile my best wishes for your work in the West. I know you will do something very creative.

I quite agree with you about the resignation from the Am[erican] Friends of German Freedom,[1] to which I have incidentally given very little time in recent months because of the pressure of other duties. I am not sure that I agree with you about the German freedom business. But that is a different problem. If we should win it your approach to the Germans seems to me too moralistic. I don't think nations can be quarantined or isolated until they are good. They have some elements of health, even when they are very sick. We do not know how much health there is in the German body politic. But whatever health there is there cannot be strengthened by purely repressive measures. For that matter our whole civilization is pretty sick, as now becomes more and more apparent. The German disease happens to be virulent and ours is some kind of consumption. Reconstruction will have to consider Western civilization as a whole. Wish I could really talk with you about these things. Letters are so inadequate. I confess that I am beginning to lose courage about the war. I don't see how or when it can be won. I believe it can be won eventually, but meanwhile it may take so long that the whole of our social fabric may be endangered.

You are right about Waldo.[2] Have been wanting to write to him to express my admiration, but I don't know how to reach him. That kind of a crisis brings out the best in him.

With affectionate regards,

Yours,

Reinhold

1. *A group of like-minded intellectuals and students interested in the welfare of Germany.*
2. *Waldo Frank; author and mutual friend.*

Union Theological Seminary
New York, NY
May 25, 1944

Dear Lewis:

Thank you very much for your letter. I have been wanting to write you for some days and didn't know whether you were back in the East.

Ursula and I are leaving for a few weeks in the country on next Monday. I shall be in New York in June only on the 19th, 20th, and 21st. If you are coming down at that time I hope that we can get together.

The reactions to your book [*The Condition of Man*] have been intensely interesting. One cannot of course attack the basic presuppositions upon which most of the reviewers stand, without getting the kind of reactions to which you are subject, but I was glad to see that practically all of the reviewers recognized the greatness of the book.

I assume, just judging by the fate of some of my other friends who had planned a trip to Britain, that the invasion has put your trip off. I am wondering what your plans in regard to the trip are.

With affectionate regards,

Yours,

Reinhold

Union Theological Seminary
New York, NY
October 31, 1944

Dear Lewis:

Thank you so much for your letter. You are quite right, one becomes conscious of the awful limits of the human imagination when in one moment one enters so fully into the grief of a friend and recognizes in the next moment that this participation is only momentary compared to the hours and years in which one's friend bears the sorrow of a young life snuffed out, so full of promise and goodness. What you write of the moral and spiritual maturity of Geddes[1] is most cheering because I know what it will mean to you and Sophie throughout the years. For the knowledge that a son had gone through the trying years of adolescence and found so fine a source of inner serenity means that the life was complete, though remaining horribly incomplete in being cut off before the whole promise of it is fulfilled.

You say that we will have to be very good to be worthy of the goodness of such young men. To me the deepest tragedy of life is the certainty that we will not be. Not that their sacrifice will prove finally availing. But the world will obviously pass through some pretty terrible decades and perhaps a century before these sacrifices will bear fruit.

Our love to you and Sophie. I am terribly sorry that I will not see you before the New Year.

Yours,

Reinie

1. *Geddes Mumford; Lewis's son, serving as a U.S. soldier in Europe, had been killed.*

Union Theological Seminary
New York, NY
July 23, 1945

Dear Lewis:

It was a great pleasure to have your letter and to know of your agreement with us on the Japanese issue. I took the liberty of publishing an excerpt of your letter in the issue of *Christianity and Crisis* which goes to press this morning. Since I did not have time to get your consent I am publishing it anonymously.

I think you are quite right about the conscription issue too. I have talked to quite a few educators about that and they are almost all opposed to turning over the young men for a year to the Army, primarily because they regard the Army as a very bad educator except on the immediate military task. I think your alternative is an awfully good one.

The address by Thomas Mann arrived only this morning and I shall take it with me to read on the train.

I am awfully glad to hear that your health is restored. I feel very much deprived since it has been so long since we have been able to look at the affairs of the world together. I do hope I'll have a chance to see you in the fall before you finally go off to Dartmouth.

Affectionate regards from Ursula
and myself to you and Sophie,

Yours,

Reinhold

[This letter from Lewis Mumford appeared in *Christianity and Crisis* on August 6, 1945, the date the United States dropped the atomic bomb on Hiroshima. The previous issue of *Christianity and Crisis* had questioned the policy of obliteration bombing of Japanese cities as being warranted by military necessity.]

"The coming of *Christianity and Crisis* today reminds me that I had wanted to write you after reading your dedication about obliteration bombing in the last issue: what you said there I have felt for a long while and would have expressed in public if I could have found the right time and place for saying it. We have taken over the totalitarian theory of warfare without any critical examination; without even perceiving that its immorality may also, from our point of view, be inefficiency. Even from a strictly military standpoint air power has been overrated, just because it has been over-publicized: thousands of lives were lost, precious weeks and months were wasted, because our army, being under the delusion that airpower would achieve the knock-out blow, never provided enough heavy artillery and never ordered a sufficient number of shells to do the work; they relied upon the air forces, at the mercy of the weather, to do what only artillery could accomplish. In 1942, when I spent a week in Washington, the question of whether air power could be used to subdue Japan without heinous *moral offense,* was still being debated in the inner circles. The air arm won that argument, apparently; and we are going ahead on those lines without worrying what will happen when we try to pacify and govern a country whose organs of political and social life have been annihilated. Your declaration should be followed up; I think you would get many laymen with no religious affiliation to join with you, as I for one would not have joined with the more pacifist statement of the other group, even though I approved their purpose."

Union Theological Seminary
New York, NY
March 6, 1946

Dear Lewis:

I am in complete agreement with the statement of your group about the atomic bomb. I have only a minor suggestion, and that is that paragraph 3 ought to be paragraph 1. I should think it might be extended to read that we make a solemn declaration to the nations that we will never be the first to use the atomic bomb in warfare, and that in proof of our sincerity we dismantle the bomb, and so forth.

We are just getting out a statement on foreign policy for the UDA [Union for Democratic Action] in which this will be one of our various points, but a very important one. I am convinced that this line of attack is more important than any possible constitutional proposal at the present time.

Cordially yours,

Reinhold

Heath, MA
June 30, 1946

Dear Lewis:

Your kind letter arrived just before I left for the country. I mislaid it and hence am very tardy in answering it. You raise an interesting point about Thomas Aquinas'[s] doctrine. I don't know enough history to know why and when Catholicism departed from his more moderate teachings on sex. I'm going to try to find out.

Am working hard up here on a new book [*Faith and History*] which I hope to have finished by fall. It's on the interpretation of history.

We'll try to stop in for a chat on our trip back to town, which we must make occasionally.

Affectionately,

Reinhold N.

New York, NY
April 1, 1952

Dear Lewis & Sophia:

It's nice to hear from you. I am already a reformed character and I hope I can be more creative if I don't run around so much. My left hand is slightly lame so I can't use the typewriter for six weeks. Convalescence is boring, but I expect to be alright—in time. It was good of you to write. Love from us both.

Yours,

Reinhold

Amenia, NY
August 14, 1965

. . . Ursula's hour with us, Dear Reinhold, was all too brief: but what a pleasure it was for both Sophie and me—all the more because it suddenly brought back such vivid memories of that summer back in the thirties—The thirties!—when you both used to drop over. And thank you again for challenging Washington's illusions of omnipotence. I fear what may happen when the whole structure of misinformation, falsehoods, and self-deceptions cracks open in public. But for the present, as Ursula may have reported, my mind is temporarily anesthetized by my absorption in my new book: an attempt, against the broadest possible background, to re-interpret technics' relation to the whole development of man. The news of your present recovery cheers us, dear Reinhold, and before too long we hope to run over for an hour's chat.

Warmly,

Lewis

Yale Hill
Stockbridge, MA
September 10, 1965

Dear Sophia and Lewis:

It is a shock to realize it is over a month ago—or—about a month or four weeks since I stopped for that (for me) most delightful 3 hours—with you both.

It was marvelous for me, and thank you both very much indeed for your kindness and generosity of time. I enjoyed it tremendously in every way, the sights and sound of you both, the chat—*and* food & drink.

Since Reinhold's illness, now 13 years ago, the casual or arranged seeing of friends have naturally & necessarily been reduced. So "dropping in" had a special feeling of freedom and of being a rare treat—which indeed it was.

Reinhold was so pleased to hear about it all when I got back, and every word I tried to remember and report with faithful accuracy. And your letter later was a great gift and tonic.

Two other details to pass on: when our daughter Elisabeth heard that I had stopped in to see you both, she was most excited, as apparently she had met Lewis at the White House last September for the Freedom award occasion.[1] "I forgot to tell you, Ma, how angry I was with you, in all that we and you had talked about Lewis Mumford, you *never* told me how beautiful he was"—in tones of outrage over the telephone. "Rubbish," I said, "I am sure I did, and also how beautiful *Mrs.* Mumford was, and what a magnificent couple they are." "I wanted to see her, but some White House squirts were hedging her in."

I was amused—and perhaps both of you will be too. It—the whole occasion—sounded rather odd; no food, which Christopher found most disappointing. . . . History is such a funny mix-up of many layers of details, isn't it?

Then a fortnight ago, I heard from my sister Barbara, who lives in Constable-land in Suffolk (her address is Ancient House, & there are Tudor roses on some of the beams, and pargetting on the external plaster), as follows: "Be careful about over-using your hands gardening. . . . May I say this?—as I discovered my thumb-joints got nasty when I started abusing them. Radiant heat lamp, a proper kind we got through a medical friend, now keeps trouble at bay for both of us."

So, Sophia, you have company in aches, and I hope yours are better. My gout is—really better, but I am wary about the drugs.

My sister was funny about the English weather this summer; she says, "Everyone is inclined to melancholia. Everything droops, too. So we're going to Spain earlier in mid-October, despite Mr. Wilson."[2]

Forgive this spiel. The world gets more and more difficult. I find our U.S. attitude more and more offensive—in preaching "Peace" to Pakistan & India.

Do come and see us whenever it is possible & convenient for you.

Gratefully & affectionately,

Ursula

1. R.N. and Lewis Mumford received the Presidential Medal of Freedom in September 1964.
2. Prime Minister Harold Wilson devalued the pound, making trips and purchases overseas more costly for British residents.

Amenia, NY
September 27, 1965

. . . We sometimes have guests, dear Ursula, who are almost as welcome as you are: but none of them write such charming letters: so we are aching for another visit before we leave for Cambridge at the beginning of November.

But some fine October day soon we'll be phoning *you* to find out if you and Reinhold will be "at home" in the middle of the afternoon. Washington was very lively and it gave me a fine chance to try out some of my unorthodox ideas about man's early development on a tough but unexpectedly sympathetic group of scholars: so I returned here greatly refreshed, despite the hot humid weather that dogged us to our doorstep. Your weather news from your sister in England somehow cheered us, as being entitled, restrospectively, to our misery. As for your remembering to report what your Elisabeth said about me—what a heavenly act of grace it was for you to remember it and pass it on: all the more because I can scarcely bear to gaze at the sinister mug that scowls at me in the mirror each morning. And what you added about Sophia made her cup run over, too.

Here's to our meeting again soon!

With affectionate greetings to you both,

Lewis

P.S. I hope you've found a satisfactory resolution of your teaching dilemma.

Amenia, NY
October 19, 1965

. . . This happens to be my seventieth birthday, dear Reinhold, and your new book [*Man's Nature and His Communities*] is one of my best birthday presents, even if an unintentional one. I've read all but the last chapter and have earned the right to express my admiration for this marvelously succinct summing of your views, which puts all your earlier work in perspective, with just those marginal corrections and changes of emphasis one has a duty to make at the end, even if not everyone is either as lucky or as courageous as you in taking the opportunity to make it. I read the paragraph that closes "Changing Perspectives" aloud to Sophia: but I couldn't finish the last two sentences because I found myself choked with years.* Your tribute to Ursula spoke for the reality of every good marriage. But I have an old debt to you, which I take this opportunity in passing to express to you: your positive recognition of the "energies" and "vitalities" that underlie all "idealities" was a salutary corrective for my generation, like your recognition of original sin: you helped me more than anyone except Dostoevsky to recognize the constant interplay of demonic and angelic qualities in man. And though we have often differed sharply I have profited as much by those differences as by our agreements. So in addition to thanking you for *Man's Nature and His Communities,* I thank you for the many invisible gifts you have bestowed on me without knowing it. . . . The paper I am herewith sending you is by no means to be taken as a return: it is just a glimpse of one of the main themes of the book I am now writing. . . . When I last wrote Ursula we had every expectation of running up to see you even before this. But last week Sophia spent mostly in New York, to have a cyst removed from an eyelid: a "minor" operation that proved exhausting: and today, while her eye is still bothering her she came down with the flu. So I fear it will be impossible for us to visit you before we leave for

Cambridge on November first. We are desolate, for the mere taste of Ursula quickened our appetites to see you both. If the weather and the gods are kind, let us hope for a meeting in February.

Meanwhile our affectionate greetings.

Lewis

*Read "tears"—this is too classic a Freudian slip to be erased.

Yale Hill
Stockbridge, MA
October 21, 1965

Dear Lewis:

You are a dear friend, writing me your letter of appreciation about my new book, presumably my last.

Being an author you no doubt know that when one launches a new book, one is anxious, wondering what people will think about it. There is no one in the world whose judgment is more precious to me than yours. So I thank you with all my heart.

Ursula was grateful and excited after her visit with you and Sophie. I am sorry your stint at Cambridge will prevent another visit from our favorite couple; but we will look forward to the visit in February.

It seems best to stay here till Thanksgiving on account of the necessity for therapy, more available here than in NYC. Meanwhile I have just read proof of an article slightly redundant, to be published by the *Saturday Review* on "Lessons Learned from Life."[1] I have not learned too many lessons, but at least I have been copious, I am afraid a little too much so, in recording them.

I am glad you and I are in such agreement on foreign policy. As a lifelong Democrat, I confess to apprehension about the course of the master politician in the White House.

Ursula joins me in affectionate greetings to you and Sophie.

As ever in friendship,

Reinhold

P.S. Hearty Congratulations on your 70th birthday. I am glad we are growing old together.

R.N.

Many happy returns of *the* day! Was it festive?—Or did you celebrate chez vous.

We are *so* sorry Sophie had this trouble, with eye, & then flu. Please tell her to rest, relax, eat & drink & wax fat & well!

Reinhold has only been home a week after a few days' sojourn in Pittsfield General Hospital. The circulation in the leg where the embolism hit him last year—was not to good, so—a stitch in time, I hope, & he is back on anti-coagulents, etc. He feels rather low in spirits & in strength, so your letter was a wonderful gift of cheer. Bless you for it.

Meanwhile, our N. York address is 404 Riverside Drive, N.Y. 10025. Where in Cambridge will you be? Please let us know! Card enclosed.

Love to you both,

Ursula

P.S. We both were melted by your sympathy re—the works of married & mutual states. Bless you both.

1. R.N.'s article "Some Things I have Learned" was published in the Saturday Review on November 6, 1965.

Stockbridge, MA
December 22, 1965

[Picture postcard of Church on the Hill, Lenox, MA]

This church pleases me so much that I *hope* it will not offend you on a post-card! This is our 34th wedding anniversary & we were married in Winchester Cathedral, so there is a sort of connection . . . So we send you both, our best love—and wishes for 1966, *and* our pleasure in & gratitude for your lives—and your shared life together.

R was quite wretched in Oct–Nov & we only achieved NY 4 weeks ago. But the very best to you.

Love and Best Wishes
—Saecula Saeculorum,

Reinhold & Ursula

P.S. R. has typed the envelope but writing is hard.

Harvard University
Cambridge, MA
December 29, 1965

Dear Reinhold, dear Ursula:

Your note came this morning and warmed the cockles of our hearts at a moment when they needed a little extra warming, for purely physical reasons that there's no need to go into. We were thinking of you, too, all the more because we'll be coming back to Amenia at the end of January. Except for a series of bedraggling illnesses (Sophia's alas!) we've enjoyed Cambridge hugely, parched as we were for human companionship other than our own.

But a black cloud hangs over all of us: perhaps the same black cloud whose foulness Ruskin was aware of long ago, though it comes from another quarter of the sky and is called Vietnam: and this adds an extra dimension to the dark moments of our individual lives—and cannot be shaken off even by health or good fortune. But these are not the proper sentiments for greeting the New Year, are they? Instead, we embrace you both and pray for restorative miracles. "Life, prosperity, health!" as the Egyptians used to say.

Affectionately,

Lewis and Sophia

P.S. Yes: I love your church, and all that went with it!

New York, NY
April 7, 1967

Dearest Sophie & Lewis:

We think of you often—sometimes I run into Babette Deutsch[1] at the cake-shop—perhaps a lesser Lewis would try to do a history of culture via the paths of food (cultivation, cuisine, *and* packaging, and, horror of horrors the yummy-yummy commercials), and we talk of the people we know and love—and this often brings you again vividly into mind. On one of the coldest days of the year, we stood on the corner of 110th Street & Broadway while we exchanged antiphonally our expressions of regards for the Mumfords. For no one (no *one*) else—would we have stood, & froze, so—ecstatically!

Then, a couple of weeks ago to see your most seemly selves at this ridiculous suicidal city—was cheering, for then we know we *are* right, we and the taxi-cab drivers who know the facts of life and the stupidity of men so well.

So this is to bring our love & hopes that we may see you again fairly soon.

Reinhold has not been too well, in fact rather wretched at times, the neuralgic-like pain in the lower intestinal tract makes sitting more painful than it should be. Drugs to relax don't help, and we hope, like last spring, that better weather & improved circulation will improve things.

How are you both? I do hope well, & that Cambridge was pleasant? We plan to migrate to Stockbridge at the end of May. Shall you be coming to the Academy?[2] Reinhold would like to go to the lunch if nothing else—I think.

Love from us both—as always—

Ever admiringly,

Ursula

1. *Secretary of the National Institute of Arts and Letters; noted poet.*   2. *American Academy of Arts and Letters; a group of fifty members of the National Institute. R.N. and Mumford were members of both and saw each other at the annual May meeting.*

Yale Hill
Stockbridge, MA
December 10, 1968

Dear Lewis:

Thank you so much for your affectionate letter on my book of original writings *Faith and Politics*. I know how busy you are working on your own books and probably you will have no time to read this rather obvious collection of occasional writings, but I appreciate your comment on it. [This does not sound like R!—U.M.N.]

Thanks so much for inviting us to your nice home in Amenia. We won't be going to New York for months. The doctor has ordained that after a heart attack, it will be better for us to stay here in Stockbridge. Perhaps there is a chance that you and Mrs. Mumford will visit us some weekend from Cambridge. I am glad that you are teaching at Harvard. Ursula and I found our stay at Harvard most rewarding.

Affectionately yours,

Reinhold

P.S. From under a hair dryer from Ursula M. N.:

This letter was dictated over 10 days ago, & the nice stenographic lady whose entire family of 4 children had been sick, told me she was not sure if she read her shorthand right. . . . So forgive delay & probable not quite correct transcription. *But* the point is—

1. Reinhold was more than pleased, in fact incredibly moved to get your letter. It meant so very much to him, & the sense of cheer and friendship has stayed with him.

2. We both would love to see you both, whenever you feel you might be able to come this way. I doubt if Reinhold is up to going back to N. York, so we shall be here.

3. What do you think of the world? of Nixon? Is it all right for Pat Moynihan to go in? I hope so. How is the next generation & the Brooklyn grandchildren? What are you on now? or, correctly (?) "On what, Mr. Mumford, are you now working???"

Happy Hanukkah & Happy Christmas to you both.

Amenia, NY
August 18, 1969

. . . This is the last, dear Reinhold, of many *unwritten* letters to you. Unwritten because I first wanted to read your new book, or because I hoped that, even if I hadn't, I might find time to run up for an hour's visit with you, or because, to make a further delay, I wanted to congratulate you on your forthright words about Nixon's using the White House as a revivalist pitch.

But my book held me in its grip and none of my letters found their way to paper. *This* I fear is not much better than no letter at all: just a sorry apology for all my good intentions. Meanwhile I've learned from the mayor of Jerusalem—how can one call him "Teddy" without smiling?— that Ursula made a dashing impression there, "as usual" I am tempted to add.[1] We hope to see you both before we return to Cambridge in October: but until I actually turn in my ms. to Harcourt's I dare make no promises.

> *Meanwhile, affectionate greetings*
> *from "house to house."*
>
> *Lewis*

1. *Teddy Kollek; mayor of Jerusalem. U.N. and Mumford were members of the Jerusalem Committee that advised the mayor.*

Yale Hill
Stockbridge, MA
August 19, 1969

Dear Sophie and Lewis:

We long to see you. . . . Are you fairly well? Is the book finished? And—are you going back to Cambridge in October? (or September?)

I *did* go to Jerusalem. We—first—decided "no," especially when I discovered you were not going, as it would have been nice to have been in your train. Then pressures started—Christopher had some connections— and our friends here, including the doctor and the nurses who variously help me with Reinhold and his physio-therapeutic exercises—and the Adolf Berles[1]—these all combined to push me off. Not on any grounds except it would be good for me!

However—whatever the motive or effective cause—I found the few days there quite marvellous. The obvious—double or trebled—or many-layered history that one had always read about coming with the situation today, that was to me the centre *and* the context of and for everything.

The assembled group, very oddly eclectic, Tagore's nephew; Isamu Noguchi—lots of architects, a nice large one from Ceylon, Geoffry Bawa, and of course Bruno Zevi—who quite intrigued me, and who also always enlivened any discussion. . . . Your name was mentioned—& I nodded—in a sort of "hear, hear" fashion. Bruno Zevi looked at me—questioningly. I passed him a note to explain that I liked L.M. "and his stuff"; Bruno Zevi passed back a note "*Stuff??*" I sent it back—"his ideas, his books, his style of writing." This seemed O.K. Then Bruno Zevi sent me another note— Ask him [Lewis Mumford] what he thinks of *my* stuff?!! So—?? I am ignorant of his stuff, but realise he is lively. So—enlighten me. . . .

But—you MUST go to Jerusalem. Please—I want to go back.

Love,

Ursula

Can we see you ever? Reinhold a bit up & down, but friends are the best tonic.

---

1. *Adolf and Beatrice Berle; summer neighbors. Adolf and R.N. had served together on the executive committee of the Liberal Party of New York state. Beatrice was a doctor; Adolf was a lawyer, professor of law, authority on corporations, and diplomat who served in the State Department and was Kennedy's ambassador to Brazil.*

Yale Hill
Stockbridge, MA
September 2, 1969

Dear Lewis:

Thank you so much for your generous letter on my little piece on Nixon's "established religion" in the East Room of the White House.[1] I am glad you approve of it. I hope that we shall see you and Sophie before the summer is over and you are on your way to Harvard. I have my own problems of ulcers which disturb my creativities, so it is nice to know that one of the leading intellectuals of our time approves of our stand, particularly since Billy Graham's cohorts have written me a liberal spate of hate mail.

Ursula and my affectionate regards to you and Sophie, and we hope we have a visit from you on your way to Harvard.

Affectionately yours,

Reinhold

R. was so cheered by your note. I think the hate mail was rather tonic for him, & he did [have] some good letters of support. Love to you both.

Ursula

1. *R.N.'s article on religious services at the White House, "King's Chapel and King's Court,"* appeared in Christianity and Crisis *on August 4, 1969.*

Amenia, NY
August 1, 1970

Dear Reinhold, dear Ursula:

It isn't for lack of thinking about you both that you haven't heard from us, or that we haven't turned up on your doorstep some fine afternoon; neither is it because there haven't been very many fine afternoons! Our attempts to get together with you remind me of that famous act of W. C. Fields, in which he gets involved with some flypaper, and in the act of struggling to get it off becomes desperately and madly ever more stuck with it. Most of the flypaper we've been struggling with is made of incipient Ph.D[s], besieging me for information about Waldo Frank, Patrick Geddes,[1] and Paul Rosenfeld: they come armed with tape recorders and trivial questions, sometimes with sentences extracted from my own writings almost fifty years ago, ideas long repeated—or repudiated!—which they would like me to explain or justify. The worst specimen of flypaper was really a nice little man, a librarian who reminded me of the pathetic character whom Melville puts at the beginning of *Moby Dick:* a few years ago he took on himself the horrid task of doing a bibliography of my published writings; and after doing an astonishing amount of file-ransacking, he came here to check on my files, to find to his consternation a mass of *New Yorker* Sky Lines and Art Galleries[2] that they had never put in the out-of-town edition that went to his Cleveland libraries. After *four* days the total haul now amounts to a thousand items; and the very thought of all that print makes me feel as if I had an albatross slung around my neck. As if all this weren't bad enough, I suddenly realized I had deadlines to meet on introductions to two books left by dead friends, one of them being Waldo Frank's incomplete autobiography, which I persuaded the University of Massachusetts Press to bring out. And what a problem Waldo is! To do justice to him in even a half a dozen pages, I've had at least to run through, and sometimes read carefully whole chapters, of most of his books; and to explain to myself why a man with all his obvious gifts nevertheless was disliked by his contemporaries and is completely neglected, almost, by the present generation. No easy task that! One can't even explain his fate by his devouring ego; on matters that concerned his physical courage, for instance, the ego was non-existent; for he even called off a longer lecture tour, on his last return from South America, because American audiences wanted him only to talk about the physical attack the Fascists in Buenos Aires had made on him. Perhaps he suffered from a superabundance of original gifts; and in his early years was never toughened by poverty or rejection. Well, I haven't solved that problem yet; and probably won't!

All this is a circuitous approach to the real point: the last fatal envelopment in flypaper. For a year, Sophia has been handicapped by a "bad knee," whose worst arthritic touches, if such indeed was the cause, were abating—when suddenly, slipping on a slithering ice-cream cone someone had dropt on the sidewalk on Amenia, she fell flat on her face and wrenched her thigh badly. True, it might, at our age, have been even worse; but it makes going about difficult; and it may be weeks before she is back in a semi-normal state. That is why this chit-chat must take the place of our presence.

It might also be made to explain to Teddy Kollek why I can't go to the Symposium[3] in December, though he was hoping that Ursula would persuade me. But there were even better reasons than this for my not making that journey; and the chief one is that I am a slow traveller, and like the Indian, feel that my soul needs a lot of time to catch up with me, if I too quickly leave my native haunts. Between Ursula and Bruno Zevi I should be well represented, or perhaps, it would be more just to say, well obliterated. If I didn't send you the Brooks-Mumford letters, though I certainly meant to, please tell me: they're the sort of literature you can pick up at any moment and drop without the slightest sense of missing anything; and what is more, they are better than sleeping pills to quiet you down at night. I am not pleased about the selection Spiller made, for he deleted some of the most interesting parts of the correspondence in order to bolster up a thesis about our relationship; and had I known he approached his task with the fixed idea that ours were "parallel lives," dedicated to the same task, I wouldn't have given my consent to their publication. Our relationship was far more complex, and more ambiguous,* too, if I may reluctantly admit that odious fashionable term, than Spiller's Plutarchian thesis permitted him to see. Someone will have to do the job over again, alas!, and that means further feeding for the Ph.D. mill.

I commiserate with you, but with Reinhold particularly, over this humid weather; and if it is not too sticky or flypaperish, let Sophia and me embrace you both!

Affectionately,

Lewis

*Yes—and ambivalent, too!

1. *Scottish town planner.* 2. *Mumford regularly contributed articles under these rubrics for* The New Yorker. 3. *The Symposium was a special meeting of the Jerusalem Committee for town planners and architects.*

August 10, 1970

Dear Lewis and Dear Sophia:

Oh, dear! Oh, dear! How sorry we were to hear of the slip on the slithering ice-cream cone. How infuriating and how painful, and we do sympathize. I am ashamed to say that despite my sympathy, I love Lewis'[s] alliterative sentence—"Sophia suddenly slipped on a slithering ice-cream cone someone had dropped on the sidewalk." I realized in a flash the tension between Art and Life. Wystan Auden so often has preached to me about the literary value of sorrow, e.g., St. Augustine, "You can take away my friend but you cannot take away my grief." So, I hesitate to say I enjoyed hearing about Sophia's slip, yet, didn't I enjoy Lewis'[s] description! But, we really are *terribly* sorry and also selfishly disappointed. We would so love to see you. Anyhow, your letter came on my 63rd birthday and we tasted the letter and re-read it with great enjoyment, after a festive cup of tea (yes, tea) and, would you believe it at the age of 63, a slice of birthday cake.

Reinhold enjoyed particularly your delightful descriptions of your struggle with flypaper. We have this as a constant "extra" in our life, too. So often I write to some flypaper character, who has come across a statement Reinhold made, if not a hundred years ago, at least forty years ago, and wants to know how he feels about the issue on which he commented then. Of course, Reinhold's reaction, inevitably, is "I wouldn't care less and am not interested in what I said forty years or more ago."

What you wrote about Waldo Frank also touched us, in both senses of that word. It moved us, as both of us were very fond of Waldo, and neither of us quite tackled the problem of why he didn't come off. Both of us resisted him, perhaps in different ways. Perhaps we felt he asked too much of us; this probably *was* his ego; for one was to give him *lots* of love, *lots* of attention, *lots* of appreciation. Yet, if we were with him, he was charming and delightful as a companion; also, to be honest, perhaps we felt he was sometimes a little whiney. Also, we both found his novels ghastly.

Yesterday, I had a copy of Teddy Kollek's letter to you. He and his colleagues and the members of the Committee, were so hoping you would be there for that meeting. You are not just a person, but a total approach, and that is what they hoped for. The December meeting will be more technical—architects, planners, etc. I feel with you about the rate of motion. I do not approve of suddenly arriving at a place where one should spend a lot of time getting to. What can we do about it? Let me know if you have any ideas. A leisurely sea voyage would be the perfect convalescence for Sophia, and think of the wonderful leisure of shipboard existence—bouillon and deck tennis and recumbent somnolence.

Meanwhile, we'll hope all goes well. Perhaps, if Reinhold and the help situation stabilizes (ghastly word), might I come over and see you?

Later: Alas, my efforts and my intentions never are fulfilled. Reinhold suddenly sprang an infection, vaguely chest-y, (he wheezed) and so became more quintessentially the centre of the universe, for me. (I am the night nurse, evening nurse, lunch-time nurse, everything that isn't 7:30 A.M. to 12:30 A.M. as well as being cook & bottle washer & rather absentee gardener and letter answerer et al.) But his temperature is down today & one of the alternating nurses is coming between 4 & 6 to give me "time off." So at last this started letter should go off, with our love & sympathy.

Ever belatedly,

Ursula

P.S. Just have had an airmail from my brother-in-law in England, to tell me that my sister is in hospital after surgery to remove a shattered knee cap. Coming back to Suffolk after a theatre in London, she fell face forward flat. I am devastated, yet I note, the alliteration again?!

We have not read your & Van Wyck Brooks' letters . . . & would love to.

Amenia, NY
September 17, 1970

Dear Reinhold, dear Ursula:

Your letter of August 10th found us in the midst of worse troubles than those you responded to: so I won't say anything about them, except that the ultimate cause was the deep fatigue that afflicted both of us after a very harassing year and a half, whose outcome in the finished *Pentagon of Power* was nothing short of a miracle. A copy of that miraculous book should reach you during the next month: but first let me tell you about the huge joke that life has played on us. Probably I've told you that the Book-of-the-Month Club chose this far-from-popular treatise as their selection, at first for March 1971, but they later changed their mind and decided on December, which means that the book will appear in the bookstores on 11 November. That was quite enough to stagger me, for they had turned down *The City in History,* a much more readable, though perhaps less exciting work. I greeted this, I confess, with "modified rapture" because by now we have quite a comfortable income, without my devilling at articles and lectures: so all that this juicy bonus will do is to guard us, for a while, against further inflation. But on top of this the *New Yorker,* or rather Shawn, the editor, was so enthusiastic over the galleys that he plans to publish more than half the book in four installments during October—with a payment quite as flabbergasting as that of the Book-of-the-Month Club's first installment. As I told my publisher, Jovanovich, I am well fortified for meeting rejection and disparagement: but I have no armor to protect me against success. Some foolish sentry has been sleepy enough to admit me to "the Pentagon of Power"! We shall doubtless survive these blows; but I confess that I never anticipated the time when a superfluity of money would make me anxious, almost superstitiously frightened. At a less wicked moment than this, and in a less wicked world—and of course if we were as much as ten or fifteen years younger!—I think I'd have reacted somewhat more exuberantly to this windfall.

But the world, as you know, is more wicked than ever, and leaves a bitter taste even in the ice-cream.

The Arab high-jackers haunt my sleep, for a son of our dear Dartmouth friends, the Stearns Morses, is one of the high-jack captives; and we both live with a sense of their unbearable anguish. As for you, dear Ursula, I trust you have given up all thought of that Jerusalem visit: to go on with your plans would not be courage but foolhardiness; and since the meeting, though important, is not urgent, all your going would do would be to express your human solidarity with this beleaguered people—whom I confidently expect will be betrayed by the American government, which keeps on, in preparation, shifting all the blame to them.

I was charmed by your literary exegesis of my description of Sophia's slithering downfall—from which particular misfortune, I am happy to report, she was by now fully recovered, helped by supersonic therapy, though I suspect that she might have been equally aided by old fashioned hot baths. Since of course I was not consciously sliding into alliteration you illustrate a point that most academic critics are never sufficiently aware of: that it is the contents itself that creates the style, and any attempt to deliberately juggle the words to express contents almost ends up by making the reader feel it is artificial and forced.

And I am comforted by what you report about your and Reinhold's feelings toward Waldo. I think I have got to the bottom of Waldo's weaknesses both as a man and a writer; but this doesn't make my task any easier. On my reading of his memoir and my reflections over his total literary achievement, his great handicap is that he had too many natural gifts and was at the beginning too well-favored in every way. A boy who was reading Dostoevsky and Tolstoy at twelve, and who refused to take a course in Shakespeare because he felt he knew more about the plays than his teacher was not merely singularly gifted, but exposed to the sin of pride, with nobody around him, apparently, either capable or willing to take him down. And that was *our* fault, too: none of us, I am sure, was ever ruthless enough to Waldo about his weaknesses and failures; and the only friend that dared to risk his friendship by saying what Paul Rosenfeld said in *Men Seen,* promptly lost Waldo's friendship and earned his pitying contempt. His early successes in the twenties, with lecture audiences, with popular magazines, and with a whole succession of women increased his insolence: He had few good words for anybody or any institution, not even for Shakespeare. So it was in fact he who rejected his contemporaries before they, quite naturally, began to reject him. Though I wrote two reviews of his books that were critical, I now feel a little guilty that I never tackled his work as a whole and pointed out the curious thinness and parochialism of his religious conceptions and the "solution"—the "deep revolution"—that rested upon them. His "Great Tradition" excluded half the human race, and how he was going to make the world over without their help I can't possibly guess. And yet, almost alone among his contemporaries in America, Waldo recognized the central importance of religion; and if this finally came to make a central place in my own Weltanschauung, it is to Waldo, and through him to Reinhold, that I owe an immense debt. I think that half his work, the half he subsumes under "History" is important; and that in his most unsatisfactory books, like *Chart for Rough Water* and *The Rediscovery of Man,* even his errors are fruitful, or would be if one examined them rigorously and sought to counter them. But how am I to convey this in an introduction without betraying my trust, indeed undermining in retrospect our whole friendship? I haven't solved that question yet; and fortunately I've had a reprieve on my deadline: so I am still mulling it over. The only thing that makes it possible at all is that Waldo's memoir is so candid, so self-revealing, so brutally honest, and in the end—as in his last letters to me—so full of humility and almost a child's bewilderment over how it came about that a life so rich, so varied, so many-sided, so gifted as his own had come so completely to grief. Was the fault really his? He almost admits it. He had never lived up to his own deepest convictions, yet he unsparingly castigated others for not accepting those convictions. You both have Christian insights into this terrible dilemma, which has dogged all religions even at their highest moments: some of Reinhold's best passages grapple with this very problem.

What misery that Reinhold has been afflicted with apparently the same ailment that brought me low in August: though it didn't settle on my chest it produced such horrendous fits of coughing, veritable seizures, the muscles of my back, involuntarily responding, ached for days at a time. I hope he finally has gotten over it, though it took two series of antibiotics to counteract my infection, and both Sophia and I still show lingering affects, though the depression and washed-outness that resulted has vanished.

What a long letter to write to a busy woman! Fortunately, you could drop it at any time, which is more than you could do with an equally tedious visitor. Don't bother to comment of the Brooks-Mumford letters, even if you should ever have time. They were edited to correspond with a pre-existent thesis in Spiller's mind, which unhappily omitted much and falsifies our actual relationship: the best that can be said for them is that they have astonished many reviewers by a single feat: we both managed to write intelligible English without erasing a line! Mumble is the literary style today.

Our love to you both,

Lewis

**Yale Hill
Stockbridge, MA
October 18, 1970**

Dear Lewis:

Your new book [*The Pentagon of Power*] is a masterpiece. It draws the proper pessimistic conclusions from the advance of technology, which every scientist implied. But you alone broke with 18th-century evolutionary optimism definitively. What an achievement to challenge the modern Urban Utopian. Your book will be a milestone in the history of culture.

Love to Sophie. Ursula returns from her vacation tomorrow.

Affectionately and admiringly yours,

Reinhold

**Yale Hill
Stockbridge, MA
October 28, 1970**

Dear Lewis and Sophia:

I have just come back from England, to find your book and copies of the *New Yorker* here. It is quite intoxicating to have your words about, and most tempting, so that I cannot even unpack with any measure of resolution. I found Reinhold very thrilled, and I gather he has written you a letter all by himself, typed with one finger on his specially equipped typewriter. Were it not for the fact that I am feeling the effects of those lost five hours flying across the Atlantic, I would barricade myself alone with the book, but alas! I am back at the job of keeping the home fires burning, and my dear man does have to be fed and cared for.

But, thank you very much not only for the gift of the book, but also for what you have done in writing the book. I feel, perhaps, slightly messianic about it—"Now are these words being fulfilled . . ."

Briefly on other matters—I hope Sophia's hurt has healed and that she is really comfortable. I also hope that all the excitement of the book being out does not give you too many interruptions but a well-earned rest and leisure. Therefore, to be consistent, you must not answer *this* letter—I do not like to think of you having to answer telegrams, letters, telephone calls, etc., from your enthusiastic friends and public, when you should be living in peace and in the ease of contentment! Let me remind you that "The Lord rested on the seventh day" after His work of Creation. You had said, on the telephone a few weeks ago, with engaging modesty, that you were surprised to find when you re-read your book that it really was quite good. This is right and appropriate, but it does involve the necessary consequence, ". . . and God saw everything that He had made and behold it was very good . . . and He rested on the seventh day from all His work that He had made."

Quoting the Hebrew Scriptures reminds me that I saw the ineffable and ebullient Mayor Kollek in London. He and Mrs. Kollek were there very briefly, and I was lucky enough to see them, and some old English, and even American, friends at a big party that George Weidenfeld had for Mayor Kollek and Lord Sieff.[1] And, then the next day, he and Mrs. Kollek came and spent some time with our dear and old friend, Lady Stansgate, whose son, Anthony, was in the Labour Government as Minister of Technology. Anthony, who is a perfect darling, needs to know and understand much of what you say in your book, and I am going to send it to him to read, mark, learn, and inwardly digest.

To return from this digression to Teddy Kollek . . . he hopes very much that you will comment on the plans that will be sent to you from Jerusalem. For my own sake, I hope you will have time to do this, as I am fascinated by what is going on in Jerusalem, much of which, because of the wretched political situation, cannot be bruited abroad.

I am enclosing a copy of what appeared in the *Times* of London, Thursday, October 15th, about the Mayor and the possible future of Jerusalem.

Peggy Stansgate and I pressed him (as no one else was there) about the back-drop of Russian power and the whole Near Eastern situation. He replied, "Let's put it like this. We are trying to build a good ant-hill, the best ant-hill in the world, and we need the advice and help of all our friends, because it is an ant-hill that is important to so many people around the world. But know what happens, sometimes, to an ant-hill? A great big foot can come and stamp it out, and that is the end of the ant-hill." He was talking, of course, about Israel generally not just Jerusalem, but the courage and "guts" of the Israelis are so magnificent that one can only hope and pray that the ant-hill survives.

No more now, although there were other things in your September letter, particularly about Waldo Frank, that one wants to go on. I was worried when I read some of your letters in the Van Wyck Brooks book that I had been tactless and ungenerous about Waldo in my earlier letter. Now, I shall not worry so much about that. Anyhow, I had never finished a note to thank you for the book or to tell you how much I valued and enjoyed those letters and relished even all the minor points you wrote about. Reinhold, meanwhile, was surprised that someone so large and magnificent as you, would bother to comment about the minor details of life. This sort of reaction of Reinhold's never fails to amuse and surprise me. He is so large and natural, himself, and yet he expects that other large people are more God-like and not subject to the minor strains and stresses of life which he knows so well himself. In a sort of a way, it is a tribute of his admiration for you and an expression of his own modesty, and I find it, as I said, both charming and amusing. (Somehow I feel Sophia would understand.)

My dear sister who "fell flat on her face" also is fairly well recovered. She also had to go into hospital for various therapy treatments and exercises, while her enchanting husband and I felt that warm baths and patient exercises done at home were even more beneficial.

It was wonderful to see them and to be in England. London seems so clean and tended, in spite of strikes of sewage treatment workers. What a world!

Later: Why does the Lord, or Fate, never allow me to finish a letter. *Mea Epistola interupta est—meae epistolae interuptae sunt.*

Reinhold was supposed to be put into hospital for observation. His plumbing system, he is on a catheter, has to be checked, possible stones in his bladder. The wretched system doesn't always work, and nature's plumbing is better than the surgical substitute. *But,* the hospital postponed his visit, on account of a hepatitis scare (drug addict hepatitis?). So much rearranging, and un-arranging.

Hence, the delay.

> *But it comes with our love*
> *to you both.*
>
> *Ursula*

P.S. Erik Erikson follows in your train. He looks a wee bit frail, having spent six weeks in Beth Israel Hospital. . . .

> *Ursula*

1. *George Weidenfeld, now Lord Weidenfeld, publisher. Lord Sieff, English department store owner (Marks & Spencer), had just published his autobiography.*

Cambridge, MA
October 29, 1970

Dear Reinhold, dear Ursula:

Your generous letter about my book was promptly followed by Ursula's postcard: both heralding happily her return. So many unexpectedly good responses have been evoked by my book, from people of such diverse backgrounds, even before its publication, that most of my preliminary qualms have been banished. Naturally I look forward to equally violent attacks—but they should be useful in keeping me tethered to realities. What a joke "success" is at this point in one's life! Like old age, one's heard about it but never believed it!

Once more we're happily settled here—the quarters themselves a little cramped, but the view of the sky, the river, and the sea gulls still enchants us. The students seem quieter—apart from the dwindling number ravaged by drugs—perhaps experience has chastened them. . . . Sophia's "bad knee" and painful shoulder are now almost normal: and the reason I report this is because her improvement came, not thru any physician's treatment, but from massive doses (1250–1500 mg) of Vitamin C daily. After a month or so she was surprised to find that the pain had disappeared and she could walk more easily, almost normally. If ever you're afflicted, dear Ursula, remember this!

After many painful but persistent efforts I've at last finished my Introduction to Waldo's *Memoir*. To strike a balance between his intellectual virtues and his spiritual defects was the hardest task—as hard as doing this with Tolstoy. But he himself provided, in this autobiography, the clue I had always lacked: so I shall be eager to see, later on, what you make of it.

We embrace you both and only wish these gestures were not so wraithlike!

Affectionately,

Lewis

Yale Hill
Stockbridge, MA
January 13, 1971

Dear Lewis:

Your Christmas letter was wonderful to get. Thank you so much for it. Reinhold had rather a "down" spell just about that time, and only the last couple of days have been a bit better. So, your letter was especially cheering to get. Many times I was tempted to ring you up just to say "thank you" to you and Sophia.

There are so many things to talk about. I reacted, as expected, to the review in the *N.Y. Times Book Review,* and realized that the author of the review (whom I don't know personally) was expressing what Mr. Holmes called the "unspoken major premise" of his own stock-in-trade. I gather my general impression was right, on the basis of what you wrote last week in the *Review* . . . how tiresome and how stupid!

. . . I recall many very minor instances of the same sort of thing with Reinhold. He wrote something in a book on the Structures of Nations and Empires, which was fairly critical, as you might imagine, of the scientific and technical point of view on political matters. We were in residence at the time, in the Institute of Advanced Study at Princeton. I recall Robert Oppenheimer was obviously miffed or hurt by what Reinhold said, even though in conversation he and Reinhold always seemed to agree. I suppose a kind of professional vested interest involves the practitioner? But shouldn't there be an effort to get outside those interests?

But, about Jerusalem? I am longing to see your memorandum, and again had to control myself from ringing you up, when I read the *N.Y. Times* with its story about your "bomb shell." How good it was that you wrote, and it really justifies Mayor Kollek's having got the group together, that experts like you and Bruno Zevi can challenge the Plan. But, of course, I want to know more . . . I have been bothered and puzzled by trying to make sense of the Master Plan in relation to the accounts I read in periodicals and the *Jerusalem Post* about what is going on. Also, the Master Plan, as described, did not quite make sense in view of some of the other things we had described—and shown—to us when we were there last year. I had written asking Mayor Kollek more details about some of these "gaps," especially in relation to . . . the Moshe Safdie Habitat plans,[1] for opposite the old Arab village of Malcha. Yesterday's *Times* (Jan. 12th) in Peter Grose's dispatch, shows that there must be a great deal of resistance even locally.

I am hoping your memorandum will bring light to me out of this comparative darkness.

If Reinhold's health were better, I would want to go and do some listening to people and various groups. Any usefulness I may have, I feel, is because I am not an expert and I am supposed to know a little bit about history; and what the *N.Y. Times* reported and you were saying, does involve that Jerusalem's history should be honored. So, I await your wisdom.

Do you like the choice for Harvard's new president [Derek Bok]? He sounds rather good and our friends, so far, have been cheering about him. I hope the New Year will be good to you and Sophia.

Forgive this typed letter. I try to write letters at night, but so often my writing is quite un-readable. I had to give up doing accounts also at night, as a kind of automatic control took over, and I persisted in writing cheques for "Harold Wilson" (our snowplough man is also a Harold), and even endorsed a pension cheque, made payable to "Nixon, Hickel" instead of "Berkshire Bank & Trust."

Do you know the Eriksons? They came in for tea and talk on Sunday—being old friends and neighbors—when Reinhold was at a very low state. He sat by Reinhold's bed—Reinhold looked at him, and said, "You know, Erik, I don't want to live." Erik replied seriously, "I know." And Reinhold relaxed and they had a wonderful chat. And they talked about you while Joan and I assisted, in the French and English senses of the word. She is a beautiful person in the way Sophia is—all the way through. He and she expect to be in Israel this summer, as they are going to do a study of children at play (that is not what it is called) & may first go on one of the fantastic Doxiadis "Trips" to the Greek Islands—with Margaret Mead & Buckminster Fuller. (I would love to see those two together, wouldn't you?)

. . . Are the Norton lectures in Design currently "on"? Deborah (the older daughter of Waldo) Caplan's husband, Ralph, is apparently helping Mr. Eames with the lectures. When Wystan Auden was so pleased with himself for being so pure & good in turning down the Norton lectures in Poetry because he had nothing to say, I suggested that he take on Ralph Caplan, but Wystan ignored my suggestion, being lost in pleasure at his own virtue . . . Dear Wystan!

Love—to you both as always,

Ursula

1. Safdie, a Canadian/Israeli architect, proposed a plan for housing in the old city of Jerusalem. The presentation of the Master Plan and other suggestions had met with tremendous arguments and criticism so that Mayor Kollek called another meeting a year later to ask for further suggestions.

Sixteen

Arthur M. Schlesinger, Jr.

Arthur M. Schlesinger was a very good friend. Reinhold found him most congenial and saw a good deal of him in the later forties and early fifties. Both of them were actively involved with the Americans for Democratic Action, holding various offices in that organization.

Reinhold found Arthur's knowledge of American history and his grasp of contemporary political problems most "impressive" (a favorite adjective of Reinhold's) and very helpful. Arthur reciprocated this regard, and in 1957 dedicated his book *The Crisis of the Old Order* to Reinhold.

After Reinhold's first stroke in early 1952, Arthur was most thoughtful and understanding. His visits to the hospital, and later to our home, always cheered Reinhold. Later that summer, after the Democratic convention in Chicago, Arthur went to work for Adlai Stevenson, also a friend of Reinhold's. A couple of times Arthur telephoned from Springfield, Illinois, asking for ideas on what seemed to be the important ethical and political issues in the campaign. Reinhold was recovering from another vascular incident, and these requests were most tonic and therapeutic for him.

Later still in the fifties, when Reinhold recovered to a certain degree from his illness, he resumed his regular preaching at Harvard University, and again we saw the Schlesingers. After the service and a good rest for Reinhold, we would repair to the Schlesingers' house for Sunday dinner. Arthur would have assembled a few of his good friends, and along with a splendid repast, we would enjoy a feast of friends. After these many years, these memories of friendship remain.

New York, NY
September 11, 1951

Professor Arthur Schlesinger, Jr.
Department of History
Harvard University
Cambridge, MA

Dear Arthur:

. . . I made a brief trip to Europe and spent the rest of my summer working on a little book on the role of irony in American history. Since I am treading on ground which you know so much better than I, I am almost tempted to send you the manuscript if you have any time to read it, in the hope that you will save me from some bad errors.

> *With affectionate regards to you and Marian,*
>
> *As ever,*
>
> *Reinhold*

Harvard University
Cambridge, MA
November 10, 1951

Dear Reinhold:

Ursula said that you were about to deliver the mss. of your book to the publishers; so I thought I would airmail my reactions, for whatever value they may have. I will return the mss. itself the first thing next week.

It occurs to me that the comments are valueless without page references. . . . I am not sure that I grasp with precision the larger design of the book (since I have not seen the first and last chapters); but this torso is splendid—wise, valuable, and illuminating. I only wish that you had put in more direct comment on the American experience. So many of your observations are good—as the one, for example, stressing the similarities between the Calvinist and Jeffersonian analyses—that I wish you had let yourself go in this field more often.

One irony deserving comment somewhere perhaps is the relationship between our democratic and equalitarian pretensions and our treatment of the Negro. This remains, as John Quincy Adams called it in 1820, "the great and foul stain upon the North American Union"; and I think you might consider mentioning it.

A few specific comments: Actually the Jeffersonians were willing to increase the power of state governments; their unrelenting opposition was to the increase in the central power. The Jeffersonian tradition had strong tendencies toward local control of economic life.

Moreover, I am troubled here (and later) by the use of the phrase "our traditional theory" or "the Whig-Republican theory." Actually the Jackson-Populist-Progressive-New Deal tradition calls for a considerable measure of state intervention and control. The present political climate lays emphasis on the anti-statist elements in the American political tradition; but there are considerable statist elements which should not be overlooked because of their current neglect.

We hope to see you soon—for lunch on Sunday, December 2, unless the [James] Conants pull rank on us.

Yours ever,

Arthur

Union Theological Seminary
New York, NY
November 14, 1951

Dear Arthur:

It is awfully good of you to go so carefully over a part of my manuscript, and I will incorporate and take heed of all your criticisms. I am a little concerned what to do about your justified criticism of my phrase "our traditional theory" or "our semi-official theory." I know that this is primarily the theory of the business community, and I have mentioned that several times. On the other hand it constantly goes beyond that—a New Deal or Fair Deal administration uses it constantly in its Voice of America; the recent Freedom House Statement, written I think by our friend Archie MacLeish, is pretty full of it. I was embarrassed to have to get off of the committee which wrote that statement because they didn't seem to know what my criticisms meant—particularly my criticism of the assumption in the document that justice would flow inevitably from freedom.

Just a word about the general thesis of the book, which appears a little bit more clearly in the three chapters that you didn't see. I am really using the concept of double irony as developed by Cervantes in *Don Quixote*. I am suggesting that Don Quixote represents an absurd imitation of the sentimentalities of the age of chivalry which convicts chivalry itself of absurdity, and that communism is a kind of demonic Don Quixote which gives the illusions of a bourgeois age, demonic potency.

My concluding chapter is an analysis of the relationship of ironic, tragic, and pathetic elements in our experience.

Thank you again for looking at all this. I was anxious to have you do so and yet I didn't want to bother you.

With affectionate regards to you and Marian,

Yours,

Reinie

Union Theological Seminary
New York, NY
May 29, 1952

Dear Arthur:

Your letter arrived this morning just after Jim[1] called. I have been deeply touched by the loyalty of my friends during my illness—I may say particularly by yours and Jim's. Now you embarrass me still further by initiating this generous gift of a television set[2]—which incidentally, whatever anyone may say about television, is a tremendous boon to the politics of our country. It will be so particularly in a presidential year. I am embarrassed almost beyond words by your kindness to me. I will also try to express my gratitude to the many friends who have participated in this when I receive the list.

Incidentally, I wanted to write you today in any event, to express my appreciation of your review of Chambers'[s] book.[3] I read it with great enthusiasm because of the shrewdness and fairness of all of your estimates, and I hope my enthusiasm was not prompted by your generous reference to me. The conclusion, which you criticized, is of course fantastic. It is another revelation of how ex-communists, as well as communists, can still be involved in an either/or proposition. One could write quite a chapter on the debate between rationalists who assume that reason is an organ of sanity, but do not recognize that a rational procedure which does not examine its presuppositions can be a source of confusion, and religious devotees who believe that democracy is based in religious humility but do not recognize how easily the worship of God can become the source of a covert idolatry. Incidentally, the *New York Times* has asked me to review the book and I am rather sorry that my sickness prevented me from doing it.

> *With kind regards to you and Marian,*
> *and renewed thanks not only for what*
> *you have done but for what you are*
> *to me in all of your work,*
>
> *Affectionately,*
>
> *Reinie*

---

1. *James Loeb, former executive secretary of Americans for Democratic Action, was working for the Stevenson campaign; in June 1952 he switched to Averell Harriman.*   2. *Schlesinger and Loeb had organized the collection of contributions from ADA friends to purchase a television set for R.N. so that he could, during his convalescence, watch coverage of the presidential campaign.*   3. *Whittaker Chambers's* Witness.

Union Theological Seminary
New York, NY
June 5, 1952

Dear Art:

Thank you for sending me the Congressional Record with Adlai Stevenson's speech. I don't know what other theological friends he has. I certainly didn't write to him a few weeks ago, and while I have expressed the sentiments in general terms which he quotes, I didn't use some of the specific similes, so I think Stevenson must have another good theological friend.

The television set has arrived and is going to be installed today. Every time I look at it I think with gratitude and some embarrassment of your's and Jim's friendly concern during my illness.

As always,

Reinhold Niebuhr

Heath, MA
July 27, 1952

Dear Arthur:

You have been in the enviable position of being both an observer of history in the making and a maker of history. When I heard Stevenson's acceptance speech all my misgivings about his coyness were overcome by gratitude for such a candidate. For there is a quality of urbanity and sophistication in his utterance which we have not had for a long time in public debate. There is also a recognition and acknowledgment of the seriousness of our times which has become unusual. I'm afraid Harriman didn't have a chance against these obvious advantages. But I don't fully understand the desire of our crowd to throw the South out, nor Stevenson's willingness to risk some northern states in order to keep the South loyal. The provisional conflict between the ADA and Stevenson is still a mystery to me. But the final results are most heartening. I congratulate you on your part in them.

I make very slow progress, but it is now steady. But I won't be able to do anything beyond a single class this fall. I am gradually learning how to use an electrical typewriter with one hand.

With cordial regards,

Reinhold

**Harvard University
Cambridge, MA
August 6, 1952**

Dear Ursula and Reinhold:

I am back in Cambridge to order my affairs before going back almost immediately to Springfield. I have agreed to work full-time for Stevenson until college begins.

The convention, as you can imagine, was most exciting. I think that the liberals were absolutely right in forcing the issue on the loyalty pledge. One trouble was that the pledge was misrepresented, by both sponsors and opponents, as binding all delegates to support the candidates—which would have been intolerable. Actually all it did was to bind the delegates to see that the candidates got on the ticket on the Democratic line; once they had done this, the delegates would be perfectly free to do anything they wanted. In the end, the liberals won on the substance of the issue, and should probably have settled for substantial compliance instead of insisting on the letter of the pledge. Their refusal to do this permitted the bosses (led by Arvey[1]) and the southerners to administer what appeared to be a smashing defeat to the liberals—though in fact the liberals won on the substance issue. The resentments of this defeat, exploited by the Kefauver people, almost turned many of the liberals against Stevenson. Fortunately Humphrey and Harriman stopped this and prevented Stevenson from emerging as the Dixiecrat candidate.

My admiration for Harriman increased steadily throughout the convention. He played a gallant and selfless role; made a clear-cut stand on the issues; and gave the liberal position a dignity and a strength it might otherwise have lacked. I saw a good deal of him in his most intimate and troubled moments; and he behaved with a dignity, a decency, and a clearsightedness which were most impressive.

I think there are great possibilities in the Stevenson nomination. He is the one person in either party who speaks with an authentically new voice. Where Eisenhower, for example, utters the cliches of the right, and Harriman the cliches of the left, Stevenson speaks with his own fresh voice. One has the sense of a personal vision which may lift us above and beyond the increasingly sterile party debates of the past generation and move us into a new political climate. I believe that Stevenson bears the imprint of an original political personality and has great creative possibilities. On the other hand, it must be admitted within the family that he is much less good on most issues than Harriman. Still [Woodrow] Wilson, for example, was a "good-government" governor of New Jersey, rather conservative on national issues, until necessities educated him; and I have the feeling about Stevenson that he is entirely educable.

I have put a discretionary label on this letter because I am most anxious that my views do not get into circulation. Stevenson naturally expects full loyalty from his staff, and will get it from me; the expression of reservations might destroy my usefulness at Springfield. Thus I would be grateful if you would not mention any of this to Frankfurter, MacLeish, etc.

One trouble is that Springfield is terribly isolated. If you have any ideas about what we should be doing, please write me at the Stevenson Campaign Headquarters, Springfield.

Of all the many idiotic reviews of Reinhold's book [*Irony of American History*], the most idiotic is probably the one I enclose (from *The Freeman*—John Chamberlain's reactionary magazine).

We hope that Reinhold continues to mend. Why teach at all in the fall? Far better to read, think, and write! Anyway, have a good rest this summer; and *let me have all possible ideas, suggestions, etc., at Springfield.*

Marian joins me in sending the best of love to you both.

Devotedly,

Arthur

P.S. Adlai had all 6 of us to dinner when we were at Springfield. He could not have been nicer, and Stephen and Katharine [Schlesinger's children] were wordless with excitement. [Stevenson's campaign manager] Wilson Wyatt (who is doing a good job) was also present. Chrissie [a Schlesinger daughter], less impressed, asked her mother on the way home: "Which one was Stevenson?"

1. Col. Jacob Arvey; Democratic leader of Chicago, Illinois.

Union Theological Seminary
New York, NY
June 25, 1953

Dear Arthur:

I am glad that we can count on you for that address in September. Of course we pay traveling expenses and I have immediately arranged to take care of the very modest honorarium which you suggest, namely, our book on *Christian Faith and Social Action*. I have asked Professor [John A.] Hutchinson at Williams College to send you the book, and I am delighted to know that you should want it. Perhaps it will have some interest to you because in at least Hutchinson's and my chapters we deal with the social gospel movement and the gradual dissipation of Marxist convictions in it.[1]

Ursula is being operated on this morning. We hope it's nothing serious, but we'll know more about it this afternoon.

With affectionate regards to you
and Marian,

Reinie

1. *Many of R.N.'s journalistic essays were composed for* Radical Religion, *founded in 1935 as the magazine of the Fellowship of Socialist Christians. In 1940 the magazine was renamed* Christianity and Society. *The organization became the Frontier Fellowship and, in 1951, Christian Action. A volume of essays to honor Christian Action was compiled in 1953 and was dedicated "To Reinhold Niebuhr—CHRISTIAN, THEOLOGIAN, PROPHET, STATESMAN. With the grateful affection of his fellow-workers and friends this book is dedicated without his knowledge." A special leather-bound copy was presented to R.N. in September 1953 when Arthur Schlesinger, Jr., spoke. But R.N. was unaware of these plans at the time of this letter. At the end of the volume he had written, "The task of any movement devoted to social Christianity must be therefore, not so much to advocate a particular nostrum for the solution of various economic and social evils, but to bring a full testimony of a gospel of judgment and grace upon all of human life."*

Harvard University
Cambridge, MA
May 9, 1956

Dear Reinhold:

As you know, I have been working for some time on a multi-volume history to be entitled *The Age of Roosevelt*. The first volume is due to come out in the fall. If you do not mind, I would like to dedicate this volume to you. The reasons for this are self-evident; and I can only add that friendship with you and Ursula has meant more for Marian and me than I can easily say, or than this inadequate gesture can express.

Yours ever,

Arthur

Union Theological Seminary
New York, NY
May 14, 1956

Dear Arthur:

Ursula and I were deeply touched by your letter saying that you wanted to dedicate the first volume of your magnum opus *The Age of Roosevelt* to me. I don't think the reasons are self-evident, at least they are not so self-evident to me that I am amazed of the honor you wish to do me.

Ursula and I have always been grateful, more than we could express, for the friendship with you and Marian. I gratefully accept the dedication as a witness to that friendship, even though I am conscious of the fact that you have many friends to whom you might, as an academic kudo, more fittingly dedicate such a book.

Jim and Ellen [Loeb] came to see us on the way back from the convention, full of enthusiasm about it.

With affectionate regards from Ursula and me to you and Marian,

Yours,

Reinie

Union Theological Seminary
New York, NY
May 17, 1956

Dear Professor White:

Thank you for your thoughtfulness in sending me your article on "Original Sin, Natural Law, and Politics," and for your great desire to be fair in argument. If you have not always been fair as your desire, you have been much fairer than most polemical arguments turn out to be, including my own.

Could I make some observations and criticisms? Why put me in a class with [Walter] Lippmann, when you quite fairly say that we hold opposite political convictions? I can find only one reason for these categories in your statement, "Niebuhr's Augustinian doctrine of original sin is neatly matched by Thomistic doctrine of natural law in Lippmann." Neatly matched? What have they to do with each other? Aquinas was not Augustinian in his doctrine of sin; and Augustine had no doctrine of natural law. And the two contemporaries whom you criticize have contradictory political opinions. These categories seem to me to be more polemical than empirical. Perhaps I am conscious of the power of categories in polemical argument since Professor [Charles] Frankel in his *Case for Modern Man* lumps me together with Toynbee and Maritain, though I disagree with about 90 per cent of Toynbee's convictions and with at least half of those of Maritain. We were all religious and that put us in the same category. But I must not wander because I am dealing with your article and not with Frankel's book.

You admit that [John] Dewey was rather too optimistic about human nature, but you do not cite the chief criticism I made of his social theory.

That was the criticism of his opinion that the "scientific method" could be applied with the same validity in the historical as in the natural realm, if only, in the warfare between science and religion, a truce had not been made prematurely delivering the historical sciences to the interference of "State and Church" and therefore condemning them to permanent inactitude. I think this is the root error of modern culture, resting on the failure to recognize the intimate relation between reason and interest and passion in all historical judgements.

I have been called an "irrationalist" for holding to this conviction, though I would not think it irrational to call attention to empirical evidence of the taint of interest upon the purity of reason. I know of no political scientist or historian, many of whom share my convictions, who are accused of irrationalism. It must be that I was foolish enough to call the fact of the inevitability of self-regard in various forms "original sin" instead of inventing some modern equivalent for it. I think I learned about that fact empirically, and I did not establish it by an "a priori" as you suggest. When I began to speculate about the mystery of the universality of inordinate self-regard and the paradox of our feeling of responsibility for our selfishness, I restudied my own presuppositions more carefully and came for the first time on Augustinian thought and through Augustine discovered Paul. I had heard of the latter in church for a long time, but, being a liberal Christian, I was rather ashamed of being associated with him. You try to prove that I believed these things "a priori" rather than empirically by calling attention to my early socialist convictions. I want to make a rueful confession of the exact chronology of my movement of thought. I became a socialist in opposition to a pacifist and to pietist or to rationalist liberalism, (there wasn't much difference in those days between the pious who expected all men to love one another, and the rationalists who wanted to establish the kingdom of justice by the "scientific method," despite the polemics between them). I meanwhile became a theological professor and for the first time really studied the history of thought. I became a critical student of Augustine because his presuppositions seemed to throw light upon facts that had perplexed me. It was not the other way around, that I looked at the facts from a rigorous "a priori!" I thought I learned from Dewey that even an empirical method cannot dispense with presuppositions, which you call "a priori" but that it must be rigorous enough to reexamine its own presuppositions. This latter trick is unfortunately more difficult than Dewey imagined, which is why neither he nor you nor I engage in it very frequently. Arthur Schlesinger has proved with rather embarrassing accuracy that I expressed socialist political convictions long after my basic presuppositions seemed to contradict these convictions.

This inconsistency may be due to many things, including the fact that the Augustinian presuppositions were not as intellectually respectable as the Marxist ones were, and it may also have been due to my intimate friendship with Sir Stafford Cripps. You see I think that other people's reason is as frail as my own. Incidentally, you commit only one grave error in your treatment of my thought. You accuse me of going back to Hegel's dialectic when I confront the paradox of responsibility and inevitability in man's self-regard, but you will remember that Kierkegaard had his own dialectic and that was taken straight from him—I didn't have to go back to Hegel.

I must add that an examination of the whole nature of man's historical freedom led me to an espousal of more of the Christian faith than I possessed in the beginning (I mean the whole range of realities comprehended in the ideas of responsibility, sin, and grace). More recently I have been so shocked by religious obscurantism on the one hand, and religious self-righteousness on the other hand, that I would like to be as polemical against various religious manifestations as I have been against the complacency of the rationalist in the past decades. But I hope it will be empirical in constructing my categories so that I will not condemn the charitable souls together with the self-righteous prigs. The net effect of this pilgrimage has been to make me a rather extreme nominalist, too afraid of general concepts, to do creative thinking.

With gratitude for your kindness,

Sincerely yours,

Reinhold Niebuhr

Union Theological Seminary
New York, NY
May 18, 1956

Dear Arthur:

Enclosed is a copy of a letter I sent to Morton White in answer to one of his, and the article which he enclosed from the *Partisan Review*. I regret that my letter is defective in many respects, including the lack of paragraphs in it, but at least you will be apprised of my debate with him. I am rather amused by my debate with every consistent rationalist to find that argument tends to make all of us unfair, no matter what our creed.

Elisabeth was accepted by Radcliffe today, so you will have another member of the Niebuhr family to bother you for another four years.

With love to Marian,

Affectionately yours,

Reinie

Harvard University
Cambridge, MA
July 16, 1956

Dear Reinhold:

Just a line to say that I am going to Chicago in a few days more or less for the duration. I will be doing the same sort of thing that I did four years ago. If you have any thought about things that might be said and done, I hope you will let me know. Perhaps governor Stevenson has already written you about the acceptance speech; but, if not, we would all very much appreciate your own thoughts as to what might be in the speech—indeed, as to what the main issues of the campaign are as you see them.

Our love to Ursula. It was, as always, a great delight to see you both at Commencement.[1]

Yours ever,

Arthur

1. All the Niebuhrs attended a party at the Schlesingers after the Harvard Commencement, at which Christopher Niebuhr graduated. Also present was Senator John F. Kennedy, who had received an honorary degree.

Chicago, IL
July 31, 1956

Dear Reinhold:

Thank you for your suggestions about civil rights and foreign policy. They both express the spirit in which we are trying to approach things; but it is hard to achieve a formulation on civil rights which can be at once politically, morally, and intellectually adequate. I agree with you about some kind of development of the governor's suggestion on nuclear tests. Please let us know if you have any further thoughts on this or on anything else.

Please give my regards to Christopher before he disappears. And also tell Elisabeth that we should be delighted to have her use our names at Radcliffe.

Yours ever,

Arthur

P.S. You will be interested to know that Bill Miller is here, working across the desk from me. He sends his regards.[1]

1. *The Rev. William Miller; a professor at Yale Divinity School, who was writing for the Reporter, a bi-monthly periodical.*

Heath, MA
August 10, 1956

Dear Arthur:

I am very grateful for your letter, especially as it is written in the pressure of things. We were thrilled this morning by Stevenson's statement on civil rights. Coming before the convention it was a master stroke and no one can accuse him now of being the candidate of the South. It solves many problems.

I wonder what can be done on the foreign issue in such a way that the nation will not be unduly alarmed but at the same be made conscious of the fact that the issues are more complex than the simple contrast between communism and democracy; and that the Administration's complacent moralism is absolutely inadequate for the issues of the day. After Stevenson's statement my defeatism was overcome and I see the possibility of victory.

Give Bill Miller my regards. I am glad he is working in the camp. His article on Dulles was first rate.

Affectionately yours,

Reinie

Union Theological Seminary
New York, NY
September 17, 1956

Dear Arthur:

Ursula and Marian talked on the phone last night and Marian has kindly offered to provide a bed for Elisabeth last night. Elisabeth will be registering at Radcliffe today. It was through this conversation that I got hold of your address and I am delighted to hear that you are busy in the campaign, and I take the opportunity of making a few suggestions.

Incidentally, I haven't written Adlai Stevenson since his nomination. He is always so thoughtful in answering letters that I felt it pretentious to bother him with a letter which he thought would have to be answered, since he obviously has a press of so many duties. I was thrilled by the turn of events at the convention, and equally thrilled and hopeful by the turn of events since.

My suggestion is that in foreign policy, as the campaign goes on, the governor ought to spell out more what is meant by the contention that we are losing the Cold War. In spelling it out I think a sharp distinction ought to be made between the actual mistakes of the administration, such as trying to contain the social revolution in Asia by military pacts, and the developments for which the administration is not directly responsible, which are due to the new flexibility of Russian policy, about which it is so complacent, and tries to persuade the American people to be complacent. I think if a sharp distinction could be made between these two points both points would be more effective.

I was, as you know, partly defeatist before the campaign began, but like every other good Democrat I am beginning to get hope that Ike will be beaten.

With affectionate regards,

Yours,

Reinie

Harvard University
Cambridge, MA
May 4, 1957

Dearest Ursula and Reinhold:

I have been meaning to write for the longest time, but everything is more than usually chaotic this spring. As you know, we are going abroad with the children, and everything has crept up on us in the most appalling way. We leave on the 17th, and are most inadequately prepared, itinerized, reservationed, etc. I find myself unable to believe that any of this is really going to happen, so I sit, paralyzed both by a sense of unreality and by the conviction that I would be unable to cope with reality should I begin to perceive it.

[Robert] Oppenheimer is here and speaks with great enthusiasm about your descent on Princeton next year. I find him much more likeable than I expected—curiously sweet and gentle; also awfully idealistic and highbrow. He makes me feel even more impure, worldly, philistine, and

corrupt than usual. The lectures have been a great success as a performance; rather less, perhaps, as a communication.

Barbara Ward was a great personal success. As you know, she is to get
an honorary degree here (big secret).

If we stop off in NY more than an hour on our way to the boat, I
hope we can get together.

> *In the meantime, much love to you*
> *from us both,*
>
> *Arthur*

Union Theological Seminary
New York, NY
May 7, 1957

Dear Arthur:

Ursula and I were so glad to hear from you. We saw you several times
on television and felt rather deprived that we didn't see you in person. We
are glad that the whole family is going to Europe, and I hope you will
continue to be as inert and irresponsible as you claim to be now. It is
much the best way. Let the wife take care of all the details—at least I have
found the irresponsibility of my condition very rewarding. But after all you
have two arms rather than one, and so Marian may make more claims
upon you than Ursula does upon me nowadays.

What you say about Oppenheimer is most interesting. He is certainly
very sweet and gentle and rather other-worldly, but when you say he
makes you feel "impure, worldly, a Philistine, and corrupt" you are merely
affirming that you are more worldly-wise than he, which is certainly the
truth. We had a very nice visit with them a month ago, and among other
things I talked about Einstein's childlike naïveté in all political matters;
Oppenheimer said very simply, "Actually I think that kind of naïveté is a
resource for physical scientists. It gives him a very pure vision." I thought
that remark was very revealing.

I do hope that we can see you on your way to Europe, and I hope
both you and Marian will have a wonderful time, despite the impediment
of family.

> *With much love to you both,*
>
> *Yours,*
>
> *Reinie*

Wellfleet, MA
July 21, 1960

Dear Ursula and Reinhold:

I wish so much that we could have come to see you in Santa Barbara, but the phone talk was a good deal better than nothing. As you probably gathered, I came away from the convention rather depressed. I never anticipated the emergence of a strong draft-Stevenson movement, and I was terribly torn when it appeared. If I had known it was coming, I would of course have stayed with Stevenson. But I believe the movement was a great error. It exposed Stevenson himself in his worst posture—the posture of indecision; and, for this and other reasons, may well have cost him the State Department. From what I saw of him in Los Angeles, I am sure that, if nominated, he would have been cruelly beaten in the election. It is a tragedy since he is by far the best and most intelligent man to appear in our public life this generation. He has a dimension that all these other fellows lack. But he lacks the will to command and the will to victory.

Kennedy has these qualities in abundance. He won the nomination and deserved it. He is a man of first-rate intelligence, authority, and decision. Yet my liking for him and confidence in him declined in the course of the convention. I have come to agree with you about the Johnson nomination; I am willing to concede that it was not only politically sound but also conceivably a wise and brave move. But the dissimulation and deceit with which Kennedy brought Johnson out were depressing. I believe on the basis of L.A. that Jack has all the lesser qualities of F.D.R. Whether he has the greater qualities too one cannot say now, any more than one could say about F.D.R. in the autumn of 1932.

It seems to me inevitable that Kennedy should have beat out Stevenson. The Stevenson movement was too amateur and unserious to win; it was like a club of intelligent, civilized people, all of whom liked each other very much. There is no "we happy few" nonsense about the Kennedy movement. Nonetheless the fact remains that I was a member of the Stevenson club; and I fear that my enjoyment of national politics is now at an end. I do not think Kennedy will ask me to work for him during the campaign; and, after L.A., I really don't care. Working in a Kennedy campaign would not be nearly so much fun as working in a Stevenson campaign. On the other hand, he will probably win not an insignificant consideration.

I didn't mean to inflict all these thoughts on you (they are, of course, for you and Ursula alone). My chief reason for writing was to say that we left Stephen [Schlesinger] behind on the coast. He is presently staying with Tom Braden at Oceanside, California. I have given him your address with the thought that he might come through Santa Barbara at some point and you might give him a bed for the night, or get him one somewhere. He probably will never show up, being a shy boy; but, if he should call, this is what it is all about.

Our best love to you both,

Arthur

Center for the Study of Democratic Institutions
Santa Barbara, CA
September 3, 1960

Dear Arthur:

Thank you so much for your letter. I am sorry we missed Stephen but the trip to Colorado was better. Am glad that Kennedy has even converted Marian, both because I trust her judgement and the intuitions of her sex. I've only seen him once, at your party two years ago. My prejudices are due to the excessive use of money in the primaries and to this brother Bob. The latter prejudices are irrational, being due to hearing his flat nasal voice at the Senate hearings and to the report of the newspaper boys of his conduct at the convention. Of course I recognize the cool intelligence of the young senator; and I know he will be a good president, if not a great one, but even the latter is a possibility.

A young friend of mine, John Cogley, former editor of the *Commonweal* and now staff member here on the religion project, left last night to join the Kennedy headquarters in Washington. He is an expert on the Catholic religion and liberal politics, but I told him I did not see what he could do since most of the arguments will be phoney, Texas oil using Baptist bigotry as a shield.

Ursula and I are spending the last weekend here. The summer has been successful, despite the remnants of the Mortimer Adler influence which are partly ruining the studies. The only two really good staff members are Cogley and Paul Jacobs on the labor project, with Clark Kerr of U of Cal. as the head of the project. I've enjoyed chewing the rag with Harrison Brown of Cal Tech, Adolf Berle, and Harry Ashmore. Brown has made me aware of the real dimension of the nuclear dilemma, because he thinks that the "arms to parley," a slogan which both candidates will probably use, does not meet the increasing peril of the arms race, the increasing willingness of the Russian technicians to bargain on a technical level, and the growing Russian fear of China. Brown was one of the negotiators of the scientific aspects of the Antarctic treaty, which was not significant politically but he thinks we have not exploited the sense of a common predicament which the Russian and Western scientists share.

I hope you will visit us in NYC. I have started the first two chapters on a new study of international relations on which I will be working this year on a Rockefeller grant.

> Love to you and Marian
> from both of us,
>
> Yours ever,
> Reinie

Harvard University
Cambridge, MA
September 10, 1960

Dear Reinhold:

I thought your statement on Peale-Poling excellent.[1] I think also that it has had considerable effect.

Do you think that more could be done to put Nixon on the spot? At present he is enjoying all the benefit of Peale-Poling without suffering any of the obloquy. Why should he not be challenged to make an explicit repudiation of the Peale movement? Of course, he might do so; but any repudiation coming so long after the fact and in response to challenge would not be very effective. Certainly he should not be permitted to avoid direct comment on Peale, as he has done up to this point.

What is Elisabeth's address? She sent such a nice farewell letter, and I want to send her an appropriate answer.

> Yours ever,
>
> Arthur

1. R.N. was interviewed by NBC-TV about his endorsement of Kennedy. He stated that the popular preachers Dan Poling and Norman Vincent Peale supported Nixon on economic grounds, not religious ones.

340 Riverside
New York, NY
Tuesday, October 25, 1960

Dear Arthur,

Perhaps you know all about it, but today *Life* called up. [Billy] Graham asked for an extra day of prayer. Asked me to keep ready to write the piece on Friday if necessary. Called up again this afternoon. Billy had received an inspiration to write another article asking all Christians to take the election seriously. Thus ends a curious chapter in religion and politics.

Yours,

Reinhold

New York, NY
January 2, 1961

Dear Arthur:

Day before yesterday I wrote both Dean Samuel Miller [of Harvard Divinity School] and Prof. Robert McCloskey of the [Harvard] government dept., promising to accept the joint invitation they proposed. I know you had much to do with inspiring this offer, and I am grateful to you for this as for many marks of your interest in my future. I have certain misgivings about meeting the high standards of Harvard academic life, and a original hesitancy about the government dept. But McCloskey wrote a very encouraging letter. Meanwhile Ursula was due for a sabbatical so it works out all right. I am working on a new book on international relations, and I think I might use the material for my lectures.

The Kennedy administration has made a brilliant start, partly by moving the Harvard faculty to Washington. I hear various rumors about your acceptance of this or that position in the administration, and I have a suspicion that you will end up in Washington, and I have mixed feelings about that, as about every brilliant teacher and scholar who is put on an executive grindstone. But you won't need or want my mixed feelings.

Our affectionate greetings and best wishes for the future to you and Marian, whether you are to be at Harvard or Washington. Naturally I have some private and thoroughly unpatriotic reasons for wishing the one, rather than the other, alternative.

We are spending January in Washington where I will try to learn something at the Center for Foreign Policy Research presided over by Arnold Wolfers[1] and, in the past, by Paul Nitze. They are both thrilled and grieved by his loss to the center.

Affectionately yours,

Reinie

1. Long-time friend, a European émigré, authority on international relations and formerly professor at Yale.

Miyako Hotel
Kyoto, Japan
September 8, 1968

Dear Reinhold:

In case this Prague dispatch never reached the U.S., I send it along.[1] I congratulate you on your transmutation into a Czech poet!

I am over here as a guest of Japanese TV with my younger daughter Christina. In a few more days, she will go on to India (she graduated from Radcliffe in June) and I, gloomily, back to New York. What a sad year this has been! The murder of Robert Kennedy terminated my interest in the campaign, and perhaps in American politics for some time to come. Hubert [Humphrey] seems to me a burnt-out case, emasculated and destroyed by L.B.J. and unlikely ever to become a man again; [Eugene] McCarthy an ungenerous, self-pitying man who has no concern for the other America and no belief in the presidency. When George McGovern became a candidate, I rallied round; as you may remember, George is a very close friend of mine, and he seemed to me better qualified to be president than the other two. But of course his candidacy was never realistic.

What do we do now? I have always supposed that anyone would be better than Nixon. But, if Hubert and Nixon have pretty much the same Vietnam policy, might it not be better to have Nixon on the ground that it will be easier to block further escalation if the Democratic party is opposing a Republican president than it would be if half the Democratic party feels it must go along out of loyalty to a Democratic president? Certainly Goldwater, had he been elected in '64 and pursued the identical policy pursued by L.B.J., could never have got so far with it because the entire Democratic party would have been mobilized against it.

I hope you had a tranquil and productive summer. I will be back in another ten days or so and will give you a ring. Love to Ursula.

Yours ever,

Arthur

1. *Clipping from* Japan Times, *September 8, 1968.*

"Poem Advises Czechs on Life

PRAGUE (Kyodo-Reuter)–A poem recited on Prague television and printed in the trade union newspaper Prace Friday morning appears to set the guideline for a Czechoslovak living under occupation. It goes:
  Calm, so I can accept things which I cannot change.
  Courage, to change things which can be changed.
  Wisdom, that I can tell these two apart."

This was a surprising adaptation of the famous "Serenity Prayer" written by R.N.

Yale Hill
Stockbridge, MA
September 23, 1968

Dear Arthur:

Thank you so much for your letter and for the enclosure which identi-
fies me as a Czech poet. It is nice to have news of your family and to
know that you have been active in India. I am afraid the election is going
to be a dismal affair. Our friend Hubert is probably going to be defeated
and ought to be since he can't extricate himself from the fateful embrace
of that great man in the White House, L.B.J., on the great issue of Vietnam. The American people are sick of this futile and bloody war and I am
afraid that Hubert will suffer the consequences.

We are going to be in Stockbridge until the new year. We will hope to
see you on our return to New York.

> *Affectionate greetings from Ursula*
> *and yours truly,*
>
> R.N.

The City University of New York
New York, NY
June 1, 1971 [Day of R.N.'s death]

Dear Reinhold:

You have probably forgotten that in 1950 you gave the baccalaureate
address and I the commencement address at Muhlenberg College in Allen-
town, Pennsylvania. I only remember because I have just returned from
giving the commencement address there again, 21 years later. I am ap-
palled by that statistic—21 years!—but it does recall the high pleasure of
the occasion nearly a quarter century ago.

I suppose we were more hopeful then. (I am trying to find a copy of
my earlier talk in order to find out what was on my mind in 1950.) I find
myself still a long-term optimist (i.e., I think we will blunder through)
but something of a short-term pessimist, at least about America. I attach a
copy of the 1971 talk—you will note, I think, a number of Niebuhrian
points, which suggests how penetrating, and fortunate, your influence was
on my generation, and how that influence endures.

I reread *Moral Man and Immoral Society* the other day in preparing a
lecture on that old chestnut, Morality and International Politics. Your analysis applies to so many of our contemporary confusions; but why is it that

we have to go through the same argument anew every generation? Who could have predicted the rebirth of utopianism—or really of antinomianism—among the young?

I don't know whether you see Stephen's magazine, *The New Democrat,* an outlet for the young who came into politics with Kennedy and McCarthy in 1968 and who want to work within the party system but, who feel, that, if the system is to work, the Democratic party must be radicalized. In any case, I enclose a couple of recent issues.

Much love to Ursula.

Yours ever,

Arthur

The City University of New York
New York, NY
June 2, 1971

Dearest Ursula:

On Sunday I gave a commencement talk at Muhlenburg College where, 21 years ago, Reinhold gave the baccalaureate and I the commencement address and we both received degrees. The occasion suddenly filled my heart with memories of the past; and, on my return, I dictated—too late—alas—a letter to Reinhold. I attach a copy now.

I don't think I need say to you how much Reinhold meant to me through the years. He had more intellectual influence on me than anyone I have ever known; and, even more important, his combination of penetrating and realistic intelligence with total sweetness and unlimited generosity proved to a hopeless agnostic what a truly Christian man can be. We all loved him so much, learned so much from him, and will be in his debt for the rest of our lives. And in your debt too—I can imagine how difficult the last years have been for you, and I know how marvelous you have been and how indispensably you recreated a life for him.

I mourn with you the death of a great and beloved man and send all love to you, Elisabeth, and Christopher.

All love,

Arthur

Seventeen

John Strachey

John Strachey, when we met him in 1960, apparently had been what Reinhold often called an "unknown friend." We had read him with interest, including the early books, *Coming Struggle for Power* (1932) and *The Theory and Practice of Socialism* (1936), although we did not always agree with his political views.

The son of a former editor of the *Spectator,* he had reacted to conservatism while at Oxford. He was elected as a Labour M.P. to Parliament in 1929, but lost his seat after the formation of the national government in 1931. This was when the former socialist Ramsay MacDonald had in the crisis over the budget betrayed the labor movement and the working classes, and had moved to combine with the liberals and the conservatives in favor with the bankers. This, in the words of a later prime minister, Clement Attlee, "was the greatest betrayal in the political history of the country."

Many besides Strachey reacted to this "betrayal." He joined the Communist Party, and then took part with many others in the Spanish Civil War. In 1939 he left the Communist Party.

His wartime services were varied and distinguished, ranging from air-raid warden in the blitzed London, to wing commander and intelligence work. It was in the difficult years of postwar England, however, that his gifts were recognized as outstanding.

In 1946 the worldwide shortage of grain threatened starvation in many parts of the world and hit Britain very hard. The Attlee government was committed to feeding not only Britain but also the British Zone of occupied Germany and famine-stricken India. The U.S.A., after negotiations, agreed to send grain to the British Zone in Germany as well as to the American, and to regard India as a special famine case, but only on the understanding that Britain would relinquish its own expected wheat supply from the U.S.A.

This precipitated a social and political crisis in Britain. Bread riots were expected, and Strachey as food minister knew that food rationing was necessary. In July 1946 bread rationing was authorized, which continued for two years.

The British government, exhausted after wartime efforts, was also involved with India. In 1947 it was decided to send Lord Mountbatten to

India, and to withdraw the Raj and declare India's independence. But at home the food crisis continued, followed by a fuel crisis and an unprecedented cold winter. Strachey was fully occupied. Later, in 1950, he became war minister.

An amusing tale is told of him at this time. He wished to publish some poems, but cabinet ministers could not publish a book without the consent of the prime minister. John wrote to Mr. Attlee to the effect that he did not think the prime minister would want to see the book as it only consisted of poems. Mr. Attlee nonetheless asked to see it. After sending it to him, Strachey heard nothing, so he telephoned after a while to enquire. Mr. Attlee himself came to the telephone. "You can't possibly publish. The lines don't scan."

We had the pleasure of meeting John Strachey in 1960, in Cambridge, at the house of Arthur Schlesinger, Jr., after one of Reinhold's preaching dates at Harvard. Later, we saw more of him in New York. Reinhold and he discussed all sorts of subjects—political, philosophical, and personal.

One Sunday evening I shall never forget. We had asked Wystan Auden to have dinner with us to meet Strachey, whom he did not know although they had both been in Spain during the Civil War, supporting the Republicans against Franco.

Sitting in front of our fireplace after dinner and after Reinhold, obeying doctor's orders, had gone to bed, the two went on talking, comparing notes of their ideological journeys, similar in part and yet different. Wystan asked, "When did you . . . ?" But the question did not have to be finished. John would start to reminisce, and Wystan too. They went on talking, as if it was to themselves, each one recollecting.

I sat by the other side of the fireplace, occasionally filling up a coffee cup or glass. They were completely held by their memories, gazing at the fire, talking as in a duet.

Wystan spoke of the shock of finding churches locked in Spain, John of other details. Much of their conversation I do not now remember. Yet the memory of it remains.

House of Commons
Westminster, S.W.
London, England
June 28, 1960

Dear Niebuhr,

I felt that the least that I could do after our delightful meetings in New York this spring was to start reading your books. So I have read

The Nature And Destiny of Man. I am very glad I did so because I find it highly relevant to the work I am trying to do about the abolition of war in the nuclear age. [Strachey's *On the Prevention of War* was published in 1962.] I want to set down my impressions of the book while they are fresh. So I do so in the form of this letter to you, which you may or may not find worth reading.

You will certainly find these impressions almost comically naive, in many respects; but then you must remember that I have literally never opened a book on theology before in my life. Therefore I have had to try and translate your theological terminology into what I think you would call "naturalistic" terminology, in order to make it comprehensible to myself.

The most important theses of your first volume, from my point of view, seemed to me to be as follows: religion, in one essential aspect, is an insight into the nature of man. This traditional religious insight sees deeper than do all forms of secularism with their assumption of the essential goodness of man. For the central message of the religious insight into man's nature is that he is originally sinful.

You really *are* a Lutheran, are you not?! But your extended meditation on original sin was fascinating to me. Now comes the part which I have no doubt you will find comically naive. For the life of me I cannot make anything other of your concept of original sin than the assertion that an essential aspect of human nature, as it has evolved on this planet, is aggression, or as you call it in various passages, the "will to power," or "the propensity to dominate," or what you will. I entirely agree that it is vital to emphasise the existence of this aspect of human nature, in order to avoid disastrous utopian fallacies. But what I find difficult to understand is that there is any mystery about it all. In a word, I can find little place for the doctrine of the Fall. Original sin in the sense of aggression appears to me only too readily explicable. How could man, as the most evolved of organisms, be without this built-in characteristic? For aggression, the will to power, the propensity to dominate, has been shown by millions of years of experience to be one of the best ways—though not the only way—to survive.

Naturally I was particularly interested in your magnificent passage on Marxism (pages 46, 50, etc., in Volume I). I entirely agree that experience has shown that Marxism has a residual and disastrous utopianism on this issue. It fails to see that aggression or the will to power, as I call it, or original sin, as you call it, is deeply built into us by evolutionary experience and cannot possibly disappear all of a sudden with the creation of a classless society.

Moreover your disquisition on original sin, in this sense, gives me a clue as to the root of pacifism. After all the will to power is by no means the only basic characteristic of human nature. Equally important, in my view, is the converse will to submission. And the origin of this converse will is equally simple. To submit is an alternative, and in some circumstances an obviously more successful, way of surviving. Many millions and millions and millions of individual organisms have survived by means of passive submission, just as other millions on millions have survived by means of aggression and the will to dominate. In my context of the abolition of war, these two basic, although polar, human impulses seem to me to be the key to the situation. Until we get a view of human nature which recognises their primacy, we cannot begin to tackle the problem. And yet most modern political theory rests on unspoken, and quite childish, assumptions as to the perfectability (proximate as in liberal theory or ultimate as in Marxist theory) of human nature. Or more recent political theory (as in Fascist theory or in Nietzschean theory) rests on equally unthought out views of the irredeemable evil of human nature.

Then I was immensely interested, as you can imagine, with your disquisition on the traditional Christian concept of anxiety, round page 180 of your book. The two basic impulses which I postulate above obviously interact dialectically, since both are based on the will to survive. The will to aggress is clearly and obviously partly based on fear. In terms of modern war, man bombs because he fears being bombed. Thus, as you say, anxiety is in many respects the ultimate sin—only I should simply call it the ultimate danger. (The only innocence is that of the lilies of the field. But when they fester how they do stink.)

Again, your concept of the nation as the partial collectivisation of the will to power is very valuable. It is almost incredible to think of the absurdities into which even great men like Fichte and Hegel have been led by their blind nation-worship, is it not? Your quote from Fichte in particular is staggering. Just think of the elemental power and persistence of nation-state worship or patriotism! And yet we have got somehow or other to get it under control if the human race is to survive in the nuclear age! As you say moreover round about page 210, we now have religious nationalism, in particular communist religious nationalism, to deal with on top of ordinary common or garden nationalism.

Going back to Marxism, as you do in various passages in the middle and towards the end of the volume, I am still inclined to say, you know, that a classless society, in the Marxist sense, really would significantly reduce the tensions, and therefore the aggressions, of social living. Therefore, if only the Marxists would be a little bit more sophisticated, they would be preaching a relative truth, at any rate, on this issue. But no doubt it would take decades, if not centuries, of living in a classless society before the reduction in aggressions became very marked. Incidentally you are awfully good, if I may say so, on the Marxist view of human nature. One can sum it up, can't one, by saying that the Marxist view of human nature is, in practice and for the present world, rather too pessimistic and cynical. On the other hand in theory, for the future, for a classless society for after the revolution, it is far too optimistic and utopian. The Marxists are too pessimistic about the way in which people behave here and now; they allow absolutely nothing for disinterestedness. And they are far too optimistic in supposing that disinterestedness will reign unchallenged in a classless society.

I realise that there is an appalling flatness in thus reducing the vast tragic myth, or poem, of original sin to the statement that the struggle for survival has made us into creatures who are by turns so aggressive, and then so submissive, as to find social co-operation very difficult. But may not this terrible flatness be precisely the inevitable effect of letting in "the common light of day"? Such a reduction to sober prose does, in my view, *explain* the poetry and the myth; but does not explain them away.

Volume II

One of the main things I got out of your second volume was what I would call "the menace of the finality illusion." Our *angst* drives us with imperious force towards finding "a final solution" for life. This accounts for the sudden breakdown of Marxist super-realism into a very simple form of utopianism the minute the revolution has taken place. Your no doubt already famous quote on page 184 that it is ". . . a good thing to seek the Kingdom of Heaven on earth but very dubious to claim to have found it" hits the thing off superbly.

Nevertheless once again, in the current atmosphere of socialist disillusionment, I am inclined to think that we are apt to go to the other extreme, and to underestimate the limited but very important benefits which classlessness really will confer.

One other point on this political issue: of course you are right that it is vital to deny these "finality claims," or else you get the typical modern fanaticism of believing that all crimes are justified in order to reach the finality of your "solution." Freedom goes by the board immediately. For freedom is, isn't it, a sort of social "uncertainty principle"? Unfortunately Marxism was built on the analogy of 19th century physics, with its much more fixed certainties about the physical world than contemporary physics. I remember once having an argument with R. Palme Dutt, by far the most intelligent of the British communists, about post-revolutionary freedom in Russia. At the end of the argument he said: "Oh well, I dare say in a few decades, when there is no danger at all, it will be quite all right to allow people to say twice two are five if they want to." What struck me even then was his absolute certainty that his general explanation of human society was as certain and scientific as the proposition that twice two are four. He had absolutely no conception that there was still need for a social uncertainty principle, by which people should be allowed to grope for the truth on a broad front.

Finally, of course, you raise the whole question of what I think is called, is it not, in traditional philosophy, "the absolute"? You make it very clear how indispensable an absolute is, if one wants to express value-judgement at all. One cannot be normative without a norm. No doubt those of us who go along quite happily without feeling any conscious need for such an absolute, or norm, are merely unconsciously and therefore quite uncritically, assuming some traditional absolute or norm as our standard of value. Incidentally, at one level, don't you do this to some extent yourself? You never feel the need to define the words "good" or "evil" at all. You assume quite tacitly that there are such things as good and evil, and do not feel any need to define them. I suppose your answer is quite simply that good is the will of God as revealed in the Bible.

This made me wonder what my norm was. And again at the risk of more naiveté, it seemed to me that consciously or unconsciously what I was doing was assuming that my absolute or standard of value was as follows. The word "good" meant that which lay along the evolutionary axis; the word "evil" meant that which pointed in the reverse direction, down the evolutionary axis on the time scale, or branching off from it at too sharp a tangent.

I imagine that you will say that this is all because I am still under the illusion of the doctrine of progress. I think I would argue that this is not so. It does seem to me to be an observable and testable fact that there has been a development of organisms, in the sense that they have become more complex, more powerful, and more self-determining. If you take a line from a beetle to Beethoven, this seems to me undeniable. And the biologists might say that there is an even longer line of development from the virus to the beetle. Moreover it is surely possible to extrapolate this line of development beyond Beethoven, at any rate in conception. I repeat that the "good" seems to me that which lies along this line of development. (In this connection have you read this extraordinary Jesuit "science-mystic" Pierre de Chardin's book *The Phenomenon of Man?* No wonder the Holy Office barred it during the author's lifetime, for a more heretical work from either a Catholic or Protestant point of view I cannot imagine! I did not think it particularly good, but it does give a sense of the evolutionary sweep. But its weakness, which is where your work comes in, is that it has no conception of evil in it at all, except in a sort of rather absurd appendix. The Holy Office must be getting pretty slack to allow it to be published—even after the author's death, I should have thought!)

Of course I can give you no justification for defining the "good" as that which lies along the axis of evolutionary development. If I could, it would not be my absolute. For obviously one cannot explain or justify one's absolute standard in terms of anything else, or it would cease to be absolute. But then I take it just the same considerations apply to your absolute of the will of God: you could give no reason why the will of God was good. Good is just your name for the will of God, just as it is my name for "along the evolutionary axis."

I judge from your final chapters that you might say that my definition of the "good" might be all right as far as it went (although it was rather prosaic and flat) so long as I abstained from perfectionist illusions. You say that original sin will develop and unfold, step by step, with the marvels of evolutionary unfolding. You would say, wouldn't you, that while Beethoven was a billion times as wonderful and as complex as a beetle, he was also a billion times more capable of sin and error. Indeed you would add, wouldn't you, that he would actually commit a billion times worse sins? This is the doctrine, which I think you more or less accept, don't you, of the anti-Christ's appearance at the same time as the second coming?

I should be inclined to say that I simply did not know about this. I should be inclined to suspect your view as being as dogmatically pessimistic as the perfectionists are dogmatically optimistic. I should have thought that the growth of consciousness really might make it, in some sense, easier and more common therefore, to move along the evolutionary axis than heretofore. Anyhow I should prefer to trust blindly in whatever is visibly propelling creation along that axis: whither it will take us, I would be the first to agree, is unknowable.

Partly perhaps for this very reason the evolutionary perspective is to me infinitely inspiring. On the other hand, I would entirely agree—indeed I think I would be more sceptical than you in this sense—that evolutionary development remains precarious. It might be set back; it might even conceivably be totally cut off. That is probably unlikely, even in the event of a series of thermo-nuclear wars; but development of the organic really might be set back even for tens of thousands of years. No doubt on the total time scale that would be a hardly noticeable regression. Yet to us it really would seem a great pity. And I am inclined to think, don't you, that our main pre-occupation for the rest of this century should be to avoid getting such a setback. We can only do so by organising the world in such a way that war becomes dispensable.

Yours sincerely,

John Strachey

Center for the Study of Democratic Institutions
Santa Barbara, CA
July 18, 1960

Dear Strachey:

I am tremendously grateful to you for your delightful and thoughtful letter, reacting to my book *The Nature and Destiny of Man*. The letter accentuates my wife's and my gratitude in having had a chance to meet you and exchange thoughts with you. You now graciously continue the exchange of thought and I will do my best to do justice to the quality of your letter. Incidentally, just before writing this letter, I had a phone call from Schlesinger at the Los Angeles airport. He attended the Democratic convention, of course, and I told him of my delight in your letter. We agreed that the young Democratic nominee was a tough, intelligent, shrewd, and partly unscrupulous politician. I didn't get a definitive answer from Arthur whether he was more or less unscrupulous than F.D.R. This is the eternal problem of the relation of morals to politics.

Before reacting to the substance of your letter, let me also say that since our meeting I have read your *End of Imperialism* with great enthusiasm and much profit. Since I have just written a book on "Nations and Empires" [*The Structure of Nations and Empires*], I also suffered from a tremendous inferiority feeling of an amateur theologian and amateur political philosopher, dealing with the thought of an astute thinker who is master of the empirical details of the political order about which I can only speak in broad generalities. If I had only read your book earlier, I would have been saved from many errors.

Now as to the substance of your letter: You are right that I approach both religion and politics from the standpoint of the validity of their interpretation of the human situation. I have moved in my thought considerably since I wrote the book, but I still believe that a Pascalian position which seeks to do justice both to the "grandeur and misery of man" is superior, not to all forms of secularism, but to consistently optimistic and consistently pessimistic interpretations, for which Locke and Hobbes are convenient symbols.

You say, "You are a Lutheran, are you not?" I would answer that I am a Lutheran in opposition to Thomas and Aristotle, to Locke and Comte or to Hegel, to mention a few thinkers who believe that rational man is also virtuous man. But I am consistently anti-Lutheran in politics, that is, where Lutheran pessimism, like that of Hobbes, supports political absolutism. In that book, I did not pay enough attention to Milton, who among the great figures of history expresses a position somewhat like my own. Indeed some of the 17th-century Puritans seem to me now to combine the valid portions of both the humanist and the Christian position more than anyone I treated in the book.

About the concept of "original sin," I now realize that I made a mistake in emphasizing it so much, though I still believe that it might be rescued from its primitive corruptions. But it is a red rag to most moderns. I find, that even my realistic friends are inclined to be offended by it, though our interpretations of the human situation are identical. The book was the culmination of my reaction to Comte and to Marx. Comte was represented by the American liberalism of John Dewey. Reacting to this liberalism, I first embraced the mild socialism, a rather irrelevant creed in America, popular in professional circles. Then I found that Marxism was provisionally more pessimistic and ultimately more optimistic and utopian than liberalism. Hence I reverted to more classical forms of the Christian tradition. My consistent purpose has been to detach "realism" from reaction and place it in the service of a "progressive" political program.

I think you may be right in suggesting that I make too absolute a distinction between "good" and "evil" and do not define the terms except by implication. I commit this error despite my constant preoccupation with description of the mixture of good and evil in all historical phenomena. I would be inclined to challenge your definition of, what I define as evil, as "aggressiveness." I would define it as all forms of preoccupation with a partial as distinct from a more inclusive purpose. Ambition and will to power and vanity in individuals is more significant than aggressiveness. And the imperial ambitions of Britain, America, and Russia are not basically, but only incidentally aggressive. I certainly do not do enough justice to the provisional creativity of the ambition of a statesman, for instance, or the provisional creativity of the imperial ambition of nations. I confess I do not know what the dividing line between creativity and destructiveness of partial interest or individual or collective egotism is though we are all agreed that Hitler and Nazi Germany exceeded the limit. That is an unsolved problem in my mind, and I suspect that all our judgements are themselves ideologically tainted. Communist imperialism is certainly not as different from American imperialism as I am inclined to think when I am embarrassed by the fact that Khrushchev is shrewder than Eisenhower.

On one point I think I am in complete disagreement with you. You say, "I am still inclined to think that a classless society in the Marxist sense would significantly reduce tensions and therefore aggressions in social living." The original Marxist dream of a classless society has been refuted by the fact that the Russian society has followed the inevitable historical pattern of social stratification related to social function, so your statement may be true, but I regard it as irrelevant.

I can't do justice to all the great problems you raise, but one more point of partial agreement and partial disagreement with you is on the "evolutionary sweep." Undoubtedly, mankind, as man, is subject to historical development, and I should have been clearer in stating that this development is "good" in itself. This is proven by the fact that a comparison between Beethoven and a beetle is pointless as you suggest. But our present nuclear dilemma proves to me that historical development in the social and moral sense solves no social problems. It only enlarges them. The symbol of Christ and anti-Christ for this dilemma of history may be archaic, but still it is closer to the facts than a simple idea of historical progress.

I haven't done justice to your whole letter, but I am deeply grateful for the fact that you should have taken the trouble to exchange thoughts with me and enlighten me on many points.

My wife and I join in personal regards and the hope of a new encounter with you.

Sincerely yours,

Reinhold Niebuhr

Postlude:
Letters to a
Dear But Departed
Spouse

I started these pages when thinking about our lives together and the many unfinished "conversations" on major and minor subjects. Friends encouraged the "conversations to a dear but departed spouse."

An editor of the *Christian Century* picked these up when visiting and asked if he might publish a couple of them. Later he suggested changing the "conversations" to "letters to a dear but departed spouse."

On April 15, 1987, the *Christian Century* published "Easter Memories," and on July 29 and August 5 of the same year an earlier version of "Cheese and Dill Pickles."

1. Breakfast: Cheese and Dill Pickles

Breakfast was your favorite meal. Often you said so. Sometimes you would remember that the Dutch had cheese with their breakfast, and that you liked. I would be interested, but stupidly never thought of giving you cheese for breakfast. Why was that? Of course, we had cheese for lunch, and my housekeeping mind may have thought, "Well, we can't have cheese for two meals, can we?" Perhaps you would have liked cheese for breakfast and then we might have had eggs for lunch? But often you weren't at home for lunch and you ate somewhere else, either on the go, traveling, or at some committee lunch, where probably the food was ghastly, or with students in the cafeteria at Union Seminary, where you swallowed your food whole because you were talking at the same time.

Anyhow, my sense of guilt remains with me, that I was not "imaginative"—that word which you used so often where I might have used the word "sensitive," and I did not produce cheese, not only cheese, but all *sorts* of cheeses, for breakfast! I am haunted by this, when I am abroad, not only in Holland, but in Israel where there are all sorts of good things—like cheese of various kinds—for breakfast. Then, I hear you saying, "In Holland, they often have cheese for breakfast."

I suppose all these memories are part of the vested capital left by a very happy marriage. But I find myself amused that minor details, that is, if food be a minor detail, remind me of so many places where I lacked imagination or was too engrossed in habits of behavior and sequence to respond to things you might have liked to have had or to have done. Perhaps life isn't long enough. We were married for nearly forty years, forty years except for six months, and yet that was not long enough. One of the favorite lines you used to quote was from that little poem by Ralph Hodgson, "Time, you old gypsy man, will you not stay, put up your caravan for just one day?" And I might add to that a line from a pious hymn about "eternity being far too short." I believe it was in the context of praising God, but perhaps I would want to say far too short for showing love in little ways as well as big. And so, because food is always with us and we have to eat several times a day, and we go to the grocery store more often than perhaps we go to church, it is food so often which reminds me of my lacks.

Yet, this in a sense is silly, because you were the most ungreedy of people, in fact not too discriminating about food. Wystan Auden often used to say, in that nasty, brotherly way, "Of course, Ursula doesn't have to be a good cook, because Reinhold would eat almost anything." Of course, he said this to get a laugh and to poke fun at us because this was part again of the dramatic set that our family gave him, where he could put me into the role of the sister he teased, and I would respond and make him the naughty but nice brother. Incidentally, this little game he used to play at other times. I remember at the Academy of Arts and Letters, some good person came up and asked if Wystan Auden and I were related. Of course, we were talking English rather than American, although both Wystan and I loved to use Americanisms and sprinkled "OK"s and other expressions to show how broad-minded and American we were—but anyhow, this person asked if we were related and the devil entered into me, and I said, "O, yes, he is my naughty younger brother." This rather baffled the enquirer who was seized on by some VIP and Wystan and I giggled like a couple of school children, and he said, "I do hope that gets abroad. It will be such fun for the biographers."

I remember a time in the sixties when my daughter Elisabeth and I drove from Stockbridge over to Hudson, New York, to meet a friend who was coming up on the train from New York City. We wandered about that interesting town, which, despite its depressed and neglected state, had all sorts of attractions—historic and, for us, also architectural—as well as its scenic setting on the Hudson. Getting somewhat hungry in the course of our peregrinations, we looked for a place to pick up sandwiches and coffee. We found a delicatessen that provided what we wanted, and, as we bade the owners farewell, we bought a few extra items, including a jar of dill pickles.

When we got back home to you, you began to talk about dill pickles. And what you related was quite a saga indeed. When you were a small boy in Lincoln, Illinois, you used to deliver groceries for the saintly owner of a grocery store in the town. I don't suppose that anyone had heard of child-labor laws in those days, because you seem to have been incredibly young for that job. Anyhow, you put together and delivered grocery orders, and you and the other delivery boys were allowed to help yourselves to a dill pickle from a barrel as a little bonus when you left for the day. You told me that the owner's daughter, who was the cashier for the store and sat in a kind of iron cage, noticed but she said nothing when you and the other boys sometimes took more than one pickle each.

Your telling me this tale prompted the two of us to write to Florence Denger, the lady who had sat in the iron cage, and thus began a delightful correspondence. We were in touch with her at the time of your increasing weakness and illness, and she wrote to us about what life was like in Lincoln, Illinois, when your family was there and your father was the local parson. She mentioned a number of things that you had never told me and was also informative about your father. But it wasn't until after you died that I was able to visit her. She was a marvelous old lady, and I love to think of her when I think of your boyhood in Lincoln.

A dill pickle was not only something that you enjoyed eating: it was bound up with your life and the community in which you grew up and to which your father ministered. Your biographers will not bother to think about dill pickles when they write about you. But I like to think about them. At the same time, I am bothered by the thought that for all those years I failed to pander to your love of them. Of course, you could have bought the pickles and brought them home. But I don't think you ever did buy things at grocery stores or delicatessens to bring home. It's odd to recollect that, but I don't think you did. I suppose that when you were a parson, much food was showered on you by your parishioners.

And that reminds me of the stories you did tell me about your father's parish in Lincoln—for example, about how farmers' wives would bring you geese, vegetables, and so on from the farm because to give these to the parson (the "holy man") was a way of keeping the evil eye off the crops. But also, since your mother was such a fantastic cook and provider, you probably did not develop the acquisitive instinct to shop for yourself.

So there we are. Sometimes very pious admirers of yours tell me how sure they are that you are in heaven—and if not sitting at the right hand of God, at least comfortably ensconced. I find it quite difficult to suppress my impulse to say, "Yes, I am sure he is eating cheese and dill pickles." But why not? I am reminded of Jesus' words foreshadowing the messianic banquet: "I shall not drink of the fruit of the vine until the Kingdom of God comes." And although presumably there is no eating or drinking or giving in marriage in heaven, yet we do like to think of bountifulness and satisfaction for the souls of the righteous.

Oh dear, how symbolic it all is. You and I were—and are—skeptical about many aspects of so-called Christian belief, including the doctrine of the resurrection. Yet, I suppose, the instinct to project and prolong the meaning and value of life stays with us. Our marriage was celebrated before the host of heaven and for all eternity. So I like to think of you as, if not seated on a cloud and playing a harp, at least as eating cheese and dill pickles.

2

I wish I had known you when you were a little boy. Of course, that's quite impossible, as you were fifteen years older than I. But I always liked to imagine your life in Lincoln, Illinois. You weren't born there, you were born in Missouri. I remember when you went to the White House in the days of President Truman you discovered you shared with the president that privilege, which all natives of Missouri possess, of "wanting to be shown!" Anyhow, I always talked about Missouri as if it ended in an "a" rather than an "i," just to show I know the proper way. Knowing some of the descendants of the first French settlers, I talked about St. Louis, not about St. Lewis which, as you used to explain to me, was the usage after the Germans, the forebears of the later beer barons, arrived. I remember hearing about one time you were coming back from, I think, the University of Missouri—was it at Columbia—and you were being driven to St. Louis, and you stopped for hamburgers at some wayside joint. You asked the university people who were driving you what was the name of this dump. They inquired of the host of the hamburger bar, who told you all it was Wright City—then you said with joy and rapture, "Heavens, this is where I was born!" You told me this, and then one of the academics I met many years later also told me. I *wish* I had been there; again it could have been an occasion; the hamburger joint man should have produced a can of beer and you could have, oh dear, done all sorts of things.

You were born in Wright City, Missouri, and then a year or so later your father was appointed to a church at St. Charles, which is quite close, in fact almost a suburb of St. Louis. You took me there once: I thought it was rather a nice place with nineteenth-century houses, and you took me to the church. Here again I have guilt feelings. It was a dreadful little church: there was *nothing* beautiful to redeem it. It had the most ghastly stained glass, which even you admitted was pretty bad. But I should have had a sense of piety about it because it was where your father ministered. Yet, I suppose conditioned by the old village churches in England and abroad, this little building with varnished yellow-brown woodwork and dreadful glass shocked me, and there was not a redeeming feature in the church to lessen or qualify that shock. I suppose if I had been at a service there, the human, social, and religious atmosphere might have made the ugliness less obtrusive.—O dear, I *do* feel guilty about my conventionality in reacting to these places where you and your family had been. After all, as a student of history I should have felt and sensed the historical associations and not been so immediate in my emphatic reactions. Anyhow, you probably put it down to my English provincial standards, and you did not resent my reactions. You were always very large about my lacks, bless you. Your father did not stay in St. Charles very long, for he was appointed to a church in Lincoln, Illinois, and that was where you and your sister and brothers grew up.

You used to tell me quite a little about life there, but nothing in much detail. Yet it gave me a little sense of what life in a small middle-western town was like in the end of the last century and the beginning of this one. I remember you telling our Elisabeth, when she was about twelve, how your friends there and the people of the church were worried that the man who looked after the cemetery in which your father (and later your mother) was buried, was Catholic and of course he *should* have been a Protestant of German descent! Elisabeth, not only born and brought up in New York, was habituated to ethnic and religious and political pluralism. "How *awful,* Daddy!" she exclaimed. You laughed and said, "Yes, in Lincoln they didn't like Negroes; they didn't like Jews; they didn't like Democrats, in fact, they didn't like anybody who wasn't like themselves." We were, of course, properly shocked, and I realized how that background may have helped to provoke and propel your critical sense about the sin of racism and all the other factors that divide community. Community, the word and the concept, were very important in your thinking and writing. Yet you were very aware of the perils of a homogenous community. I thought of this just a couple of years ago, when attending a meeting in New York, the annual Scholars' Conference on the Holocaust, and Eberhard Bethge, the biographer of Dietrich Bonhoeffer, was giving the dinner address at our opening meeting. He had been a visiting professor at Union Theological Seminary that term, and this was his farewell speech before leaving. He described the north German village in which he grew up where everybody was exactly like everybody else. He depicted this rather well, not laying it on too thick, and said that this was so in school and in gymnasium also, and then mentioned parenthetically that Dietrich Bonhoeffer at least was luckier than he because he had been educated in Berlin, and there he met Catholics and Jews. Further, he described how in the family Bible all the illustrations had blond figures; Jesus was a blond, the disciples were blond. His description, in the quiet way he gave it to us, was startling as well as horrifying. I recalled you saying when Elisabeth was so shocked at your description of Lincoln, "Yes, they liked people to be like themselves."

I suppose we all do this, we talk about people, our sort of people, "Have you congenial neighbors?" We always need to detach ourselves from, again, a norm that we construct as "the kind of person," "the kind of interest" characteristic of ourselves. Perhaps this is why marriage between people of different backgrounds, even of different races, may be fraught with peril for some, but be also extraordinarily creative for others. Thus one partner can begin to think and feel with the eyes and ears of the other and vice versa. But it may take a long time. It took me many years before I really appreciated a middle-western voice; of course, I loved *yours,* with its exaggerated r's and that dreadful way you talked about "Amurrica." Even New York secretaries (do you remember Dr. Coffin's secretary?) used to object to that! But again this is the point, because I loved you, I liked the way you talked. Now I remember one time in London hearing somebody from the middle west talk and my heart leapt up, and I thought, "Heavens, he is from the Middle West, how lovely! I must go and give him a hug." Of course, he was a dreadfully ordinary American tourist with a ghastly wife in tow, with a voice also of the Middle West but not as nice as his. However, you see the problem? Inspired by love of you, I was welcoming the man's voice, but found his wife awful. I expect people said that about us, so I'll stop there!

The pickle lady in Lincoln, Illinois, Florence Denger, not only wrote me but when I went to see her told me much about you and your family. She was devoted to your father and told me how he used to start his sermons: "Speaking as a doubting Thomas . . ." She remarked en passant, "What ordinary pastor would start a sermon like that?" I had the feeling from her and from others that you were very like him. He was not as tall as you, but he had the same kind of energy, intellectual energy if not physical. He was perhaps too much the German to assume that other people did the domestic jobs that you did so willingly, such as sweeping the kitchen or rushing about doing chores with more energy than they really needed. Obviously you and he were very congenial. He must have been extraordinarily gifted as a pastor, because he had very little to help and enrich him in that village. Apparently his only really congenial friend was the village atheist who was the doctor. You told me how they used to play chess together occasionally and enjoy a bottle of wine. Presumably the doctor also was German. But the parish was composed of lower-middle-class workers, and farmers in from the countryside and miners. I am rather vague as to what miners are doing in that part of Illinois, but you and your mother mentioned the miners, because sometimes they were on strike or the mines were closed down and things were very difficult indeed. This is where the father of our friend the pickle lady came in. He, being the owner of a local grocery store, gave credit to his customers until he, a couple of times, was bankrupt. This man made a profound impression on you, because he was so good and so generous, and often in your sermons you referred to him as an example of unselfishness. Do you remember when we started writing to his daughter?

I kept a letter we received from her in 1971, only a few months before you died. She wrote and told us that when Mr. Adam Denger, her father, died, an old colored woman came in at the back door to see him in his funeral casket. Her mother, Mrs. Denger, said, "Of course, but you didn't have to come in at the back door." The colored lady stood at the coffin and wept and said, "Mr. Denger always made me feel like a white woman when I came into his store." So, in spite of a homogeneous character of Lincoln, Illinois, saintly good men like that redeemed the community.

She often mentioned how she went to see you in the parsonage on Fifth Street in Lincoln in the evening. Your father would be reading, your mother would be watering the petunias, and she could remember how sweetly the flowers smelled. And you and your brothers were turning somersaults while Hulda, who was the eldest of your siblings, and she gossiped. In her lonely old age, she thought of your father's pastoral counsel. She recalled his prayers when he visited the house and his Lenten services. She wrote, "I remember them so well—[his saying] 'I am by nature a doubting Thomas,' and his always saying, 'Just stick to this.'" You had told me that your mother, who was violently anti-alcohol, had reasons for it because there was a good deal of drinking in the town, so there was a citizens' meeting at the courthouse, to consider what Miss Denger called the corruption in the saloons. She said your father rose and in his deep, gutteral German accent said, "I am no prohibitionist, but I *am* for law and order!" She commented that he always said what he thought and let the chips fall where they would. That must have been, of course, before Prohibition, but I was intrigued that your mother was very ardently prohibitionist, probably because of the situation in the parish, while your father due to his German heritage did enjoy a good bottle of wine.

So you see I try and get the picture of Lincoln, Illinois. You weren't too much help to me, but you did describe quite vividly as a small boy going to pick berries at some of the farms in the countryside. I think that was because you earned your first money in that way. You were a great earner, because you earned enough money, not only by picking berries and then working at that grocery store and later on working in the shoe store in St. Louis, to pay your expenses at the Yale Divinity School. You often used to speak of the sensation of being in a nice warm cozy barn, with the smell of the hay and the smell of the cows when there was a thunderstorm or rainstorm, and you felt safe and warm and secure. This must have been very vivid to you because you so often mentioned it.

You never said too much about your early relations to your brothers and sister. Hulda, being the eldest, was good, the little mother to you three younger boys. Walter, the next, was handsome and successful and obviously popular. He almost becomes the conventional bright boy spoiled by early success. He had health problems, a hearing defect, brought on by some early infection of childhood. Then also, H. Richard, who was younger than you.

Often you spoke about the family being where the norm of love operated. When we were engaged and in our first year of marriage, you were working on *Moral Man and Immoral Society*. Often I questioned your easy assumption about family life, and how often would I use your own quotations about justice against your sentimentality about the family! It was partly in jest, but not altogether, for we were trying to look at how to relate your sense of responsibility about your mother, with the fact of our own marriage and a new family.

You had liked to think of yourself as cynical, but I was *far* more cynical, particularly about the family. In your family, you obviously were the dominant person, and perhaps being so vital and such a strong personality, you did not realize that very vitality may have taken an unknown toll of other members of the family.

You used to tell me how when you were boys, you and Helmut, or Richard as he was known later to his colleagues particularly at Yale, would go to pick berries and stay at one or other of the neighboring farms. But Helmut would get homesick and be very miserable and would have to return home. So you worked very hard to earn enough pocket money for both. Later on, because obviously he was not as vigorous as you, perhaps not as healthy, he did not earn so much money and you earned enough for him to go to Eden Seminary and later to help to get him to Yale. But, do people *like* to be helped as much as you helped him? As the younger brother, less vigorous and less energetic than you, did you perhaps take something from him?

3

Quite obviously you were your father's favorite. This comes out in what other people said, and even in what you told me. First of all, you must have been awfully like him. Judging from that dreadful portrait that your eldest brother Walter had painted after your father's death, and other photographs, he had that same rather piercing look and warm energetic and searching gaze as well as the same shaped, slightly bulging forehead and features of the upper face. I always wished I had known him—he must have been terribly nice. But you obviously found him the most interesting person in that small town and you wanted to be like him and do what he did. When quite a boy, you showed this interest and he started you in Latin and Greek, so that you could do what he did. Yet he himself had not been a foreordained theological scholar, had he?

He was a younger son of a landowner in Lippe-Detmold. He had left Germany because he didn't like authoritarianism either in the family or the state, Prussianism at home or nationally. You told me that Abraham Lincoln and Teddy Roosevelt were his heroes, and he came to this country because there was not a future for him as a younger son. His elder brother was going to inherit the estate, another brother was going to study and teach, but your father pulled out and came to this country. He had not even finished at the gymnasium at Lemgo and resisted his father's authoritarianism. He went to stay with relations of some workers from the family farm who had settled in the Middle West. He stayed with these good, pious—I suppose from our angle, fundamentalist—farm folk in Illinois, and went with them to church; you described how they all went along in the farm cart or buggy and he shocked them because he was so profane and lusty in his language. But their simple piety and their sheer decency converted him; so he prepared himself to be ordained in that immigrant church known as the Evangelical Synod. I think the story is rather nice, that this German lad found his, I dare to say, identity (using the Eriksonian work) with these decent farm folk of central Illinois.

You at—what was it?—twelve years old or so were schooled and shaped by your own interest and love of your father and by his love for you into the eager scholar. Later in Illinois you went to Elmhurst, now a college, but in those days it sounded like a mixture of an English boarding school for sons of clergy and a junior college with the Germanic tradition of education. You said all you got out of it was grounding in the classics, again the languages Greek and Latin. But you also enjoyed the literature classes, and obviously, particularly, acting in Shakespearean plays. Your brother followed in your train. Again, was he just taking the lines of least resistance, or was it the unconscious conditioning of these two powerful personalities, his father and older brother? He did not have the same happy and easy relationship with your father as you did. You told me that your father, although he reacted against German authoritarianism at his home in Germany, yet was quite conventional about behavior and authority in his home in Illinois. You mentioned one thing that I found rather shocking, that he locked your brother up in a closet as a punishment. Something else may have been locked up beside the physical little boy by such actions.

Hulda, your older sister, again was very much influenced by your father. German Protestant churches, as also the more evangelical wing of the Church of England, had been influenced by the movement that reestablished deaconesses to serve and minister the church. I remember from my childhood in England the Mildmay Deaconesses. In the German tradition, the deaconesses often were trained as nurses, and the deaconess hospitals survive to our day. Your father started the Deaconess Hospital in Lincoln, Illinois. Your Aunt Adela, your mother's younger sister, was ordained a deaconess after she had done her nursing training. Hulda, your sister, apparently went through an agonizing time as an older adolescent wondering if she ought to follow the same vocation. I wonder who it was who released her from that felt imperative? Did your mother have the wisdom and common sense, and know it was not for her? Anyhow, Hulda apparently was the traditional parson's daughter. She played the organ in church, taught in the Sunday school, did all the useful things at home and in the parish. Your father's passionate Americanism did not extend to education for women, but that was rather general at that time, I suppose. After all, Hulda must have been born about 1890.

When your father died in 1913, Hulda no longer had any job or vocation. She had not been trained to earn, and I remember you told me how conscientious she was, going to night school and learning to type, so that she could get some poor paying job addressing envelopes and licking stamps until she could save up enough to take more academic training. However, she worked on and on, and when I first knew you, she had been teaching religious education at the School of Theology at Boston University. She had been able to use her experience as the dutiful parson's daughter in this work—work that she continued both at Madison Avenue Presbyterian Church in New York and then as professor at McCormick Theological Seminary in Chicago, until her death.

But somehow, I felt that she as Helmut was still very much bound to the influence of your father. Perhaps also I felt that your personality somehow continued because you were so much like him. Your mother, whose clinging to you was such a threat to our married life at the beginning, told me quite innocently that she really did not miss her husband when he died, because you took his place! Although that was rather a shock for me to digest, it was profoundly illuminating. Somehow, I think in the family you stepped into the shoes of the paterfamilias. And, more cynical than you, I had my suspicions about the family all being peace and love. After all, your brother had two very bad nervous crack-ups. Your sister also did, just about the time we became "involved" and engaged. I remember you getting off the boat at Southampton when you came over to visit my family in 1931 and telling me, "Our future happiness depends on the frail thread of my sister's health." Again, I was overcome with a mixture of mirth and horror, as it was not what an ardent fiancé was supposed to say when he met his loved one! Then characteristically, you inquired about the news in England: Were we going to go off the gold standard? You had promised some journal a report from England, and of course you had your little portable typewriter along so you could get off a column. However, I swallowed both expressions of your interest, and recalled to myself my theory that if a man were interesting, you either had to accept his interests or get rid of the man!

I was dithering, indeed, as to whether I *did* want to get rid of the man, and that was why you had come over to see me and get a taste of me and my life. To be quite frank, you were not particularly interested in me and my life. I mean, you were, I am frank to say, very much in love, but I don't think you were really interested in what I would call the archeological, sociological, personal side of me—my family, my background. I was very much interested in yours, but then you see I like to dig in people's history. As a child, I loved "Puck of Pook's Hill" by Rudyard Kipling. As the youngest member of a family, I heard other people talking about Roman roads and British villages; local history to me was fascinating. We lived in a historic part of England and my, perhaps fantasy, life was fed with material culled from old records, old maps, parish registers, and the like. So, we were very, very different. Which of course makes life, married life, more interesting. Yet, I realized I was more interested in your background and in your life than you ever would be in mine. I think this may continue with our children. I realize they are not very interested in my family—I don't mean my brothers and sister, but in the whole heritage that comes down to one from one's forebears. So that is part of the reason I wanted to think about *you* and your background for my own sake and perhaps for theirs, our children and grandchildren. After all, you *did* tell me quite a lot about your family over the nearly forty years of our life together!

4. "Shoe Salesmanship" and Your Education

When going through all the papers I have, I came across a little piece you wrote for a St. Louis paper, with your cynical reflections on working as a clerk in a shoe store. You were rather nasty about the ladies who pretended that they had smaller feet than they had. Of course, that is dated now as even famous beauties have no compunction about having enormous feet. It was a little brown and tattered piece of newspaper that made me think of you, the energetic, vibrant young theological student trying to fit St. Louis ladies with shoes! I am sure I would have melted completely if I had been one of them, as I am also sure that, despite your cynicism, you were awfully nice. In all the photos I have seen of that period and later, your grin was very taking. People used to tell me much later how much they enjoyed your sermon—you had such a wonderful grin even when you were talking about sin! The fact those two words grin and sin rhyme always made me want to compose a little limerick, but somehow it never happened. However, in St. Louis you were studying at Eden Seminary and selling shoes on Saturday so that you might earn enough to take you to Yale Divinity School.

Elmhurst, where you had been to college, was not in those days accredited. So when you applied to Union Theological Seminary, New York, there was not a chance of your being admitted. You explained that Yale, on the other hand, needed students, as it had been going through a rather low period, and was accepting, apparently, uneducated creatures from the outer reaches of the Bible Belt and people without a proper college education. So you got in at Yale Divinity School! Dr. Press, who had done so much for you, was very anxious for people who had studied with him to continue, not only their academic studies, but also to travel and get away from the narrow and local confines of their denominational background. You and a good friend of yours, Cornelius Kruse, who taught classics for so many years at Wesleyan, were some of the first fruits of Dr. Press's concern and policy.

I used to ask you about your coming to Yale. Obviously it was a very varied experience. You described yourself as a yahoo from the Midwest arriving at this seat of education and culture. I don't believe you had read Jonathan Swift or knew what the expression "yahoo" meant in *Gulliver's Travels*. Anyhow, you liked using the phrase, "A yahoo from the Middle West!"

College and university years are very important for many—not only for people like you and me, coming from rather provincial backgrounds, so that the university represents the wide world of thought and culture and learning, but for many others, whether from the economic upper classes or from the lower classes. The marketplace of ideas, and the heady excitement of being able to wander about that marketplace and perhaps pick or choose among the different wares being offered for one's interest and pleasure— this is what I coveted for my own students at Barnard College and Columbia. But the American undergraduate curriculum was, in the forties and fifties, very predetermined, so there was neither the leisure or the opportunity for that wandering. Perhaps I idealized my own years at Oxford and tried to let a little of that be available at least in my small area of responsibility. I remember my colleague William Haller, the seventeenth-century historian, sympathizing with my efforts, and saying, "Perhaps part of our job is to buck the system." But, as a faculty advisor, I used to resent having to say to undergraduates, "Have you *had* your Lab Science? Have you *had* English A? Have you *had* this requirement, that requirement?" as if a college education were something where one had shots of this and that, innoculation for this, innoculation for that. Yale Divinity School for you and my undergraduate years at Oxford for me were very important and as far as I was concerned for me at Oxford, enormously pleasant.

Oxford was great fun. The beauty of the place—I was always thrilled just to be in the Bodleian Library, or to walk about, going from my some-what occasional lectures to weekly tutorials, and the magic of the place laid hold upon me and stayed with me. But I do not know if Yale was such great fun for you. Of course, you worked awfully hard, as you always did. I remember trying to get you to tell me how you worked. You worked furious-ly, not exactly in fits and starts, but you couldn't sit for too long, you had to rush out to do something and then come back to your books. Then also there was the time you told me about, when you had scarlet fever and lost all your savings and your hair. In those days there was no health insurance, and you were put into some isolation wing and your friends came and gossiped and fed you grapes from outside through the window.

I suspect at times, you were a bit bored at Yale Divinity School. You said so, quite frankly, particularly with respect to Professor Douglas Macintosh's interest in epistemology, which you did not regard as so very enthralling. That was why you tried to change and instead study in the university. That was the early beginning of World War I, because the dean of the graduate school, who was professor of German, and German himself, got caught in Germany and was interned. Again, your inadequate college background meant that you were a dubious candidate for proper graduate work in the university. But by then, Wilbur Cross had become dean, and allowed you to try for a term and if your marks stayed high enough, you would be admitted as a graduate student in Yale University. This you achieved, and I remember you told Wilbur Cross this—when he was governor of Connecticut, and also a member of the cor-poration and trustee at Yale University—when he escorted you on the occasion of your receiving an honorary degree.

Your father, meanwhile, had died, and you felt you should leave aca-demic life in order to give your mother and sister a home. Your mother had not been left well off, so things were difficult. Now one wonders why your mother did not work. After all, she was only in her early forties, but I suppose clergymen's wives or widows in those days were not expected to earn and support themselves.

5. Easter Memories*

Well! Easter is over. I thought, perhaps naturally, of you very much during the past days of Holy Week and Easter. Not only because that festival

*Previously published in the Christian Century, April 15, 1987.

is a dying and also a hope, but because we talked so much about the problem of Easter—how to interpret it, how to celebrate it and yet be true to what we thought and think about the New Testament story.

Partly because I was thinking about this, I wrote a column for *The Berkshire Eagle,* which they published on Easter eve. It was not terribly good, it was rather one-dimensional and I think it was a little more conventional or orthodox than somehow I meant it to be. But I had the problem of eight hundred words, something that you coped with very well in all the columns and editorials you wrote for *Christianity and Crisis* and other papers. Also, I was rather worried that I did not write anything about Passover, which had started on the previous Wednesday. Other years, and in other contexts, I have tried to interpret the meanings of both, as sacraments of time and eternity.

But I remember so many times when we talked about the problem of Easter. I recall voicing some of my doubts with Harry Emerson Fosdick, whose Gothic church (Riverside, NY) was surrounded by throngs of avid church-goers, all dressed up for Easter. You were a little nervous lest I should sound too critical, but Dr. Fosdick was responsive. He said something like this, "When I see the serried rows of people in their best clothes and the ladies with their Easter bonnets, I wish I could speak as honestly as did Amos and cry out, 'I hate, I despise your solemn feasts.'" Then, you relaxed, and you and he talked about the problem of preaching sermons on Easter Day, how often they degenerated into a paean upon spring, or alternatively a rather incoherent burbling upon the doctrine of the immortality of the soul.

You, perhaps too easily, said, "Why don't we let the liturgy take care of what we want to say and cannot say. It is better to sing these hopes especially if you don't understand what is being sung."

I remember another time, when we went to the Cathedral of St. John the Divine together on Easter Day. Again, that vast place was for the occasion filled, and it was all rather magnificent, with trumpets and the western doors opened. Yet, in those days of the thirties, a rather inadequate sermon by Bishop Manning brought us closer to earth! I felt you bristling, your journalistic instinct was at work, and sure enough, out came the back of an envelope and a pencil and you began to scribble notes. The result was a rather wicked article in the *Christian Century.* I ought to look it up, but I remember the occasion with a certain amount of pleasure.

I remember also a friend of ours, Frederic Fox, a former advertising man, who, after World War II came to Union Theological Seminary to study for the ministry. He had corralled Christopher, who was then about twelve, to help him do an Easter display for the seminary bookstore. This display was full of Easter hams, bunnies, Easter eggs, advertisements for new hats, and all the rest. I was shocked and raised questions with Christopher. "Mummy," he explained, "Fred feels as you do; we are cutting out advertisements to show how silly it all is, you must come and see them." Of course I did. I remember one vividly, a full-page ad from *Life,* or one of the glossy big magazines, for a new car at Easter with the background of a gothic church and people going up to it. There was another one, and this of course dates the story because ladies wore hats in those days, "Every woman's right at Easter!" And this "right" was for a new hat! And so on, and so on. What worried me was that the clergy who did not challenge this, even our dear friend Dr. Fosdick; I wish he *had* been Amos in the pulpit. But, the motives may have been economic, many parishes depended upon the Easter offering. Also, it was one of the few times a year, Christmas no doubt being the other, with carols and candlelight, when churches were full, and no one in their senses mocks at a full house. Yet is rather silly to talk about idolatry when it is practiced so much in all the churches.

I remember another Easter occasion. It was just after Easter, I think the Tuesday after Easter, when we were asked to lunch at the home of the banker Thomas Lamont with the Arnold Toynbees. I had written an Easter editorial, for your paper—for which you never asked me to write, but you had been abroad and so whoever was running it asked me to do something, and so I had raised some of these questions in a very, very mild fashion. Mrs. Thomas Lamont was a little worried because I had raised questions about Easter bonnets, and said rather sensibly, "But it is so good for the economy for women to buy new hats for Easter." Somehow, although she was quite liberal both politically and generally, my article had not gone down too well. Then, I remember Arnold Toynbee, rather charmingly said, humming the Gilbert and Sullivan line, "Flowers that bloom in the Spring, tra la." I appreciated that, while we were having lunch in their sun parlor at the top of their townhouse. The flowers that were in boxes all around the room were terribly faded and dead. I wondered whether even the empire of Thomas Lamont was shaking; the butler who had answered the door when we arrived was busy wriggling into his coat as he opened the door, and the coat really needed a brush. I wondered if the revolution for which her left-wing son Corliss no doubt prayed was starting? Anyhow, it all belongs in my bundle of memories about Easter.

And the puzzle and the problem of Easter remains. As I was saying to a journalist friend recently, "We cannot explain the birth of the Christian church by an Easter bunny popping out from the tomb." Sometimes, I rather wish I could do an Easter story and combine the Peter Rabbit material with the gospel story. The gardener in the Garden of Gethsemane should be rather like Mr. McGregor in the Peter Rabbit story, and the dialogue with the Marys should be conducted I think with a mixture of idiom. However that will have to wait. I am often rather amused when in Jerusalem, the tomb in East Jerusalem to the north of the Damascus gate is presided over by a very British colonel, Dobie. The tomb is not regarded by archeologists as the place where Jesus was laid—The Church of the Holy Sepulchre is theoretically and, perhaps more authentically, regarded as the locale of the place where Jesus lay—but General Gordon decided it looked as if it was. So, since that day, it is known as the Garden Tomb and does a brisk trade with the tourists. Colonel Dobie, a conservative Protestant whose name is associated with the defense of Malta in the Second World War, came out to Jerusalem a few years ago to preside over it, and a fundamentalist Dutch couple were assisting him. When the Dobies flew out, their belongings including their clothes followed by boat. There was a strike, however, in the container cargo line, and all their stuff was impounded at Haifa. So, in the rather warm weather of Jerusalem, dear Colonel Dobie presided in a heavy tweed suit over the Garden Tomb.

This Easter, however, has been very full of deaths and dyings. So the Easter story does help, I think, with words of comfort. We went to a funeral on Easter eve. Another friend died suddenly on Easter Sunday. I have had letters from friends who lost husband or wife, and who wrote at this time about their feelings of loss and the way their hopes find expression. This is right and fitting. The eternity of love. It is easier to think of that than of the immortality of the soul. Whatever things be good and true and beautiful—they remain. So, perhaps it was the instinct that people who express the good, as the human life and human words of Jesus did, do remain and last and are pointers toward the realm of the mysterious transcendent. So in that sense, we can sing "Alleluia, He is risen."

Index

Devil, 234
Dewey, John, 72n.1, 73, 378, 379
Dibelius, Bishop Otto, 197 *and n.3*, 198, 236
Dictatorship, 335
Disarmament, 317
Discerning the Signs (Niebuhr), 223
Dodd, C. H. (Harold), 13, 16, 153–54, 156, 171, 193, 257, 258, 263
Dodd, Phyllis, 153–54, 156
"Does the State, or the Nation Belong to God or the Devil?" (Niebuhr), 120
Dombrowski, Jim, 38 *and n.1*, 42, 53, 55, 57, 63, 76, 88, 93, 98, 102
Dulles, John Foster, 258, 259n.4
Dun, Angus, 81, 258, 259, 299
Dutch Reformed Churches of South Africa, 315

Easter, 420–23
East Germany, 266
Economics, 334
Economist, The, 97, 173n.18
Ecumenical movement, 260
Eddy, Sherwood, 76, 114
Eden, Anthony, 97 *and n.4*
Eden Seminary, 419
Edinburgh, Scotland, 144–53
Education, 266
Egyptian religion, 69, 70
Ehrenstrom, Nils, 215, 216n.3, 237, 238, 245
Einstein, Albert, 384
Eisenhower, Dwight D., 375, 383, 403
Eisenhower, Milton, 266, 269, 270, 273
Eisenhower administration, 307, 311, 316n.1
Eliot, Tom, 168, 170, 177, 179
Eliot, T. S., 124–25, 154, 173n.11, 173n.26, 285
Elliott, Harrison and Grace, 47 *and n.3*, 57, 102
End of Imperialism (Strachey), 401
England. *See* Britain
English Congregational Church, Congressional Union of, 163, 165n.3
Epistle to the Romans (Barth), 15
Erikson, Erik, 364, 367
Essential Reinhold Niebuhr, The (Brown, ed.), 129n.8
Ethics, 47, 49, 56, 59, 62, 63, 73, 233, 239, 334
Europe: post WWII, 216–17; pre WWII, 336
Evans, Luther, 266, 270
Evil, 399, 400, 402
Evolution, 399, 400, 403

Fahs, Sophia Lyon, 102, 104n.4
Faith, 239
Faith and History (Niebuhr), 345
Faith and Politics (Niebuhr), 352
Faith for the Living (Mumford), 337
Fall, the, 396
Family, 415
Fascism, 335, 356, 397

Fear, 397
Federal Council of Churches, 70, 71n.1
Fellowship of Reconciliation (FOR), 53, 54, 56, 245
Fellowship of Socialist Christians, 80, 246, 377n.1; conference of, 101, 114
Fichte, Johann G., 397
Flesseman, Ellen, 222, 224, 225, 226, 228, 258, 260
Florovsky, George, 260, 261n.1
"The Foolishness of God and the Wisdom of the World" (Niebuhr), 247
Foreign Office Committee, 170, 181, 190
Foreign Policy Association (FPA), 71, 72n.3
Forgiveness of Sins, The (Williams), 283
For the Time Being (Auden), 283
Fosdick, Dorothy, 33, 93, 108
Fosdick, Harry Emerson, 19, 33, 111, 421, 422
Frame, James, 33 *and n.1*, 37, 43, 44
France, 266, 336
Frank, Oliver, 217, 218n.1
Frank, Waldo, 341 *and n.2*, 355, 356, 358, 360–61, 363, 365, 367
Frankel, Charles, 378
Frankfurter, Felix, 261, 376; correspondence with Niebuhrs, 298–323
Frankfurter, Marion, 298
Freedom, 398, 399
Freedom of the Press Commission, 220
Freeman, The (Magazine), 376
Fund for the Republic, 317, 319n.2

Gandhi, Mohandas K., 27, 29, 32, 328
General Assembly of the Church of Scotland, 153, 175 *and n.1*, 178, 179
German Evangelical Church, 193n.1
Germany: Nazi, 114, 122, 123, 124, 129, 145, 155, 157, 167; Niebuhr on, 341; post-war occupation, 188, 195–206, 394; religious and political climate, 246, 327–32
Gifford, Lord Adam, 144
Gifford Lectures, 4, 132, 139, 144, 149, 150, 151, 157, 158, 162, 202, 339, 340
Gilbert, Bishop Charles K., 81, 218, 220n.1, 227, 298
Glasgow Cathedral, 169, 176
Gnosticism, 55
God, 290, 328; and power, 335; will of, 400
Goldwater, Barry, 323, 389
Gollancz, Victor, 172, 173n.21
Good, 399, 400, 402
Gordon, King, 55, 56n.1, 236
Gospel, 239, 247, 290
Grace, 150, 380
Grace Church, N.Y., 125, 126
Graham, Billy, 355, 387–88
Greece, 190, 268
Greek Church, 244
Greer, Billy, 257, 258

Guild of Episcopal Scholars, 285, 286n.1
Gwyer, Barbara, 124, 125

Hagen, Paul (Karl Frank), 119, 129n.3
Halifax, Lord Edward, 28n.1, 32, 155, 228
Hall, R. O., 191, 192n.1, 230
Harlow, V. T., 10, 29–30
Harris, Wilson, 172, 230
Harvard Divinity School, 111, 388
Harvard University, 5, 135, 148, 181, 184, 219,
    290, 300, 352, 367; Board of Preachers, 298;
    Law Review, 322; R. Niebuhr teaching at,
    319–320 and n.1
Heath, MA, 80, 81, 132, 140
Hebrew law, 233, 234
Hegel, Georg W. F., 380, 397, 402
Henotheism, 234
Henson, Francis, 55, 57
Heroes, 280
Hetherington, Sir S., 168, 176, 211, 221
Heuss, Theodor, 188
Hinduism, 62
Hiroshima, bombing of, 343
Hitler, Adolf, 122, 123, 125, 129n.2, 145, 153,
    196, 197, 198, 204, 267, 330n.2, 334–36,
    402
Hobson, J. A., 43, 61
Hodgson, Leonard, 70, 71n.2, 273, 291 and n.3
Holland, 123, 210, 211, 212, 215, 221, 222–23,
    242, 255, 271; religious life in, 225, 243
Holland, Sir Thomas and Lady, 150–51
Horkheimer, Max, 109, 114
House of Commons, 121, 122, 155, 173n.23,
    190, 228, 230, 234, 299
House of Lords, 120, 121, 168, 172
Human Values (Parker), 30
Humphrey, Hubert H., 375, 389, 390
Hungary, 260, 270, 309
Hunter, Bishop Leslie, 172, 173n.22, 174, 216,
    227, 228, 229n.1
Hutchinson, John A., 376–77
Hutchinson, Paul, 77 and n.1, 102
"Hymns for Worship," 132

Idea of the Holy, The (Otto), 14
Iknaton, 234
Impatience of a Parson, The (Sheppard), 127
Imperialism, 402–3
India, 257 and n.2, 260, 270, 289–90, 394, 395;
    religion in, 70
Indian Committee, 56
Indonesia, 255
Institute of Advanced Study, Princeton, 309,
    310n.1, 366
Institute of Social Research, 109, 114
International Students Service, 270
Interpretation of Christian Ethics, An (Niebuhr),
    91
Interracial conference, 101, 106

Iraq, 268, 269
Irony and ironic hero, 280–81
Irony of American History, The (Niebuhr), 281,
    303, 376
Irwin, Lord. See Halifax, Lord Edward
Isenberg, Max, 320 and n.1
Isolationism, 162
Israel, 269, 311, 312, 360, 363, 366; creation of
    state of, 192n.2. See also Jerusalem
Italy, 114, 122

Jackson, Dr. Foakes, 43, 44, 48, 55
Jacobs, Paul, 317, 319n.3, 386
James, Henry, 285
James, William, 144
Japan, 156; and WWII, 282, 343, 344
Jeffersonian tradition, 371
Jerusalem, 353 and n.1, 354, 360, 363, 366, 423
Jewish Agency, 191
Jews, 300, 301n.2, 309; immigration to Palestine,
    188, 189; nationalism, 189
Johnson, Arnold, 35 and n.2, 37, 38, 45, 71
Johnson, Howard, 234, 236
Johnson, Lyndon B., 385, 389, 390
Jones, Jack, 163, 164
Journey to a War (Auden; Isherwood), 156

Kagawa, Toyohiko, 88 and n.1
Keedy, Allen, 37 and n.1, 45
Kempthorne, June, 152
Kennedy, John F., 317, 318, 323, 354, 381, 385,
    386, 387
Kennedy, Robert F., 318, 386, 389
Kennedy administration, 388
Keppel-Compton, (Mother of Ursula) 11–12, 32,
    58, 59, 86, 105, 326
Keppel-Compton, (Father of Ursula) 10–12, 32,
    58, 59, 86
Keppel-Compton, Barbara, 10, 32, 65, 66, 86,
    94–95, 96, 261, 326, 347, 359, 364;
    marriage to G. Witt, 205
Keppel-Compton, Robert H. and Marjorie, 36,
    118, 261
Kester, Howard, 102, 104n.3, 114
Khrushchev, Nikita, 316 and n.1, 403
Kierkegaard, Søren, 3, 280, 282, 283n.1, 284,
    285, 380
King, Martin Luther, 311
"King's Chapel and King's Court" (Niebuhr), 355
    and n.1
Kollek, Teddy, 353 and n.1, 356, 358, 363, 366
Kraemer, Hendrick, 222, 223 and n.1, 226, 260,
    261n.1
Kruse, Cornelius, 104, 105n.1, 106, 419

Labor Party (Dutch), 226, 236, 241, 243, 244
Labour Party (British), 121, 122, 123, 128, 171,
    228, 243
Lambeth Conference, 257, 258, 259

Lansbury, George, 93, 94n.1, 98, 102, 121, 122, 123, 128
Law, English, 62
League for Industrial Democracy, 56, 57
League of Independent Political Action, 72 and n.1
Leaves from the Notebook of a Tamed Cynic (Niebuhr), 35, 167, 232, 243, 245
Lehman, Paul and Marian, 71, 72n.1, 113
Lei Tim Oi, 230, 231n.1
Lewis, C. S., 259, 291
Liberalism, 236, 402
Liberal Party, 177
Liberia, 269
Life magazine, 387
Life of Jesus (Noel), 154
Lightfoot, R. H., 184 and n.1, 186
Lincoln, IL, 409, 411, 412, 413, 414
Lippman, Walter, 316, 378
Lister, Reverend Hugh, 91, 95
Literalism, 262
Literature, 15
Liturgical reform, 293, 294
Liturgy, 239
Loeb, James, 220, 221n.3, 226, 373 and n.1, 374, 378
London Monetary and Economic Conference, 80
London University, 174
Lords Spiritual, 121, 129n.5
Love in the Western World (de Rougemont), 245n.1, 339
Loy, Myrna, 266, 272
Lucas, Martha, 266
Luther, Martin, 3, 328, 339
Lutheranism, 196, 236, 242, 246, 248, 331, 402; Scandinavian v. German, 246
Lyman, Eugene and Mary, 62, 64n.1, 71, 87, 93, 102

McGovern, George, 389
MacKay, John, 237, 239n.1, 258
Mackie, Robert, 236, 254, 262
MacLeish, Archibald, 315, 319, 372, 376
MacMurray, John, 89, 90n.3, 93, 105, 183 and n.2, 185, 212, 213
Malin, Pat, 47, 57
Mann, Thomas, 341n.1, 343
Man's Nature and His Communities (Niebuhr), 348
Markham, Virginia, 234, 237
Martin, Hugh, 165, 166n.1
Martin, Kingsley, 167 and n.2, 168, 179, 183, 184, 185, 190
Marxism, 243, 328, 377, 380, 396, 397, 398, 402, 403
Maud, John, 267, 268n.1, 271
Meade, Mrs. (R. Niebuhr's secretary), 135, 136n.1
Men Seen (Rosenfeld), 360
Middle East, 172

Miller, Samuel, 388
Miller, William, 382 and n.1
Mind and Heart of Love, The (D'Arcy), 215n.3, 235, 242, 246
Ministry of Information (MOI), 167, 170, 172, 173, 175, 186
Moffatt, Dr. and Mrs. James, 29, 31n.1, 46, 47n.1, 102
Monotheism, 234
Moore, John, 33 and n.2
Moors, John and Ethel, 81, 132, 133, 138, 140, 141, 298
Moot, Oldham's, 172, 173n.26, 181, 184
Moral Man and Immoral Society (Niebuhr), 26, 30, 82, 83, 91, 121, 189, 390, 415
Morgan, Charles, 108
Morgan, Lloyd, 15, 26
Morris, William, 334
Morrison, Charles C., 77 and n.1
Morrison, Dorothy, 58–61
Mother love, 64–65
Moynihan, Patrick, 353
Muller, Ludwig, 328, 330n.2
Mumford, Geddes, 342, 343n.1
Mumford, Lewis, correspondence with Niebuhrs, 334–67
Mumford, Sophia, 334, 342, 347, 348, 360
Murry, John Middleton, 86, 96, 104, 108
Mussolini, Benito, 122, 335
Mysticism, 62
Mysticism of the Apostle Paul (Schweitzer), 62

Nation, The, 3, 45, 54, 73, 167n.2, 173, 177, 185n.1, 234, 236, 300
National Conference of Radical Christians, 113
National Council of Churches, 71n.1, 288, 304
Nationalism, 397
National Socialism, 328, 329, 331
Nature and Destiny of Man, The (Niebuhr), 158, 177, 202, 223, 246, 284, 396–401
Nazi Germany. *See* Germany
Nazi party, 236
Nazi-Soviet pact, 156
Negro Conference of the South, 101
Negroes, 310, 311, 371
Neil, Bishop Stephen, 259 and n.2, 272, 273
Netherlands, 210, 242, 271
New Castle Cathedral, 174
New English Weekly, 170, 173n.11, 179
New Republic, The, 20–21, 102, 283, 284
New Statesman, The, 103, 167n.2, 169, 172, 177, 179, 185n.1, 234
New Yorker, The, 103, 334, 357n.2, 359, 362
New York Times, The, 3, 103, 176, 177, 179, 305, 316, 366, 373
New Zealand, 271
Niebuhr, Beulah, 33n.3, 36, 54, 204
Niebuhr, Christopher, 132–42 passim, 145, 151, 154–55, 216, 221, 225, 235, 245, 271, 319,